SOCIOLOGY CONFRONTS THE HOLOCAUST

SOCIOLOGY

CONFRONTS THE

HOLOCAUST

Memories and Identities in Jewish Diasporas

EDITED BY

JUDITH M. GERSON

AND

DIANE L. WOLF

DUKE UNIVERSITY PRESS   DURHAM AND LONDON   2007

Printed in the United States of America on acid-free paper ∞

Designed by Heather Hensley

Typeset in Adobe Jenson Pro by Keystone Typesetting, Inc.

Library of Congress Cataloging-in-Publication Data appear
on the last printed page of this book

Duke University Press gratefully acknowledges the support of
Rutgers University Research Council, which provided funds
toward the production of this book.

CONTENTS

ACKNOWLEDGMENTS

This book represents the culmination of considerable hard work by many of our colleagues and the support of several organizations, and we are pleased to have the opportunity to express our appreciation to each of them for their assistance. The initial impetus for the international conference on which this book is based grew out of informal conversations between the two editors as we found ourselves involved in our respective Holocaust-related research projects without sufficient intellectual guideposts within sociology to analyze our findings. We planned a working conference on the Holocaust and post-Holocaust life to include primarily sociologists and other scholars working in the related fields of collective memory, diaspora, identity, gender, and transnationalism as a means to present work in progress and encourage an intellectual exchange between researchers involved in specific Holocaust-related projects and those in areas relevant for framing. In some sense, we hoped to bring the study of the Holocaust and its aftermath up to speed in sociology.

That conference, held in October 2001 at Rutgers University, had the support of the American Sociological Association and of the National Science Foundation's Fund for the Advancement of the Discipline. There is no question that we could not have proceeded to attract supplementary funding without the initial funding from this important program. We are also grateful for the crucial support of the Lucius N. Littauer Foundation, as well as of our home institutions, Rutgers University and the University of California, Davis. Within Rutgers, we had significant support from the Research Council, both for the conference and again for subvention for publication; from the Faculty of Arts and Sciences; and from the Departments of Jewish Studies and Sociology. In addition, the Institute for Women's Leadership hosted our conference, and with the help of two of its member organizations—the Institute for Research on Women and the Women's and Gender Studies Department—we were able to provide a suitable intellectual setting for our work. The Departments of Jewish Studies and Sociology at the University of California, Davis, provided significant funding as well. Several Rutgers colleagues also aided our efforts. Miriam Bauer expertly organized the multiple sources of financing and billing; Joanne Givand guided us through the labyrinth of university rules and procedures; Beth Hutchison generously shared her expertise on conferences and collections; and Karen Small organized Michal Bodemann's keynote address.

There are a few others whose efforts and commitments proved crucial to the success of the conference and the completion of this book. Lynne Moulton did the work of three people as conference coordinator with great foresight, intelligence, and good cheer. Raphael Allen initially guided us and our manuscript at Duke University Press. Jane Le worked tirelessly and systematically to format the final manuscript. We are indebted to Colby Chlebowski for her superb assistance in the last stages of manuscript preparation when all the pieces of the puzzle needed to be put back together again. Many of the final revisions took place while Judy Gerson was a visiting fellow at the Center for Advanced Holocaust Studies, United States Holocaust Memorial Museum. Though the statements in this volume remain those of their authors, the intellectual environment created by colleagues at the center coupled with an incredible library provided important antidotes to some of the technical demands of the book. Daniel Magilow, a fellow fellow, provided crucial emergency support and a stream of much-needed humor during the last stages of word processing. Though they remain unnamed, we also want to thank the two anonymous readers who carefully and thoughtfully reviewed our manuscript for the press.

At Duke University Press we have been truly fortunate to work with Reynolds Smith and Sharon Parks Torian. Reynolds is a sagacious editor whose astute advice on a wide range of matters both intellectual and practical guided us through the completion of this book. Every conversation with him was enlightening, often in ways that surpassed the demands of our project. Sharon Torian, a senior editorial assistant, facilitated our work at every stage of the manuscript submission and preparation process. Our thanks to Petra Dreiser who used her copyeditor's wisdom, saving us and our authors from numerous traps, and to Justin Faerber who responded to an enormous range of last minute requests.

Finally, we want to thank our families, friends, and colleagues whose support has been unconditional and deeply meaningful. Working together on this book often seemed like participating in an academic obstacle course specifically designed for two *yekkes* like us. We faced serious computer crashes, major e-mail glitches, and even mail fraud as our manuscript seemed to vanish after leaving the post office on its way to the publisher. Although we have encountered more of Murphy's Law than usual during the journey from conference to published book, we thank each other for our friendship and shared feminist sociological commitments begun years ago while we were graduate students at Cornell. It is perhaps no coincidence that we are both daughters of German Jewish refugees and have come to this project in midlife.

1

RECONSIDERING HOLOCAUST STUDY

INTRODUCTION

Why the Holocaust? Why Sociology? Why Now?

JUDITH M. GERSON AND DIANE L. WOLF

Contemporary sociological research is marked by a profound silence in relation to the Holocaust (Bauman 1989; Kaufman 1996; Markle 1995).[1] The chasm is acute in the sociological literature written in English, the focus of our attention, though the lacuna is also evident in other fields such as anthropology and cultural studies. To rephrase Virginia Dominguez's (1993) critical scrutiny of anthropology, it appears as if sociology might also have a "Jewish problem" (621). Few sociologists, regardless of their religious or cultural identity, have focused their academic work on the Holocaust or post-Holocaust life. Those who have tend to be in Jewish studies programs, and thus their work is often regarded as marginal to most disciplines. But the question, of course, should not be limited to why more Jewish sociologists do not focus on the Holocaust or post-Holocaust life; rather, we should ask why not more sociologists in general are not taking up such research.

Comparable problems are apparent in the piecemeal study of immigration. Jews initially presented the ideal type for the concept of diaspora (Clifford 1994; Safran 1991), so much so that the term was initially more or less synonymous with the Jewish experience. Contemporary scholars have frequently lost sight of this earlier case and instead have explored the notion of diaspora among dispersed Third World peoples without appropriate reference to or comparison with the Jewish diaspora (Boyarin and Boyarin 2002; Gold 2002). Like previous scholars, we do not wish to suggest that a Jewish diaspora is or ought to be hegemonic. Yet there are dangers of " 'transcend[ing],' evading or erasing Jewishness in cultural studies of the new diasporas" (Boyarin and Boyarin 2002:13).

Omitting the case of a premodern Jewish diaspora permits erroneous assumptions, such as that diasporas are twentieth-century phenomena or that Jews are questionable multicultural subjects. A broadened, more inclusive notion of the concept of diaspora "offers rich material for a reinvigoration of Jewish thought. But the converse is also true: analyses of non-Jewish diasporas will be most fruitful when they engage in dialogue with the specific Jewish context in which the term originated" (Boyarin and Boyarin 2002:7).

Similarly, contemporary discussions of refugees are increasingly represented in the literature as "first and foremost a 'Third World problem'" (Malkki 1995b: 503). In immigration studies, numerous authors (Basch, Glick Schiller, and Szanton Blanc 1994; Portes and Rumbaut 1996) have argued how post-1965 immigrants or refugees from the Third World differ from earlier European immigrants due to the postcolonial context, the global economy, and the racialized nature of U.S. society. Yet the proposition that the same analytic models do not pertain to pre-1965 immigrant groups precludes analyses of similarities and differences between Holocaust refugees and more recent migrants. Furthermore, though many assume that transnationalism is a contemporary postmodern phenomenon, Jewish experiences before and after World War II were and continue to be transnational, yet they have not been analyzed in such terms. Given the multiple diasporic migrations of pre- and post-Holocaust European Jews, comparative analyses with, for example, Indians in East Africa or the Chinese in Vietnam (Bhachu 1985; Espiritu this volume) could enable important new understandings of immigration processes and outcomes when there are multiple cycles of displacement and resettlement rather than a single occurrence.

In Holocaust studies, the concept of survivor has increasingly dominated research and public discourse, precluding appropriate comparisons with other stateless refugees. Today in the United States, moreover, the term *survivor* can pertain to almost anything—from someone who was a victim of incest to someone who remains employed after a corporate merger—whereas formerly it had the specific connotation of referring to Jews interned in concentration camps. In other words, the intellectual isolationism that pervades studies of the Holocaust and maintains its marginal status vis-à-vis sociology has made it more difficult to draw appropriate comparisons with relevant phenomena; it also inadvertently permits inappropriate assumptions and conclusions.

Moreover, there are constructs central to the sociological enterprise—including race, ethnicity, minority group, assimilation, and insider/outsider status—

JUDITH M. GERSON AND DIANE L. WOLF

that have shaped Holocaust scholarship (Biale, Galchinsky, and Heschel 1998; Boyarin and Boyarin 1997). While these works appropriately draw on rich intellectual traditions, there are few sociologists directly connected with these endeavors, and thus some of the most recent and best work on race and ethnicity, for instance, remains absent from these projects. That said, it continues to be both significant and necessary that Holocaust scholarship was originally devoted to documenting the past, to developing the historical record of what happened, where and when it happened, and if knowable, how it happened. Yet increasingly writers have come to recognize that the historicity of the Holocaust must be understood both in and of itself and as a reflection of how we interpret and represent our knowledge of the past.

Collective memory, according to the sociologist Maurice Halbwachs (1992), refers to the ways in which the present molds how and what we recall of the past—a quintessentially sociological project. We remember and forget as members of particular groups in particular social locations, and through these processes, identities are formed and reformed. To a considerable extent, groups shape their own memories (Novick 1999), and thus how a group remembers its past reveals the group's sense of itself and its understanding of the past. Similarly, Hirsch and Smith (2002) elaborate this concept with their reference to "cultural memory," which they understand to be "an act in the present by which individuals and groups constitute their identities by recalling a shared past on the basis of common, and therefore often contested norms, conventions, and practices" (2002:5). And yet curiously, though historians and others in the humanities have relied heavily on notions of collective and cultural memory to analyze the Holocaust, such endeavors have remained limited in sociology (see Bodemann 1996c; Levy and Sznaider 2005; Olick 1999a; Olick and Levy 1997; and Olick and Robbins 1998 for notable exceptions).

The dynamic link between collective memory and collective identity constitutes an important focus of this book. It is generally accepted that the Shoah plays a crucial role in Jewish collective memory and, therefore, in the constitution of Jewish identity. Indeed, scholars note with concern the increasing prominence of the Shoah as the basis, and sometimes the sole basis, of contemporary Jewish identity (Goldberg 1995; Novick 1999). It is clear, however, that not every generation has the same memory of the Holocaust because of its respective historical positions and life experiences, and much of what we understand to be "the" memory of the Holocaust is actually post-memory: "Postmemory is distinguished from memory by generational distance and from history by deep personal connection" (Hirsch 1997:22). Thus the post-memory of the second or third generation differs considerably from the memory of Holocaust perpetrators or survivors because only survivors or perpetrators witnessed these events. For the rest of us, post-memory of the Holocaust is filtered through a variety of sources including records and documents, memoirs and narratives of the destruction written and compiled by survivors, perpetrators, and bystanders, and contemporary research, textual accounts, and artistic portrayals of the Holocaust.

Several of the authors in this volume rely on the framework of collective identity and memory to examine daily practices of identities. Similarly, other writers consider the differential relationships of survivors and the "1.5" and second generations to the diaspora, as well as to processes of collective displacement, resistance, and resettlement.[2] How do survivors of genocide experience their collective identities in the aftermath of trauma, and how does that vary among generations? Such questions intersect with several important themes in immigration, diaspora, transnational, and refugee studies.

Thus we recognize the need to expand intellectual exchange between researchers working on the Holocaust and post-Holocaust life with North American sociologists working in the fields of diasporic and transnational studies, immigration, and collective memory. We do not want to suggest that Jewish experiences are either unique or hegemonic, but instead seek to understand how our knowledge of immigration and transnationalism, for instance, would change if the case of a post-Holocaust diaspora were brought into that literature, and conversely, how that research tradition might complicate our thinking of post-Holocaust immigration. The current state of these intellectual separate spheres has helped maintain Holocaust studies as an area of inquiry onto itself, one located in an academic ghetto distant from sociological practices particularly in the United States and in Canada. Ultimately, this intellectual bifurcation impoverishes both Holocaust studies and sociology. Within Holocaust studies, this separatism has meant that research proceeds without comparative knowledge from sociological areas of study that might deepen our understanding of the precursors, dynamics, and consequences of the Holocaust, thereby buttressing the presumptive claim of the Holocaust's uniqueness without exploration.[3] Conversely, the missing case of the Holocaust in North American sociology means that many theories and substantive generalizations have not been tested on what is arguably a defining moment of the twentieth century.

In addition to the issues emanating from the sharp divide between these areas

　　　　JUDITH M. GERSON AND DIANE L. WOLF

of inquiry, the virtual absence of a comparative study of the Holocaust introduces another set of problems for researchers.[4] Arguments about the uniqueness and incommensurability of the Holocaust actually assume a series of implicit comparisons and judgments about whether those comparisons are justified. In other words, claims for the uniqueness of the Holocaust or any other phenomenon are premised on comparisons. For example, the idea that the Holocaust is genocide derives from the knowledge that the Holocaust shares several properties with other genocides. Comparisons enumerate both similarities and differences. The Holocaust is not identical to other genocides, but it is sufficiently similar to be categorized as genocide. In other words, assertions about the Holocaust's uniqueness depend on implicit comparisons, while at the same time precluding the possibility for subsequent explicit comparisons by insisting on the principle of the Holocaust's incommensurability.

And yet it is the responsibility of social science scholars to analyze as well as document, and making these implicit comparisons explicit remains a central goal of this volume. We believe that studies of comparison and generalization enable a more sophisticated understanding of the Holocaust. Appropriate comparative study of the Holocaust does not diminish its importance, but instead enables a more sophisticated and refined understanding. This approach points to an intellectual agenda that includes questions about which comparisons about the Holocaust are made, contested, and refused, by whom and under what conditions. We also ask what forms of comparison prevail in popular and scholarly discourses and how they influence each other. In ethnographic research, we want to know how people use comparison and generalization in their speech and silence about the Holocaust. And to our presumptive critics, we want to make clear that adopting this approach will not diminish or defame the Holocaust or its legacy. Rather, it promises to widen and deepen our understanding and produce more sophisticated knowledge.

The authors in this volume thus refuse the practice of separating sociological inquiry, on the one hand, from Holocaust studies, on the other, and instead seek to further the richness of scholarly interchange by bringing these literatures together into comparative conversations. As a collection, these articles provide innovative approaches to studying the Holocaust and post-Holocaust life using the concepts, theories, and methods available to us working predominantly in sociology and in closely related social science fields. Primarily, we rely on recent research on race and ethnicity, immigration and assimilation, identity, collective memory and transnationalism in our studies of the Holocaust and post-Holocaust Jewish life. We seek to understand how these approaches might expand and contribute to a more complex understanding of the Holocaust. At the same time, the chapters of the current volume help move research on the Holocaust and closely related research in Jewish studies out from the academic margins onto center stage, providing new perspectives that enable us to rethink how our sociological knowledge might be revised to incorporate the insights available from studies of the Holocaust and post-Holocaust life. Indeed, the organization of this volume reflects this dual emphasis with authors who interrogate the Holocaust and its aftermath using the analytic tools prominent in recent sociological scholarship and other commentators who speak to how these works might contribute to ongoing questions in their areas of specialization in sociology and related fields.

The initial motivations behind this volume and the October 2001 conference from which it stems are simple: as feminist sociologists well steeped in the field of the political economy of gender and labor, we understood from our earlier work the need to place disparate fields of inquiry into dialogue with each other and realized that this type of interchange can yield many important insights unattainable through a more singular, solitary focus. When we began our individual research projects on the Holocaust and post-Holocaust Jewish life, we found, and continue to find ourselves wandering in what seems like a sociological desert. As we write about the Holocaust, we continually search for links with sociological constructs central to our projects. Just as academics often create the courses they wish they had had as students, we endeavor to join these different fields as both a template and a catalyst for other scholars.

While we asked authors to consider the role that sociology could play in their research, we conversely asked commentators to consider how Holocaust research might inform, expand, or challenge ideas central to their areas of study if it were more central to those areas of inquiry. The scholars in this volume incorporate a broad range of sociological theories, methods, and substantive findings into studies of Holocaust and post-Holocaust Jewish experiences, focusing attention on topics that heretofore have received fleeting consideration because of other disciplinary emphases. For example, sociologists are accustomed to considering the interface of macro social structures and microlevel interactions and thus are well positioned to articulate how state policies regarding immigration shaped collective identities as refugees, immigrants, and survivors. The content of these essays and the format of our book can only invite comparative analyses, an endeavor long overdue in reference to Jewish experiences and the Holocaust. We

JUDITH M. GERSON AND DIANE L. WOLF

have much to gain from dismantling the barriers that have for too long contained the study of the Holocaust and Jewish life in their academic ghettos.

Thus the chapters in this volume center on the themes of memory, identity, and diaspora in the Holocaust and its aftermath, which both draw on and contribute to ongoing work in sociology in these areas as they intersect with studies of race and ethnicity, immigration, globalization, and social theory more generally. We have argued for the importance of intellectual cross-fertilization by integrating work on the Holocaust and post-Holocaust life into English-language sociology and using the analytic tools of sociology to further our understanding of the Shoah. Through the research in this volume, we have already seen the intellectual advantages of relying on a broadly defined sociological approach to interpret the empirical research presented here. It is our hope with the publication of this volume that its presence will initiate many more engagements with the intellectual endeavors that bring together what until now have been distant fields of knowledge.

Notes

1. We recognize the problems of language inherent in using the phrase *the* Holocaust, setting it up as the sole, most important holocaust and the standard for other holocausts. The term *holocaust* itself is a Greek word referring to a burnt sacrifice. Hebrew and Yiddish referents represent its location within Jewish life rather than in a world event (Young 1988). The Hebrew word *Sho'ah* means "disaster" or "catastrophe," as do the less commonly used terms *hurban* in Hebrew and its Yiddish analogue *hurbn*. Yet both these terms do not directly name the Nazi genocide. Without an alternative available, we reluctantly reproduce the problem here. We use the terms *the Holocaust* and *Shoah* interchangeably.

2. While there is widespread recognition of the importance of generations to the study of immigration (Rumbaut [1976] 2004a, 2004b; Zhou 1997) and the significance of generations to collective memory of the Holocaust (Aviv and Shneer this volume; Hirsch 1997; Kaufman this volume; Suleiman 2002), there is no consensus on how best to define and measure the concept. The term *1.5 generation* was originally developed by Rumbaut ([1976] 2004a) to elucidate the differences between immigrant youth and their first-generation foreign-born immigrant elders, on the one hand, and their second-generation, native-born kin and friends, on the other. Rumbaut (2004b) operationalizes the 1.5 generation to include those who were preadolescent children of primary school age upon immigration, thus distinguishing them from ideal typical first- and second-generation immigrants. Other scholars have either failed to recognize the 1.5 generation or resorted to fuzzier age-based definitions.

3. A dearth of formal comparative research and extensive links among the Holocaust and relevant social science literatures helps secure the vexed and highly contested idea that the Holocaust was unique. Though it is not the major focus of our work here, we, like Bauer (2001), argue that the Holocaust was unprecedented yet not unique.

4. Fein's (1993) work on comparative genocide remains an important exception.

Sociology and Holocaust Study

JUDITH M. GERSON AND DIANE L. WOLF

In this essay, we consider the scholarship in sociology that focuses on the Holocaust and its aftermath.[1] We confine our review to English-language sources that might most appropriately be categorized under the rubric "sociology of the Holocaust and post-Holocaust life."[2] We begin with an overview of the field cognizant of the relative scarcity of sources.

In the opening pages of his book *Modernity and the Holocaust*, Zygmunt Bauman (1989) laments that a "glaring paucity" (xiii) of sociological scholarship exists on the Holocaust. Indeed, our review of the literature confirms these persistent concerns about the dearth of a sociological understanding of the Shoah (Gerson and Wolf 2000; Kaufman 1996; Markle 1995). Yet it would be a serious mistake to overstate this claim, and thus we turn to the available literature in sociology to identify the most prominent sources.

We discerned two distinct approaches to the study of the Holocaust within the sociological literature. We discuss each of these clusters in turn, recognizing that they constitute neither exclusive nor exhaustive categories, and that they do not make for distinct stages either. Within sociology, the first and by far the predominant approach to the study of the Holocaust was distinguished by scholars' reliance on macrohistorical methods to interrogate their subject matter. These researchers were likely to study the rise of fascism and National Socialism —specifically, mass society, propaganda, modernity, and German militarism—but tended to eschew any sustained analysis of the genocide and Judeocide in particular. In other words, the focus in sociology, much as in other disciplines, was on perpetrators rather than on victims as researchers grappled with the threat the Holocaust posed to Enlightenment ideals.

It is a commitment to positivism that most clearly distinguishes this group from the next. Researchers in this first group grappled both explicitly and comprehensively with how and why the Holocaust occurred, and they relied on a broad range of core sociological constructs such as social order and cohesion, racial ethnic prejudice and conflict, bureaucracy and modernization, and power as a means to try to comprehend the destruction and mass murder of the Holocaust. Within this cluster, there exists a notable subspecialization on the study of social movements and political sociology, and here researchers have documented and explained patterns of Nazi party membership.

In contrast to the work in this first cluster, a second, more recent cluster emphasizes interpretative approaches. Included under this rubric are microlevel approaches and meta-analyses—local ethnographies, case studies, autobiographical and biographical narratives often written from victims' perspectives. And yet our review begins with a group of scholars who challenged this dichotomy and instead understood their work in both positivist and political terms.

The preponderance of sociological scholarship on the Holocaust during the war and in the years immediately following it was to be found in the writings of refugee scholars, and among them, members of the Frankfurt Institute for Social Research were best known for their work on fascism. Initially the main areas of interest of Max Horkheimer, the intellectual leader of the group, Theodor Adorno,[3] and their émigré colleagues, many of whom were living temporarily in the United States, fell squarely within a Marxist philosophical tradition, but with the rise of Nazism and the scholars' escape to the United States, those interests took a decidedly more social-psychological turn and shifted increasingly to the relationship of personality to anti-Semitism and authority (Coser 1984). The group's research culminated in a series of empirical works, *Studies in Prejudice*, which included the renowned volume, *The Authoritarian Personality* (Adorno et al. 1950). Although that volume was based on an earlier text, *Autorität und Familie* [*Authority and the Family*], which emphasized structural and particularly class factors, the newer book, written in collaboration with American colleagues, was more characteristic of liberal individualism (Coser 1984) as it sought to understand authoritarianism by analyzing personality. Personality alone explained ethnocentrism and fascism without any need to consider external conditions that might have produced this personality type. Consequently, for its authors, the world was cleanly divided between proto-Nazis and their victims. What remains notable today about *The Authoritarian Personality* is not its actual findings, many

JUDITH M. GERSON AND DIANE L. WOLF

of which its authors and other critics subsequently discounted. Rather, the text serves as an early template for how to study Nazi atrocities and for its absolution of everyone but the Nazis for these crimes. After the war, members of the Frankfurt Institute for Social Research ([1956] 1972) developed a sociological explanation of prejudice that analyzed anti-Semitism in Nazi Germany as an example of a more general instance of racial hatred. Some have criticized the work of the Frankfurt Institute as limited by its members' assumptions concerning the uniqueness of the Holocaust and their attendant failure to interrogate its historical and comparative links (Bahr 1984; Bottomore 1984:21,72). Yet members of the institute also need to be recognized for their use of multiple methods and theories in their search for an objective understanding of Nazism and fascism, which they pursued in hopes that their knowledge perhaps could help prevent future disasters.

Even before Germany declared war against Poland in 1939, a number of immigrant and native-born sociologists sought to understand the growing popularity of the Nazi party. In 1934, one year into the Third Reich, the American-born Theodore Abel convinced Nazi party authorities that he be allowed to sponsor an essay contest among early joiners of the party. Six hundred essays were submitted and analyzed, and Abel ([1938] 1986) described a wide range of motives, rather than argue the now more common interpretation that the earliest members were dissatisfied and lower middle class. Hans Gerth, a German refugee, analyzed the shift in Nazi party leadership in its earliest years from charismatic authority to increasingly one that fused charisma with bureaucratic power. With this shift came a concomitant change in party membership from earliest members, who tended to be young and economically disadvantaged, to subsequent members who were more likely to be older and civil servants. Published in 1940, his words are prescient: "The anti-Jewish riots of November, 1938, the swift efficiency in raiding synagogues, offices, business establishments, and homes of Jews revealed the increased rationalization of the terror as compared with the Kurfürstendamm raid in the summer of 1935" (Gerth 1940:541). Rudolf Heberle ([1945] 1970), an émigré sociologist, was also interested in understanding Nazi party membership. Concentrating on the largely rural state of Schleswig-Holstein, he used an ecological approach to map the growing acceptance of the Nazi party in the region. Support came particularly from the middle strata that included small farm owners and small entrepreneurs, groups at the margins of an industrializing economy. In the introduction to the book's second edition, Heberle notes the connection between his work and "certain recent political tendencies and movements (somewhat vaguely called the 'extreme right') in the United States today" (Heberle [1945] 1970:vii).

Travel, study, military or governmental service in Europe enabled a few U.S. sociologists to have firsthand knowledge of Germany. Though most of the work in this genre was empirical and concentrated on the Nazi party in its early years and subsequently the perpetrators and bystanders in the aftermath of the war, all of the articles seem to respond to the authors' implicit questions about how the destruction could have happened. In 1935 and 1936, Edward Hartshorne used his firsthand observations of Germany, and British and German statistical data, to study the effects of National Socialism on German universities. He reported the attrition of many faculties, with the worst losses in the social sciences given the dismissal, harassment, and/or exile of many professors. Academic governance and collegial relations were terminated as well, thus destroying the fabric of free inquiry and liberal learning (Hartshorne 1937). Serving as an intelligence officer after the war, Morris Janowitz (1946) interviewed a hundred Germans and found that even though most had basic knowledge of the concentrations camps, they nonetheless denied knowing the specifics or the extent of the atrocities, repressed such knowledge when confronted with it, and deflected blame for the genocide on the Nazis and the ss. While today the complex relationship of the perpetrators to their crimes is better understood, Janowitz must have been among the first to propose it. Janowitz also collaborated with the chief of intelligence of the Psychological Warfare Division in a study of German prisoners of war and their loyalty to Hitler (Gurfein and Janowitz 1946). In addition, Edward Shils and Morris Janowitz (1948) studied the structure of the German army and found that strong social ties within a soldier's company best explained infantrymen's behaviors and beliefs. In the summer of 1945, Clifford Kirkpatrick (1948) also conducted a survey of the reactions of "well-educated Germans" to their defeat. These responses revealed considerable confusion about how to assess Nazi responsibility, and also distress about both the concentration camps and the Allied bombings. Kirkpatrick was explicit about his concerns about the limited utility of sociology in understanding the war and concluded that only afterward, "unclouded by war hysteria" (1946:67) would sociological thinking about Germany prove appropriate. He derived ten sociological generalizations about guilt, responsibility, bias, and in- and out-groups, which seemed most relevant for Americans rethinking their peacetime relations with a defeated Germany—propositions that appear not to have inspired further research.

JUDITH M. GERSON AND DIANE L. WOLF

Talcott Parsons's work on National Socialism is probably better known to readers today than many of the above-cited works, but even his nine articles on the subject are not as widely read as are his other texts.[4] Parsons's approach to the rise of National Socialism derived in part from his interest in understanding structures of authority and power in political systems. He was troubled by the ways in which racialized laws and practices had replaced individual-based evaluations of merit and represented a rupture of universal standards of rational knowledge, human rights and liberties common in democratic life (Parsons [1942] 1993a, b).

Uta Gerhardt, Parsons's biographer, traces his strong stance against National Socialism to his belief in liberal learning and universalistic religion, both of which he considered linked to modern capitalist economic structures and crucial for Western civilization (Gerhardt 1993a, 2002). Unlike other democratic nations, Weimar Germany had retained a significant landed aristocracy with elements of feudal and traditional societies, resulting in both a formality and patriarchal authority in social life that Parsons associated with that democracy's demise. Although Parsons ([1942] 1993a) also acknowledged the importance of external factors such as the treatment of Germany by the Allies in World War I, economic crises, and so forth, he reasoned that domestic social patterns made it harder for many to become more fully integrated into an increasingly urban, industrial society, which consequently kept Germany a divided society rather than a unified, rational one (Parsons [1942] 1993c).

Parsons also argued for the usefulness of basic sociological principles to comprehend fascism. Within a culture or subculture of deviance, Parsons found that compulsive conformity developed. He viewed Nazi Germany as the extreme case of deviance at the state level. In Parson's opinion, anti-Semitism, a form of group prejudice, and crime relied on similar mechanisms, although their outlets differed. Anti-Semites in Nazi Germany belonged to mainstream society and scapegoated one particular group, whereas criminals rebelled against the broader society. He called for dissecting the roots and meanings of fascism as a revolutionary movement, arguably "the most dramatic single development in the society of the Western world in its most recent phase" (Parsons [1942] 1993d:203). In addition, Parsons published three articles in *Psychiatry*—the first on propaganda and social control in which he argues for a more generic understanding of propaganda, defined as any technique used to achieve a goal (Parsons [1942] 1993c). In March 1944, Parsons was invited to the Conference on Germany after the War, at which its participants tried to articulate a social and cultural rather than a political and economic response to Germany's anticipated defeat (Gerhardt 2002:110). Parsons outlined a program of necessary changes, which included ending the high degree of hierarchy, authoritarianism, and formalism evident in German institutional structures.[5]

Although sociological writing on the Holocaust in the 1940s and 1950s was not extensive and those writing confined their work to the rise of fascism and militarism, by the 1960s, the seeds of a more expansive sociological inquiry had become evident. Everett C. Hughes (1962) published "Good People and Dirty Work," a frequently cited article that explores how the ss, the inner fanatical sect of the National Socialist government in Germany "perpetrated and boasted of the most colossal and dramatic piece of social dirty work the world has ever known" (1). Concentrating on the Final Solution as a case, Hughes does not single out Germans from others as more culpable for committing dirty work. Instead, he argues that dirty work is a phenomenon evident in all societies, be it the lynching of blacks in the United States, worldwide disease and hunger, crimes in South Africa, and so forth. Visiting Germany in 1948, Hughes found it remarkable that rather than remain silent, ordinary Germans, whom he considered "good people," actually discussed the atrocities.[6] But how do good people enable dirty work to happen? Hughes reasoned that they increasingly defined Jews as a problem, categorized them as out-group members, and distinguished themselves from the Jews. Yet good people were not the perpetrators of the Final Solution; that was a fanatical core in a militant social movement legitimated by the state and eventually by the general population. All societies, Hughes concludes, have "smaller, rule-making and disciplining powers . . ." (1962:11) including the family, religious orders, political parties, and so forth. The Nazis wanted to replace these other institutions with their own laws and forms of control. The problem for civil society remained how to sustain these other institutions to ensure a social and moral order.

In addition, several sociologists in the postwar years considered fascism and Nazism in their work, often as counterevidence in their more general writings on democracy. Certainly this is evident in Seymour Martin Lipset's (1960) *Political Man*, in which he analyzes electoral support of various political parties in order to understand the rise of fascist parties to power. To a lesser extent, this is also the case in Jessie Bernard's (1949) *American Community Behavior*. More generally, the popular sociological writings of the period focused on questions that troubled postwar democracies—questions of community, civil society, and anomie. While often understood as a response to worries about the Cold War, it seems eminently reasonable to us that these texts might also be read as a response to the aftermath of the Holocaust, even though it remains a tacit, unspoken rejoinder.

It was not until the 1970s that sociologists began to grapple more fully with the mass murders and atrocities of the Holocaust. Among the earliest sociological studies of concentration camps was Anna Pawełczyńska's ([1973] 1979) *Values and Violence in Auschwitz*. Written by a Polish member of the resistance and a political prisoner at Auschwitz-Birkenau, the work remains remarkable for its detailed analysis of the social organization of this camp. Though Pawełczyńska recognizes the importance of the larger political context of the Third Reich and is unequivocal in her condemnation of the regime, she reserves her most forceful and nuanced analyses for the routine structures and patterns of interaction that defined prisoners' existence. Camp prisoners were strategic rather than passive in their conformity. They sought to retain as many of the shreds of their values as possible, realizing that they had to adapt. Inmates adjusted norms of caring to attend to the person physically or emotionally closest to them or the one most in need. Pawełczyńska concludes that camp prisoners relied on a diminished set of human values to sustain themselves biologically and retain "their attitude of protest against force and violence in relation to the human person" ([1973] 1979:137). Writing at a time when there was heightened public interest in the ostensible absence of Jewish resistance to the Nazi reign of terror, Pawełczyńska's analysis of conspiratorial and resistance organizations in Auschwitz is particularly noteworthy.

Pawełczyńska was not the only sociologist with firsthand knowledge of the concentration camps. Paul Neurath, a Jewish political prisoner, was arrested on April 1, 1938, sent to Dachau and, a few months later, transferred to Buchenwald. After being released from the second camp in May 1939, he made his way to the United States, where he won a predoctoral fellowship to study sociology at Columbia University (Fleck, Müller, and Stehr 2005:279–311). He wrote his dissertation based on his concentration camp experience using ethnographic methods, recalling from his recent memory what daily life in the camps had been like. He also interviewed ten other inmates. They all readily concurred with his account including almost all of the specific facts, disagreeing, as Neurath tells his readers, only in the slightest of details. Although he successfully defended his dissertation before a committee of ten in June 1943, he did not seek a publisher for two more years. By that time, in Neurath's words, "publishers didn't want to print any more about concentration camps without gas chambers" (qtd. in Fleck, Müller, and Stehr 2005:297). Neurath's text is a precise social account of daily life in the two camps, including his initial impressions of the camps, the daily routine, different prisoner groups, the guard system, and the organization of work. The intensity of these descriptions is followed by a chronological record of increasing forms of harassment and brutality. Neurath refuses to rely fully on description and grapples with the vexed issue of minimal inmate resistance. He considers how prisoners' spirits were broken during their transport and analyzes the camps as sites without meaningful civilized life. He recognizes that when prisoners personalized their conflicts with the guards, resistance proved more effective (Fleck, Müller, and Stehr 2005; Neurath 2005:245–67).

Most sociological research was not, however, based on firsthand evidence. As we will see, writings in the postwar period tell us as much about the Holocaust as they do about the state of sociology. Barrington Moore Jr. (1978) recognized the importance of a comparative historical approach to the Holocaust, as is evidenced by his volume titled *Injustice: The Social Bases of Obedience and Revolt*, the hallmark of a sociological approach to the study of inequality, injustice, and moral codes. Moore identifies the conditions that either evoked or precluded moral outrage against social injustice. Focusing on the dual processes of atomization and cooperation that operated among concentration camp inmates at Theresienstadt and among the Chamars or untouchables in India, he argues that either too much social support or support unsuited to the situation prevents people from resisting injustice. In his search for recurring patterns of resistance or its absence, he returns to the universal problems societies face—the distribution of goods and services. Ultimately, Moore's explanation of the actions of Holocaust victims and perpetrators proves a deeply sociological one, emphasizing societal organization around mechanisms of reciprocity and social cooperation as key to understanding the occurrence of subversion.

Similarly, Helen Fein has developed an intrinsically sociological analysis of the varying "successes" of the Final Solution, which she argues must entail an explanation of "how Jewish victims were disintegrated from the social systems by which they were usually protected" (Fein 1979:33). She stresses the importance of studying the citizenship rights of Jews before the war, as well as the varied experiences of Jews throughout Europe. As such, the proper unit of analysis for Fein is neither perpetrators nor victims but the nation-state. Using a range of methods, she develops mathematical models to explicate where the Final Solution was more successful and where it proved a relative failure. Fein identifies the importance of the size of the prewar Jewish population and its concentration, the dominance of the Roman Catholic church, the success of anti-Semitic movements before 1936, warning time to extermination, native governments' degree of collaboration, and the activities of local *Judenräten* (councils of Jews responsible for enforcing Nazi rule and adjudicating Jewish communal affairs) among other variables as significant in explaining the outcomes to the Final Solution. In subsequent research on anti-Semitism, Fein (1987) analyzed its commonalities with other forms of inter-group conflict, studied its impact on Nazism and the Holocaust, and considered its effect on more contemporary issues of national identity, the state, and current forms of harassment. Today, Fein remains probably best known for her comparative work on genocide (1979), which she originally conceptualized as premeditated and organized state-sanctioned murder. In subsequent work, she expanded this conceptualization to include all purposeful acts to physically destroy a group through biological or social reproduction, perpetrated despite victims' surrender or lack of threat (Fein 1993).[7]

Other sociologists have also studied state-sponsored genocide and have done so within a comparative historical framework. Leo Kuper focuses on "domestic genocides," which he defines as internal to a society and not a direct outcome of a war (1981:9). These genocides, which include the Holocaust, occur in pluralistic or divided societies in which minority groups have recently been granted enhanced civil rights. Yet these are also societies with long-standing traditions of exclusion directed at these minorities, and increased integration also generates escalating hatred and violence. Irving Louis Horowitz concentrates on the nation-state and argues that state-sponsored bureaucratic apparatuses, rather than theological approaches, are essential to understanding the structural and systematic destruction of a people. For Horowitz, "totalitarianism is the essence of the genocidal process" (1982:202). Although he concedes qualitatively distinctive aspects of the Jewish Holocaust, Horowitz urges readers to adopt a sociological perspective that places the Holocaust in a cross-cultural framework.

Ranier Baum (1981) concentrates on cultural values as a mode of explanation and points to a moral indifference among German elites in government, academia, the economy, and the armed forces. Modern Germany had a long-standing desire to be an imperial power, but it was also characterized by fundamental regional and class differences in values. As a consequence, there were multiple and competing sources of moral authority, and a dearth of public discussions of moral issues. With values and morality fractured and public discourse diminished, an unexamined amorality could more easily develop.

Exemplary of the macrohistorical approach is Zygmunt Bauman's (1989) *Modernity and the Holocaust*, in which he argues that only a modern bureaucratic state with norms and institutions that emphasized rationality, science, objectivity, planning, and efficiency could provide the necessary foundation for the Holocaust. Though such a state was capable of mass destruction, it also required leadership committed to a particular vision of an ostensibly perfect society, which necessitated destroying all those who threatened such a vision. Bauman's attack on modernity centered on his contention that systematic murder was made possible through modern bureaucratic society's destruction of human moral capacity through the production of social distance and the replacement of abstracted technical responsibility for individual moral responsibility (Bauman 1989; Smith 1999). In a subsequent work, Bauman reconsiders the idea of "categorical murder" in which "men, women and children were exterminated for having been assigned to a category of beings that was meant to be eliminated" (Bauman 2004:26). Mass killings of Armenians, Jews, Gypsies, homosexuals, Jehovah's Witnesses, and Tutsis all amounted to categorical murder, which Bauman understands as a unidirectional consequence solely of their assignment to a group to be eliminated.

Adopting a similar approach of trying to understand how the social organization of mass murder routinely functioned, Wolfgang Sofsky studied concentration camps. Originally published in German in 1993, *The Order of Terror* (1997) offers an in-depth empirical investigation of concentration camps, looking specifically at the social organization of a camp in terms of time and space, the dynamics of absolute power, the organization of work or "terror labor," and so forth. His analysis provides readers with a thick description of the routine lived experience in the concentration camp, including how power and terror functioned.

Whether or not the potential for comparison with other extremist political movements motivated scholars, years later the political-sociological interest in Nazi party membership witnessed a scholarly resurgence. A number of sociologists documented membership patterns in the Nazi party. Who joined, when did they join, who was most likely to remain, and who was the most apt to drop out or be expelled? Using party membership data, scholars argued that membership was more representative of the whole of German society than initially believed (Brustein 1998a). In Munich, Nazi Party membership between 1925 and 1930 was evenly spread among city districts and generally proportionate to social status and most occupational distributions (Anheier and Neidhardt 1998). Economic self-interest, according to Brustein (1998a, 1998b), was a major motivator in party membership, making the early joiners of the Nazi party much like other citizens who choose parties or candidates according to their distinct economic interests. Based on careful data analysis of more than forty thousand party members, Brustein demonstrates the success of the Nazi party in crafting economic policies to meet the needs of ordinary German citizens. Others have argued for a more multifaceted explanation that underscores the importance of various social structural and political processes (Anheier 1997; Anheier, Neidhardt, and Vortkamp 1998). Some have investigated the effects of preexisting social networks on party membership (Anheier and Neidhardt 1998; Ault and Brustein 1998) and tried to understand gender differences in party membership (Anheier and Neidhardt 1998; Berntson and Ault 1998).

In his most recent book, Brustein (2003) returns to the question of anti-Semitism that Fein (1979) originally explored in her work. Both scholars examine national variations in anti-Semitism, which Fein concludes helped explain the different rates of Jewish victimization among nations. Brustein concentrates on the pre-Holocaust period and seeks to understand the foundations of European anti-Semitism and its varying formulations across five countries—France, Germany, Great Britain, Italy, and Romania. An exemplar of historical comparative research, Brustein's work identifies empirical evidence for four strains of anti-Semitism between 1879 and 1939—religious, racial, economic, and political—each of which relies on a particular configuration of anti-Jewish beliefs that vary over time and space.

Studies of the post-Holocaust era are even scarcer than those dealing with the Holocaust period itself, which speaks to the enduring epistemological chasm between Holocaust studies and immigration research, and the ways in which the unprecedented nature of the Holocaust has effectively erased questions of diaspora, immigration, and resettlement in postwar inquiry. Yet several notable exceptions do exist: Davie's (1947) survey of European immigration to the United States, Berghahn's (1984) monograph on Austrian and German Jewish refugees in England, Helmreich's (1992) work on Holocaust survivors arriving in the United States in the 1940s and 1950s, as well as Rapaport's (1997) and Bodemann's (2005) studies of second-generation Jewish Holocaust survivors living in Germany. Research on post-Holocaust life speaks to a phenomenology of surviving—that is, how people express their agency under genocidal conditions and their aftermath—thereby complicating assumptions about the universality and totality of the Holocaust genocide (Linden 1993).

Completed shortly after the end of World War II, the report of the Committee for the Study of Recent European Immigration (Davie 1947) examined hundreds of national and local refugee organizations in the United States, seventy-four of which committee members studied in depth; they surveyed a representative sample of 11,233 refugees, and collected over two hundred life-history narratives. Comprehensive in scope, the report covers refugee attitudes toward Americans, as well as American perceptions of the refugees, settlement patterns in the United States, problems on arrival and during subsequent years, and the contributions refugees made to the economy and social life. A significant portion of the analysis is devoted to specific occupational groups—businessmen and manufacturers, physicians, artists and writers, among others, and to young refugees, whom the reports characterize in generally positive terms. Berghahn (1984) interviewed first and 1.5 generations of immigrants, as well as children of the first generation born in Britain, about 180 people all together, concentrating on questions of assimilation and integration. Binary models of assimilation that posit either integration or its absence prove inadequate for Berghahn's data, which instead reveal new flexible forms of ethnic identity among the refugees and their offspring that combine elements of British, German, and Jewish cultures. While the formulation of ethnic, national, and religious identities forms distinctive dominant patterns for each generation, respondents indicated that they had frequently reconsidered the meanings and relative weighting of the various elements of their identities. Influenced by earlier studies of assimilation, Helmreich explains why most Holocaust survivors were relatively successful when measured by various personal, social, and economic indicators. To some extent, Helmreich's study mirrors a shift from viewing individuals as victims to seeing them as social actors with agency. This study counters a number of previous psychological studies of survivors, which focused almost exclusively on their resultant trauma and pathology (Krystal 1968; Niederland 1964).

Increasingly, scholarship on second-generation Holocaust survivors and perpetrators has become evident across disciplines, and sociology has also begun to contribute. *Jews in Germany after the Holocaust* is Lynn Rapaport's (1997) study of the vexed aspects of Jewish identity among eighty-three second-generation Jewish women and men living in Frankfurt. They vary in their affiliation to the organized Jewish community, religiosity, occupation, class, education, marital status, and, furthermore, by their parents' wartime experiences of the camps, exile, or hiding. Using one extended family as his focus, Michal Bodemann's (2005) most recent book consists of narratives from interviews with the three brothers who survived concentration camps and their children. This Eastern European Jewish family ended up homeless, stateless, and in displaced persons (DP) camps in Germany after the war but stayed on, becoming an important part of the contemporary Jewish community in Germany. The reader is immersed into the lifeworlds of these younger Jews born in Germany who are there because the Nazis failed to murder their parents. Such intimate portraits expose the range of dilemmas and inner turmoil experienced by Jewish families in post-Shoah Europe, as well as how assimilation and anti-Semitism challenge the identities of the second generation. One of the several contributions of this particular approach is that Jews are normalized and seen as social agents, foibles and all. Although not intended to be a book specifically about the Shoah, Bodemann finds it was constantly evoked and present in the lives of this family, particularly among the second generation who confronted identity struggles not wholly unlike those of contemporary second generations elsewhere.

The interpretative turn in Holocaust and post-Holocaust studies has taken place largely outside the social sciences, but increasingly sociologists have been influenced by the interdisciplinary scholarship on gender and the extant literatures on culture, narrative, and collective memory. Here the emphasis shifts from the importance of evidence to confirm or disconfirm hypotheses and positivist arguments to the interpretation of evidence presented most commonly as case studies. This shifting focus is reflected in the sociological literature on the Holocaust and constitutes what we term the second cluster.

Among the most prolific sociologists writing in this tradition is Nechama Tec, who in addition to her autobiographical volume *Dry Tears* (1984) has published a study of Christians' rescue of Polish Jews (1986); a biographical account of Oswald Rufeisen, a Polish Jew who passed as a Christian and used his connections and power to aid victims of Nazism (1990); a study of Jews who helped rescue other Jews (1993); and most recently a study of gender and the Holocaust (2003). Largely social-historical and documentary, her work is important for the ways in which it appropriately complicates the analytic categories of *victim* and *rescuer,* and for its focus on the many Jews who were active not only in their own survival but also in rescuing other victims. Although Tec's work differs from that described in the first cluster in that she is less interested in proving a claim or a particular pattern, it has clearly made an important and enduring set of analytical contributions to the literature.

Increasingly, gender scholarship comprises a significant element of this interpretative cluster. Since its inception, analyses of gender and the Holocaust have had to contend with the critique that attempts to define the catastrophe and its victims in gendered terms "will trivialize or banalize the Holocaust" (Ofer and Weitzman 1998:14) and "may lead to invidious comparisons and distract us from the real cause" (1998:15). But as many of these scholars have begun to show us through their research, rather than defile the Holocaust, analyses of gender contribute an important specificity to our knowledge of the Holocaust; without it, partial or distorted knowledge persists.

Although research on gender and the Holocaust is most prominent in social history and literary studies (Baumel 1998; Bridenthal, Grossman, and Kaplan 1984; Kaplan 1998; Koonz 1987; Zerubavel 2002), sociological scholarship in this area has become increasingly visible and instructive. Among the first sociologists to focus on gender was Linden (1993) who adopted a postmodern approach to study female survivors, thereby compensating for an earlier emphasis on men and the marginalization of women in Holocaust studies. Unfortunately, like some other postmodern researchers, she inserts herself vis-à-vis her own history, reflects on the interviews, and as a result, the reader sometimes learns more about her than her subjects.

A central collection on gender and the Holocaust edited by Ofer and Weitzman (1998) avoids the traps of gender essentialism and in many instances goes beyond mere description of women and men. Weitzman, the lone contributor who is a sociologist, eschews these pitfalls as she effectively analyzes why women, given a gendered division of labor and their duties as household providers, found themselves in a better position to live successfully on the Aryan side and survive the Nazi regime in Poland. Unlike circumcised men, women were less easily identified and thus more confident of their abilities to pass. Women were more likely to have attended secular schools and were consequently more assimilated, less religious, and had more Catholic friends. In addition, gendered patterns of socialization had taught women to be more sensitive to others, a functional skill when trying to pass. Weitzman considers the ways in which daily survival constituted a form of resistance, albeit an invisible one. Moreover, she analyzes women's participation in organized resistance activities that despite their real dangers, tended to go unnoticed and unrecognized because the work was assumed to be helping male leaders.

Diane Wolf's (2002a) oral history of a male camp survivor furthers a gender analysis as she demonstrates that some male inmates of the death camps were as caring if not perhaps more caring than some women. Her case study of a camp survivor, Jake Geldwert, raises the question of whether both women and men who survived the camps and their aftermath had available to them, and used, a greater range of skills and knowledge typically associated with either men or women than they might have had living under normal conditions.

Nechama Tec's (2003) recent book, *Resilience and Courage: Women, Men and the Holocaust* is replete with evidence of women's and men's behaviors and responses to Nazi policies, the accelerating brutalization of Jews, and survival strategies in hiding and in ghettos and camps. During the early years of the Third Reich and in the ghettos, Nazis prohibited Jewish men from fulfilling their masculine obligations to provide for and protect their families, and as a result, they were often demoralized. Recognizing the void created by the constraints on men's lives, Jewish women sought to compensate by expanding their work for their families and communities. Social class appeared to exacerbate gender differences as working-class Jewish men, for example, were better able to cope with the demands of physical labor and the deprivations of war than more economically privileged Jewish men. While Tec argues that women and youth were often the ones to urge their families to confront the inevitable doom of the Nazi regime, there is conflicting evidence about whether women or men were better able to survive, and Tec refuses to make what she considers a premature conclusion about gender and survival. She demonstrates how survival in the death camps required cooperation and caring among inmates—more traditionally feminine behaviors. Women appeared to be better able to endure the suffering than men, but men also seemed to have experienced more brutal treatment than women.

Israeli-born and Ireland-based Ronit Lentin has crafted a compelling book about the Shoah that stands out in the literature as a model of feminist sociological imagination. In *Israel and the Daughters of the Shoah: Reoccupying the Territories of Silence*, Lentin (2000) proffers a gendered analysis of the Shoah and its role and image in Israeli society. While Israeli society and the ideal *sabra* (a native-born Israeli) constitute highly masculinized images, she explains how the diaspora (*Galut*) and the Shoah were feminized, thereby stigmatizing and emasculating its survivors. Her book focuses on the personal narratives of nine Israeli daughters of Shoah survivors—writers and filmmakers—as she analyzes national discourses of Zionist and Israeli ideologies. She then links a gendered examination of the nation and the Shoah to the ways in which these discourses are utilized to justify Israel's sense of entitlement to the occupied territories. She returns to the gendered memory and narratives of the daughters of Shoah survivors in subsequent writing, questioning if these accounts are beginning to unsettle the dominant masculine codes of an imagined Zionist community even as the Zionist narrative remains intact (Lentin 2004a:59–76). Summoning several interdisciplinary approaches, including most notably postcolonialism, Lentin charts a sophisticated theoretical understanding of gender and the Holocaust within Israeli society.

The importance of gender scholarship to interpretations of the Holocaust is fully realized in Jacobs's exemplary ethnographic research on the collective memory of Holocaust memorial sites in Eastern Europe. Focusing on how memorial sites at concentration camps visually depict inmates, Jacobs (2004) contrasts the tendencies to remember genocide in religious terms through male ritual practices to the commemoration of ethnic genocide "through images of the subjugated female body, photographs of naked and starved women whose memory has come to represent the worst of Nazi atrocities" (231–32). Jacobs avoids the problems inherent in reproducing female and passive representations of Holocaust victims by understanding the insufficiencies of relying on descriptive ethnographic reports. Instead, Jacobs asks that she and others "interrogate not only the gendered realities of ethnic annihilation but the problems inherent in representing the victimization of women through the lens of sociocultural objectification" (235).

Particularly in the more recent works cited above, the importance of a gendered analysis of the Holocaust and post-Holocaust life is apparent. These projects surpass a descriptive and essentialist approach of merely bringing women and men into evidence and consider how gender both shapes and is shaped by the conduct, atrocities, and remembrance of the Holocaust. These texts challenge the assumption that a gendered understanding detracts from alternative approaches of Holocaust study, and they conversely demonstrate that analyses of genocide are incomplete, distorted, or limited without it.

Similarly, integrating research on Roma or Gypsies, as well as on lesbians and gay men, would arguably also advance our understanding of the Holocaust. More inclusive scholarship stands to complicate a unified narrative and promises to yield more sophisticated and nuanced knowledge of the subject. That said, the existing scholarship on Gypsies and the Holocaust in the social sciences remains sparse, and an apparent void exists in sociology. Among the social science contributions is Barany (2002), a political scientist who examines the changing statuses of Gypsies in the modern period across different political regimes and six Eastern European nations. He attributes the dearth of research on the Gypsy Holocaust to unreliable demographic information and a paucity of Nazi records on Gypsy deportment and death due to their extreme marginality. While he refuses to argue based on "precise numbers," Barany demonstrates the importance of Nazi policies in promoting anti-Roma practices in some but not all the nations studied. Concentrating on Germany, Margalit (2002) finds that in some regions, treatment of the Gypsies did not vary significantly between the Weimar and early Nazi years as practices were already restrictive and harsh before the Nazi rise to power. Importantly for social scientists, Fraser (1992) and Margalit (2002) compare Nazis' racialized policies toward the Gypsies and the Jews, but they differ on the extent to which Gypsies, assumed to be marginal to social and political life, were the objects of sustained political attention in Nazi writing and policies. Nonetheless, Gypsies particularly from Eastern Europe were deported and killed in massive numbers. Unlike the Gypsies living in Germany, who retained their romantic existence in the minds of many Third Reich leaders, Roma in Eastern Europe lacked such cognitive protections and the Gestapo collaborated with local leaders to exterminate them (Margalit 2002:25–55).

The social science literature about homosexuals during the Holocaust is also quite limited, in part as a consequence of postwar stigmatization and the criminalization of homosexuality, which helped sustain an intellectual disregard of gay men and women (Elman 1999; United States Holocaust Memorial Museum n.d.). Nazi policies concerning homosexuality were intertwined with concerns about Aryan birth rates and popular prejudices about lesbian sexuality, which trivialized women's same-sex relationships. These worries about reproduction resulted in some protection for both lesbian women, whom the Nazis reasoned could still bear children for the Reich, and for gay men living outside of Germany and the occupied territories whose sexuality could not augment Aryan births.

When read together, the texts on gender, Roma, and homosexuals demonstrate the advantages of studying specific groups—not only among victims but among perpetrators and bystanders as well. Such specificity helps generate an appropriately more complex understanding of the structures and processes of the Holocaust as these cases stand to complicate overgeneralized knowledge and foster appropriate comparisons. The sources cited above make clear that gender, Roma, and homosexuals do not function as essential identities but that, instead, their meanings are particular to the situation, often constructed in tandem with other cultural values. The salience of social and cultural factors alongside comparative empirical analyses suggests, moreover, that both interpretative and empirical approaches are important, and distinctions between the two are less than absolute.

A major part of this interpretative trend is the work on collective memory, and among the most important contributions to the study of social memory in the post-Holocaust era is Jeffrey Olick's work. Broadly framed by a sociology-of-knowledge approach, Olick has articulated collective memory as a negotiated process of meaning production in political culture, thereby effectively challenging more commonly held assumptions that the Holocaust functions as an unchangeable constant (Olick and Levy 1997). In subsequent work, Olick (1999b) argues against more presentist approaches and persuasively for the importance of a context-specific approach to the commemoration of May 8, 1945, in the Federal Republic of Germany. He demonstrates the usefulness of a "genre effect" that concurrently evokes the past and present (Olick 1999b:384).

Comparing collective memories of the Holocaust in the United States, Israel, and Germany, Levy and Sznaider (2005) contrast particularistic memory forms that define a specifically Jewish tragedy with German perpetrators to a universalistic form that understands the Holocaust as a breakdown of human civilization and values. The authors trace the transition from national to cosmopolitan memory cultures, the latter term referring to the processes of internal globalization that invoke both transnational and local dynamics. They demonstrate that the sociological relevance of the Holocaust lies in its location between these two distinct configurations of modernity, shifting from a particularistic conceptualization of the Holocaust centered on German perpetrators and Jewish victims to collective memory cultures that transcend national and ethnic boundaries. In contrast to the dominant research tradition within Holocaust studies arguing that memories of the Holocaust are defined by the political and cultural imperatives within each nation-state, Levy and Sznaider provide a compelling case for a deterritorialized and reflexive understanding of the received meanings of the Holocaust based on a dialectical relationship between local and global configurations.

If people remember as members of various groups, it follows that collective identity would also interest sociologists studying the Holocaust. Bodemann

(1990) has pursued questions of ethnic identity specifically with reference to postwar German Jews. He documents and interprets the "ideological labor" German Jews performed after 1945 for the West German government, and compares those practices to Nazi definitions of Jewish ethnicity. In subsequent work, Bodemann grapples with the complex linkages between collective memory and identity in his analysis of the five-stage reconstruction of the Jewish community in West Germany (Bodemann 1996a) and tensions over competition for commemorations of the *Kristallnacht* and German reunification in East Germany (Bodemann 1996b).

Robin Ostow (1989, 1990) has pursued the study of identity by investigating the anti-Jewish policies that practically decimated the Jewish community in the German Democratic Republic in 1952–53. Comparing these measures to attempts to resurrect the Jewish community following Stalin's death, Ostow documents the important role of the state in defining ethnic and religious minority groups. In later work, she examines how Jews in East Germany functioned as antifascist monuments in the 1980s but after reunification lost their unique status as "the 'victims' of German history" (Ostow 1996:241).

Intellectual memoirs and personal narratives, several written by sociologists, represent another form of collective memory. Reinhard Bendix (1986) describes his family's life in Berlin and their exile during the Nazi period. Reflecting on his early years in the United States, he recognizes the importance of the university to easing his own resettlement. Guenther Roth (1990) came to the United States after the war to work on a study of de-Nazification. He reflects on the meaning of his early years in Germany for his life's work on Max Weber. A second-generation Holocaust memoir writer, Anne Karpf (1996) speaks of her parents' erasure of their past, her own feelings of marginality, and her obsession with death. Her understanding of the Holocaust changes with growing public awareness of it, which enables her to recognize that what she once considered personal experience is also the collective experience of many refugees' children.

Probably nowhere is this interpretative turn more forcefully and poignantly articulated than in two recent volumes, *Cultural Trauma and Collective Identity* (Alexander et al. 2004) and *Re-presenting the Shoah for the Twenty-first Century* (Lentin 2004b). Covering a range of topics that includes the Holocaust, slavery, postcommunist societies, and September 11, 2001, Alexander and his coauthors develop a cultural model of trauma, which they offer as a corrective to commonsense understandings of trauma. Their theoretical exposition of cultural trauma argues that the meanings of any event cannot be taken for granted nor are they inherent in the events themselves. Thus the facts of a catastrophe, like those of any other event, need to pass through an "interpretative grid" to be understood at a collective level. Such grids are themselves located in time and space, and thus knowledge of the Holocaust would have been very different, for instance, had the Allies not been victorious. We cannot take for granted that the Holocaust would come to be understood as trauma or as evil, nor can we assume that its meanings would shift from primarily ones of Nazi atrocities to ones of its Jewish victims.

Lentin's (2004b) collection also engages questions of how we understand and represent our understanding of the Holocaust in its aftermath. Although our historiographic knowledge of the Shoah is now quite sophisticated, a vexed confusion remains about how we can understand it. Tension revolves around persistent debates about whether the Holocaust is comparable to other phenomena, and about whether or not we have the analytic categories that would permit Holocaust study, speech, and commemoration. While some argue that we can never understand the Holocaust because its uniqueness deprives us of the necessary intellectual capacity to know it, others have persuasively shown that the Shoah is unprecedented as a consequence of modern social life (Bauman 1989:12; Lentin 2004c:5) and "must be accessible to representation and interpretation" (Lentin 2004c:2), however inadequate. Yet Lentin cautions readers against simplistic comparisons that invoke the Holocaust, which she believes can erase the Holocaust.

It is our purpose in this collection to expand the ways of interpreting the Holocaust and post-Holocaust Jewish life by bringing the analytic tools of sociology and related fields of inquiry into dialogue with recent Holocaust scholarship. Our collection goes beyond prior scholarship and makes a distinctive contribution by proposing that we open up the interpretative grid that defines Holocaust scholarship to include an emphasis on questions of identities, diaspora, and collective memory with attention to key factors such as transnational relations, disaster and trauma, gender, and ethnicity where relevant. Our expressed goal remains to provide a model of intellectual cross-fertilization that will inspire Holocaust scholars to take fuller advantage of the intellectual resources in sociology and encourage sociologists to bring the Holocaust as a case into their work. Since we call into question monolithic notions of identity and memory, we deliberately refer to identities and memories in the plural. Indeed, many of the essays that follow argue that ethnic, religious, and national identities

JUDITH M. GERSON AND DIANE L. WOLF

were often in flux, a matter of ongoing contestation and negotiation, and rarely if ever understood to constitute a single, stable configuration. The contributions in this collection incorporate recent theoretical and substantive advances scholars have developed outside the field of Holocaust studies primarily in sociology, but also in interdisciplinary fields of inquiry such as cultural, postcolonial, migration, social movements, and gender studies. Many chapters focus on the past, and for most of them, memory constitutes a crucial operating principal, while still others consider contemporary Jewish life, practices, and identities.

The essays in this volume center on the themes of memory, identity, and diaspora in the Holocaust and its aftermath, both drawing on and contributing to ongoing work in these areas as they intersect with studies of race and ethnicity, immigration, globalization, disaster research, and social theory more generally. We have argued for the importance of intellectual cross-fertilization integrating work on the Holocaust and post-Holocaust life into sociology more broadly and using the analytic tools of these disciplines to further our understanding of the Shoah. Through the work of our commentators in this volume, we have already seen the intellectual advantages of relying on a broadly defined sociological approach to interpret the empirical research presented here. It is our hope with the publication of this volume that its presence will initiate many more engagements with these intellectual projects.

Notes

1. Although we were tempted to use a more expansive definition of sociology and sociologists, we have adopted a more conservative approach and defined the disciplinary boundaries as being isomorphic with those generally recognized as its professional practitioners (see Abbott 1988). Had we taken a more flexible stance and given more weight to the content of the ideas regardless of their authorship, Hannah Arendt surely would have been the first among those we would have considered as professing sociological knowledge of the Holocaust. As Ira Cohen has astutely argued in a personal communication, Arendt's (1963) analysis of the "banality of evil" is "sociology at its best." It is not possible to justly deal with Arendt's contributions here, but hopefully a reminder to our readers will suffice. Arendt proposed a framework for understanding how evil was perpetrated initially though routine acts and then reproduced through patterned actions.

2. Restricting our review to English-language sources (largely in the original, though some in translation) is not merely a matter of convenience. Knowledge never is universal knowledge but instead changes over time and place. Thus we wish to specify the boundaries of our arguments. Though historical scholarship still dominates studies of the Holocaust and post-Holocaust eras in Europe and Israel, social science research on

the Holocaust seems more in evidence in those countries than in the United States. Nonetheless, in a recent article on the development of sociology in Israel, Hanna Herzog (2000) maintains that the Holocaust has not been studied extensively in Israeli sociology.

We used multiple methods and sources to identify sociologists who studied the Holocaust. We searched journal articles and books using the commonly accepted ways of locating materials. If we did not know whether an author was a sociologist, we resolved this question using several criteria and sources. We read authors' acknowledgments and citations for ties to known sociologists and sociological work, which usually yielded the necessary information. If there were remaining questions, we consulted the American Sociological Association's *Directory of Members* and Nicholas C. Mullins and Carolyn J. Mullins' (1973) *Theories and Theory Groups in Contemporary American Sociology* to determine if a person was listed in either of these sources. See especially Mullins and Mullins' methodological appendix. This process meant that we might have inadvertently omitted sociologists who were less well known and/or were not affiliated with the American Sociological Association. We also compared our resources to Porter and Hoffman's (1999) *The Sociology of the Holocaust and Genocide: A Teaching and Learning Guide* to ensure that we had not overlooked materials, which we had not. We take some solace in realizing that Zygmunt Bauman, a scholar whose work we hold in highest regard, discusses only three sociologists who have analyzed the Holocaust (Bauman 1989).

3. A Nazi refugee, Adorno (among many others) was plagued by the horrors of the death camps, and his writings through the mid-1960s reflected his terror (Jay 1984).

4. Two books by his biographer Uta Gerhardt (1993, 2002) highlight Parsons's work on National Socialism and partially correct this gap. But even Gerhardt refers to Parsons's writing on National Socialism as a "special phase" of his work (2002:58).

5. Although Parsons's writings on Nazism were not particularly provocative, some of his postwartime activities have generated concern and controversy. Weiner (1989), Gerhardt (1993b, 1996) Porter (1996), Wrong (1996), and Oppenheimer (1997a, b) have analyzed Parsons's involvement with the Harvard Russian Research Center and his connections to the governmental intelligence community.

6. Goldhagen (1996) assumes and tries to make a case for the opposite conclusion—that is, that ordinary Germans were active in the brutalization and extermination of the Jews because of widespread and extreme anti-Semitism.

7. A few other sociologists have also used comparative historical approaches to study the Holocaust and genocide more broadly. See Irving Louis Horowitz's (1984) work on national cultures of totalitarian states; Chalk and Jonassohn's (1990) attempt to develop a typology of genocide; and Thompson and Quets (1990). Fein's 1993 volume on sociological perspectives on genocide includes nonsociologists because of the paucity of published work in the discipline. The penchant among sociologists to discover generalizable patterns as a means to understand the Holocaust is probably best exemplified in William Gamson's (1995) presidential address before the American Sociological Asso-

ciation. Gamson builds on Fein's (1977) idea of a "universe of obligation," which refers to the people to whom we are accountable. Gamson refers to the Holocaust and other cases to analyze how the "most blatant forms of action exclusion, which includes genocide, and indirect exclusion, which is characterized by subtle forms of exclusion," operate (1995:1). Furthermore, in a recent issue of *Contemporary Sociology*, in the lead article Oberschall (2000) wrote about genocide prevention as part of a more varied collection of essays on "Utopian Visions." Whether these works mark the beginning of a trend in sociological research on genocide or are an anomaly remains uncertain.

2

JEWISH IDENTITIES IN THE DIASPORA

The essays in part 2 focus on Jewish identities in the diaspora in the post-Holocaust years. Debra Kaufman begins with a focus on post-memory, which she argues influences not only the cultural memories but also the social and political practices of Jewish young adults. Unlike older generations, today's youth in the United States emphasize the importance of the survival of a Jewish culture given the destruction of the Shoah. Using Marianne Hirsch's concept of post-memory, more typically associated with the children of Holocaust survivors, Kaufman describes how among those with no direct familial links to the Holocaust, fragmentary knowledge of the Shoah enables them to focus on an imaginary past destroyed by the Nazis. This romanticized version of a Jewish past—whether in terms of community life, culture, music, or food—represents fond recollections of what might have been and what might now be revived through their concerted collective practices.

Caryn Aviv and David Shneer also address identity issues among young American Jews and consider how their sense of themselves as Jews is formed in part through the organized tours they often take to Israel and Eastern Europe. This travel forms a central element of the diaspora business, that is, the wide-ranging transnational organizational landscape dedicated to building strong(er) Jewish identities. These tours tend to represent Israel as the site of Jewish renewal and life, and Eastern Europe as the post-Holocaust site of Jewish death and destruction. Yet as the authors indicate, these oppositional definitions of place are neither permanent nor stable. Intermittent violence in Israel, the inclusion of many Eastern European countries in the European Union, and heightened security concerns in the United States stand to alter the current associations of place and identity, and ultimately reconfigure both the popularity of some sites and their meanings in the production of diasporic Jewish identities.

Chaim Waxman's chapter shifts our attention to the influences of Orthodox Jews on Jewish identity within the organized Jewish community in the United States. Orthodox Jews were disproportionately the victims of the Holocaust, and they also were disproportionately represented among survivors and refugees. The arrival of Orthodox Jewish refugees after the war reversed a decline in Orthodox Judaism in the United States and led to a significant revitalization of organized Jewish life and consciousness both inside and outside the Orthodox community. More recent developments leave open the question as to whether a revitalized Orthodox presence will ultimately lead to greater unity or disunity within the larger Jewish community.

Arlene Stein opens up the discussion of the foregoing essays by focusing on storytelling. Trauma stories have recently become more common as members of many groups—including lesbians and gay men, sexual abuse victims, recovering drug and alcohol users, as well as Holocaust survivors—have begun to speak publicly. While it is important to recognize this more general trend, Stein argues, it is also necessary to situate these stories in time and place. In the period immediately following World War II in the United States—a time that emphasized assimilation, the Cold War, and suburbanization—there were few public accounts of the Holocaust. Holocaust survivors did not easily fit within this context, and not surprisingly, their stories were barely voiced or heard. Yet Jewish communities have varying relationships to so-called Holocaust talk, and Stein points to changes over time, as well as to differences in religious observance, national identities, and generations as she maps how various Jewish communities have denied or encouraged talk about the Holocaust. Though cognizant of the reactionary potential of survivor stories, Stein ultimately remains hopeful that when marginalized people narrate their suffering, it will ultimately result in greater recognition and inclusion.

Social theory promises to transcend specific cases, as Richard Williams reminds us, enabling us to make more general statements about social life. Extreme or unique cases test the limits of any social theory and thus provide the means for theorists to judge the inclusiveness and validity of their work. If the theories are found deficient, aberrant cases often contain the evidence suggestive of needed revisions. Williams begins his analysis recognizing the virtual absence of the Holocaust and Jewish identity in theories about the social construction of identity. Yet as Williams convincingly demonstrates, Jewish identity and the Holocaust are legitimate cases, and their omission proves problematic for social constructionists of identity. To ameliorate this situation, he considers how people cognitively create identities, that is, notions of similarity and homogeneity, on the one hand, and ideas of difference and heterogeneity, on the other. Using evidence from the previous chapters, Williams demonstrates that a unified Jewish identity is not sufficient to explain the beliefs or behaviors of group members. Even the Holocaust, widely assumed to unify the identity of diasporic Jews, fails to create a homogenous collective identity. Indeed, the extant differences in identity confirm what theorists have understood for some time, namely, that people select elements to construct a basis for a homogenous identity. As he writes in this volume: "The cases show that responses to the Holocaust have been heterogeneous, based on social and cultural differences, although Jewish identity, as an assumed homogenous category, is always a potential resource for shaping collective beliefs and actions." He suggests, moreover, that social constructionist theories of identity do not yield an easy resolution to questions about the uniqueness of the Holocaust. The Holocaust and Jewish identity represent "messy cases"; in other words, they do not provide simple or clear-cut evidence of collective identity trauma. Williams proposes that a more productive way to approach studying the issues linked to collective identity trauma is to attend to the full range of responses to such traumas among members of a group and ultimately compare those conditions and responses to other groups who have experienced collective trauma.

Post-memory and Post-Holocaust
Jewish Identity Narratives

DEBRA RENEE KAUFMAN

> Comprehending our past depends upon our
> ability to make it speak our language; in
> doing so, equally, we give it a voice with
> which it can tell us things about ourselves.
> —Steven Buckler, "Historical Narrative,
> Identity and the Holocaust"

Dominick LaCapra (1998) contends that one job of history is to
critically test memory and "to work through a past that has not passed away" (8).[1]
The sociologist's job is to analyze the ways different cohorts revise memory
depending on the national, cultural, ideological, religious, economic, and political
context. The post-Holocaust identity narratives of young Jewish American
adults (not necessarily children or grandchildren of Holocaust survivors) I gathered as part of a larger project about Jewish identity clearly reflect a past "still
alive or invested with emotion and value" (LaCapra 1998:8). These identity
narratives provide insight into the ways through which dynamic social forces
help formulate something we call cultural memory. They also reflect and contribute to the "ongoing process of imagining and presenting the Holocaust along
specifically American lines" (Rosenfeld 1995:5).

In this essay I am suggesting that contemporary identity narratives should be
treated, in part, as indicators of the ways in which post-memories about the
Holocaust are positioned in the cultural memory and individual consciousness
we sometimes refer to as American Jewish identity. Marianne Hirsch has coined
the term *post-memory* to distinguish between the post-Holocaust memory of

survivors and post-memory of the Holocaust of survivors' children.[2] I am expanding Hirsch's use of memory to extend beyond that of Holocaust survivors' children to include identity narratives of contemporary young adults. These identity narratives are prisms that reflect post-memories of the Holocaust by a generation for which memory is fast becoming history. Hirsch sees photographic "sites of memory" as prisms through which to study "the postmodern space of cultural memory" (1997:13). For her, that cultural space is composed of "leftovers, debris, single items that are left to be collected and assembled in many ways, to tell a variety of stories, from a variety of often competing perspectives" (13). Identity narratives offer yet another kind of prism from which to study the "postmodern space of cultural memory" (13).

Important to the ongoing debates about collective memory and history is Pierre Nora's (1989) understanding of memory as an actual living entity associated with "the remnants of experience still lived in the warmth of tradition, in the silence of custom, in the repetition of the ancestral . . ." (7). If, as David Cesarani (2001) believes, we live in "an epoch preoccupied by memory and memorialization" or a "confessional culture" in which the individual recollection is assigned the highest priority, the language and meaning embedded in identity narratives become important components of collective memory (231).[3] In the personal narrative, Cesarani suggests we "tend to recall things that are important in our society and culture, events of political significance as well as personal dramas" (231). Personal dramas, I argue, include what each of us brings to or reimagines as being part of our ethnic/religious histories, therefore, identity narratives are simultaneously collective and individual.

The following identity narratives explore the perspectives of seventy young adults from twenty to thirty years of age, a cohort that is frequently underrepresented in Jewish identity research. Their identity narratives might be seen as future sites of memory or current narrative forms of post-memory for understanding the peculiarly American shaping of an ever-evolving post-Holocaust collective memory.[4] The identity narratives of these young American Jewish adults reveal a form of post-memory not necessarily specific to Holocaust survivors or their children. The identity narratives of this twenty- to thirty-year-old cohort are steeped in a profusion of Holocaust memorials, media presentations, curricula, literature, and ongoing survivor and children of survivors' testimonies and writings.

Hirsch and Spitzer (1993) ask how current narratives might advance the inquiries we make about the Holocaust. Although they are referring to Claude Lanzman's film *Shoah* (1985) their discussion provides a way of viewing the post-Holocaust identity narratives of the seventy young adults I studied. Like Hirsch and Spitzer, I contend that when respondents narrate their identity stories, such narratives are never fully "theirs," nor are their identity stories ever "unmediated representations" of the past and its relationship to the present (Hirsch and Spitzer 1993:14). Moreover, although their post-Holocaust identity stories may be fragmentary, mediated, and subject to historical inaccuracies, these young adults' narratives represent a way of bearing witness to the Holocaust, or as Hirsch and Spitzer put it, of "witnessing about the event without witness" (14). I hope to show how the narratives of these young adults have been affected by their presence in the largest and most powerful diaspora Jewish community in the world. By analyzing identity narratives, both as individual identity and as one set of themes relevant to a collective cultural post-memory, we may gain insights into the fluid ways that cultural memory is shaped and reshaped by time and circumstance.

Jewish History and the Holocaust

In *The Holocaust in American Life*, Peter Novick (1999) critically describes the way in which Holocaust memory has been shaped and manipulated by Jewish organizations in the United States and Israel. He is particularly concerned about the way in which the Holocaust has been manipulated to nurture a Jewish American sense of community and identity.[5] Novick assumes that the Holocaust plays a major role in Jewish American identity and that it is correlated to identity in the way in which he presumes it to be. He is not alone in his presumptions. Although, as Diane Wolf (1998) points out, there is no monolithic Jewish collective memory, many contemporary scholars suggest that the Holocaust comprises one of the most important bases of American and Israeli Jewish identity, a Jewish "civil religion" (Woocher 1986; Goldberg 1995). According to Meyer (1990), for most Jews prior to the Holocaust, American Jewish identity either was a religiously based morality or a loose bond of ethnic solidarity (see Kaufman 1998, 1999). A rise in awareness of the Holocaust, claims Meyer (1990), has produced in many individuals a much more "determined" Jewishness (56) and has become a major factor in sustaining Jewish identity since World War II.

Despite the lack of empirical data or research about identity among contemporary young adults, Chaim Seidler-Feller (1991) argues that in the absence of a positive motivation, the Holocaust becomes critical in sustaining Jewish identity. Charles Silberman (1985) reported almost two decades ago that there were well over seven hundred courses on the history and literature of the Holocaust in secular American colleges and universities and that those courses attracted more students than any others in Judaic studies. Seidler-Feller (1991) reasons that the steady diet of Holocaust films, novels, memorials, museums, and courses are the institutional ways in which this generation of young adults create their identities (see Kaufman 1998). The focus for most young people, claims Seidler-Feller (1991), is on victimology, a political identity based both on perceived and real anti-Semitism and the historical reconstructions of being the victim. Alvin Rosenfeld (1995) writes: "This tendency to relativize and universalize the Holocaust has been a prominent part of the American reception of Holocaust representations from the start. It is strong today and seems to be growing, especially within those segments of American culture that are intent on developing a politics of identity based on victim status and the grievances that come with such status" (17).

More speculative than certain, Jonathan Webber (2001) conjectures that Jewish cultural and political memory tends "to activate itself constantly with reference to past tragedy and catastrophe" (237). Like Novick, Webber (1992) wonders whether the renewed interest in the Holocaust might provide a new basis for secular Jewish self-identity, especially in countries where there is little significant anti-Semitism. But unlike Novick, he does not necessarily tie this insight to political manipulations by Israeli and American Jewish leaders. For Novick, victim identification may lead to a potential battle among ethnic groups over whose victimization is greater. For Webber, such identity constructions are a way of providing a moral discourse about human history, a way of getting others to "see their own Auschwitz in Auschwitz" (Webber 1992:1). Novick, on the other hand, questions the value of such a moral discourse since it requires too facile a moral consensus to be of any ultimate political value. However, such speculations about the bases and maintenance of Jewish identity are just that, speculations.[6] We have little empirical data to support any of the above assertions one way or another.

Survey data from the American Jewish Committee reveal that in 1997, 94 percent of respondents believed that Jews should "keep the remembrance of the Holocaust strong, even after the passage of time" (Penkower 2000:128). Two years later, respondents cited the Shoah, above religious observance or the state of Israel, as important to their Jewish identity (Penkower 2000). However, these quantitative data leave much unexplained. For instance, does keeping the Holocaust strong over time and the recognition of the importance of the Holocaust to Jewish identity necessarily translate into a political identity based on victimhood? Indeed, large quantitative surveys rarely can attest to any of the important narrative information needed to assess identity issues. Reflecting on the American Jewish Committee's studies to determine what people in several countries know about the Holocaust, Rosenfeld (1995) notes that although Europeans did better on basic information about the Holocaust, paradoxically, Americans seem to care more, "with large percentages of those polled replying that it is 'essential' or 'important'" that Americans "know about and understand the Holocaust" (2). Popular culture often provides better clues about the meaning of the Holocaust in Jewish identity than survey research. For instance, in *The Americanization of the Holocaust*, Amy Hungerford (1999) and Joyce Antler (1999) explore the ways in which Holocaust themes play a part in the popular expressions of American Jewish identity. Earlier, Paul Breines (1990) presented Israel as the macho antidote to the powerless diaspora Jew.

The seventy identity narratives offered in this essay form a part of a larger project I am engaged in about Jewish identity among young adults in the United States, Great Britain, and Israel. In the present article, two issues are of interest: how dominant, if at all, is the Holocaust in the identity narratives of the young adults I interviewed, and in what ways, if at all, is the Holocaust expressed in their identity narratives? In other words, which, if any, aspects of the Holocaust are "remembered" and "how" by a generation for whom the Holocaust is an historical event. These data represent narratives from a generation some sixty years beyond the Holocaust living in one of the most powerful diaspora communities in the world.

The Postmodern Space of Cultural Memory and Jewish Identity Narratives

Stuart Hall writes, "identities are the names we give to different ways we are positioned by and position ourselves within the narratives of the past" (qtd. in Silberstein 1994:4). One such potential narrative, for the young adults under study, is the Holocaust. Despite the pivotal role young adults play in understanding Jewish identity (a topic of profound interest in the sociology of Judaism), this is a cohort for whom we have very little data. Addressing many of the shortcomings of current and past identity studies, Egon Mayer (2001) offers a concept he calls "outlook" as a useful corrective to most identity research. Outlook, he claims, is "drawn directly from the ordinary experience of the everyday life of people and employs a metric or method of measurement that emerges directly from the language of that experience" (Mayer 2001:5). In my research, I am assessing identity through the language and stated worldviews of the respondents. I focus on their subjective self-understandings rather than on behavioral or affiliative measures of identification (see Kaufman 2005 for more on methodological issues and needed correctives in identity research). I contend that narrative takes up the many challenges typical identity research presents.

The seventy respondents under study were primarily middle to upper middle class, urban young adults currently residing in the northeastern part of the United States. The average age among the interviewees was twenty-three. All are either in school, continuing with their education at the graduate or professional level, and/or currently employed. All have had some or are currently engaged in postsecondary education. The estimated family of origin incomes (combined if both parents worked during their years growing up) reported by the respondents ranged from $65,000 to $250,000, with almost all parents in professional and/or business careers. Although the sample was heavily concentrated in the northeastern part of the United States, other areas of origin included Montana, Oregon, Texas, California, Illinois, Ohio, and Mississippi. The sample consisted of thirty-four women and thirty-six men. Respondents were interviewed through a snowball sampling technique, using what I call "structured conversations," a set of prepared questions that guided our recorded conversations. The interviewees were not necessarily relatives, grandchildren, or great grandchildren of Holocaust survivors, and, for this study, I was not interested in this particular constellation. I was interested in exploring whether and to what extent the Holocaust provides themes and metaphors around which contemporary Jewish identity is constructed and positioned by contemporary young adults.

For the young people in my study, the Holocaust represents one expression of their Jewish identity, although not necessarily the most important or primary one. One thirty-year-old male explains his position this way:

I think there are a lot of people whose Jewish identities are very structured by memories of the Holocaust and the establishment of the state of Israel, and they are things I feel strongly about. Neither one is the primary event, however, that structures my Jewish life . . . I really think . . . an emphasis on either of those two things really de-emphasizes the way in which one can, or sort of understand a Jewish experience that's in the present. (Kaufman 1998:52)

Although anti-Semitism is certainly a component in the construction of Jewish identity, the strongest issues emerging were not couched in terms of perceived or real anti-Semitism, but rather in the need to belong to a group one could call one's "own." When asked what was specifically Jewish about that kind of group identification, almost all believed that it had to do with belonging to a group of people who had a unique and long history and a distinctive culture. One twenty-six-year-old male put it this way: "I was born into this 5,000 year tradition, of which I am proud . . . I feel an obligation to continue and perpetuate it" (Kaufman 1999:52). A twenty-seven-year-old stated that the most "comfortable" part of being Jewish is that he identifies with "a community and a history and a tradition." "Notice," he says, "I didn't bring up God . . . whether God exists, or doesn't . . . it doesn't change our history or tradition, or all the great things about the Jewish people one way or another" (Kaufman 1998:52). Moreover, contrary to Seidler-Feller's (1991) expectations, while the Holocaust subtly infuses their identity narratives, historical reconstructions of being the victim do not. One twenty-eight-year-old female claims:

Judaism is not just about the past . . . the Holocaust is a BIG PROBLEM (emphasis hers). I mean, it's CRUCIAL (emphasis hers), that we remember it. I've been to Poland, and I studied it, and read books, and it's awful. It's the worst thing to happen to the Jewish people, or any people, and we have to remember it, and read books, and tape testimonies from people and make movies, and have it immortalized, but what we CAN'T (emphasis hers) do is become a cult of the Holocaust, where our sole identity is based upon guilt that we survived, or determination that it will never happen again, or just rooted in the tragedy . . . Judaism is much more than that. . . . It has an affirmative message which predated the Holocaust, and which will go forward from that and that has to do with the land, and Jerusalem, and the food, and the music, and the culture, and the way you live your life. (Kaufman 1998:52)

A twenty-year-old male put it this way: "I don't like to think of it as something where the Jews have suffered through history and we have to protect it . . . I don't deny it happened, that Jews have suffered a lot throughout the ages, but I don't think that's the reason that I choose to go on being Jewish . . . I don't want to think of myself as a victim of history" (Kaufman 1998:52).

Others were very specific about their belief that the United States actually went to war to liberate or save the Jews. One twenty-year-old said quite firmly: "I never quite understood until I went to the Holocaust Museum in Washington how important it was for us (U.S.) to save the Jews. I mean . . . I am not sure . . .

you know . . . just what we knew during the War, but once we knew there is no doubt that we wanted it made known to the World that this will never happen again."

When I asked to whom "we" referred, she was quite clear that it meant the American soldiers and the U.S. government. Another twenty-year-old male stated that he understood quite completely how it was so easy to fight in World War II. He notes: "We had to go to war . . . those crazy Nazi fascists were trying to take over the world. We were and still are the strongest democracy in the world . . . we just had to go to war." This connection between democracy, liberation themes, the Holocaust, World War II, and American Jewish identity should not be very surprising given, as but one example, the location and presentation of Holocaust museums in the United States. Vivian Patraka (1997) asserts that one of the main ideological underpinnings of the U.S. Holocaust Memorial Museum in Washington "is to create a 'meaningful testament' to the values and ideals of democracy, thereby inscribing it within the history of American democracy, if not American history per se" (62). Both the opening and the closing images of the museum are taken from the perspective of American troops liberating the concentration camps. Patraka notes: "If what is critical for the museum's project is to extend our fictions of nationhood by the premise that a democratic state comes to the aid of those peoples outside its borders subjected to genocide, then the conferring of liberation becomes the story of American democracy" (Patraka 1997:62–63).

Liberation themes are clearly situated within the identity narratives of the young adults I studied. Moreover, as the following quotes indicate, the emphasis is as much on being American as on being Jewish. "We liberated them," one twenty-five-year-old tells me. He continues: "I lost no family in the Holocaust and I know very few people who did, but I know that one of the reasons we went to war was to free those victimized by the Germans." The distancing between himself and "them," and the insistence that "we" went to war because of those who were "victimized by the Germans" reveals an interesting take on the entrance of the United States into World War II and on being victimized. A twenty-two-year-old woman recounts her first visit to the Holocaust Museum in Washington. "I guess you could kind of call me a conscientious objector," she says, but then adds the following: "But I do know that the one War, especially seeing how many people were persecuted because of their race, religion or sexual preference, I would not have objected to was WWII. It is our duty, you know, I mean, as Americans to make sure that this never happens again to any person anywhere in the world."

For this population of young contemporary Jews, the Holocaust is the historical marker against which all other atrocities are compared. When the Holocaust is used as a historical marker, it brings into focus not only events after World War II but also those that preceded it. Perhaps, unwittingly, this results in a kind of revitalization and reshaping of earlier moments of Jewish history and/or personal biography. One twenty-seven-year-old female suggested that after visiting the Beit Hashoah–Museum of Tolerance in Los Angeles, she decided to do a genealogical search. She comments:

I don't know, it just hit me, there but for what go I. I mean here I am, I haven't been touched by the Holocaust directly, not my parents or my grandparents, but then I began to wonder about my mother's family in Poland. Why didn't the whole family leave at the same time? You know, the distant cousins, what happened to them . . . what was life like for them? I mean what did they do prior to the War that maybe kept them in Poland longer, what kind of lives did they lead? I think some of my family were musicians, you know Klezmer stuff, at least I think it was Klezmer. We are a part of a family tree and I wanted to know what the early branches looked like.

Others found that Holocaust-related themes led them to an interest in Israel and the belief that Israel is most important in preventing any such cataclysmic event from happening again. As one twenty-year-old male puts it:

You know, I have read some of Elie Wiesel's work. It is awesome. It makes me think, how do people go on after such stuff? . . . I get so angry. I am sure that if Israel had existed during the time of Hitler, so many Jews might not have died. I have some reservations about the current political role of Israel, but I am never willing to have her jeopardize her safety or our claims to that land, ever.

Those who were members of Hillel House on their respective campuses found themselves frequently celebrating what they classified as nonreligious holidays (Chanukah and Passover, for instance) more than attending weekly religious services or even high holiday services. Both Chanukah and Passover celebrate themes of liberation and victory. The increasing celebration of *Yom Ha'atzmaoot* (Israeli Independence Day) among this age group might be yet another signal for the way in which they envision themselves as victors rather than victims (Kaufman 2003).

It is clear that the Holocaust is not necessarily the most salient component of these young people's identity narratives. Yet links to the Holocaust are evident in the ways in which they connect their identity politics and the Shoah's legacy. Liberation and democracy are closely tied in these young adults' narratives. These twenty- to thirty-year-old adults, as "liberators," extend their American Jewish identities to include contemporary Others. For example, of those who claimed social action as key to their Jewish identities, most did so as a sensibility and sensitivity of Jews to others' suffering. For men and women, active social engagement is clearly linked to their concern for other Others. For many, political engagement stands as a testament to the larger cultural narrative of "never again." For those expressing their politics specifically as a connection to the Holocaust (and not, for instance, as part of their religious duty as Jews to other Jews), "never again" specifically meant never again to *any* people. This was seen most clearly for those involved in what was formerly Yugoslavia. Others felt their work with Oxfam expressed their obligation never to see a population "die out." For still others, it was human rights activities directed at South America, Africa, or Asia (Kaufman 1998:54).

While many male and female respondents tied their Jewish identities to their political commitments to others, gender differences emerged when respondents spoke of their connections to others socially. Jewish identity as "unique," "separate," and "different" appeared to be more troubling for women than for men. For instance, women more than men seemed to connect their concerns about Others with their own connection to the Jewish community. One twenty-two-year-old wondered about the lack of non-Jewish friends in her life. Another complained that the lack of diversity within her friendship circles "probably makes me a very narrow person." Another woman says: "Being involved with the Jewish community has made my social life much too homogeneous and that's something that I'm trying to do a little bit more outreach on and to try to cultivate some other relationships" (Kaufman 2003:8).

While both men and women understood the Holocaust as an extreme version of racism, men and women described it differently. One twenty-two-year-old male put it this way: "We need to be ever vigilant about racism. I think racism is very much about the way you think, the ideas you have about people, especially around differences . . . you know, I think any thought that you can have equality with difference is a very mistaken idea. I don't believe in 'different but equal.' The idea of equality is critical in doing away with difference and consequently differential treatment" (Kaufman 2003:7–8).

Women were more likely than men, in all of their identity stories, to narrate their concerns from a more practical and grounded basis (for a discussion of the theoretical implications of this, see Kaufman 1999, 2003). They were more likely than men to offer details and specific examples in making their points. One twenty-three-year-old woman suggests the following:

If you want to make a difference then you have to put your money where your mouth is. Look, if you want to make a difference get yourself dirty, get into the community, get in there. I worked for several years as a playground supervisor in the summers in a ghetto community near my hometown. I won't say it was easy or that I wasn't frightened some of the time, but I thought if I am going to make a difference you got to get in there and experience it. Did I make a difference, I don't know. Do I think it's part of my duty as a Jew, you bet.

For women, the experience of being grounded and embedded in one community informs the way in which they draw conclusions about how to be connected to others not of the same group (see Kaufman 2003). Similarly, if mentioned at all, women were more likely to be concerned about the notion of a "chosen people" and the consequences of such a perspective. "It's very hard to think that you are part of a chosen people and still feel you are part of all people," complains one twenty-seven-year-old female. Another twenty-two-year-old suggests that she intellectually understands what "chosen" means, that is, "a light unto nations," but worries that "actually" it is expressed as a feeling of "superiority." "This is no way to be a light," she concludes (see especially Kaufman 1999 and 2003 for a fuller discussion of the same issues).

My data suggest something both similar to and different from the ways in which earlier writers I have cited conjecture about the Holocaust and American Jewish identity. In my sample, identity narratives, at both the personal and collective level, often go beyond the particularistic understanding of victim. The current and historical recountings offered by the young adults in my study reflect a complicated, if not, at times, contradictory, understanding of being a victim. And while the Holocaust is clearly present in their identity narratives, it is often interwoven with other identity themes of equal importance to them. Indeed, only 60 percent of the sample *spontaneously* referred to the Holocaust during the conversations we had about identity. If, for instance, at the end of the interview the respondent had not mentioned the Holocaust in any thematic way, each was asked: "How important, if at all, is the Holocaust to your feelings about yourself as a Jew?"

Clearly, the identity narratives reported here are more than historical reconstructions of being the victim and themes of anti-Semitism. These young adults envision their identities in ways that move them beyond their immediate communities, beyond victim to victor (liberator) in their historical recounting, and in ways that vary by gender. These identity narratives reflect the fluid and complex interaction at both the cultural and personal level in the telling of identity stories. Philip Gleason argues that one's identity "may be shed, resurrected or adapted as the situation warrants" and that there is a dimension of individual and group existence "that can be consciously emphasized or de-emphasized as the situation dictates" (Gleason 1998:55). Novick suggests that post-Holocaust narratives among contemporary Jews, especially in the United States, are so banal that they become uncontestable platitudes against racism and genocide. However, the post-Holocaust narratives, at least among the young adults I studied, do reflect very engaged and politically active responses to the reductive platitudes Novick bemoans.

Identity Politics, the Sociohistoric Moment, and the Holocaust

The young people in my sample inherit a set of memories and memorials that feed into their identity narratives in both expected and unexpected ways. While their identity narratives borrow from images and stories based on novels, poems, plays, films, television programs, magazine articles, and newspapers, it is clear that the themes represented by the United States Holocaust Memorial Museum in Washington and the Beit Hashoah–Museum of Tolerance in Los Angeles have a place in many of the respondents' post-memory configurations as well. At least two distinct themes, found in these two very differently oriented museums, are articulated by many of the respondents (these themes are not mutually exclusive, for traces of each can be found in the very same interview): themes about liberation and themes about the victimization of other Others. In contrast to the United States Holocaust Memorial Museum's stress on the role of the United States in liberating oppressed groups, the Museum of Tolerance focuses on the ways in which violations of human rights have taken place and continue to take place in the United States. Patraka (1997) suggests that the Museum of Tolerance "articulates the history of the Holocaust to an American landscape of prejudice and racism, a more liberal narrative" (70). The concern for other Others articulated in many of the identity narratives I gathered, and in very specific ways by women, resonate with worry about our "own oppressed" in the United States, those beyond the Jewish community.

Young (1993) contends that as "events of World War II recede into time, the more prominent its memorials become" (1). He suggests that

as the period of the Holocaust is shaped in the survivors' diaries and memoirs, in their children's films and novels, public memory of this time is being molded in a proliferating number of memorial images and spaces. Depending on where and by whom these memorials are constructed, these sites remember the past according to a variety of national myths, ideals, and political needs . . . all reflect both the past experiences and current lives of their communities, as well as the state's memory of itself. (2–3)

While there is no direct influence of one on the other, it seems that the American narrative of victor and liberator (the state's memory of itself) has helped shape the identity narratives of the cohort I sampled. The worry about the oppressed Other that appears in many of the identity narratives suggests that other cultural memories and meanings are also present in the narratives of the young adults I interviewed.

Pierre Nora, write Gedi and Elam (1996), holds an unorthodox view of memory: "His view is radical to the extent of substituting the monument for living memory, thereby turning it into the actual location of 'collective memory.' The end result is that because history and memory stand in opposition to one another, he has to declare *lieux de mémoire* as 'another history.' We thus no longer deal with events but with sites" (10). Once created, as Young (1993) notes, memorials take on a life of their own. "New generations," he reasons, "visit memorials under new circumstances and invest them with new meanings" (3). Such meanings, he concludes, become part of a collective cultural memory and individual identity. Interestingly, when the specific motto "never again" emerges in their Holocaust narratives (borrowed from the collective cultural Holocaust narrative), the young adults I interviewed are clear that it means never again to any people. Perhaps, as Allan Rosenberg and Gerald Myers (1988) might conjecture, the young adults I studied are distanced enough from the Holocaust to be capable of integrating memory about the Holocaust into their moral and intellectual lives. Many of the young people in my study seem to have moved beyond a particularistic and/or historical recounting of victim status to a more general concern for other Others.

Conclusion

The relationships among post-Holocaust identity, memory, and history represent a complex phenomenon. In this essay, I have chosen to show how some young adults' modes of political and social practice reflect a number of the ways in which the Holocaust has become part of their Jewish identity narratives. Through a sophisticated analytical schema, Dominick LaCapra (1998) suggests that social action may be one way of remembering traumatic events in a desirable way. In that sense, perhaps these young adults' social and political activism represents a form of contemporary mourning for the Holocaust.

This generation of young adults has appropriated a connection to the Holocaust that is akin to Hirsch's concept of post-memory. That is, like children of survivors, they have a historical distance from the Holocaust. And like children of survivors, not only do they seem to have an investment in remembering the Holocaust but their experience of it is dominated "by narratives that preceded their birth" and "shaped by traumatic events that can be neither fully understood nor re-created" (Hirsch 1997:2). Their narratives present one way of sociologically analyzing what Hirsch might refer to as "the postmodern space of cultural memory." That is, as sites of remembrance, these identity narratives represent indirect, fragmentary stories that reflect and contribute to cultural narratives of Holocaust post-memory. Carl Becker (1958) observes: "The kind of history that has most influence upon the life of the community and the course of events is the history that common people carry around in their heads. . . . Whether the general run of people read history books or not, they inevitably picture the past in some fashion or other, and this picture, however little it corresponds to the real past, helps to determine their ideas about politics and society" (61).

The Holocaust, with its mandate to witness and not to forget, becomes, then, the subtle marker for both past and current events. LaCapra contends that events that occurred before the Shoah cannot be understood or read in the same way today. This is apparent to me in the ways in which the young adults in my study reinforce their commitment to all that preceded the Holocaust and to a communal present. Many place a great premium on Jewish survival. They speak of what Judaism has given to the larger culture. For many, their revisioning of a mythic past comes from what they envision as having been destroyed by the Holocaust. Therefore many place a great identity premium on that which preceded the Holocaust (shtetl life, ethnic foods and customs of another time and place). With the Holocaust as a key historical marker, historical precedents are reimagined and reflected in their contemporary identity narratives and constructions of Jewish identity. Moreover, their narratives reflect the current cultural presentations of the past that emphasize a liberator rather than a victim mentality. This victor ideology extends to participation in political and social activism. And finally, their identity narratives evoke a collective consciousness created by Holocaust representations in memorials, museums, films, literature, courses, and testimony. These post-Holocaust narratives, influenced by the socio-historic moment may find their revised way back into the cultural collective consciousness, a consciousness that may well become a part of tomorrow's post-memory of the Holocaust.

Notes

1. In his introduction to his edited volume, *The Sixties: From Memory to History*, David Farber (1994) reinforces LaCapra's claims about memory and history. Farber refers to the movies and books of the 1990s that tried to bring order to the "still powerful rush" of vivid experiences of the 1960s (1). He argues that memory is the emotional counterpart to history, giving us direction and helping us to understand what is important in motivating us to explain history. In this sense, as some authors have conjectured, memory has been stereotypically drawn as the feminine counterpart to masculine history.

2. In my discussion of post-memory, I am most indebted to the work of Marianne Hirsch (1997). I am also indebted to Diane Wolf for reconnecting me to Hirsch's work, although she is not responsible for my unorthodox take on that rereading. Although Hirsch is using photographs rather than narratives as sites of memory, it is her interpretation of their place in history that makes her work so appealing to me.

3. Again, the main point for me, as Stier (1996) also indicates, is that the processes of collective memory reveal a contemporary sense of identity as it depends on the past. He writes: "Memory is about the present, or, more precisely, it is about a particular way of imagining and representing the present by turning attention towards the past" (10). Wolf (2002) writes that the production of cultural memory is pivotal in creating and per-petuating links for the "second generation" (5). My interpretation is that "the second generation" does not refer only to Holocaust survivors or their descendents.

4. Although relevant to the topic, it is not possible to delineate here the growing scholarly debates about the meaning of collective memory and history. Maurice Halbwachs's (1980) work on the topic has been a key source for many scholars. Important to his argument is the distinction between what he calls history—a scholarly scrutiny of the records of the past, presumably detached from the pressures of the immediate political scene—and collective memory. Yael Zerubavel (1995) writes: "Halbwachs's seminal work made a major contribution to the study of collective memory by identifying it as a form of memory that is distinct from both the historical and the autobiographical. By high-lighting the importance of understanding collective memory within its social frame-works, Halbwachs has inspired a growing body of research on the social and political dimensions of commemoration" (4). She ends her paragraph by noting that Halbwachs understands collective memory as "an organic part of social life that is continuously

transformed in response to society's changing needs" (4). In this essay, identity narratives are critically connected to collective memory as one source of post-memory.

5. Kaplan (2001) writes that Novick is concerned that this sense of community "defends against anti-Semitism by establishing favourable instead of unfavourable images of Jews, whether as victims or heroes or both at the same time" (313).

6. James Young argues "over time the only 'common' experience uniting an otherwise diverse, often fractious, community of Jewish Americans has been the vicarious memory of the Holocaust . . . if to entirely disparate ideological ends" (1993:348).

The Holocaust, Orthodox Jewry, and
the American Jewish Community

CHAIM I. WAXMAN

If we look at the impact of the Holocaust on American Jewry in terms of
the number of survivors who immigrated to the United States, it may not seem to
be very significant. During the years 1937–48, an estimated 200,000 to 250,000
European Jewish refugees arrived in the United States (Wischnitzer 1948). In the
years following World War II, approximately 120,000 Jews arrived in the United
States, with the highest number, about 41,200, arriving in 1949 (Rebhun 2001).
The Jewish population in the United States at the time numbered about 5 million,
which means that the total immigration during the postwar period amounted to
about 2.4 percent of the total Jewish population.

In reality, however, their impact was far greater than their actual numbers. In
both religious and secular communal institutions and organizations, the Holocaust survivors played significant roles in intensifying both "extrinsic" and "intrinsic" Jewish culture.[1] The Holocaust immigrant had an especially significant
impact on religiously traditional branches of American Judaism, especially Orthodox and, to a lesser extent, Conservative Judaism.

More than 90 percent of contemporary American Jews are of Eastern European background. In 1880, there were approximately 250,000 Jews in the United
States, most of Central European background. Between 1881 and 1923–26, close
to 3 million Jews from Eastern Europe, most of whom had lived in small towns
and villages (*shtetlach*), immigrated. For all intents and purposes, the only form of
Judaism with which they were familiar in Eastern Europe was what has become
known as Orthodox Judaism. As a result of the immigration, the "heyday of New

York's Orthodoxy"—which was essentially American Orthodoxy, since the overwhelming majority of Orthodox Jews in the United States lived in the New York area—occurred in the 1920s and 1930s (Joselit 1990:2).

In the United States, however, many of them and their children left Orthodoxy for Conservative and, to a lesser extent, Reform Judaism. If American Orthodoxy was self-assured and optimistic about its future in the 1920s, the sense of elation and self-confidence dissipated rather quickly. As Joselit (1990) put it,

> By the 1940s the English-speaking Orthodox rabbinate had suffered somewhat of a reversal and was forced to take stock of its future. Now muted, its characteristic buoyancy and optimism was succeeded by a barely disguised sense of thwarted expectations, especially pronounced among the second and third generation of RIETS [Rabbi Isaac Elchanan Theological Seminary] students, as the interwar years gave way to wartime and the fifties. To the modernized Orthodox Jews, once confident that their form Judaism would become the dominant religious expression of second-general Americanized Jews, it now seemed as if a true modernized Orthodoxy could found only in isolated instances, in "pockets," and that the anticipated orthodoxization of middle-class American Jewry would not materialize. "A lost cause," reflected a RIETS graduate of 1942, "Orthodoxy was not going anywhere." (80)

One of the problems was that when immigration was feasible, the most traditional and Jewishly educated of Eastern European Orthodox Jewry, and especially its rabbinic intellectual elite, most resisted migration to the United States, for several reasons. As a rule, the more traditionally religious are the most resistant to geographic mobility, in part perhaps because of its negative consequences on religious participation. Namely, as the empirical research suggests, there is typically an inverse relationship between geographical mobility and religious participation (see Finke 1989; Irwin, Tolbert, and Lyson 1999; Stump 1984; Welch and Baltzell 1984; Wuthnow and Christiano 1979). Eastern European Orthodox Jewry was further discouraged from migrating to the United States because of negative reports about religious life there. For example, New York's Rabbi Moses Weinberger (1982), who had immigrated from Hungary, wrote a sharply critical portrait of Judaism in New York in the 1880s. He viewed American society as totally materialistic and bemoaned the low levels of Jewish education and observance of dietary rituals in the country. His book was, in large measure, a warning to his fellow Jews in Eastern Europe that the United States posed a spiritual threat to religiously traditional Jews.

In the early 1890s, Rabbi Israel Meir Hakohen of Radun, Belarus, one of the most revered rabbinic authorities of his generation and one widely known by the title of one of his works, *Hafetz Hayyim* [*Desires of Life*], published his own warning to Eastern European Jewry about the dangers of immigrating to America. In the conclusion to *Nidhe Yisrael* [*The Dispersed of Israel*], work clarifying some of the basics of traditional religious law, *Halakha*, for those in "distant countries," especially the United States, the author warned of the risks of leaving Eastern Europe and asserted that the economic opportunities were not worth the price of losing one's Judaism or that of one's children (Hakohen 1893).

Several years later, in 1900, Rabbi Jacob David Wilowsky, the renowned rabbi of Slutsk (Belarus), publicly proclaimed "that anyone who emigrated to America was a sinner, since, in America, the Oral Law is trodden under foot. It was not only home that the Jews left behind in Europe, he said, it was their Torah, their Talmud (Oral Law), their *yeshivot* (schools of Jewish learning)—in a word, their *Yiddishkeit*, their entire Jewish way of life" (Davis 1963:318).

There was at least one further reason that the majority of the Orthodox rabbinic intellectual elite remained in Eastern Europe and did not participate in large numbers in the massive emigration of Jews to the United States during the peak years of immigration, 1881–1923. The words and actions of several of them on the very eve of the Holocaust suggest that some remained because they felt that they had an obligation, as leaders, to tend to their followers in Eastern Europe.

The prevalent leadership of Orthodox Jewry was, apparently, not quite equipped to overcome the challenges of the open American society. As Marshall Sklare (1955) put it at midcentury, "Orthodox adherents have succeeded in achieving the goal of institutional perpetuation only to a limited extent; the history of their movement in this country can be written in terms of a case study of institutional decay" (43).

The Holocaust changed much of this. Although many Orthodox Jews had resisted coming to the United States in earlier years, there was now no choice for them, and they decided to come and transplant their religious culture to the United States. The available evidence suggests that Orthodox Jews were disproportionately represented among Holocaust refugees who immigrated to this country. As William Helmreich (1992) found in his study of Holocaust survivors, which entailed in-depth interviews with 170 survivors, approximately 41 percent identified as Orthodox, as compared to the 10 percent or less in the larger American Jewish population.

Lest it be argued that Helmreich's interviewees may not be representative, my own analysis of data from the national survey of Jews in the United States, the 1990 National Jewish Population Survey, indicated similar patterns. Looking at respondents who stated their current religion as Jewish, I found among those who were born elsewhere and arrived in the United States during the years 1937–48 20 percent identifying as currently Orthodox and 45 percent identifying as raised Orthodox. Among those of comparable ages born in the United States, 6 percent identified their current denomination as Orthodox and 19 percent identified the denomination in which they were raised as Orthodox.

This pattern manifests itself with respect to Jewish organizational membership as well. Among those who were born elsewhere and arrived in the United States between 1937 and 1948, about a third (32 percent) stated that they belonged to two or more Jewish organizations, compared to 22 percent among those born in the United States. Among the latter, 59 percent stated that they did not belong to any Jewish organizations, as compared to 53 percent among those who arrived in 1937–48. The 1937–48 immigrants also had slightly higher rates of volunteering for Jewish organizations than did their U.S.-born counterparts. Finally, whereas 20 percent of the U.S.-born cohort had more than eight years of formal Jewish education, 36 percent of the wartime immigrants did.

Most of the immigrant survivors settled in existing centers of Jewish population, although some ended up in Jewishly remote areas, such as the close to one thousand refugees settled in Oswego, New York (Gruber 2000; Lowenstein 1986). It has been reported that more than 90 percent of the four hundred European displaced persons (DP) settled worldwide were placed in urban areas (Meyer 1953). According to the United States Displaced Persons Commission, most of the post–World War II DP admitted to the United States between 1947 and 1952 settled in the ten largest states, with 31 percent settling in New York State and about a quarter settling in New York City (Dinnerstein 1982; United States Displaced Persons Commission 1952).

There were also other, more remote, places where Jews settled. According to Morris Zeldich (1950), the United Service for New Americans (USNA) "settled more than 2,800 persons in 122 communities in 37 states during 1948 . . . [and] by the end of July, 1949, 7,716 arrivals under the DP Act had been assisted to their destinations in 334 communities in 43 states" (195).[2]

A number of newly arrived Orthodox leaders had been heads of advanced rabbinical seminaries, *yeshivot gedolot*, in Eastern Europe and, almost imme-

TABLE I. Number of Hebrew Day Schools: Year, Types, and Enrollment

	Day Schools	High Schools	Total Enrollments	Number of Communities
1940	35		7,700	7
1945	69	9	10,200	31
1955	180		35,500	68
1965	323	83	63,500	117
1970			72,000	
1975	425	138	82,200	160

Source: Chaim I. Waxman, *America's Jews in Transition.* Philadelphia: Temple University Press, 1983.

diately on their arrival in the United States, set about to reconstruct those yeshivas on American soil. Such leaders as Rabbi Aaron Kotler, Rabbi Abraham Kalmanowitz, and Rabbis Eliyahu Meir Bloch and Mordechai Katz reestablished their advanced yeshivas in Lakewood, Brooklyn, Cleveland, and elsewhere in the Eastern European mold and helped spawn a generation of knowledgeable and ideologically committed Orthodox Jews, many of whom were to subsequently establish other advanced yeshivas in dozens of American cities.

As a first step, the National Society for Hebrew Day Schools, Torah Umesorah, was formed with the objective of encouraging and assisting in the founding of Jewish day schools—elementary and high schools that would provide intensive Jewish education along with a quality secular curriculum—in cities and neighborhoods across the country.

As the above table indicates, the number of day schools grew from 35 to 323 and enrollments grew from 7,700 to 63,500 between the years 1940 and 1965. By 1975, there were a total of 425 day schools, 138 high schools with an enrollment of 82,200. These schools were located not only in the New York metropolitan area but in thirty-three states across the country. By 1975, every city in the United States with a Jewish population of 7,500 had at least one day school, as did four out of five of the cities with a Jewish population of between 5,000 and 7,500. Among cities with smaller Jewish populations, one out of four with a population of 1,000 Jews had a Jewish day school (Waxman 1983).

It should be noted that instituting this type of day school was in itself an adaptation to modernity. Many of the very same rabbinic leaders who spirited the day school movement, especially Rabbi Aaron Kotler, had been adamantly opposed to this kind of school, which combined both sacred and secular education. Although a number of day schools had been founded early in the twentieth century, their numbers and, hence, their impact had remained relatively small. With the efforts of the new immigration's leadership, the picture changed dramatically. As indicated, a virtual boom in the growth of the day school movement occurred between World War II and the mid-1970s, and since then, day schools have become recognized as valued institutions within conservative and Reform Judaism as well. Indeed, by the 1990s, non-Orthodox day schools were the fastest growing phenomenon in the American Jewish community (Alexander 1998). As indicated in a 1994 study by the Avi Chai Foundation analyzing the self-identified denominational affiliation of day schools in the United States, of a total of 221 schools surveyed in New York State, 204 were Orthodox, 11 conservative–Solomon Schechter, 5 nondenominational community schools, and 1 Reform. In the rest of the country, a total of 280 schools were surveyed: 170 were Orthodox, 55 community, 43 Solomon Schechter, and 12 Reform (Avi Chai 1994). Thus in New York State, the Orthodox schools represented 92 percent of the total number of day schools, but the picture was very different outside of New York State. There, although Orthodox schools still constituted a majority, they represented only 60 percent of the total.

As for the impact of day schools on Jewish identity, an analysis of the 1990 National Jewish Population Survey data on baby boomers indicates that day school education correlates with almost all measures of Jewish identity and identification,[3] and for many of those measures, the correlation is much higher than it is with other types of Jewish education (Waxman 2001).

Also among the refugees were many members and some leaders of Hasidic sects such as Belzer, Bobover, Chernobler, Lisker, Munkatcher, Novominsker, Satmarer, Skverer, Stoliner, Talner, Tarler, Tasher, Trisker, and Zanzer, to name some of the more prominent ones. The Hasidim, perhaps even more than others, were determined to retain their traditional way of life even within the modern metropolis, and they were largely successful in achieving that goal (Daum and Rudavsky 1997; Mintz 1998).

This new infusion of ideologically committed Orthodox Jews provided the numbers and the manpower for the renaissance that was to manifest itself more than a quarter of a century later. It also played a role in the intensification of religious belief and practice among the Orthodox, as well as in the increasing rift between them and the non-Orthodox (Freedman 2000; Waxman 1998).

Interestingly, in contrast to the assertions by several critics of this phenomenon, the increased religious zealousness and the growing rift between the Orthodox and non-Orthodox denominations within American Judaism do not represent a distancing of Orthodox Jews from American society. Quite the contrary. Indications suggest that they are increasingly attached to the larger society and view living their Orthodox lifestyle as a right *within* the larger society, rather than viewing it as setting them apart from it. One indication of their emotional attachments to the larger society may be reflected in the widespread display of American flags on homes and businesses in heavily Orthodox neighborhoods following the World Trade Center disaster of September 11, 2001. The national office of Agudath Israel, a prominent *haredi*, or "ultra-Orthodox," organization, sent out strongly worded letters imploring its members to contribute to the fund for families of firefighters and police victims of the disaster. These actions appear to indicate a deep sense of identification with the tragedy as Americans.

As Diamond (2000) points out in his study of the Orthodox Jewish community in suburban Toronto, a series of vibrant Orthodox Jewish suburban communities have developed across North America, and the key to their success is the combination of the socioeconomic affluence of their constituents with their religious commitments that require them to live within a single neighborhood— Orthodox religious law prohibits driving on the Sabbath, setting the framework for a communal structure in which its members are in close physical proximity to each other.

Orthodox Jews sufficiently modern as to have achieved relatively high educational and economic status and who internalized modern conceptions of aesthetics and social organization pioneered the suburbs for Orthodox Jews and built small communities that subsequently, once there were communal foundations, attracted larger numbers of Orthodox Jews. In contrast to the stereotype of Orthodox Jews as being concentrated in the lower socioeconomic strata, many of them are fairly affluent. It should be noted, however, that according to the 1990 National Jewish Population Survey, as a group, Orthodox Jews continued to have annual family incomes lower than conservative and Reform Jews. Yet compared to the general North American population, even the Orthodox have above-average incomes (Waxman 2001).

There is an irony in the fact that the new Orthodox communities, developed by modern Orthodox Jews and reflecting modern Orthodox norms and values, are abandoning many of those norms and becoming much more traditionally Orthodox (Diamond 2000; Freedman 2000; Waxman 1998). In part, this is due to the fact that with the Orthodox communal development, increasing numbers of traditional Orthodox feel free to move there. This pattern manifests itself in a range of Orthodox communities in New York—such as Borough Park and Flatbush in Brooklyn, the Five Towns in Nassua County, and Monsey in Rockland County—as well as in Baltimore and Toronto, among others.

Be that as it may, these Orthodox communities are tied together by technological innovations in communications and transportation as a variety of national institutions, organizations, and activities that make them part of one larger North American Orthodox community (Diamond 2000). In addition, they have been assisted by the replacement, within the larger American society and culture, of the ideology of the melting pot with that of cultural pluralism, as well as by the emergence of multicultural marketing (Halter 2000), which was one factor in the growth of the kosher food industry, as well as the phenomenal increase in the production and availability of a wide range of Judaica, including Jewish religious items, books, art, music, and the like.

American Orthodox Reactions and Responses to the Holocaust

Just before the outbreak of World War II, in 1939, the Vaad Hatzala (Rescue Committee) was established by the Union of Orthodox Rabbis of the United States and Canada to save as many Jews as possible. It represented highly traditional *haredi* Jews, who were largely unknown to the wider public and the leadership of the U.S. organized Jewish community at the time. Its initial efforts were directed toward fund-raising to save as many rabbis, yeshiva students, and their family members as possible.

The Vaad's efforts, however, sparked a controversy within the American Jewish community. The major American Jewish organizations favored a single, united fund-raising and relief effort, with the funds to be raised domestically by the Council of Jewish Federations and Welfare Funds (CJFWF) and to be disbursed in Europe by the American Jewish Joint Distribution Committee (JDC). They saw the efforts and activities of the Vaad Hatzala as competitive, splintering, and self-defeating. The Vaad's leadership publicly proclaimed its support and admiration for the work of the JDC but insisted that practical and ideological issues made its formation a necessity. Many of the non-Orthodox were at a loss to understand why the Orthodox felt that they had to act independently of the JDC, especially since the European office of the JDC worked diligently to save Jews there, as well as to assist refugee communities abroad that had significant Orthodox populations such as the ones in Kobe, Japan, and in Shanghai (Kranzler 1976; Warhaftig 1988). Yet much as the Vaad and the JDC leadership publicly played down their mutual ambivalence, the very existence of the Vaad remained a sore point that, at times, bordered on open conflict (Zuroff 2000). In broader terms, the establishment of the Vaad marked the first major instance of separatism from the larger Jewish community on the part of Orthodoxy in the United States.[4]

Relations between the larger organized American Jewish community and American Orthodoxy were further strained by the political activism of the Vaad. In contrast to the quiet diplomacy of the communal leadership, the Vaad Hatazala organized campaigns to publicize the plight of European Jewry, especially its rabbinic elite. In October 1943, it organized four hundred Orthodox rabbis in a very public march on Washington. This was one of a handful of public protests engaged in by the American Jewry. The Vaad also undertook a number of other unconventional actions in its rescue efforts, such as having elderly, long-bearded, and black-frocked rabbis attempt to influence members of Congress to pass legislation to help Jews in Nazi-occupied Europe, none of which appear to have had any substantial results (Grobman 2004; Kranzler 1987; Vaad Hatzala 1957; Zuroff 2000).

During the 1950s and 1960s, when American Jewry and the organized American Jewish community began to grapple with the significance and impact of the Holocaust, it emerged as a central myth and symbol (Woocher 1986), and the public commemoration of the Holocaust, accompanied by a religious liturgy, was adopted as a central ritual within the American Jewish community. Given the disproportionate number of Orthodox among the survivors, it often seems ironic that the more traditionalist *haredi* have been the most resistant to adopting Holocaust Memorial Day and to instituting special prayers to commemorate the tragedy.

In fact, however, the position of the sectarian Orthodox may not be as ironic as it appears. As David Ellenson (1996) points out with respect to the similar resistance of these Orthodox to implement liturgies for the state of Israel, "The failure of Orthodox liturgies to take cognizance of the Jewish state is hardly a reflection of Orthodox disinterest in or indifference to the Jewish state. It rather reflects an Orthodox reluctance to tamper with the received liturgy" (121–22n19). As far as Holocaust Memorial Day is concerned, there is an additional problem for the sectarian Orthodox that involves the specific date selected for commemoration. Holocaust Memorial Day falls in the springtime, on the equivalent of the twenty-seventh day of the Hebrew month of Nissan, and was selected because it is believed to be the date of the outbreak of the Warsaw Ghetto uprising. The Orthodox, however, urged that one of the traditional days of mourning—such as the tenth of Tevet, the seventeenth of Tammuz, or the ninth of Av—should be adopted to commemorate the Holocaust, especially since the month of Nissan is traditionally a joyous month in which memorial services are not recited (Brin 2002). Consequently, although many Orthodox Jews, "ultra" or not, commemorate the Holocaust in a variety of ways—in the privacy of their families, as well as within their own Orthodox communities[5]—they are often looked on with disdain as separatists because of their nonparticipation in the larger communal commemorations.

Another reason for the Orthodox resistance to Holocaust Memorial Day commemorations is that many of their leaders portray the Holocaust as but another manifestation of the kind of anti-Semitism that has existed since the very beginning of the Jewish people. To these Orthodox thinkers, the Holocaust was not qualitatively unique and, therefore, does not require any special commemoration (see Hutner 1977). Interestingly, although Debra Kaufman (2001) gives no indication of the denominational affiliation of her interviewees, many of them likewise tended to view the Holocaust within the framework of Jewish history, rather than as a totally unique phenomenon.

Finally, there are some Orthodox who because of their inability to grapple with the Holocaust religio-philosophically, refrain from participating in Holocaust commemorations (Caplan 2002; Schweid 1994).

Conclusion

The Orthodox, and especially the more highly traditional among them, were disproportionately affected by the Holocaust, and they were disproportionately represented among the immigrant refugees. The influx of Orthodox Holocaust refugees reversed a trend of decline, in both quantitative and qualitative terms, and sparked a revitalization of Orthodox Judaism in the United States.[6] This revitalization of American Orthodox Judaism contributed, as well, to the intensification of Jewish consciousness in the larger organized American Jewish community. Nevertheless, some of the specific stances of the Orthodox community, and especially those of its more religiously conservative elements, have contributed to a sense of estrangement and polarization between the denominations

CHAIM I. WAXMAN

that comprise American Judaism. The question thus remains whether, in the face of rifts such as these, organized American Jewry will be able to retain its communal-like character. To put it in the terms of the German sociologist Ferdinand Tönnies, will the relations among America's Jews continue to be *Gemeinschaft*-like or will they become *Gesellschaft*-like. In the *Gemeinschaft*, he says, people are essentially united despite all of the things dividing them; in the *Gesellschaft*, they are essentially divided despite all of the things uniting them (Tönnies [1887] 1957). Within that context, the question is whether the memory of the Holocaust will serve to sustain or to weaken *Gemeinschaft*-like relations among Jews in the United States.

Notes

1. As Milton Gordon (1964) uses these terms, "*intrinsic* cultural traits" refer to such patterns and traits as "religious beliefs and practices," "literature," and "a sense of a common past" among others, while "*extrinsic* cultural traits" refer to such patterns and traits as "dress, manner, patterns of emotional expression, and minor oddities in pronouncing and inflecting English (79).

2. The National Council of Jewish Women assisted in the formation of the National Coordinating Committee of Refugee Problems, which became the National Refugee Service and, later, the United Service for New Americans. In 1954, USNA merged with the Hebrew Immigrant Aid Society (HIAS) and the JDC Migration Department into the United HIAS Service.

3. The concept "Jewish identity" is one that numerous scholars have attempted to define (Herman 1989; Levitz 1995; London and Chazan 1990; Phillips 1991), but a precise conceptualization remains elusive. Indeed, there appears to be a basic difference in the way in which psychologists conceive of identity when compared to the way in which sociologists conceive of it. Also, despite Herman's (1989) distinction between identity and identification, most social scientific studies of Jewish identity infer identity from indicators of identification (Phillips 1991). Indeed, Herman (1989) himself, having emphasized the distinction, nevertheless writes, "While it is useful to bear in mind the distinction . . . between 'identification' and 'identity', the two concepts will frequently intertwine in the analysis which follows" (39–40). To complicate matters, within the framework of the newer postmodernist conception, Jewish identity is something that individuals create for themselves and entails how they think and feel emotionally about their Jewishness (Rubin-Dorsky and Fishkin 1996). It is, therefore, much less susceptible to measurement by responses to survey questions. As Kleinman (1991–92), a Jewish communal professional, points out, "Because of its vagueness, it means all things to all people. . . . Without a shared meaning for discussion, without guidelines to understand the language we use, any effort to discuss continuity and outreach is of little practical

value to our professional practice" (140). Given the semantic and conceptual complexities, I have chosen to refer to the variables selected as indicators of identity and identification. Since no other reliable criteria for analyzing Jewish identity are yet available, the empirical data in the National Jewish Population Survey (NJPS) that reflect Jewish identification are also taken as indicators of Jewish identity.

4. On the development of Orthodoxy in imperialist Germany as a separatist, sectarian community, see Breuer 1992.

5. To cite just two examples: For one, a number of prominent Hasidic rabbis wrote special lamentations to commemorate the Holocaust that have been appended to the traditional lamentations recited in the morning prayer service on the ninth day of Av, the traditional anniversary of the destruction of the Temple in Jerusalem. In another example, almost immediately after the Holocaust, the Rabbinical College of Telshe, transplanted from Lithuania to Cleveland, Ohio, in 1941, adopted the twentieth day of Tammuz as a day of prayer to commemorate the destruction of the parent community.

6. For a different perspective on the state of Orthodoxy between the world wars and subsequent developments within that community, see Gurock 1996.

Traveling Jews, Creating Memory: Eastern Europe, Israel, and the Diaspora Business

CARYN AVIV AND
DAVID SHNEER

We say life isn't just about learning, it's about putting what you learn into action.
Don't just be a tourist, make a difference.
—Livnot U'Lehibanot (To Build and Be Built) Programs in Israel Web site

Many young American Jews have participated in organized tours to Eastern Europe or Israel in the past ten years. These pilgrimages are designed to encourage a strong sense of Jewish identity for the rest of one's lifetime. There are hundreds of programs that send Jews of all ages to Israel to dig for archaeological treasures, pray in synagogues, fire guns, excavate bones, scuba dive, learn a little Hebrew, and pick olives or oranges, among other pastimes. These tours and trips often situate Eastern Europe as the center of Jewish suffering and death, America as an exilic place of weakening Jewish identity, and Israel as the center of Jewish life. Tours to these Jewish places of death and life are used to consider how participants might translate their memories of travel into action at home, that is, in America or other communities around the world. Israel and Eastern Europe have been used as a theatrical backdrop on which to construct and strengthen Jewish identities for Jews in America and around the world. We call this kind of Jewish tourism and identity travel the "diaspora business."

The diaspora business is a broad institutional and organizational terrain that complicates the questions of home and abroad, centers and peripheries, in a shifting, global world of capital, people, ideas, memories, and national borders

(Appadurai 2001; Clifford 1994; Ong 1999). A major aim of this business is to shore up the religious, ethnic, and cultural identities of individuals, perceived as diminishing in Jewish communities around the world, while simultaneously benefiting Israel, the United States, and now Eastern Europe through finance, tourism, cultural exchanges, product import and export, and employment (Kirschenblatt-Gimblett 1998). Particularly in the case of young Jews, this travel industry is less about sustaining already existing connections and memories between individuals and communities than it is about *inventing* new relationships between American Jews and other Jewish places. The diaspora business includes educational and historical tours of Israel and Eastern Europe, intense group experiences within particular religious worlds (such as Orthodox yeshivas), and volunteer work opportunities for Jewish teens and young adults as a way of strengthening the allegiances and solidarity of Jews from different countries, and of creating a sense of global nationhood, usually with Israel at the center of that tourist universe. Similar forms of travel exist for other ethnic groups (Basch, Glick Schiller, and Szanton Blanc 1994) and even for Israeli Jews of immigrant origins (Levy 1997), but within the Jewish world, this form of diaspora business constitutes the *foundation* of global Jewish tourism, and as such, it garners both intense academic scrutiny and serious communal investment (Saxe et al. 2002). Jewish parents and communal leaders send children around the world to find their Jewish futures—not in Israel, but "at home."

A History of Jewish Youth Travel

Prior to the 1980s, few trips existed to bring Jews to communist Poland, and most trips to Israel focused on developing and deepening Jews' commitment to Zionism and Israel, rather than using Israel as a means to strengthen identity at home. The collective effort of Jewish communal organizations to view Israel and Poland as important places for creating and/or solidifying rooted, global Jewish identities is relatively new.

Palestine, and then later Israel, was initially a place where American Jews could remake themselves into full-fledged Zionists and potentially become citizens of a new Jewish state. The Zionist kibbutz and youth movements The Young Guard (HaShomer Hatza'ir) and Young Judaea provided the initial infrastructure and ideological foundation for travel to Palestine and Israel from the 1930s through the 1950s (Kelner 2002). These programs explicitly touted resettlement to Israel as the highest virtue and expression of commitment to the nascent Jewish nation-state.

Although the idea of *aliyah* (immigration to Israel) has been supported in theory by Jewish communal organizations, this promotion has never resulted in concrete action plans. Instead, global Jewish organizations increasingly use Israel as a backdrop for different purposes. The sociologist Shaul Kelner (2002) writes, "The classical European Zionist argument that acculturation and assimilation were inevitable in open societies, and that communal boundaries and cultural integrity could be maintained only by physical resettlement in a self-determining Jewish state, was so far from communal consensus that no serious plan for promoting mass emigration was ever put forward in the central organs of American Jewry" (13).

After the founding of the state, the postwar economic expansion of the 1950s proved to be a golden era in the establishment of the diaspora business infrastructure as the type of programs that offered youth-oriented travel to Israel expanded (Kelner 2002). Young Judaea and American Jewish denominational movements established summer programs in the 1950s attended by many young Jews who later assumed key leadership and policy-making positions in these movements' communal organizations (Kelner 2002). In 1955, Hebrew University began offering one-year study abroad programs for foreign students, and in 1971, the university opened its foreign studies school, now called the Rothberg School for Overseas Students, to create an institutional infrastructure for potential immigrants.[1]

Rabbis, Jewish educators, and other community leaders staffed early programs as unpaid workers in exchange for the trip to Israel. Meanwhile, the World Zionist Organization and local outposts of American denominations recruited Israelis to serve as cultural and ideological liaisons with American Jews. As global travel increased through commercial airline services in the 1960s, the Histadrut (Labor Zionist trade union) steadily developed and devoted resources to create an Israeli tourism industry and professional vocational training. This organizational structure also served as a pipeline for young Americans interested in casual employment and became an important pathway for many people engaged in gradual migration—extended visits, temporary employment, and other semipermanent relationships to Israel.

Gradual migration and the burgeoning diaspora tourism business accomplished several important objectives. Not only did they increasingly link American Jews to specific people and places within Israel through organized programs but they also funneled critical dollars to the emerging state to build the Jewish homeland. As in the prestate period, American Jews continued to support Zionism with their financial resources, but not necessarily by becoming citizens. This support translated into opportunities for Zionist impresarios both at home and in Israel through marketing campaigns for Israel Bonds, cultural exchanges with Israeli dance troupes, and elaborate stage productions, as well as travel. Jeffrey Shandler (2001), a cultural historian, writes, "American Zionists championed the need for a Jewish state abroad while continuing their commitment to maintaining Jewish communities in the United States" (56). The development of tourism also created a physical structure for the growing presence of American Jewish communal and religious organizations, something foreign to the very secular Zionist establishment. Finally, tourism provided employment to Israelis and, in some cases, to American immigrants who had chosen to move there.

In the 1970s and early 1980s, several key diaspora business organizations were founded to provide the logistical and educational support structure for emerging relationships between global tourist groups and Israel as a tourism site/international Jewish homeland. Melitz (a Zionist education center) was established in 1973, the Kibbutz Program Center was created in New York in the late 1970s, and American denominational programs during that time became more sophisticated and entrenched in providing a steady circulation of people and capital between Israel and North American Jewish communities as part of the larger project of youth education.

The hallmark of these early trips was, and continues to be, their shared emphasis on pilgrimage and building Jewish identity through carefully planned educational programs, rather than on simply touring for pleasure. From its humble beginnings as a vehicle for kibbutz labor to contemporary, postmodern forms of mass tourism, the diaspora business has consistently focused its efforts on designing, promoting, and implementing programs with specific educational objectives based on the different ideologies and goals of organizational sponsors.

Making Jews More Jewish

In 1990, the National Jewish Population Survey, conducted by the Council of Jewish Federations, released data that suggested decreasing levels of Jewish communal affiliation, increasing intimate relationships between Jews and non-Jews, declining group cohesion, and an overall "waning of Jewish identity" in the United States. The impact of this study on the Jewish community cannot be underestimated, and it resulted in deep reflection, anxiety, and a shift in organizational priorities. One clear change was a new emphasis on the role Israel could play in shoring up American Jewish identities (Saxe and Kadushin 2001).

Even though the majority of Jews around the world choose *not* to live in Israel,

CARYN AVIV AND DAVID SHNEER

the country has long been situated as the symbolic and emotional "center" or "home" of global Jewry (Aviv and Shneer 2005). However, most of the programs, organizations, and companies engaged in diaspora business work are wholly transnational, with offices in several countries, Web sites in multiple languages that can be accessed from anywhere in the world, and daily e-mail communication. Organizational staff, donors, tourists, and students freely travel back and forth between "home" (wherever that may be) and abroad. In true global fashion, this constellation of relationships and organizations, moving across international boundaries, often blurs the lines between private enterprise, Israeli state funding, the nonprofit world, and philanthropy. For instance, the Jewish Agency, which is based in Israel, sends *shlichim* (messengers or cultural attachés) to America and elsewhere, who in turn are supported by local American Jewish Federation initiatives to raise money for Israel, which in turn supports the work of Israeli social service organizations.[2] Where is the global and where is the local?

Using tropes of history and biblical inheritance, diaspora business organizations offer an emotional promise to visitors to renew their spirituality, their Jewish identity, and their sense of place in a hostile world. This is true across the spectrum of organizations and ideologies, as both resolutely secular and deeply religious groups claim Israel as a homeland, although using divergent language, images, and metaphors. The programs provide carefully marketed and tailored experiences for their participants. They offer an opportunity to explore a particular ideological perspective, a set of practices and behaviors, and a specific emotional vocabulary in which participants can construct, interpret, and authenticate meaning and changing notions of selfhood (Wolkomir 2001). These experiences induce powerful emotions such as pride, religious awe, anger at the historical persecution of Jews, camaraderie, a sense of entitlement toward the "land of Israel," nostalgia, and a longing for a "return to Zion." Participants who experience emotional and identity transformations through these organizations are encouraged to translate those feelings into action. For young American Jews, this involves several possibilities: dating and marrying other Jews, joining Jewish organizations, taking a professional job with a Jewish communal agency, getting engaged with the Jewish political establishment, donating money, or simply creating a social circle of other like-minded Jews.

Saving the Jews

The diaspora business, in effect, is a reflection of the emergent consensus among Jewish communities around the world that educational travel offers a key way to construct, maintain, and ensure the reproduction of Jews (Saxe 2004). If Jews participate in the diaspora business, so the logic goes, then they will come home with a reinvigorated or newly minted sense of passion and excitement for what it means to be Jewish, and will want to somehow translate that enthusiasm into tangible practices connected to specific Jewish communities *at home*. This can range from lighting candles on Friday night to usher in Shabbat to stepping into a Hillel for the first time in a college career, taking a Jewish studies course, or deciding to keep kosher.

The programs run the gamut of religious practices and political affiliations, from thoroughly secular to *haredi*.[3] They tailor Israel experiences for different groups based on age, class, sexuality, family arrangements, and level of institutional involvement.[4] These educational and tourist organizations create itineraries and experiences that revolve around central, ideologically vexing questions of identity, representation, and contested claims made about who belongs in the land of Israel, who is a Jew, and what Judaism is. Programs range from intensive yeshiva study run by Orthodox Torah seminaries to informal secular summer tours that put American kids on a bus and zigzag across Israel. Some even meld yeshiva study and participation in a kibbutz. In modern Orthodox circles, it is possible for young men to spend a year combining yeshiva study with a short course of basic training with the Israeli army (called *hesder yeshivot*). At the other end of the Jewish ideological spectrum, the North American Jewish Federations offer recent college graduates a work-study program that emphasizes the principles of *tikkun olam* (repairing the world), secular Zionism, and egalitarian, religiously pluralist Jewish study. In this essay we focus on Taglit–birthright israel and March of the Living (MOTL), two popular yet very different programs designed to foster a sense of place, belonging, and identity among Jewish young.

TAGLIT—BIRTHRIGHT ISRAEL

In 1999, several philanthropists offered a multimillion-dollar challenge to the Jewish community to organize free trips to Israel for young people as a way to counteract the alarming trends the National Jewish Population Survey of 1990 had outlined. Participants hail from all over the globe—including Australia, South Africa, Russia, Eastern Europe, and South America—although the majority of donors come from North America. These North American Jewish philanthropists initiated birthright israel with the expectation of matching funds from Israel's Ministry of Education and the United Jewish Communities, the American network of Jewish federations. In March 2004, the Avi Chai Foundation donated 7 million dollars to rescue birthright israel after the Knesset significantly reduced its funding share to the overall budget. By late 2004, Taglit–birthright israel had sent more than sixty thousand Jewish young adults to Israel.[5] The essential element of birthright israel is a ten-day tour for Jews aged eighteen to twenty-six who have never been to Israel before in which participants visit all the major secular and religious tourist destinations in Israel—including Masada and the Western Wall—as well as spend leisure time in resort areas like Eilat. Birthright's actual programming is subcontracted with different global organizations that range in ideology, denomination, mission, and type (both for-profit and nonprofit maintain contracts). To routinize the process and avoid the duplication of efforts, birthright israel provides logistical coordination and support, and also maintains basic curricular requirements for all organizations. The itineraries are standardized and based on established logistical considerations and constraints. The trips include holy sites, hikes, *mifgashim* (managed encounters with Israelis), visits to places of historical and contemporary significance (such as the Israeli parliament), and some socializing. Since the program's inception, but especially since the second intifada began in 2000, all tours avoid visiting sites in the West Bank and the Gaza Strip. This sidesteps potential danger, but also avoids confronting a central fact of Israel's contemporary condition: conflict, occupation, and militarism as key elements of everyday life.

In addition to leisure activities, and days of shopping, the program organizes structured group discussions at each tourist site visited. Participants learn master narratives about Jewish peoplehood, history, and politics and are encouraged to frame their individual life stories as part of those narratives. Michelle, a twenty-year-old college student, described her experience as follows:

The goal of birthright is to just get them to go, and a lot of the people who go aren't really Jewish, they don't go to services, and aren't into the religious aspect. . . . The other intent was to get us in touch with our Jewish roots. There was one huge conversation about whether our roots mattered to us, and it was overwhelming how many people felt like our roots were irrelevant to contemporary Judaism and identity. That's one of the problems with birthright— everything was discussed to death, and people just wanted to have a vacation.[6]

Michelle's experience points to the tension between the organizers' goals and participants' desires. Birthright israel provides the opportunity for participants to simultaneously have fun and revise their personal and "the Jewish people's" history. The hope is that participants will experience such powerful emotions about place and people that they will want to rethink their own biographical narratives and place them squarely within contemporary discourses about Jewish identity and belonging. But what the students do with this opportunity in fact remains up to them. After a few years of birthright israel trips, program organizers instituted the Charlie Awards (a cash award of several thousand dollars, named after one participating philanthropist) as an incentive to parlay the participants' tourism experiences into Jewish communal service at home.[7]

THE EVER-PRESENT PAST: MARCH OF THE LIVING AND TOURISM TO EASTERN EUROPE

Unlike Israel, which has been the focus of diaspora business travel for the past fifty years, the haunted places of the Holocaust have only recently become a central focus of Jewish youth travel. But the Eastern Europe depicted in Jewish youth identity travel is far different from the contemporary Eastern Europe facing dilemmas of globalization, entry into the European Union, and rapid economic change. Eastern Europe in Jewish identity travel is negatively depicted as the site of Jewish catastrophe, a diasporic place of forgotten and long-lost shtetls, murdered Jewish ancestors, and death camps. Oren Stier (2003) writes, "In this most highly negotiated and deeply appropriated genre of the contemporary cultural memory of the Shoah we also find more ways in which memory is made meaningful—ways it engenders commitment in the present and to its own future" (151).

What drives this new tourism is as much a combination of memory and nostalgia for a lost or imagined past as it is a symbol of the increasing shrinkage of the global world, in which travel to formerly forbidden or unfamiliar places has become de rigueur. Eastern Europe represents the romanticized birthplace of American Jewish folklore as represented by *Fiddler on the Roof*, while it simultaneously evokes fear of persecution and represents the twentieth century's geographic center of genocidal anti-Semitism (Kirschenblatt-Gimblett 2001). A trip to Eastern Europe for American Jews of Eastern European background is becoming a central rite of Jewish passage for adult children of Holocaust survivors and affluent baby-boomer American Jews. But for the children of Jewish baby boomers, who have little direct memory or connection to these places, the emphasis of Jewish identity travel hinges on *inventing* the link between the destruc-

CARYN AVIV AND DAVID SHNEER

tion of the past and the possibility of their own Jewish futures (Kugelmass 1994). In the context of fading direct memories of the Holocaust, the diaspora business takes young adults to witness the ashes, crematoria, cemeteries, and somber memorials to the dead Jewish communities of Europe. The burden of remembering the genocidal horrors of the Holocaust has assumed new urgency as survivors, the narrative storytellers that implore us to remember, age and pass away. Debbie Findling (1999), who has studied Jewish tourism to Eastern Europe, writes: "A paradox exists for the generation that survived the Holocaust. In the immediate aftermath, many survivors simply wanted to forget and move on with their lives, while imploring the next generation to remember" (1). But witnesses to the Holocaust have grown older and are starting to pass away. The looming threat of lost memory and the absence of living survivors, coupled with the imperative in Jewish tradition to honor memory, has motivated and mobilized Jews around the world to devote millions of dollars and countless hours of creative energy toward documenting and rendering visible these ghosts—in the form of monuments, memorials, museums, books, films, archives, and Web sites.[8] It has also led to the creation of March of the Living, which introduces young Jews to the ghosts of the past through direct experiential engagement with the physical structures that stand as silent witnesses and legacies of Eastern European Jewry's absence.

As an example of how global the diaspora business has become, MOTL was established in 1988, not by American philanthropists as a challenge to renew American Jewish identity, but by the Israeli Ministry of Education, as a way to "evoke a strong connection between the participants and their past/heritage through a Zionist ideology of history" (Stier 2003:153). March of the Living uses the Holocaust and the founding of the state of Israel as two axes around which to mark Jewish time—the Holocaust as the Jewish past and Israel as the Jewish future. According to Findling (1999), the March of the Living "is clearly a symbolic journey whose message is one of rising out of the metaphoric and literal ashes of Poland to life and future in Israel" (35). The anthropologist Jack Kugelmass (1994) concurs, suggesting "the death camps in Poland act as condensation symbols for the entire Jewish past, while Israel, the end point of the journey, is schematized as the Jewish future."

March of the Living brings teenagers from over fifty countries to Poland and Israel to explore the enormity of the Holocaust through direct, physically embodied contact with the sites of genocide.[9] Its mission, according to MOTL's Web site (http://www.motl.org), is "to create memories, leading to a revitalized commitment to Judaism, Israel and the Jewish People. It will allow Marchers to educate their peers about the Holocaust and to fight those who would deny its history, while forging a dynamic link with Israel, with many returning to strengthen that connection."

In a carefully scripted unfolding emotional drama, March of the Living offers a compelling, stark contrast of dichotomies: between the living and the dead, grief and elation, mourning and celebration, destruction and renewal, past and future. According to Dafna Michaelson, a MOTL participant and former director of the organization for the New York region: "[March of the Living] is our opportunity to reaffirm that there are Jews all around the world, that we're a strong people, that we'll continue to go on and make great changes in terms of hate and intolerance and bettering this world. Hitler, you did not win."[10] After being part of and leading thousands of Jews from around the world marching through the Polish countryside, Michaelson argues that MOTL's main purpose is to reaffirm communal solidarity through memory, sadness, and fear. In the past twenty years, Israel and Poland have become the places many young Jews go to discover and make meaningful their own sense of what it means to be rooted and Jewish in a global world. This is not why their parents go to Eastern Europe: Their interest in the Holocaust is more likely to send them to a Holocaust museum, while a trip to Eastern Europe is an exploration of roots and lost pasts. It is a trip driven more by nostalgia than identity building.

Although preparation for the march begins months before the plane touches down in Poland, the actual MOTL itinerary begins in Warsaw with visits to the Jewish Museum, the Noczyk Synagogue, the Jewish Cultural Center, the Warsaw Jewish cemetery, and a *Yom Ha'Shoah* (Holocaust Remembrance Day) ceremony at Rappaport Memorial located in the former Warsaw Ghetto (Stier 2003). Students experience powerful emotions of solidarity and sadness during the "March of the Living," a one-mile somber silent walk between Auschwitz and Birkenau (also known as Auschwitz II), on which everyone wears identical blue jackets draped with Israeli flags. Students then travel to Treblinka and Majdanek and conclude their tour of Poland in "Jewish Krakow," visiting the Ramo synagogue, Schindler's factory, Plaszow, and several empty synagogues before flying to Israel.

Participants retrace and reenact grisly scenes of suffering to pay homage to the memory of victims. As the organization's Web site states: "As one of the March-

CARYN AVIV AND DAVID SHNEER

ers . . . you will experience Jewish history where it was made. This time, however, there will be a difference. It will be a March of the Living with thousands of Jewish youth, like yourself, marching shoulder to shoulder. You will participate in a memorial service at one of the gas chambers/crematoria in Birkenau, which will conclude with the singing of Hatikvah, reaffirming 'Am Yisrael Chai—The Jewish People Live.'" At Auschwitz/Birkenau, participants view mountains of stolen luggage and victims' shoes. They stand in the courtyard next to the wall where thousands of Jews were shot at close range. They wander silently through gas chambers, their mouths open in shock, horror, and disgust that the very ground on which they stand was the site of so much death. For the participants of MOTL, walking through the quiet, placid, almost eerie physical structures of genocide shatters the conventional distinctions between here and there, memory and reality. As the Holocaust scholar James Young points out, a visit to the site of a Polish extermination camp is not simply a visit to a memory site, like visiting a memorial or a Holocaust museum, because the events of the past happened there. Visitors can picture the violence that took place in the spaces that they now occupy (Young 1994).

Organizers prepare students to see Poland as dead, frozen, and fearful, despite the fact that through the 1990s it had a booming economy and entered the European Union in May 2004. By seeing Poland and Eastern Europe as dead, the participants cannot perceive them as real places in which Jews were once rooted. They cannot serve as a "home" with the possibility of return for Jewish youth who participate in MOTL. In a global world, "home" comes to be the places where these students live and the Jews' "eternal home," Israel.

After students have been emotionally drained by their encounters in Poland, they fly to Israel. The sociologist Jackie Feldman (1995) writes: "After the gray deprivation, vulnerability and death of Poland, Israel is constructed as the land of milk and honey, sexy soldiers, military force, sun, beach, and abundant falafel and chocolate. Israel is an idealized 'future of the Jewish people' world" (57–66). Findling (1999) speculates that the trip is scheduled in spring not just because it coincides with the modern Israeli Jewish holidays of Yom Ha'Shoah and Yom Ha'atzmau't (Israel Independence Day) but also because it is the time of year during which Poland is often gray and Israel verdant and warm.

On arrival at Ben Gurion airport, the students are immediately whisked off to the Golan Heights, then visit a few synagogues in the area, and have a cruise on the Sea of Galilee. The next day, students visit a military base and tour the north of the country. On *Yom Ha'Zikaron* (Israel Memorial Day) students visit Tsfat, Acco, and stay overnight in Nahariya. On Yom Ha'atzma'ut, organizers link the Israeli present and future to the dead European past. The day begins with a visit to Kibbutz Lochamei Geta'ot (Ghetto Fighters' Kibbutz), whose name symbolizes the Israeli memory of the Holocaust as a moment of heroism rather than existential tragedy. Students then tour Atlit, the British detention center near Haifa that held illegal Jewish immigrants fleeing the destruction of Europe during and after World War II to remind students of the injustice done to Holocaust victims by the British. On their final two days, students plant trees, have organized meetings with Israeli teens in Tel Aviv, spend Shabbat in Israeli homes, and tour the Old City before boarding a plane to go home.

March of the Living teaches Jews a master Zionist narrative of history that moves from European death in the past to Israeli life in the future. And at the same time, the trip aims to instill in participants a sense of global Jewish unity using fear, narratives of persecution, and anti-Semitism as its main tactic.

Perhaps most important, the March of the Living uses both Poland and Israel as a backdrop for instilling a new form of Jewish identity, one rooted in the places from which these students come. Oren Stier (2003) argues that the march fosters a sense of sacredness around the Holocaust and Israel, and that it is a key component in fostering American Jewish civic religion (see Woocher 1985). Jews return home, wherever that may be, with a stronger sense of Jewish identity, more positive attitudes toward Israel, and a more developed sense of social responsibility. If the march shows American Jewish teenagers that the past is Poland and the present is Israel, it also hopes to show them that their future is simply at home.

Is Aliyah Still on the Agenda?
Religious Nationalism and Identity Travel

For a few organizations, the transformation of self in relation to one's Jewish community and Israel (as place and nation) still translates directly into the hope of immigrating to Israel (*aliyah*). However, unlike fifty years ago, when aliyah meant making a commitment to building the secular Jewish nation, today moving to Israel is an aspect of personal transformation that symbolizes not only deep religious commitment but also a public declaration of one's emotional and national allegiances (Waxman 1989). For example, Emily, a thirty-year-old American from the West Coast, described her experience attending *Livnot U'Lehibanot*

(To Build and Be Built) in the following words: "It was like a warm Jewish womb that I didn't ever want to leave. It was the first time I felt really loved, like I belonged to something larger than myself and was part of a community. I felt like the power of Judaism had so much to offer that I couldn't turn it down and I couldn't not live here. So I came back."[11] Unable to find and recreate that rich sense of community in California after her religious transformation, Emily changed her name to Zohar, grew increasingly observant, and returned to Israel for further study with no immediate plans to return to the United States.

That encouragement toward transformation and the potential promise of aliyah is often coupled with a stinging critique of pluralistic denominations in American Judaism, and of modernity and American popular culture more generally. On another Orthodox weekend program in Israel, Ya'acov, the patriarch of the American family who hosted a Shabbat lunch, proclaimed that "no Jews have any business living in *golus* [the diaspora] anymore." According to him, the diaspora has been a disastrous experiment in moral corruption and assimilation. Ya'acov lived for many years in Los Angeles prior to his move to Israel, and his religious observance was relatively recent. When asked to explain his recent transformation, he replied:

The way Judaism is practiced in America today is a *shonda* [embarrassment]. It's not really Judaism, and anyone who tells you otherwise doesn't know what he's talking about. I think it's bizarre that anyone who wants to make *aliya* today is considered crazy, when in fact, that Jew is actually doing what *Hashem* [God] wants all of us to do, what we should do if we knew what was good for us! You see, most Americans don't even know they're still enslaved in *Mitzrayim* [Egypt]. What with all the lust for material things and money, with all that garbage on television, it's hard to know what *Hashem* really wants from us. It's hard to keep the *mitzvos* [obligations and commandments] and be true to Torah in *golus*. Believe me [he points toward all of us—mostly non-Orthodox Jews under thirty], I know what I'm talking about.

What *Hashem* really wants is for us to be true to Torah and live here [he points his finger down on the table to emphasize his thought]. *Ba'aretz* [in the land of Israel], it's easy to see why *Hashem* gave us Torah *b'Sinai* [the Torah at Mount Sinai]. The beauty of *mitzvos*, the joy that we get from doing what Hashem wants us to do, it's easy to live by the *halacha* [law] ba'aretz. That's why I'm here with my family. [He leans back in his chair, folds his hands over his stomach, and smiles at the group of young Americans assembled around his table.] That's why all of you should be here too.[12]

In the case of Ya'acov, the goal of identity travel was to strengthen religious observance and further a form of religious Zionism that was a minor voice in Israel fifty years ago but now plays a major role in Israeli politics. By traveling to Israel and seeing "true Jewish religiosity," in action, Ya'acov argued that young Americans would realize the spiritual poverty of American culture and materialism and transform themselves into more religiously observant and fervently Zionist Jews.

A common strategy for encouraging and facilitating this transformation combines Jewish education programs with structured emotional, financial, and logistical support for those who choose this path. In other words, some programs blur the line between tourism and subsidizing gradual migration. For example, Mercaz Hamagshimim is the Reform movement's "soft landing," the institutional infrastructure that makes being (and potentially settling) in Israel as pain-free as possible for English speakers in Jerusalem. It provides courses, job listings, social networks, and leisure programs to make being in Jerusalem less stressful. Yeshivot provide another popular route for offering the promise of transformation with the practicalities of support. For example, in Jerusalem, Caryn met Yonatan, a *ba'al tshuvah* (newly religious Jew) from Baltimore at a Shabbat dinner in 1998. Over chicken, *cholent* (barley and vegetable stew), and challah, Yonatan (originally Jon) told her about how his lack of religious education as a kid left a spiritual void inside him as an adult. After meeting a rabbi/chaplain at the hospital where he worked in Baltimore, Yonatan became increasingly interested in Jewish textual study and religious observance. His rabbi encouraged him to pursue further study in Israel. So Yonatan came to Jerusalem to study at a very popular Zionist yeshiva with only four hundred dollars in his pocket. After an intensive four-month immersion in the religious and communal life of the yeshiva, Yonatan felt convinced that his future belonged in Israel, despite having very little idea of how he might earn a living once the program ended.

The Intifada and Costs of Continuing Violence

Since the second intifada began in 2000, the definition of safety has shifted, and Jewish youth travel participation rates have dropped, prompting detailed explanations of security measures by organizers to assuage parents' fears and anxieties about their children's safety and well-being. Parents began pulling their children out of MOTL not because of Polish anti-Semitism but because of bus bombings in Tel Aviv and Be'er Sheva. Some American universities have suspended their study abroad programs at Hebrew University (Thomson 2002). Trip itineraries

have changed to avoid potentially dangerous areas. And birthright israel organizers have made a concerted effort to conduct outreach to potential participants
in other regions of the world (such as South America, Russia, and Eastern
Europe) to stave off declining rates of Americans. But the truth, for all Jewish
travel organizers, was that no one was safe at the Western Wall—neither Jews,
who constantly worried about suicide bombers, nor Palestinians, who feared
Israeli police repression. In a travel brochure from Arza, the Association of
Reform Zionists of America, the issue of security was addressed head-on in an
anxious plea to consider the continuity of a Jewish future:

We appreciate the difficulties of travel during these trying days, especially to Israel, but we
cannot give in to our fears. If we do not continue to visit and link our destiny with Jews
everywhere, we will lose the next generation of Jews and let terrorism win. We will show
you first-hand how Jews around the globe cope and flourish as they look toward a better
future, in a way that will make you prouder and more inspired by Reform Judaism than
ever before.[13]

The complete disintegration of the peace process, the September 11, 2001,
terror attacks, and the second intifada devastated the tourism industry within
Israel. Israeli tourism advertising used the slogan "Now, more than ever, we need
you here in solidarity," in an effort to publicize severe economic losses. The
Israeli Ministry of Tourism announced a joint effort with some American groups
to sponsor emergency "solidarity missions" to shore up flagging morale. These
campaigns have to appeal to global Jews' sense of collective responsibility to
support the beleaguered Jewish state. They also attempted to allay fears by
emphasizing heightened security measures to ensure tourists' safety at a time
when the death toll of Palestinians and Israelis mounted daily.

Jewish identity travel has constructed Eastern Europe as the site of historical
danger, destruction, and death, while Israel has been essentialized as the Promised Land of refuge for diaspora Jews (Fuss 1990). But with persisting violence,
how Jews relate to these historical places has changed dramatically in a short
span of time. During the intifada, Jewish organizations' emotional appeals to
loyalty and obligation did not sufficiently convince the American Jewish public
that Israel was a safe place for travel. Trips to Israel were rerouted to other parts
of the globe (for example, Argentina), and some were cancelled altogether. Despite orange alerts and dire warnings from the American government, safety and
home were more associated with the United States than anywhere else.

These changes suggests that using Israel as a backdrop for developing American Jewish identities at home was useful at a particular historical moment. When a semblance of peace defined Israeli-Palestinian relations through much of the 1990s and the Holocaust reached its peak impact as a defining element of American Jewish identity, this strategy made sense. But that moment of optimism has changed radically, giving way to widespread weariness and cynicism, particularly among Israelis. The future seems more uncertain than ever. And as the prospect of peace has shifted once again into a relentlessly grinding and everyday violence, as the Holocaust recedes further into the past, Jewish identity travel and the diaspora business are changing. More students are rediscovering and studying the rich histories of Eastern Europe, Yiddish, and klezmer as viable routes to constructing Jewish identity. New York is now becoming a key heritage travel site. Perhaps ten years from now, diaspora business organizations will see other Jewish places like the Lower East Side of Manhattan, the Hasidic neighborhoods of Williamsburg, and the Russian neighborhoods of Brighton Beach in Brooklyn as the latest authentic sites where Jewish young people can make sense of themselves as diaspora Jews.

Notes

1. See the Rothberg School's Web site (http://www.overseas.huji.ac.il).
2. The Jewish Agency's Web site (http://www.jafi.org.il) writes: "Shlichim are sent for various reasons: some to work with local Jewish communities and Federations, some to teach in Jewish day schools, and some to lead the members of a Zionist youth movement. All of them live in a Jewish community and provide a living link to Israel." Accessed September 2001.
3. *Haredi* is a term used to denote ultra-orthodox. The range of definitions, descriptions, labels, and microdifferentiation is subject to intense scrutiny and debate among insiders.
4. For example, there are programs designed specifically for seniors or bar-bat mitzvah adolescents, gay and lesbian educational tours, programs to reach out to unaffiliated Jews searching for spirituality, expensive "deluxe" programs for philanthropists, and on and on. Segmenting to target a key audience for specific programs is crucial in staking out a claim in a crowded field.
5. See the birthright israel Web site (http://www.birthrightisrael.com) for more information.
6. Personal interview, March 2003.
7. See (http://www.jta.org).
8. The largest operation for capturing the testimony of survivors is Steven Spielberg's Shoah Foundation Institute for Visual History and Education (http://www.vhf.org).

9. Students come from all points in the global Jewish community, including North America, Latin America, South Africa, Australia, Eastern and Western Europe, Russia, Australia, and Israel.

10. Personal interview, April 2003.

11. Personal interview, January 1999.

12. Conversation recorded in December 1998.

13. ARZA / World Union of Progressive Judaism travel brochure, 2003.

Trauma Stories, Identity Work, and the Politics of Recognition

ARLENE STEIN

Stories are central to self-making and world making. They give shape to our experiences, tell us where we came from, and offer guideposts to the future, situating us in relation to families, communities, and traditions. Collective stories constitute reference points that anchor us, and we in turn adopt them as our own, using them to construct a sense of self. Recent sociological work suggests that we pay attention to the contexts—political, cultural, and individual —in which stories emerge and circulate. Under what conditions are certain stories tellable? Some stories cannot readily be told because of their traumatic or stigmatized nature; they carry particular emotional weight and intensity because of the circumstances surrounding their telling.

In recent years, as private pains are transformed into public stories, there has been a growing incitement to speak publicly about experiences of child abuse, homosexuality, drug and alcohol abuse and other previously taboo topics (Plummer 1995). For better or for worse, cultural spaces such as these did not exist fifty years ago. The recognition of a group's cultural distinctiveness, including the injuries it has sustained, has emerged as a central demand of feminism, gay liberation and other "new" social movements committed to multiculturalism (Brown 1995). This politics of recognition says to a public comprised largely of strangers: "Attention must be paid to us. You must recognize and honor that which makes us different from you, and you must be acquainted with our culture and history." The experience of lesbians and gay men provides a case in point: before the rise of the gay liberation movement, their stories remained private and personal; today, the coming-out story has become a master narrative with which individuals construct a sense of individual and collective identity, demanding recognition by others (Stein 1997).

Traumatic memories are increasingly discussed in public spaces. Survivors of rape and incest are encouraged to transform their private memories into speech; families and friends who have lost loved ones in the AIDS epidemic and the Vietnam War erect memorials and bear witness to their loss; the descendants of African slaves invoke their history of suffering during the Middle Passage (Plummer 1995; Sturken 1997). And in an ironic appropriation of human suffering, *Survivor*, one of the most popular American television shows, features contestants facing extreme circumstances engaged in a battle to outwit and outlast each other. The mantle of victimhood offers moral authority, visibility, and political clout—and is even traded as a commodity on the commercial television airwaves. The burgeoning discussion of the Holocaust should be understood, then, as the product of Jewish identity claims and demands for recognition in relation to an American culture in which such claims seem to have growing resonance.

In the following, I explore the relationship between Holocaust stories and postwar Jewish identities, primarily in the context of the United States, with sideways glances at other national contexts. How have the shifting contexts of postwar Jewishness changed the ways in which the Holocaust is publicly discussed? And how have these public discussions, in turn, altered the shape of Jewish identities? I will suggest that the growing public discussion of the Holocaust must be understood in relation to shifts within Jewish communities and beyond that have made the recognition of historical injustice an increasingly salient theme in postwar political culture, particularly in the United States.

Historicizing Holocaust Talk

Today most people are aware, even if in a hazy and shapeless way, of the destruction of European Jewry sixty years ago. This is particularly true of Jewish communities, for whom the Holocaust has become a touchstone of identity, alongside (and sometimes even superseding) religious rituals and commitments to the state of Israel. The salience of Holocaust stories today—driven by films such as Steven Spielberg's *Schindler's List* (1993), the United States Holocaust Memorial Museum in Washington, Holocaust oral testimony projects, and the growing number of memorials—suggests that the Holocaust has become a central aspect of Jewish, and perhaps even American, national identity. On many college campuses, Holocaust-related courses are filled to capacity.

In itself this is not altogether surprising: the genocide of European Jewry was (and is) an event of enormous world-historical significance whose reverberations will be felt for generations. Yet only three or four decades ago, Holocaust stories were told almost exclusively by survivors and their families, if they were told at all, and the Holocaust did not constitute a central aspect of Jewish identity, at least in terms of its public expression in the United States. Perhaps this is because stories can only be told when there are audiences capable of listening, and for two decades after the end of World War II, the audience for Holocaust stories did not exist.

Like all stories, particularly those of a traumatic nature, Holocaust stories are embedded in specific times and places and require both tellers and audiences in order to be told and heard. Yet for at least several decades, audiences were not receptive, and the potential tellers were hesitant to tell their tales. The once vibrant Jewish communities of Eastern Europe were obliterated, and communism silenced many of those who wished to revisit the past in that region. In the United States—and to some extent Canada, South Africa, Argentina, Australia, and other major Jewish centers—Jewish communities were engaged in a quest for assimilation and upward mobility rather than dwelling on the traumatic past.

In the United States, the immediate postwar era was a time of rapid suburbanization and the emergence of a triumphalist Cold War culture. Many upwardly mobile Jews embraced this culture and the assimilationist project it implied (Prell 1999). If they had communal aspirations, they turned them toward building local Jewish communities, or supporting the State of Israel. Holocaust survivors—and the sense of radical difference they embodied—did not fit neatly into such projects. Collectively, the world was not yet ready to hear the survivors' tales, and survivors were rarely, if ever, coaxed to tell their stories. Therefore, they were barely heard.

Those survivors who did speak of their experiences typically did so haltingly, often in fragmentary ways, in hushed tones, and often even carrying with them a degree of shame. As they struggled to construct "normal" families and livelihoods in new countries, they were caught between two opposing impulses: the desire to tell and the desire to repress the past (Wajnryb 2001). Their Holocaust stories were personal and familial, fragmented and tentative. They did not know how to tell them; they did not know who to tell them to. There was not yet a category of experience called "the Holocaust" within which they could situate themselves. Survivors and their families (including my own) tended to refer to the events as "the war." A conspiracy of silence preempted public discussions of their experiences (Karpf 1996; Wardi 1992).

Just because a story is not explicitly articulated, it does not mean that it is not communicated, however, and for least two decades after the war, the experience of the Holocaust maintained a powerful but largely underground presence. As Wajnryb (2001) has shown in a brilliant study of how families transmit traumatic memory through silences, the Holocaust was the "elephant in the room"—a subject barely spoken but nonetheless unavoidably present (Zerubavel 2006). After all, this was a time before therapeutic culture, before post-traumatic stress. It was an age in which psychological problems were frequently stigmatized and individuals forced to "manage" their stigma for fear that their "spoiled" selves would come into public view. It was a time in which difference constituted a source of shame, the so-called melting-pot ideal made American identity synonymous with the submergence of group differences, and Jews tried desperately to become "white folks" (Brodkin 1998). Nonsurvivor Jews conspired in these silences. Some did not know how to integrate Holocaust survivors into their Jewish worlds; others did not want to do so. Perhaps some felt guilty about not having done enough to save Jews in Europe. And newer immigrants who lost extended family members often suffered survivor guilt. Some American Jews found survivors' very presence—their experiences of genocide, their foreign accents and manners—threatening.

Of course the Jewish community was and is not monolithic, and as Biale (1998) reminds us, the "instability and multiplicity of Jewish identity" has a "long history going back to the Bible itself" (31). For some, Jewishness is largely a religious identity, performed through rituals and given in sacred texts. For others, Jewishness is primarily an ethnic identity, tied to language and secular customs and rituals. Jewish identity, then, is multiple and complex, defying easy generalizations.

Different groups within Jewish communities have had different relationships to Holocaust talk, some speaking more freely of that event than others. For example, Waxman (this volume) suggests that religious Jewish communities in the postwar United States have been more receptive to publicly speaking about the Holocaust than the American Jewish community as a whole, and that Holocaust survivors may have exerted a more significant influence on religious Judaism than on more secular Jewish communities. Perhaps Orthodox Jewish circles were not as dedicated to the project of assimilation as their more secular compatriots and were therefore not as wary of Jews who spoke with accents and sometimes wore strange garb. Orthodox Jews were less likely to be a part of the forward rush toward suburban affluence and the conformity to mainstream American values that such trajectories entailed. But since Orthodox Judaism comprised a declining share of the Jewish population in the 1950s and 1960s, this influence was barely felt in the larger American Jewish community.

National identities also divide the Jewish world, shaping the contexts of memory and giving Holocaust stories a different tenor in Argentina than in Israel, for example. In Israel, a militarized Jewish nation-state emerged, defining itself in terms of secular Jewish might and often against the diaspora Jewish world and its history of persecution. The legacy of Jewish victimhood has shaped Israeli national identity, constructing the Jewish state as a symbolic and emotional safety net for Jews in a hostile world. A host of institutions have been established to encourage diaspora Jews to immigrate to Israel, spend extended periods of time engaging in religious and other studies, and donate money to help sustain the Jewish state (Aviv and Shneer, this volume). These institutions often harness biblical sources to render selective memories of Jews inhabiting the land in order to promote Jewish nationalism and a greater Israel, including the Occupied Territories. Even if the Holocaust is not the explicit reference point for such appeals, the memory of genocide constitutes a potent backdrop against which such subjects as Jewish continuity and survival and Israel's place in the world are discussed.

So while the experience of the Holocaust has irrevocably shaped Jewish consciousness, this experience is mediated by stories that vary by national, cultural, and familial contexts. For at least two decades after the war, particularly in Jewish population centers outside of Israel, public expressions of Holocaust memories were fragmentary, repressed, and sometimes actively silenced. Since the public circulation of stories depends on the existence of the stories to begin with, tellers to tell them, and audiences to hear them, and there was little or no audience capable of listening to the survivors, their stories remained untold. In the United States, this shifted in the late 1960s and early 1970s (Plummer 1995).

Liberating Memory?

As the potential firsthand tellers of Holocaust stories become fewer and fewer in number, the audiences clamoring for these narratives seem to increase exponentially. A veritable flood of memory has come gushing forth—books, museums, memorials, educational programs—what Sturken (1997) calls "memory sites" and "technologies of memory"—affording Holocaust survivors and their families the possibility of organizing their memories of the past in a publicly accessible fashion. Oral history projects mine the memories of Holocaust victims and describe in detail the killing fields. The annual *Yom Ha'Shoah*, Holocaust Remembrance Day, is the largest and most visible Jewish event on many college campuses.

To some extent, this liberation of memory is the product of the passage of time. Because of years of suppression, Holocaust talk now emerges with particular intensity and urgency. The traumatic memories are less raw than they once were, particularly as the survivors die and their children embrace a post-memory somewhat removed from firsthand experience (Hirsch 1997). Institutional politics and power also certainly play roles. The construction of museums, the making of films, and the development of school curricula require a mobilization of resources made possible by the growing affluence and integration of Jewish communities into mainstream American life, exemplified by the establishment of the United States Holocaust Memorial Museum in the U.S. capital, a stone's throw from the Washington Monument.

American Jews at the end of the twentieth century are a "community of choice" that "constitutes a kind of intermediate ethnic group, one of the most quickly and thoroughly acculturated yet, among European ethnicities, equally one of the most resistant to complete assimilation" (Biale 1998:31). Increasingly central to an American Jewish identity that resists assimilation is the claim of cultural distinctiveness based on suffering. Along with African Americans, Native Americans and other ethnic groups whose history has been linked to genocide, American Jews embrace a politics of multiculturalism that challenges the American melting-pot ethos and suggests that the distinctiveness of identity groupings is something to be preserved, not overturned in the interest of assimilating into the whole. A Jewish politics of recognition makes claims for cultural distinctiveness partially on the basis of past injustices.

Many middle-class American Jews in their twenties who have little or no direct connection to the Shoah today embrace its memory as a badge of distinction because it has given them a sense of uniqueness as Jews (Kaufman 2003). These children of baby boomers reject their parents' and grandparents' assimilationist Jewish identities in favor of an embrace of Jewish difference. Interest in Yiddish, once shunned as the language of ghetto Jews, is now enjoying a resurgence, particularly among educated twenty-somethings in search of secular ethnic identities. Young Jewish Americans of the baby boom were encouraged to embrace Zionism toward that end; their children are often more captivated by symbols of the diaspora than the nation-state. The Shoah seems to be a malleable narrative that can be shaped and reshaped according to different needs. As

Kaufman (2003) suggests, for example, many young people excavate Holocaust memory to find a heroic as well as a tragic past.

What shall we make of this growing identification with Jewish trauma in the Holocaust? Certainly, for many survivors and their families, this is a positive development, offering the possibility for sharing their experiences publicly and finally clearing the fog of denial and repression. Psychologists tell us that in order to claim a sense of personhood and become a full citizen, it is necessary to work through our traumatic past. If the trauma is a collective one, a group must grapple with that past and incorporate it into its own self-understanding. Part of this process may involve revealing one's trauma to others so that they recognize the traumatized group's injuries (Boss 1999). The recognition of historical injustice seems to be a universal need, as witnessed by the emergence of institutions such as South Africa's Truth and Reconciliation Commission, in which the victims and perpetrators of apartheid confronted one another, working through the crimes of the past. For the Holocaust's victims, now dead, this is impossible. But for survivors and their families, and for the larger Jewish community, the growing recognition of the Holocaust is a positive development. Thanks to the liberation of memory, members of Jewish communities have growing access to information silenced and hidden in the past, and more and more citizens of perpetrator nations have been forced to recognize their complicity in the horrors.

While these developments are certainly positive, all talk, even talk about suffering, is always embedded in relationships of power and should never be taken at face value (Foucault 1978). Every discourse, or system of stories, creates new silences and exclusions, even as it removes others. So we must also ask, following Michel Foucault, how some voices get heard while others are silenced, who benefits and how—that is, we must address issues of power, empowerment, and disempowerment. For example, while the so-called liberation of sexuality during the sexual revolution of the 1960s and 1970s certainly opened up new sexual freedoms for many individuals, some feminists have charged that it also created a "pleasure imperative" that favored men and unleashed a no-holds-barred commodification of sexuality. The liberation of Holocaust memory may operate similarly, affording victims of suffering public recognition, while at the same time promoting the commodification of the Holocaust and the abuse of memory by those who reap rewards by piggybacking on the "victim bandwagon" (Novick 1999).

Increasingly, it seems, a politics of morality frames the way we see social problems. On the right, Charles Sykes (1992) charges that the United States is becoming "a nation of victims," threatening the American character. "I am not responsible; it's not my fault" is the common refrain linking compulsive gamblers, codependents in dysfunctional relationships, obese people "oppressed" by narrow airline seats, and others who claim victim status, Sykes claims. He excoriates the psychiatric profession for continually inventing new disease categories and lashes American "therapeutic culture," which he says turns everyday difficulties into certified psychological problems. On the left, Lauren Berlant (1997) suggests that "the . . . national victim has become a cultural dominant in America . . . political authenticity depends on the individual's humiliating exile from somebody else's norm. A nationwide estrangement from an imagined hegemonic center seems now to dignify every citizen's complaint" (27). As the personal and the political collapse into each other, she suggests, public discourse is impoverished. Complex political debate is replaced by "discourses of dignity and of the authority of feeling" (Berlant 1997:100).

In contrast, I would suggest that the politicization of trauma can at times be used for progressive political ends. The emergence of Holocaust talk signals the democratization of culture and a growing willingness to recognize past injuries of marginalized groups. The intensity with which the Holocaust has entered the cultural imagination is a response to the earlier suppression of the subject—much like the suppression of talk of homosexuality, sexual abuse, and other previously taboo topics. The extent to which the Holocaust dominates the American Jewish imagination, and the American public sphere, today is a direct result of its suppression for at least two decades after the war. In some sense, this is a particularly American phenomenon, though different versions of Holocaust talk circulate in different national contexts, shaped by the exigencies of Jewish communal life, the presence or absence of social movements organized around demands for recognition, and the nation's particular relationship to World War II memories. At its best, such talk affords Jews the possibility of recovering part of their lost history and forging identities that maintain continuities with prewar Eastern and Central European Jewry. For the general public, the memory of the Holocaust, and human trauma in general, could be used to encourage the development of a "species awareness" that an injury against one constitutes an injury against all (Lifton 1993:217).

Responses to the Holocaust:
Discussing Jewish Identity through
the Perspective of Social Construction

RICHARD WILLIAMS

Whether or not it is realistic, we build theories with the ideal of transcending specific cases so that we can make statements about humanity, the human condition, as a whole. Given that perspective, social theorists are particularly intrigued and challenged by cases characterized as exceptional or unique instances of social behavior. The Holocaust, without question a significant event in human history, has been the constant focus of debate regarding its uniqueness (Alexander 1994; Bischoping and Kalmin 1999; Chalk and Jonassohn 1990; Dawidowicz 1981; Eckhardt and Eckhardt 1980; White 1990). Hence we might expect that issues related to the Holocaust would significantly challenge and attract theorists working from a wide variety of perspectives. Yet that has not been true of theorists concerned with the social constructionist approach to identity.[1] The notable exception is a recent book by Alexander et al. (2004) that attempts to develop a theory of cultural trauma. Other than that, social constructionists have not commonly used the Holocaust and its relationship to Jewish identity as a relevant case to explore the social construction of identity.

I draw on the essays by Chaim Waxman, Debra Kaufman, and Caryn Aviv and David Shneer in the present volume to demonstrate that research on the Holocaust and Jewish identity can help social constructionists further develop some of the basic tenets of their perspective. Showing that these constitute legitimate cases is only one of the issues at hand, however. I also explore the reasons for the disconnect between social constructionist perspectives of identity, and studies of the Holocaust and Jewish identity.

I approach the three essays using the concepts homogeneity and heterogeneity, which capture the core of the social constructionist exploration of the cognitive aspects of identity construction.[2] Those concepts point to some of the tensions involved in establishing feelings of similarity (homogeneity) among individuals in the face of a multiplicity of factors that could indicate differences (heterogeneity) among them. Evidence of such tensions demonstrates the complexity of how social actors come to operate as cognitively unambiguous collective identities. This discussion ultimately revolves around the question of how creating collective identities (homogeneity) involves *cognitively resolving* problems connected to heterogeneity (Anderson 1991; Cerulo 2002; Cohen 1989; Douglas 1986; Jenkins 1996, 1997; Lamont and Molnar 2002; Weber 1978; Zerubavel 1991).

In addition to showing how collective identities are created, the concepts of homogeneity and heterogeneity point to the continuing social relevance of heterogeneity within the context of homogeneity. In other words, *cognitively resolving* differences is not the same as *removing* them from social life. The activities involved in resolving differences, as much as the activities involved in their continuation, are associated with actors who have specific interests. This insight is of further relevance when we recognize that identities are resources actors use to obtain social goals.

As a resource, a collective identity is an entity over which actors compete for control. Actors gain control to the extent they establish their goals as the same or similar to the goals of the group as a whole. This is a classic representation of the tension between interests and values in which the interests of a specific segment of a population compete for the position of becoming a value of the population as a whole (Habermas 1998).

Homogeneity and heterogeneity therefore point toward the complexity of social solidarity. On the one hand, they help us understand how collective unity is established in social life. On the other hand, they allow us to observe actors competing for control over established collective identities. More specifically, they prove useful as analytical concepts because they capture the manner in which actors strategically rely on claims of "we are similar to each other" and "we are different from them" as social tools for advancing their agendas. These tools can be picked up or put down according to actors' perceptions of their usefulness.

Waxman, Kaufman, and Aviv and Shneer do not use the concepts homogeneity and heterogeneity. Nonetheless, there are two reasons internal to their work that make those concepts appropriate for thinking through their essays. On the one hand, in their concern with the association between the Holocaust and Jewish identity, they flag the extent to which the Holocaust serves as a common touch point for a unified Jewish identity.[3] In so doing, they necessarily engage in a dialogue with the broader issue of the cognitive conditions under which homogeneous identities are advocated.

The authors uniformly present evidence indicating that a common response to the Holocaust, linked to a common Jewish identity, is always challenged. Their focus on that tension indicates that while the homogeneity of Jewish identity might be a common claim, it cannot be said that "Jews" uniformly rely on that claim as a guide for their behavior. The findings in these essays therefore point in the direction of the constructionist argument that homogeneity of belief does not necessarily establish homogeneity of behavior.

In this commentary I more fully demonstrate the legitimacy of viewing these essays as cases for the social constructionist position by specifically embedding the concepts of homogeneity and heterogeneity into these authors' discussion of the Holocaust and Jewish identity. I then move beyond those cases to argue that research on the Holocaust and Jewish identity creates difficulties for both theorists and researchers because their interconnection pushes them beyond their familiar boundaries. My position is that those difficulties are far from insurmountable; resolving them, however, requires that we begin by facing the fact that they exist.

The Texts

In his essay, Waxman places his primary focus on the tensions between what he calls American Orthodox Jewry, on the one hand, and the American Jewish community, on the other. According to Waxman, the historical basis of tensions between the two groups is rooted in sociocultural differences prior to their arrival in the United States. The non-Orthodox group primarily came from Central Europe during the middle of the nineteenth century. The Orthodox group largely came from Eastern Europe toward the end of the nineteenth century. There is, of course, a broader point embedded in this distinction by geography, namely, the idea that Jewish identity has been differentiated by particular sociocultural environments. In essence, the category *Jewish* has historically encompassed persons with a wide range of social and cultural distinctions (Le Rider 1993).

Differences between the two groups of immigrants are clear from the circumstances surrounding their arrival into the United States. Those from Central

Europe arrived in relatively small numbers in the late 1840s. They were commonly urban professionals who had culturally assimilated into Germany or Austria. Assimilation meant that they had moved away from some of their religious and cultural traditions, as well as from the dialects associated with Judaism in those countries. Therefore, during the early decades of their settlement in the United States, their small size, in addition to their social, economic, and cultural capital, allowed this group to live relatively inconspicuously in their new society.

Those who came from Eastern Europe arrived in the United States in large numbers at the end of the nineteenth century. They had commonly lived in shtetls, to which they had been confined by the regulations of Eastern European governments. This meant that, in general, they had been physically separated from non-Jews. Their separation had the consequence of confining this group to traditional Eastern European Jewish cultural forms. The isolation preserved aspects of older Jewish life, but it also kept that population on the periphery of what was already the periphery of European modernization during the nineteenth century. Not surprisingly, then, on arrival in the United States, the skills of this group were largely limited to those of populations from rural and village communities (Howe 1976).

With the arrival of Eastern European Jews in the United States, "Jews" became a visible social category and "Jewish" became an identity defined by religious practices, styles of dress, and speech patterns. The visibility of one of its segments therefore came to represent the identity of the group as a whole. Yet despite their "common" Jewish identity, the factors that made the immigrants from Eastern Europe visible to and separate from the larger American society made them nearly equally visible to and separate from the earlier Central European immigrants. Here, as Waxman indicates, lie the roots of a complex struggle over the goals of a collective Jewish identity.

The concepts of homogeneity and heterogeneity are useful for discussing some of the external pressures those with a Jewish identity faced from the larger society in the United States at the end of the nineteenth century and the beginning of the twentieth century. They are also useful in describing some of the strategies Jewish leaders relied on to negotiate the social pressures on their identity. Waxman shows that even though external pressures toward a unified identity existed, distinct interests internal to that identity commonly determined when actors would rely on a homogeneous or a heterogeneous identity strategy.

During the late nineteenth and early twentieth centuries, U.S. society as a whole believed in the assimilation of new immigrants into the dominant WASP cultural norms. This so-called melting-pot assumption points to the aspiration of achieving a homogeneous society through assimilation, that is, by eradicating non–Anglo-Saxon, non-Protestant cultural norms. Although it did so in different ways, the ideal of an American national identity put pressure on both segments of the Jewish community to mediate their differences with the dominant culture as well as with each other. Central European Jews had the cultural capital to embrace the homogenizing practices of the larger society. In following that strategy toward the larger society, they embraced a heterogeneous strategy toward the Eastern European group. The latter group did not have the capital to immediately embrace the homogenizing practices of the larger society. As a result, they were more likely to call for a form of diversity (heterogeneity) as the legitimate social strategy. But remaining truly separate was not an option because, despite their fundamental differences, both groups were, in the end, identified as Jews and both faced elements of anti-Semitism in the broader society.

In theory, their different responses to the homogenizing strategy of the society as a whole would simply have furthered existing tensions between the two groups. As I have previously stated, however, to the extent that both were defined as Jewish, they were perceived in the broader society as a homogeneous identity group.[4] Therefore, regardless of their attitudes toward each other, their common identity label necessarily resulted in various strategic acts of unification. Such actions logically raised the significant question of "unification under whose sense of the world?" As such, acts of homogenization were oriented toward specific goals and were logically accompanied by some conflict.

We can therefore read Waxman as stating that during the late nineteenth century and the early twentieth century, the two groups responded to social pressures in the United States with both homogeneous and heterogeneous strategies. Their responses unified them at times and at times led them to take different paths. Thus, Waxman indicates that their identity differences are as important for understanding the behavior of the actors as is a sense of a homogeneous Jewish identity. That would be the case even when looking at situations in which they acted in concert.

The Holocaust plays a central role in two of the examples that Waxman provides during his discussion of tensions between Central and Eastern European Jews. The first is particularly striking because it involves a situation in which Orthodox and non-Orthodox Jews took different actions in regard to the

Holocaust even during World War II. A simplified reading of the Holocaust and of Jewish identity would lead one to expect that the Holocaust would have unquestionably brought the two groups to support the idea of an undivided Jewish identity. But such a read would necessarily ignore their distinct life experiences, their different cultural histories, and their distinct conceptions of how to engage with the larger, non-Orthodox Jewish world. An awareness of those differences helps us understand, for instance, how and why Orthodox and non-Orthodox Jews took different positions around how Jews should be rescued from the Nazis.

During the war, leaders in the Orthodox community organized efforts specifically designed to rescue Orthodox religious leaders. The major American Jewish organizations strongly opposed that strategy, arguing instead for the establishment of an umbrella group that would coordinate the rescue of Jews in general. The non-Orthodox groups claimed that resources could be most effectively utilized if the two groups would unify their efforts. The Orthodox group stuck with its plans for a separate rescue effort, and the major organizations proceeded with a general rescue plan.

Both groups were concerned with the goal of rescuing Jews, but their different life experiences, their different perceptions of Jewish identity, lead them to develop distinct strategies toward accomplishing that goal. The approach of the Orthodox group can be understood as based on the presumption that Jewish identity constituted a heterogeneous category based on specific identity characteristics. The different characteristics were such that they translated into a greater probability of the Orthodox being identified as Jewish. Given that all Jews were at risk of death, it would follow that the Orthodox were at even greater risk of death than the non-Orthodox. Such an understanding would be one reason for the development of a rescue strategy that specifically targeted Orthodox religious leaders.

The strategy of the major Jewish organizations can be seen as based on the assumption that the category *Jew* constituted a social whole, a homogeneous identity, distinct only from non-Jews. From that point of view, all Jews were equally at risk of being interned and killed. The Orthodox point that non-Orthodox and specifically assimilated Jews were less likely to be identified as Jewish did not, from the perspective of the major Jewish organizations, significantly diminish the fact that even assimilated Jews were at great risk and thus needed to take extreme precautions in order to survive.

In this example, the concepts of homogeneity and heterogeneity provide us with a way to understand the distinct actions of the two groups as both rational and humane. These concepts also allow us to see that the use of heterogeneity to make the claim of "similar but different" and the use of homogeneity to make the claim of "similar without difference" are practices that go beyond our usual sense of theory. As strategies for addressing the life-and-death problem of rescuing people from harm, they also serve as moral justifications for actions taken.

In another instance, Waxman points to tensions between the ultra Orthodox and American Jewry around the timing of Holocaust Memorial Day. The more secular American Jewry group proposed that Holocaust Memorial Day also serve as an acknowledgment of the anniversary of the Warsaw Ghetto uprising. Ultra Orthodox Jews argued against combining the two because the uprising had occurred during the month of Nissan, a month of joy according to tradition. Holding Holocaust Memorial Day during that month would have therefore constituted a significant break with tradition. Ultimately, the position taken by American Jewry prevailed.

This example points to continuing differences between the two groups, but it also provides an example of how traditions are reconstructed. In this instance, the secular group downplayed the religious tradition of observing Nissan as a time of joy. This allowed for the creation of a new tradition that would merge the Warsaw Ghetto uprising as a sign of resistance with a memorial day for the Holocaust as a sign of respect for those killed and interned because of their Jewish identity.

Establishing Holocaust Memorial Day during the month of Nissan meant that it would be filtered through an understanding of Jewish identity constructed out of events contemporaneous with the Holocaust rather than through the older Orthodox Jewish religious tradition. The spirit of the new tradition is masterful, yet by establishing a tradition for homogenizing distinct aspects of recent Jewish identity, it represented a break with what had served as a homogenizing role among Orthodox Jews. This conflict between the two groups is a clear sign of the heterogeneity of Jewish identity in the United States. Yet the act of establishing a new tradition by changing aspects of an older one points toward an instance in which Jewish identity was homogenized as secular, at least at the public level in the United States, while bracketing a tradition that has and continues to unify Orthodox Jews.[5] At the beginning of the twenty-first century, Jewish identity in the United States has a homogeneously secular persona. The insights of Waxman's historical overview, however, point to the existence of diversity, potentially distinct cultural and social interests, within that identity group. Thinking in terms of identity in general, we can conclude that claims of heterogeneity as well as claims of homogeneity will continue to be used strategically as expressions of the distinct interest that exists within that publicly homogeneous group.

The broad focus of Kaufman's essay is on the relationship between memory and identity. She interrogates this relationship through the late-twentieth-century Holocaust narratives of young Jewish American adults. Her work can thus be viewed as specifically concerned with the outcome of filtering the Holocaust through a young Jewish American identity. Structuring her research in that manner challenges the assumption that a homogeneous way of remembering the Holocaust exists. In addition, it challenges the presumption of such a thing as a homogeneous Jewish identity. The claim, as taken by Kaufman, that specific Jewish identities shape the representation of the Holocaust is akin to arguing that Jewishness represents a heterogeneous identity. Such a position differs quite markedly from the homogeneous assertion that the Holocaust as an event has uniformly shaped the interpretation that all Jews—independent of their culture, location, or experience—have of that event.

Kaufman finds that the narratives her respondents generated were indeed influenced by their Jewish identity. But, she argues, in order to gain a clear sense of those narratives it is important to pay attention to how their Jewish identity was influenced by their American identity. In essence, she did not find "a" Jewish identity existing independent of time and place acting to determine the narratives her respondents produced. She states that for Jewish Americans in their twenties, the Jewish aspect of their identity is a personal tool to be used as they wish, rather than an identity with preconceived beliefs and expected behaviors. This is the image of Jewish identity that is tied to the idea that its members have become individuated because of the contemporary stress in American society on choice and individuality.

Kaufman focuses on the impact of the specific cultural context within which actors are socialized as important to the structure and content of their narratives. Doing so, she operates in a way that is consistent with the constructionist assumption that identity is historically shaped and thus malleable rather than fixed. Although this idea is also present in Waxman's and Aviv and Shneer's work, Kaufman more centrally touches on an added complexity for those using the social constructionist perspective. She provides a view of persons with multiple identities, one of which is assumed to be authentic because it offers inherited ties to a primordial past, while the others are seen as tied to one's present culture. A further complexity lies in the fact that the identities have differential degrees of overall societal influence. In Kaufman's work, when individuals gave prominence to their inherited Jewish identity, they stressed the heterogeneity between themselves and the U.S. culture into which they were socialized. This view points to another time and another place as dominant in shaping their Holocaust narratives. When they gave prominence to their American identity they stressed the homogeneity between themselves and their society. In both instances, individuals are participating in the construction of their identity by defining the self in relationship to the mainstream cultural context in which they live.

Despite pointing to the complexity of potentially competing identities, Kaufman is primarily interested in mainstream influences on her subjects. In taking this approach, she stresses the power of memories shaped by one's immediate cultural context over one's inherited identity. In this sense the immediate culture can be said to distance one from one's inherited identity.

Kaufman relies on three levels of mainstream culture to demonstrate how her respondents have been socialized to view the Holocaust as a distant event. One level is the geographical and military relationship of the United States to World War II and the Holocaust. Another relates to the cultural climate of the United States during the late twentieth century, when Kaufman conducted her interviews. The last relates to the remoteness between the Holocaust and the birth of those she interviewed.

Overall there were no direct geographical or cultural connections between the Holocaust and U.S. society as a whole. This was the case because World War II was not fought on American soil. Thus, despite heavy casualties among Americans, there was a sense that the war took place "over there." In addition, only a relatively small segment of the U.S. population during the war had any immediate personal connections to the Holocaust. The general attitude of Americans toward the Holocaust was thus both figuratively and literally one of distance.

The victory of the Allies in World War II became part of U.S. history, with representations of Americans acting heroically to save the world from Nazi domination and in defense of democracy. The rescue of Jews from the horrors of the Holocaust is represented as having occurred within that larger battle. This idealized American identity was passed to the next generation through history books, novels, television, films, memoirs, and plays.

The aftermath of the war resulted in an explicit move toward homogenizing white ethnics into the American middle class. In addition to general economic growth, the GI Bill, which included government-sponsored suburban housing, tuition support for higher education, and increased access to consumer goods, resulted in a general period of optimism in the society. The initial sense of distance from the Holocaust, the victorious ending to the war, and the optimism produced by upward social mobility after the war proved fundamental to shaping the "American" perception of the Holocaust. Those "American" memories were passed down to the generation of Jews Kaufman interviewed.

A further extension of the homogenization of white ethnics was noticed by sociologists during the late twentieth century. It took the form of individuals being increasingly involved in determining their ethnic identification (Alba 1990; Giddens 1991; Waters 1990). That involvement is described as individuals being more flexible about how to relate to the past. It was in a similar environment that Kaufman's subjects absorbed a sense of their right to develop an interpretation of the Holocaust that felt personal, rather than overly determined by their Jewish identity.

As young adults at the end of the twentieth century, Kaufman's respondents experienced additional cultural factors that served to distance them from a singularly world Jewish interpretation of the Holocaust. One such factor was their exposure to the results of the intense scrutiny of World War II and the Holocaust that began in the United States toward the middle of the twentieth century. That scrutiny occurred primarily in academic institutions. But all segments of society were exposed to representations of the Holocaust, the bombing of Hiroshima and Nagasaki, and the possible end of the world itself through nuclear war as an iconic event. The narratives of Kaufman's respondents were also influenced by questions of one's ability to make objectively truthful statements about social life that arose during the late 1950s and early 1960s. That sense of the multiplicity of interpretations of the past was so potent that even the ability of historians to represent "truth" was being challenged (White 2000).

Because they were young adults in their early twenties during the time of the interviews, Kaufman's respondents also had a personal distance from the Holocaust. Similar to the geographical distance of the United States as a whole, their temporal distance served to diminish the emotional immediacy of the event. That gave them room for a personal relationship to their Jewish identity, while also allowing for the development of a personal narrative about the Holocaust. We can say that Kaufman's respondents provided her with a postmodern Americanized version of post-Holocaust narratives, one based on the multiplicity of their cultural influences.

Looked at through a social constructionist lens, we can see that Kaufman is raising the question of whether there could be such a thing as a Jewish identity outside of a specific sociohistorical context. This does not suggest that constructionists assert that there is no Jewish identity. Rather, the point is that identity as such, including Jewish identity, is necessarily mediated by one's social context. From this perspective, Jewish identity is a fundamentally heterogeneous entity, precisely because Jews will tend toward being homogeneous with the culture within which they grow up. Hence a unified Jewish identity could only exist if, for starters, all Jews had been socialized into the same sociohistorical context.

The essay by Aviv and Shneer overlaps with Kaufman's in an important way. The authors focus on actors who are specifically concerned with counteracting the impact of the type of socialization that Kaufman describes. The American identity of the young people Kaufman studies is referred to by the social actors Aviv and Sheer study as the result of "exile socialization." The reference is to Jews who have grown up in post-Holocaust societies outside of, in exile from, Israel. To describe any Jew socialized outside of Israel as existing in exile is therefore to lay claim to a homogeneous Jewish identity.

Aviv and Shneer characterize their subjects as involved in the "diaspora business." In so doing, they call attention to the fact that memories and identities have economic value in today's world. Despite that characterization, however, the authors point to the belief by some in identity resocialization as a way to save the unified Jewish identity from complete fragmentation.

Those in the diaspora business are engaged in a form of truncated socialization when compared to the "normal" socialization associated with the early stages of movement through the life course. The notion of truncated socialization necessarily has an air of rescue to it because it is premised on the existence of an immediate problem of identity that needs to be addressed. In the context discussed by Aviv and Shneer, that problem refers to the impending loss of Jewish identity due to the continuing assimilation of Jews into the cultures of the nations outside of Israel. Given that definition of the problem, the identity-rescue actors must save the homogeneous group by reestablishing connections among its fragmented parts. In essence, the effort is directed toward convincing the globally and culturally diverse segments of the identity that their social, cultural, and economic diversities are more superficial than real.

From a social constructionist perspective, the temporal and attitudinal differences between the "normal" and "truncated types" of socialization are less important than are their structural similarities. Constructionists call attention to the fact that all identities result from an ongoing process of socializing new members into a sense of "we-ness." Implicit in that statement is the assumption that establishing a "we" involves a process of homogenizing individuals into one identity in the face of viable alternatives. In essence, social life is conceived of as composed of a multiplicity of possible identities. One concern of the constructionist perspective, then, is to show how social agents go about establishing one identity in the face of competition from others.

The "truncated" approach to resocialization proves valuable because it is explicitly about social actors operating with an awareness of identity competition. Competition is not always an obvious component of what I have been calling "normal" socialization. That type of socialization, especially during periods of social calm, involves individuals who are rather passively absorbing the culture of their environment.

In their discussion of the diaspora business, Aviv and Shneer provide us with a clear model of how competition for Jewish identity has become structured. In so doing, they illustrate the general competitive nature of the social construction of identity. One central component of constructing an identity is the establishment of an object that serves as a positive symbol around which individuals come to see themselves as similar. When effective, their similarity can be defined by the fact that they respond to the positive symbol in the same way (Durkheim 1974; Hobsbawm and Ranger 1983). For those operating in the diaspora business, Israel is posed as the safe haven and eternal home of all Jews. By constructing Israel as the ideal place that can protect all Jews, Israel is put forth as the location for the homogeneity of the identity.

Another central component of identity construction is the establishment of an opposing force, a negative symbol, that threatens to destroy the group's homogeneity. In the diaspora business Eastern Europe, as the location of the Holocaust, partially serves that principle role.[6] Within this context, Holocaust narratives are filtered through a Jewish identity linked to the experience of victimization when outside of the safe haven of Israel. Thus, beyond the horror of this extreme event, the Holocaust serves as a reminder of why geographical and cultural homogeneity are important. Focusing on the Holocaust from this perspective is thus a way of pointing to the past in order to justify resocializing efforts in the present (Gellner 1998).

The Holocaust remains a strong negative sign of the dangers of being Jewish in the contemporary world of the diaspora business. But Eastern Europe no longer fully serves the role of a specific danger to the homogeneity of Jewish identity. That role is now "lightly" played by "places of exile." As contemporary "locations of exile," those societies offer, as Kaufman describes it, true alternatives for constructing Holocaust narratives, and thus alternatives to Israel as the home for homogeneous Jewish identity. Such alternatives therefore point toward tensions between heterogeneous and homogeneous notions of Jewish identity.

According to Aviv and Shneer, those in the diaspora business focused on intermarriage between Jews and non-Jews, along with cultural and identity assimilation in general, as indicators that there existed ominous threats to Jewish identity in "exile" communities. They relied heavily on that claim as justification for the diaspora business's commitment to generating a homogenized Jewish identity in Israel. That initial homogenization mission of the diaspora business turned out to be ineffective as a tool for convincing large numbers of Jews to move from their home countries to Israel, however. Indeed, it was ineffective precisely because Jews are highly identified with their home cultures.

As a response to "exile" homogenization, diaspora business actors have taken a pragmatic approach to Jewish homogenization. That approach has been to build a homogeneous Jewish identity by accepting the heterogeneity of the group. They reason that even in the best of times, a negative characterization of the United States and other exile nations will only attract a small number of individuals to Israel. Those taking this homogenizing position have therefore focused on alliances with Jewish organizations in countries outside of Israel. The more pragmatic goal is to infuse a greater sense of Jewishness into Jewish youth where they are throughout the world.

As Weber (1978) points out, the degree of attachment of members to any identity is related to the extent to which they feel that its symbolic value is legitimate. That insight proves helpful for understanding another reason why those in the diaspora business have accepted the heterogeneity base of a homogeneous Jewish identity in the contemporary world. The violence connected to the conflict between Israelis and Palestinians has demonstratively diminished the role Israel can play as a safe haven for all Jews. Jews not from Israel have, in turn, traveled less to Israel and have been more reluctant to provide resources to the diaspora business in Israel. The reality is that the "exile" communities, at the moment, are generally safer than Israel. This fact has not been lost on members of the "exile" communities.

In essence, Aviv and Shneer ultimately argue that plans for the development of a homogeneous Jewish identity succeed to the extent that they operate as a compromise with the reality of the heterogeneity of Jewish identity in the world. In this instance, the ideal of a homogeneous Jewish identity works to the extent that nationally based experiential differences among those who take on that identity are accepted. These authors, similar to Waxman and Kaufman, therefore show that even the use of the Holocaust has limited power as a symbol for establishing a homogeneous Jewish identity.

That is precisely what social constructionists argue in general. In different ways, for example, Weber (1978), Douglas (1986), and Ricoeur (1988) stress identity creation as a process in which actors select from among a multiplicity of elements in order to establish the cognitive bases for a homogeneous entity. That type of activity points toward the human ability to accept the belief in social wholes without insisting on absolute conformity between what wholes imply (totality and fixity) and the world as such (fragmentating and changing).

Whether intentional or not, these authors have provided evidence that falls on the side of the argument that the Holocaust is not a conceptually unique event. In addition, they have provided evidence indicating that Jewish identity constitutes a battleground for social actors. The image that they convey is that although Jewish identity is persistent, like all identities it is always under internal as well as external stress. Focusing on the foregoing essays through a constructionist lens logically calls our attention to those two points. In doing so, it compels us to become involved in a dialogue we might not have otherwise entered.

Discussion

In each of the essays I have discussed, the respective authors' work can comfortably be looked at in terms of their presentation of tensions between claims of a homogeneous identity in the face of heterogeneous actions by identity members. Specifically, by looking at how persons with a Jewish identity have responded to the Holocaust, the authors describe situations in which the use of a unified Jewish identity remains insufficient for explaining the beliefs and behaviors of those under examination.

Based on these cases, I assert that research concerned with the Holocaust and Jewish identity can provide meaningful case studies for the discussion of broader issues related to the construction of identity. They are valuable because they do what cases at their best should do, namely, provide specific data for examining elements of a broader theoretical orientation, while perhaps pushing the boundaries of that orientation (Ragin and Becker 1992). Within that context, these cases confirm two social constructionist claims: (1) that identities are constructed out of disparate parts, and (2) that identities are constantly being transformed. The cases show that responses to the Holocaust have been heterogeneous, with variations based on social and cultural differences, although Jewish identity as an assumed homogeneous category always offers a potential resource for shaping collective beliefs and actions.

Waxman bases the heterogeneity of Jewish identity in the United States on Central European and Eastern European sociocultural differences. He shows that those differences persisted over time, despite social pressures and temporary strategic alliances to establish them as similar. Kaufman discusses how the Holocaust narratives of contemporary young adult American Jews have become infused with American culture. She thereby points toward the fact that Jewish identity is context specific and thus both fluid and heterogeneous. Aviv and Shneer describe the changing complexity of the diaspora business through which some actors have engaged in a concerted effort to construct a globally unified Jewish identity. They show that this ideal of homogeneity has had to give way to a pragmatic homogeneity that accepts the reality of the continuing heterogeneity of Jewish identity.

But how legitimate is it really to engage in a straightforward translation of these studies into social constructionist language? This question brings the discussion back to the more difficult questions of the legitimacy of using the Holocaust and Jewish identity as common cases for the study of identity construction in general. The truth of the matter is that there is no way to resolve those issues once and for all. Taking a position on them is to begin with the premise of either the homogeneity or the heterogeneity of human actors as a whole.

Without any doubt, the Holocaust did not happen to humans in general. It concerned humans specifically targeted because of their collective identity. The identity group therefore experienced collective identity trauma (Alexander 2004).[7] This then calls for sympathy toward those specifically targeted. No theoretical perspective can ignore that fact, and none that is credible would. But theorists are engaged in the task of focusing on past and present aspects of the human condition in hopes of understanding and perhaps changing the way in which we as humans treat each other in the future. Necessarily, however, theorists while in the act of theorizing are less sympathetic to the conditions of specific cases than they are to the category as a whole.

It is here that speculation about why social constructionists have so sparsely used the Holocaust and Jewish identity as examples can constructively begin. The limited use of studies tied to the Holocaust and Jewish identity is itself a "case" of the limited use of groups associated with collective identity trauma as data to develop sociological theory (Williams 2002). A potential reason for this limitation is the messiness of cases tied to collective identity trauma. Specifically, collective identity trauma leaves individual members with a range of emotional responses to the destructive event. The emotional responses associated with the trauma do not get muted even by the type of geographical and cultural distancing alluded to by Kaufman. All identity members, having equal access to historical facts, can vie for the role of what Alexander, relying on Weber, calls a "carrier group" (Alexander 2004:11). Carrier groups, in this instance, are agents who consciously attempt to transform the destructive events into a collective identity trauma.

Collective identity trauma calls specific attention to the collective, and thus it also constitutes a call for "moral responsibility" (Alexander 2004:27). Operating theoretically, Alexander discusses moral responsibility as a responsibility all humans have toward each other. But moral responsibility can also be directed in a more limited manner toward those of a collective identity who are viewed as not having been sufficiently mindful of the threat that events have implied for their identity.

The Holocaust and Jewish identity thus cannot readily be neutralized into general statements about human behavior. In some sense, those connected to it, whether by personal or cultural memory, understandably might view such an event as unique (Cuddihy 1987; White 1990). But claims of group uniqueness are precisely what theoretical perspectives argue against. One way theorists have dealt with such messiness has been to avoid it. The result is not using such cases at all, or using them sparingly, as data for research.

A more productive way to deal with this issue is for theorists to take on the challenge that comes with the study of collective identity trauma. At the most basic level, this involves moving in two directions. One way is to pay full attention to the range of responses that identity members have to the trauma. This direction helps to show that those within identities respond to the trauma differently, ranging from using it as a fundamental definition of self to viewing trauma as connected to the self only in the broadest of terms. This is precisely what the authors I have discussed do in their essays, and therein lies the value of their work.

Another direction is for theorists to make the explicit effort to show that abstractions about the human condition can provide us with information about how humans have inflicted suffering on each other, how humans have suffered, and how humans have dealt with suffering. This direction would use comparative studies that point toward our common responsibilities in each other's suffering, as well as our ability to alleviate this suffering (Alexander 2004).

But theorists are not exclusively responsible for the limited interface between the social constructionist perspective, the Holocaust, and research on Jewish identity. The literature on Jewish identity does not shy away from discussions of conflict among Jewish groups competing for control over the factors that contribute to the homogenizing aspects of Jewish identity (Waxman 1983). But to the extent that those conflicts are treated merely as historical events specific to Jews, that is, not moving beyond the boundaries of the group, the discussion reinforces the sense of the social uniqueness of that identity group. Those doing local studies could thus more explicitly use their research to move beyond the study of Jewish identity in order to reflect generally on identity creation.

The reluctance to move beyond the boundaries of the identity group is most definitely not specific to Jewish studies. My sense is that it is linked to the study of groups with collective identity trauma, however. This is so because those studying such groups face the difficult issue of becoming involved in debates about the uniqueness of the group and its collective identity trauma. On the one hand, researchers can confront this dilemma by moving in the first direction I point to above. They can turn toward the data of their work for evidence that identity members have heterogeneous responses to historical facts. In addition, they can turn to theorists for ways to treat their complex data more broadly.

Difficulties logically arise when social constructionists take on the "exceptional" case of the Holocaust and Jewish identity for the study of identity construction in general. Significantly, however, I have suggested here that such difficulties are broader than the specific issues of the Holocaust and Jewish identity. Nevertheless, I have claimed that an interface between the two, beyond being possible, can also prove fruitful. On the one hand, it can provide social constructionists with new avenues for establishing the theoretical maturity of their perspective. On the other hand, it can demonstrate to those doing local studies the relevance that specific data about Jewish identity offer for those engaging in theoretical work in the constructionist mode.

Notes

1. I am not making the claim that social constructionists are exceptional in this regard.
2. I use *identity* as a form, a subset, of social solidarity.
3. There is a distinction between filtering the Holocaust through Jewish identities and filtering Jewish identity through the Holocaust. The former indicates that distinct Jewish identities independently influence the meaning of the Holocaust. The latter is closer to a homogeneous position that the Holocaust can shape a singular Jewish response.
4. One of course could push the argument further by challenging the legitimacy of operating only with two Jewish groups, but doing so would not generate any further theoretical points.
5. In this respect, the nineteenth-century image of "the Jew" as Orthodox can arguably be seen as transformed into the twenty-first-century identification of "the Jew" with the non-Orthodox.
6. As the idealized birthplace of a segment of American Jewish folklore, Eastern Europe plays a more complex role than this, but its central role is as the negative contrast to Israel.
7. Unlike Alexander, who uses *cultural trauma* in making the excellent distinction between "extraordinary events" and trauma (2004:3), I use the term *collective identity trauma* to call attention to the fact that while it is individuals who suffer, the attachment concerns the collective identity. That distinction provides a basis for us to take account of the fact that members of the identity experience the extraordinary events in different ways. Because all members have claim to the identity, however, there will be competition for developing collective identity narratives about the identity-related events. This is the essence of what Waxman, Kaufman, and Aviv and Shneer have proved for us.

3

MEMORY, MEMOIRS, AND POST-MEMORY

Part 3 zeros in on the use of socio-historical analysis, drawing on interviews, memoirs, and testimonies about the Holocaust from those who survived. In her article, Judith Gerson considers how writers of Holocaust memoirs alternately rely on and refuse various notions of comparison and generalizability when narrating their experiences. The title of her essay, *"In Cuba I Was a German Shepherd,"* both references an oft-told joke among German Jewish refugees about life in the old country and the title of Ana Menéndez's (2001) collection of stories of Cuban American immigration and resettlement. In both instances, the title reveals a small dog's longing for an ostensibly more glorious past, and reminds us of the importance of comparison for comprehension more generally and for understanding the Holocaust more specifically. Rather than depend entirely on moral or normative responses to ongoing debates as a way to argue for or against the uniqueness of the Holocaust, Gerson suggests that scholars can gain an appropriately more complex understanding of the Holocaust if we consider when memoir writers represent their experiences as amenable to comparison and when they insist on its noncomparability.

Suzanne Vromen's essay focuses on Jewish children hidden in Belgian convents during the war. Using a multiperspective approach, Vromen recounts the collective memories of the nuns and priests who hid them; of women underground rescue workers who escorted them from their homes to the convents and returned them to their families at war's end; and of former hidden children. Integrating these three sets of accounts yields a rich but understandably vexed and ultimately complicated picture of collective identity, particularly in terms of family relations and religious identity for these now adult survivors. Often convents became places of refuge in which children could resume their childhoods and have a sense of structure and safety in their daily lives. Yet Catholic rules regarding communion forbade those not baptized from receiving the sacrament, and the resulting exclusion jeopardized the safety of the children. While some children were baptized as a result of this situation, and found their new religion a source of comfort, this was not the universal experience. At the war's end, children were not necessarily happily reunited with their families. Some remained attached to the convents that hid them, some did not remember their parents, some resented their parents for abandoning them, and some had become orphans. Overshadowing these complex relations, Vromen argues, is the absence of "hidden children" as an analytic category until the late twentieth century. Consequently, many of these children until recently labored privately and silently under the anxieties they believed were their own and not a result of larger social forces.

Diane Wolf's contribution challenges the analytic framework underlying the Holocaust testimonials collected by the Steven Spielberg project. While the fifty thousand testimonials taken by the Spielberg project are unquestionably important, they give short shrift to the postwar experience except for the regeneration of Jewish families. Thus these testimonies produce a particular politics of Jewish memory and identity that uncritically reasserts the family as a haven. Wolf's (2002a) oral history of the postwar experiences of Jake Geldwert, a Polish Jewish camp survivor, points to some harsh practices enforced on him by Jewish kin after he arrived in the United States. Using the oral history as a case study and comparing it to the video done by Spielberg volunteers, Wolf discusses the implications for analyses of Jewish post-memory and identity. Furthermore, she brings up questions concerning gender and the Holocaust, and the relevance of diaspora and transnational studies for a further analysis of Holocaust testimonials.

Irina Carlota Silber situates her commentary on these essays within the larger context of the aftermath of violence and the subsequent challenges of rebuilding lives. Working from questions of social theory, methodology, and pedagogy, Silber considers a range of issues surrounding narrative, diaspora, and the politics of memory. Survivors, Silber acknowledges, do not constitute homogeneous groups, despite their often common representations as such, and consequently it would be a mistake to think of their communities as monolithic, or of their memories as identical. Instead, she reminds us to contextualize the meaning of exile, and Silber offers several methodological tools and substantive recommendations. She urges us to articulate appropriate comparisons with other genocidal and postwar groups, as well as other migratory populations during the time period of the Holocaust and its aftermath. Her own research on the aftermath of the civil war in El Salvador serves as a reminder that there are "difference[s] along gender, generation, wartime experiences and postwar locations that are refracted through people's narrative recollections" (Silber this volume: 178) and that scholars need to read narratives and listen to testimonies while attending to these distinctions. Too often Holocaust testimonies "homogenize and romanticize 'the people' and 'the people's voices'" (Silber this volume: 180). In addition, she explores the possibilities and limitations of comparisons between Holocaust narratives and Latin American *testimonios* of violence, reminding us to consider their production, consumption, circulation, and representation. Under what conditions can and do informants talk? How are the end of military rule and subsequent attempts to restore peace and democratic processes reflected in *testimonios*? As listeners to and readers of these juxtaposed accounts, we, Silber suggests, bear witness to the atrocities of genocide and the attendant political violence as a way to work toward social justice.

In her commentary, Ethel Brooks explores the importance of contextualizing and historicizing memoirs and testimonies, as well as the concomitant problems that result if we overlook macrolevel frameworks. She considers how capitalist modernity, often understood as globalization and reiterated through U.S.-centrism, shapes representations of Holocaust and post-Holocaust lives. She compares memories and accounts of the Holocaust with her own research that analyzes the testimonies of mostly women workers involved in antisweatshop campaigns in Bangladesh, El Salvador, and New York City and develops a framework for interpreting both sets of narratives. Brooks suggests that local meanings are expressed in all testimonies but are reiterated and translated transnationally. Global and/or commodified representations shape local memoirs, and these remain important contexts to interpret testimonies. Scholars working with these narratives, moreover, need to appreciate how local experiences of familial, gendered, sexual, class, and ethnic relations shape which stories get told, how they are told and retold, which ones get repressed, and how these stories are altered. Testimony is structured not only by narrative conventions but also by the demands of various audiences at different points in time and place. Brooks cautions us against isolating the history of the Holocaust from post-Holocaust life lest we maintain the Holocaust outside of modernity. Comparisons with the contemporary situations of other refugee or survivor populations, she argues, would enable an appropriately more complex and comprehensive understanding of survival, mourning, and remembrance.

In Cuba I Was a German Shepherd: Questions of Comparison and Generalizability in Holocaust Memoirs

JUDITH M. GERSON

The first part of the title for this essay is taken from Ana Menéndez's (2001) collection of short stories by the same name. In the lead story, a dog explains to his canine companion that in the United States he may be a short, insignificant mutt, but that in Cuba he was a German shepherd. The book caught my eye when it was released because I had encountered the joke several times before in my family, and in the memoirs of and interviews with German Jewish immigrants. The version popular among German Jews usually depicts two dachshunds talking with one another lamenting their more glorious past as Saint Bernards as they and their companions stroll in a park.[1] In other words, a tale I had once considered uniquely identified with German Jewish immigrants is almost identical to the one Cuban Americans tell each other, thus suggesting the import of comparison and generalizability.

Ideas about comparison and generalizability are embedded in a diversity of claims and thus matter for researchers irrespective of their subject of inquiry. When we assert a position or point of view, state a fact, or describe a pattern, we make decisions about the applicability and generalizability of our statements—what to include and what to exclude. Recognizing that *both* Cuban Americans and German Jews, and not simply one group or the other, commonly told this joke to express a sense of loss over a once-upon-a-time more prosperous way of life, makes a difference. It does because it is more precise, more accurate to assert that both immigrant groups relied on this narrative, rather than presume its uniqueness within one or the other group. In other words, by comparing the two immigrant groups' proclivity to joke about their more glorious past, we can understand this dynamic more appropriately as generalizable to both rather than unique to one or the other. Comparison aids accuracy, and moreover, enables us to theorize about the human condition (Williams 2002; Williams this volume).

Broadly defined, comparative techniques are the central analytic tool social scientists use to determine the parameters of generalizability. Comparison enables scholars to disaggregate phenomena that initially or commonsensically appear unified. And conversely, comparison also permits researchers to see connections and unity where none were obvious earlier (Wieviorka 1992:170–71).[2] We strive to make clear what our criteria are for inclusion and exclusion, and then apply these criteria consistently. When we compare, we place ostensibly similar phenomena adjacent to one another and determine if indeed they are sufficiently similar to be analyzed together. If they appear to be virtually identical to each other, researchers commonly lump them together in a single analytic category (Zerubavel 1991). But when they are similar in some respects but not in others, researchers keep phenomena separate from another and compare them along various pertinent dimensions to discern where differences and similarities lie.

One way to articulate the core project of sociology is to suggest that all forms of social life can be apprehended as part of or related to other, more general forms of behavior. Although no single statement can ever adequately represent a discipline, I want to argue that a central theme of sociological inquiry is the study of routine, patterned forms of social life. For researchers of the Holocaust, this approach requires that we analyze its generalizability, and comparative techniques are probably most useful in this regard. We cannot determine the uniqueness, difference, or similarity of any phenomena without making comparisons. The possibility of another holocaust or genocide suggests, moreover, that sociologists interested in prevention require a comparative approach in their investigation (Fein 1993; Obershall 2000).

This essay considers the question of comparison and generalizability with respect to the Holocaust. Debates and tensions about the uniqueness or comparability of the Holocaust continue to be heard today, more than half a century after the end of World War II.[3] Scholars, survivors, and many other writers have done an excellent job articulating those positions, and I will not attempt to summarize them here.[4] Rather I want to consider a set of issues about the appropriateness of comparisons with and generalizations about the Holocaust as a sociologist, using commonly understood definitions of the discipline. I begin with typical social science methods with the research tools available to us, rather than start from the more general and normative question about whether we ought to speak about the Holocaust as one of many genocides. While I acknowledge and respect the moral positions that have guided others both in their arguments about the uniqueness of the Holocaust and in their contentions about its comparability with other genocides, my purposes here are more specific and empirical.

I am interested in understanding how we might attain a more nuanced and appropriately more complex understanding of the Holocaust if we attend to the uses of comparative methods broadly defined. In this article I seek to identify how Holocaust memoir writers and the researchers who read them deploy, evade, or refuse comparative approaches. Said somewhat more succinctly, my aim is to determine how comparison and generalizability function in Holocaust narratives. Thus I start with the question about how and under what circumstances memoir writers use notions of comparison in their narratives. Aware that memoir reading is an interpretative act, I recognize the limitations of a purely positivist approach to analyzing these memoirs and acknowledge my own position in interpreting them. My approach implies that I will bracket normative issues of whether the Holocaust should or should not be compared. Indeed, for social scientists, it may be more productive to think about if and how comparisons are made, rather than rely completely on a comprehensive position for or against comparability and generalization. I conclude with a brief discussion of whether comparing the Holocaust with other disasters such as the events of September 11, 2001, might further our understanding of the Holocaust. Ultimately, I hope that with more concrete evidence about how people use notions of comparison and generalization to understand the Holocaust, we will be better able to respond to the more vexed moral issues about its uniqueness.

Comparison and Generalization in Holocaust Memoirs

I begin the analysis of how comparison and generalization function in Holocaust memoirs with a brief discussion of my study design and sample, in which several ideas about comparison are implicit. From there I move to an analysis of how comparison operates in the writing and reading of these memoirs.

Evidence for this article comes from a larger, ongoing project on German Jewish immigrants who fled Germany between 1933 and 1941 and who had resettled in the United States by 1945.[5] The sixty-two largely unpublished memoirs I analyze here are written by people who generally claim to speak for themselves and/or their families alone.[6] In fact, many memoir writers are explicit about the point that they do not intend to portray their experiences as representative of any larger group. In other words, many writers expressly reject any notion that their memoirs should serve as a basis for a more general understanding. They write out of personal experience usually after the war, when often they themselves are middle-aged or older. At times, they have diaries and letters from years past that they weave into their narratives, but more commonly, they write from memory, which they consider to be precise even years after the events they describe. I have deliberately selected memoirs written by people who are not, nor do they consider themselves to be famous, extraordinary, or exemplary.[7]

Part of my decision to focus on this immigrant group and its relationship to the Holocaust stems from the relative scarcity of knowledge about people who escaped from Nazi Europe before the mass deportations began in October 1941. In order to document and try to understand the Holocaust, most scholars initially concentrated on perpetrators and then victims, and only more recently has their work turned to studies of bystanders, as well as to questions that extend and/or complicate these analytic categories. Within the past few years, a new research interest has emerged that focuses on people who fled the Third Reich before 1942 and resettled elsewhere. My work is part of this latter approach, and I understand it as responsive to some of the remaining gaps in knowledge by developing an appropriately more complex understanding of that era than we have had available to us heretofore.

Individuals who comprise my sample of first and 1.5 generation immigrants had a complex understanding of the Holocaust,[8] usually derived from direct experiences of increasing racial exclusion, harassment, and brutality, and indirect knowledge of the Final Solution.[9] I wanted to understand in what ways their experiences of the Holocaust and as newcomers who resettled in the United States differed from more prototypical survivors.

Yet I soon realized that the very terms used to define this group were contested. These were people who outsiders today might have labeled Holocaust survivors, but this vocabulary was not in use at the end of the war. It was not until the 1960s that the word holocaust became commonly known in English as the translation of the Hebrew word shoah. First evident in founding documents of the state of Israel, the word holocaust began to circulate widely in reports on

JUDITH M. GERSON

the Eichmann trial, which reached the American public beginning in 1961 (Novick 1999: 133–34). Furthermore, after the war, native-born Americans initially relied on *immigrant, refugee,* and *displaced person* to refer to those I study, often using the terms interchangeably. Much to the horror of these newcomers, some Americans occasionally but incorrectly also thought they were enemy aliens. The genealogy of *survivor* in Holocaust study is harder to specify. Cohen tells us that people did not use this word until the 1960s (2007: 179). It is also arguable that as the testimonies and accounts of Holocaust survival became more and more prominent, researchers and clinicians began to connect these narratives with the survivor accounts of other forms of trauma, thereby solidifying the term *Holocaust survivor.*

Preferences among those I studied for the term *immigrant* over either *refugee* or *survivor* reflects this chronology, although the refusal of these two terms serves somewhat different purposes. In the words of a key informant, "refugees referred to those who were forced to leave, while immigrants chose to leave." This distinction was confirmed repeatedly while reading memoirs and in interviews with other immigrants.[10] First and 1.5 generation German Jewish immigrants generally limit the use of *refugee* to convey constraints and expulsion, and use *immigrant* to suggest choice, free will, and emphasize a sense of their own agency. Like the word *refugee*, which partially serves this purpose, the use of the label *immigrant* serves to evade or repress remaining terrors of the Holocaust.[11] Immigrants reserve the term *survivor* as an honorific to pay respect to those who survived the war either in concentration camps, forced labor, or in hiding.

Although there is no universal understanding of the terms *refugee, survivor,* and *immigrant*, the differentiation remains significant here for several reasons. First, it obviously indicates the comparison that immigrants make when referring to themselves in contrast to refugees or survivors, and therefore it offers a meaningful distinction for them. Yet this particular configuration of immigrant-refugee-survivor inadvertently reproduces a collective silence among the immigrant group.[12] Out of respect for the suffering survivors endured during the Holocaust, immigrants distinguish themselves from those they and others refer to as survivors. This distinction helps mark survivors' suffering as the real suffering. Thus if survivors remain comparatively silent about their traumas, immigrants may also find it difficult to speak because they have less standing, less authority to speak, thereby inadvertently contributing to their own invisibility. German Jewish immigrants are neither prototypical Holocaust survivors nor refugees, and they often see themselves at the margins of groups of Holocaust survivors.

Second, the contrast immigrants draw between themselves and refugees suggests that scholars and the lay public alike need to rethink their more common assumptions that lump immigrants, refugees, and survivors together into a single category of Holocaust survivor (Zerubavel 1991) thereby erasing potentially important differences among them. As scholars, we are not required to take informants' definitions of themselves as fact, but we must account for their definitions in our own interpretations, whether or not we like or accept them. This differentiation functions furthermore as a cautionary note against overgeneralization and for specificity in research and language use. As important, it also suggests the need to think about this group as immigrants with all the resources available to us through the vast research literatures on immigration. Studying first and 1.5 generation German Jews both as part of the Holocaust and as immigrants therefore seems eminently reasonable.[13]

Memoir Reading

Although each memoir stands on its own as documentary evidence, given sociology's emphasis on patterns in social life, a sociological interpretation of memoirs benefits from reading a larger collection of memoirs and drawing comparisons among them. It would be a mistake, however, to assume that memoirs are simply individual narratives. Zussman (2000) effectively argues that "if autobiographical narratives constitute the self, those narratives are socially structured" (5). He develops the concept of autobiographical occasions to refer to those moments in which people provide accounts of themselves and therefore narrative and social structure intersect. In the following pages, I outline a range of comparative techniques evident in these memoirs.

I read these memoirs as clues for larger social patterns, relying on the methods of grounded theory to inform my investigation. Initially, I use simple content analysis to try to discover similar or contrasting patterns when reading the memoirs. Do several writers mention the same event, express concerns about similar matters, and frequently evade others? Although I initially treat each memoir as a case, I also am interested in aggregate patterns—something I can only discern by comparing these memoirs to one another. What at first appears to be an individual experience or reaction may also prove an illustration of a more generalizable pattern. Thus the most obvious form of comparison I rely on when reading these memoirs is contrasting them with each other. Closely related to this form of comparison is my reading of them within a larger sociohistorical context. I know the general history of the period, and my interpretation of these memoirs is guided by that larger context, as I will illustrate in detail below.

The first set of examples derives from the explicit comparisons memoir writers made. Invariably they referred to themselves as German Jews and often spoke about themselves as part of this group. They contrasted themselves as German Jews with other German Jews and to Germans who were not Jewish, and on resettlement to Americans, whom they usually treated as a homogenous Other. The most salient comparisons German Jews invoked pertained to their citizenship.

German Jews sought to legitimate their rights to German citizenship by proving their residence and longevity in Germany over the centuries. Through genealogical research, they proved that they had been on German soil as long as or even longer than many of their Christian neighbors. Ernst Hausmann, for example, chronicled his family's existence in Baden back to the Thirty Years' War (1618–48), and figured the chaos of those years probably meant that earlier records were destroyed. His family's genealogical knowledge created considerable trouble for one of his cousins, a Jew, who was able to prove in a school assignment that her family had been in Germany longer than any of her Aryan classmates (Hausmann 1996:1–2). Indeed, genealogical research was quite popular in Germany in the early years of the Third Reich. But unlike Mischlinge (people of mixed heritage) and Christian converts who sought to prove their Christian heritage to protect themselves from anti-Semitic attacks, German Jews looked to their genealogical records to certify themselves as Jews and as Germans.

The second major vehicle German Jews employed to justify their rights as Germans was their loyalty to the state. The paramount expression of this loyalty for many was military service during World War I, and the most telling symbol of this allegiance was often the Iron Cross, a medal awarded for valor. Men who received the Iron Cross mentioned it in their writings, but so did their wives, sisters, mothers, and children. Occasionally, a narrative revealed a sense of confusion or indignation about their status as loyal citizens having served in the military just years earlier. For example, Joseph Adler (1992) who received the Iron Cross on "January 27, 1917, Kaiser Wilhelm's birthday" (30), wrote, "I had the Iron Cross and the Front Fighter Orden (a war medal) from Hitler's government. In this respect we were a little better off than the other Jews" (51). "In Germany, as a front soldier, I still had [in 1938] certain privileges under Hitler, which made the negotiations with the Gestapo and the *Devisenstelle* (foreign exchange) somewhat easier" (56). Reiterating this theme of Jewish men serving the German state, a daughter was explicit about her resentment. "My father, like many Jews, was a good German and insisted on enlisting voluntarily in the Army in World War I. . . . How grateful the Germans were to us later on!" (Baum-Meróm and Baum 1996:93).

Legitimating citizenship rights and retaining privileges as citizens were not only individual or family matters. Many memoirs referenced the disproportionately high numbers of Jews who had volunteered to serve, as well as the disproportionately high numbers of Jews killed in action during World War I (Wolf 1969:229). Tension over the meaning of German Jewish military service was so acute during the early years of the Third Reich that a memorial book containing the names of twelve thousand German soldiers of Jewish origin who had died for Germany during World War I was compiled and widely circulated (Friedländer 1997:15), and those names and numbers were frequently cited as evidence of Jewish patriotism.

The above comparisons were articulated to substantiate claims for German citizenship. But there were also numerous references German Jews made to other German Jews, solidifying a sense of collective belonging. These passages occurred frequently and varied greatly in their content. But comparison among memoirs eventually yielded several emphases, such as the popularity of taking walks. Immigrants mentioned walking to synagogue on Saturday morning along with other German Jews (Gruenspecht 1993), taking walks or hikes with extended family or with a Jewish youth group on Sundays, walking in parks in Berlin to regain a modicum of calmness in their lives (Peters-Rothschild 1986:4), and even trying to appear as if they were just taking an early morning walk when crossing illegally into Switzerland (Ottenheimer 1995).[14] Once in New York City, they talked about walking the streets of Washington Heights to do their shopping, how walking in New York offered fewer pleasant sights, and how walking could save the five cents a subway ride would have cost. These are largely anecdotal references, and at times it is difficult to discern their meaning beyond descriptive accounts. But occasionally such anecdotes can be understood to have some greater significance.

Such was the case with what seemed initially to be curious references to the purchase of a top hat in preparation for immigration. Several men wrote about buying a top hat before they immigrated, but the significance of that action

JUDITH M. GERSON

remained unclear. Was it simply that top hats were fashionable in Germany in the 1930s? Did top hats represent something they imagined about the United States? A clue finally came in one memoir whose writer lamented all the preparation required for immigration: new items had to be purchased if funds were available to compensate for the meager amount of cash one could legally take abroad; packing lists had to be made out in detail, approved by several governmental offices; and heavy taxes and penalty fees had to be paid before permission to leave was granted. German Jews who left Germany relatively early and legally were deliberate in their preparations. What first appeared to be an individual immigrant decision anticipating and acquiring goods for life in the new homeland, when read in this larger bureaucratic context, took on additional meaning. Moreover, newspaper columns especially written for a Jewish community whose members were often anxious to leave offered extensive advice organized by country of destination about what to expect. Advertisements in one of these newspapers promoted top hats as important for men wanting to make a proper impression in their new American homeland. A subsequent rereading of the memoirs under consideration suggests a further class-based explanation. Top hats seemed to have been the object on which some men of middle-class status focused their anxieties about their status and economic well-being. Men who mentioned top hats included professional workers, shop keepers, small businessmen, and office workers—all understandably anxious about their and their families' viability.

Other anecdotes required considerably less investigation and explanation. For example, one of the most frequent greetings among German Jews when meeting each other in Germany before 1942 was, "What number do you have?" The analogue in New York among recent German Jewish arrivals was the salutation, "When did you get here?" (Grebler 1976:3). Given the extensive regulations and requirements for leaving Germany, and the quotas imposed by many receiving nations often tied to where potential immigrants were born, the import of both queries is evident. These greetings were an indirect and initially a relatively safe and polite way to initiate conversation. Their routinization suggests their salience and hence significance. As insiders, fellow immigrants understood in considerable detail how a high number in an immigration queue signaled a later departure date that in turn translated into increased probabilities of anti-Semitic exclusion, danger, and attacks. Immigrants became adept at calculating the meanings of these coded numbers to assess the likelihood of racial harassment.

In addition, there are problems of interpretation that derive from the avoid-ance of comparisons when reading memoirs. Below I cite three examples. The first pertains to German Jewish immigrants' collective definitions of themselves guided in part by nineteenth- and twentieth-century popular and scholarly dis-cussions about whether German Jews were more German than Jewish. Rooted in eighteenth-century debates over the Enlightenment and nineteenth-century debates over emancipation and citizenship, German Jews encountered ever-changing definitions of themselves as public participants. The significance of this formulation was pointedly summarized by Evyatar Friesel (1996) who wrote, "There is hardly another issue in modern Jewish historiography which con-strains the present-day researcher with so many charged concepts as the case of the relationship between Germans and Jews in Germany in the nineteenth and twentieth centuries . . . . Implicitly or explicitly, scholars have tried to understand what, in the history of the German people and the development of modern German Jewry, brought about the final destruction" (263–64).

There are numerous instances of this long-standing notion that German Jews were more German than Jewish, and the illusion of their integration into German society in the years before the Third Reich was a contributing factor to their demise (see Strauss 1982:xi). This narrative was appropriately critiqued by Henry Schwarzschild (1993) in a letter he wrote to the *New York Times Book Review* editor that I quote below to demonstrate the importance of comparative analyses.

But the more problematic suggestion, that German Jews thought of themselves as Ger-mans first and as Jews only secondarily—always put in an accusatory tone, as though they had been blindly self-destructive—provokes the following two thoughts: Political and social emancipation—in education, language, appearance, economic integration, and the like—came earlier and more completely in western and central Europe than in the eastern regions, where Jews lived in far greater numbers. The Enlightenment that brought eman-cipation to the Jewish minority also brought nationalism, the proposition that citizens of a state in which they enjoy equality of rights owe it identification and loyalty. Like the citizens of every other modern state, German Jews bore their country that loyalty. But the very point of that emancipation was that this national identity did not require the sacrifice of one's intense sense of belonging, at the same time, to the historical and religious Jewish community. Secondly, if it was blameful disorientation for German Jews to think of themselves as an integral part of Germany, consider how American Jews see themselves (leaving aside ultra Orthodox Jews). American Jews have been in this country, in the main, for a hundred years; Jews had lived in Germany for more than ten times that span.

A second example derives from instances of self-blame that occasionally appear in interpretations of personal experiences in these memoirs and in the secondary literature. Though there are many versions of this phenomenon, and they often surface quite subtly, writers seem to suggest that they should have known better. Questions and statements such as "How could I have not known?" or "I should have known better" appear with some regularity and remain unanswered. Writers thus take their present knowledge of the Holocaust and inappropriately use it retrospectively to interpret and judge their actions in the past. What others have called "hindsight bias" (Carli 1999; Hawkins and Hastie 1990; Hoffrage and Hertwig 1999), operates here to establish an impossible standard for knowing what was impossible to know at the time. In fact, if we are to read the remembrances of life in Germany in the larger social structural context of the rules and regulations regarding Jewish conduct under the Nazi state, there is a contradictory and confusing picture at least until *Kristallnacht* on November 9– 10, 1938. There was no simple, linear progression of increasing restrictions; rather, laws were passed and then relaxed by subsequent legislation or practiced irregularly; exemptions to restrictive laws were extended sometimes systematically, as was the case with World War I veterans and their ability to retain public sector jobs. In other words, when writers accord too much weight to knowledge acquired through hindsight or try to apprehend their experiences apart from a larger social-structural context, possibilities for misinterpretation flourish.

Whereas the above examples point to the potential of perpetuating a dominant but problematic interpretation if comparisons are avoided or deployed incorrectly, the third illustration suggests the difficulties inherent in making sense of a finding without any comparative awareness. When German Jewish immigrants remembered Germany, that memory was invariably located in nature. Descriptions of green meadows, mountain scenery, and beautiful hikes were common in the memoirs read. For some, nature functioned as a literal and figurative refuge. Lotte Peters-Rothschild, living in Berlin and married to a non-Jewish social worker, lamented, "And then again after a walk in the Grunewald he [her husband] would come home desperate, where in the world would we find a place to live and work as wonderful as this? So close to the woods and lakes?" (1986:4). The natural environment provided the imagined possibility of protection for Leo Grebler (1976), who admitted, "I must also confess to toying with the foolish notion of withdrawing somewhere to the German countryside if my work at the paper was terminated, to await further developments while playing music and reading books" (7). Poignantly, Liselotte Kahn (1970) described her parents' decision to escape from Nuremberg to Garmisch-Parten-kirchen and build a house: "They felt that there in the midst of meadows with grazing cows, looking out toward the eternal beauty and stillness of their beloved snow-covered mountains, away from active professional and social life, they would be forgotten and left in peace" (18). Thus it appears that the permanent, natural landscape, relatively unchanged by human intervention, was what immigrants sought to retain or comfortably recalled from their homeland. In contrast to their social relationships in Germany, the landscape remained reliable and comforting. Its beauty provided a respite, an escape, albeit only temporarily.

Read out of context, we can understand the natural landscape as a refuge in contrast to the social landscape defined by human relationships. But we also need to consider the importance of landscape more generally in both German popular consciousness and for victims of traumatic events. The centrality of forested woodlands in Germany were "simply not a matter of patriotic sentimentality but functionally important for the life of the nation" (Schama 1995:118). Grimm fairy tales and the works of scores of other writers and artists prominently featured wooded landscapes in German literature and the arts. But this does not suggest that the natural environment is invariably nor necessarily a refuge. In times of social upheaval, the natural landscape may provide a sense of refuge, but natural disasters often produce worries about the trustworthiness of the natural environment, which then can bleed into a mistrust of others. Victims and survivors of natural disasters such as floods and earthquakes often report that part of their trauma is an enduring unease or panic about the land around them, and also about their communities: "Among the symptoms of extreme trauma is a sense of vulnerability, a feeling that one has lost a certain natural immunity to misfortune, a growing conviction, even, that the world is no longer a safe place to be. And this feeling often grows into a prediction that something terrible is bound to happen again" (Erickson 1976:234).

September 11, 2001: A Question of Trauma

The terrorist attacks of September 11 prompted me to rethink some of the earlier research on Holocaust memoirs, spurred in part by telephone calls from two German Jewish immigrants who explained that they never expected "something like this would ever happen here."[15] Searching for historical parallels to understand the present is a common enterprise (Sicher 2000:78), and the events of that day generated several immediate forms of comparison. Among the initial and most common comparisons to September 11 were references to the attack on Pearl Harbor and other attacks on the U.S. government and industry both within its continental borders and in various locations throughout the world. Also evident were more problematic analogies between Osama bin Laden, the Taliban, and Afghanistan, on the one hand, and Hitler, the Nazis, and Germany, on the other. Though my thoughts are not conclusive in any respect, I want to suggest a few additional ways to think about comparison between these world events so that they might provide further insight to scholars of the Holocaust and post-Holocaust life. I write as a bystander and refer to other bystanders in the most recent terrorist attacks in the United States.

During the morning of September 11 in the eastern United States, and to some degree in other parts of the country and during the day(s) immediately following the terrorist attacks, there was considerable confusion. Although the broad outlines of terrorism were soon available to the U.S. public, the extent of the attacks could not immediately be known. In response, federal offices in Washington and throughout the country closed almost immediately. In some locations, banks and shopping malls shut down, as did public schools and universities. In the days that followed, some argued that officials had overreacted by closing various institutions, but others noted that there had been a long-standing insufficient governmental response, particularly by the defense and intelligence communities. In order to impose some semblance of meaning on this crisis, many bystanders initially resorted to overly dichotomized versions of victims and perpetrators, of good and evil. But these simplistic accounts generally did not prevail for many bystanders, although the need to make sense out of the chaos persists.

One of the most common refrains in response to the terrorist attacks, and arguably an artificial way to reassert social order, derived from the notion that the nation needed to get back to normal.[16] In the days following September 11 in and around New York City, and throughout the nation, elected officials and various others including commentators and entertainers exhorted the public to try to resume their normal lives. While I am in no position to definitively assess to what degree people heeded this advice, there are unobtrusive indicators suggesting that some approximation of daily life returned relatively quickly. For the most part within days, people went back to their jobs, kids returned to school, and advertisements were again visible on television, to cite just a few examples. Also informal conversations with family, friends, neighbors, and colleagues suggest that to some degree people have reverted to their routines, although for many bystanders the return seemed initially more superficial and piecemeal than real.

Although what we assert as "normal" is an artificial construct, what was considered normal before September 11 is different than what is normal today, a few years following the attacks. Certainly it is beginning to look more normal the further from Ground Zero one travels and the more years that pass. Outside the city, and also within parts of the New York metropolitan region, people try to act normal by going about their routines, and such behaviors appear to increase daily. Yet attempts to normalize everyday life do not necessarily suggest either apathy or denial about the import of the terrorist attacks of September 11 or some possible future form of terrorism. Instead, the range of normal behaviors and attitudes are dramatically incoherent. There are deep-seated and widespread concerns about subsequent acts of terrorism in the United States and abroad, as well as about the realities of armed conflict in various regions of the world.

Within these competing realities, trips to the supermarket and commutes to work occur regularly and do not seem to displace these fears completely, except perhaps for some time and for some people. We may simply be coping. Or if we are to believe unofficial rhetoric, we are resisting terrorism by going back to our routines, particularly our economic routines. Perhaps German Jewish immigrants also thought they were coping or even resisting the powers of the Third Reich by going about their daily lives. Scholars thus need to be cautious about overinterpreting the significance of accounts that discuss these mundane and routine activities as indicative of people's denial or repression of imminent danger. We cannot know the meanings of such actions from their recital or description without asking people directly.

Living in this moment also points to some of the problems inherent in retrospective analyses that rely too heavily on objective or more established indicators of daily life. If we do not include subjective reactions to world events, we can only have a limited understanding of objective measures such as school records, commercial activity, or electoral behavior. Although objective data are important, so, too, are subjective accounts, particularly when conflicting responses and actions are likely. That said, individual accounts such as Holocaust memoirs, when read collectively and comparatively, can reveal an appropriately more complex version of the truth than that available through a reliance on formal indicators alone. In the coming months and years, we may or may not seem foolish or dumb about the threats we face. But we cannot and do not know that now.

Similarly I would assert that German Jews were not in denial before the pogrom of November 9–10, 1938.[17] Just as we cannot now completely understand the outcome of events that started long before that Tuesday in September 2001, German Jews at that time could not have known the consequences of Kristallnacht, or the events now subsumed under the Holocaust. The Germans did not know until sometime in 1941 what they would do with the Jews. If the Germans did not know about the destruction of the Jews, how can we expect that the Jews should have known (Bauer 2001:25–26)?

Moreover, since 9/11 there is increased surveillance and policing within the United States and in targeted regions worldwide.[18] The U.S. federal government has attempted to assure the general population that these actions benefit their protection and well-being. This benign-sounding rationale—that expanded forms of control serve the common good—was also heard in the early years of the Third Reich. This similarity suggests the possibility of studying the mechanisms states use to institutionalize new social orders and forms of social control. By disaggregating the Holocaust into various parts and phases, we can better understand how it developed, rather than continue to think about it as an undifferentiated, singular event, placing it outside serious scholarly scrutiny.

In addition, certain groups have been profiled in racial, ethnic, and gendered terms and deemed a threat to the safety of ordinary citizens. Men of Middle Eastern descent have frequently faced harassment, detention, and have suffered civil rights abuses. In general, remove anti-immigrant sentiment is growing in the United States and in other Western nations. Comparing U.S. racial profiling and anti-immigration policies and practices with those the Nazi party implemented should enable a more thorough understanding of both.

The Holocaust and September 11 also suggest comparable questions about who is fully recognized as a victim or a survivor. It is obviously wrong to forget about the Gypsies, Soviet war prisoners, mentally ill Germans, or gays, among many others, who were forced into labor or died in the camps, and it is also problematic to erase the many Jews and other victims who died in countless other ways outside the gas chambers (Marrus 1987:20). Thus only certain victims and survivors—in this case Jews in the death camps—have come to represent the quintessential victims and survivors, while others are left barely visible or forgotten. Similarly with respect to September 11, undocumented immigrants—whether wounded, killed, or surviving—often went uncounted lest they, their kin, or friends be subject to other reprisals.

Finally, I raise the possibility of comparison with the events of September 11 to suggest that debates over the generalizability of the Holocaust with respect to other genocides are unquestionably important but dismiss the ways in which the Holocaust might also be compared with other kinds of trauma. Comparisons with the terrorism of September 11 may or may not be fully appropriate, and indeed it may be too early to tell. But that said, I want to urge scholars to consider questions of the generalizability of the Holocaust in reference to other types of trauma and disaster, both social and natural in origin.

Conclusions

In the foregoing pages I have developed an argument in favor of making comparisons between the Holocaust and other social phenomena. The bases and parameters of my argument are empirically driven, which I maintain might be a more useful starting point and approach for sociologists and other scholars grappling with these questions. Using Holocaust memoirs as evidence, I have identified how writers themselves refused or engaged comparative techniques in their texts. In addition, I have specified several comparative techniques useful in the interpretations of these memoirs and the problems associated with ignoring appropriate comparisons. While the actual substance of these comparisons remains important in my empirical work, I will not reiterate them here and instead leave to some future date further analyses of their significance. But several more general conclusions are appropriate now.

As I stated earlier, reading these memoirs makes clear that the issue is not whether to compare the Holocaust to other events or not, but rather how comparison functions in relation to the Holocaust. Evidence from these memoirs demonstrates that writers in many instances relied on comparisons to explicate their experiences. They referenced other German Jews with allusions to the similarities among them, and they portrayed stark contrasts between themselves and non-Jewish Germans and Americans as well. In addition, writers often revealed an astute awareness of how structural forces operated and shaped individual lives, and they recognized the importance of social contexts in developing these accounts.

The implications for researchers follow closely. Comparison is a necessary methodological tool if we are to accurately interpret meaning and be able to generalize from our findings. In this instance, comparison must minimally involve reading a memoir within a larger sociohistorical context or making explicit comparisons among several memoirs. Doing both seems preferable. It is, moreover, important for scholars to appreciate when and under what circumstances people generalize from the Holocaust, and this principle also asks that researchers scrutinize their own practices.

JUDITH M. GERSON

To date, most of the discussion within academia about the generalizability of the Holocaust has understandably centered on the question of genocide. While I will not reiterate those ideas here, in my estimation Michael Marrus (1987) and Yehuda Bauer (2001) have provided a wise analytic distinction when they assert that the Holocaust has many elements in common with other genocides, and thus has historical antecedents, but also insist that it retains distinctive features and thus remains unprecedented. In other words, the Holocaust is both comparable and generalizable—and at the same time unprecedented. If there is agreement on this point, it seems to me that this is a particularly important moment to bring comparative historical questions to bear on the Holocaust and bring findings from the Holocaust more centrally into established disciplines including, but not necessarily limited to, sociology. Interrogating the comparability of the Holocaust to other genocides and disasters is the only route toward beginning to understand if and in what ways it was unprecedented. Continued assumptions of uniqueness only offer to place the Holocaust outside full scholarly study and perpetuate a priori conclusions about its distinctiveness.

I have argued for the significance of analyzing the Holocaust through three distinct comparative approaches—memoirs, immigration research, and trauma and disaster research. But none of these approaches should be understood to challenge or deny the importance of understanding the Holocaust as genocide. These perspectives do not compete with one another, but instead complement and enhance each other. Just as it seems unproductive to argue for the uniqueness of any phenomenon or event in social life, so it seems that we only stand to gain by expanding our analytic frames when studying the Holocaust and its aftermath.

Notes

1. Though there are several versions of this joke, it basically revolves around two dachshunds out for a stroll with their owners. The latter stop to chat, and the dogs talk about life in the old country, romanticizing their more glorious former lives and mourning their end. Like other immigrants before them, these dachshunds have exaggerated tales of their more prosperous pasts. The dogs' conversation turns competitive, with the canines one-upping each other to determine who was more successful in their homeland. In an attempt to win and put an end to this competition, one of the dachshunds finally responds to the other's claims: "That's nothing. In Germany (or Cuba), I was a German shepherd (or other large dog)." Indeed, numerous writers about German Jewish immigration have referenced immigrants' proclivity to compare their lives in the United States to their former existence in Germany as the *bei uns* ("with us" or the "situation we had") phenomenon. Invariably, the result of such comparisons demon-

strates that things were better in the past. Anderson (1998), Arendt (1943), and Davie (1947) relate a version of this joke as an archetypical expression of a better past.

2. The same problem could also be framed in terms of social-classification analysis, that is, how people make distinctions among cognitive categories, the features they attend to and ones they ignore (Zerubavel 1991).

3. I recognize the problems of language inherent in using the term *the* Holocaust, setting it up to be the sole, most important holocaust and the standard for other holocausts. See Gerson and Wolf (this volume: 9), for a fuller discussion of this problem.

4. The sources here are extensive. One of the most thoughtful discussions that compares the Holocaust with other genocides can be found in Bauer (2001). Among sociologists, Fein (1979, 1993) is probably best known for her comparative work on genocide. Other sociologists have also used comparative historical approaches to study genocide. See Horowitz's (1984) work on the national cultures of totalitarian states; Chalk and Jonassohn's (1990) attempt to develop a typology of genocide; and Thompson and Quets (1990). Still other sociologists have asked more specific comparative questions of the Holocaust. Two salient bodies of work include research on the Nazi party (Anheier 1997; Brustein 1998) and collective memory (Bodemann 1996b; Levy 1999; Olick 1999b).

5. Immigrants were often forced to follow complicated routes before they permanently settled in the United States. This explains my decision to include immigrants who left Germany by 1942 in my sample, even though they may not have arrived in the United States until 1945. Using a cutoff date of the end of World War II enables me to distinguish refugees from displaced persons and other survivors who came to the United States thereafter.

6. Most of these documents are housed in the archives at the Leo Baeck Institute in New York City; others are deposited in the United States Holocaust Memorial Museum; essays for a Harvard-sponsored contest, "My Life Before and After January 30, 1933" are located in the Houghton Library at Harvard University.

7. Elsewhere I have discussed the theoretical rationale for my work in some detail, which centers around questions of daily identity practices as a means to apprehend various elements of immigrant identities—not only as Germans and Jews and Americans to be but also as women and men, family members, workers, and so forth (Gerson 2001).

8. The term *1.5 generation immigrants* refers to those who immigrated as young children, usually before adolescence, falling between older, first-generation immigrants and the second generation born in the new homeland. For a more complete discussion, see Gerson and Wolf (this volume: 9).

9. No one should interpret these sentences as suggesting that the Holocaust is necessarily less consequential or significant for people in this sample than for others who were able to survive until 1945 in Europe.

10. In addition to the memoirs read, I interviewed twenty-six Jewish refugees from Germany who fled before October 1941 and resettled in New York City before the end of the war in Europe in May 1945. I identified these individuals through various secular and religious organizations, which German Jewish immigrants frequent and through

snowball sampling techniques. Usually I spoke with respondents in their own homes, though on rare occasions relied on telephone interviews. I interviewed fourteen women, eight men, and two married couples.

11. In an oft-cited article, "We Refugees," Hannah Arendt (1943) wrote, "In the first place, we don't like to be called 'refugees.' We ourselves call each other 'newcomers' or 'immigrants'" (69). Coser (1984) contrasts immigrants to refugee intellectuals; the former generally came from lower-status positions, while refugee intellectuals came from more advantaged ones. Anderson (1998) recognizes this issue, noting that *refugees* connoted the newcomers' status in the past, while they began thinking of themselves as immigrants once they became Americans (xi–xii). Levine's (2001) respondents, German Jewish cattle dealers, did not make this distinction. The lack of consensus is intriguing.

12. There are several contributing factors to this collective silence. German men rounded up at Kristallnacht and sent to concentration camps were told that one condition of their release was to not speak about their experiences in the camps. Moreover, interviews with German Jewish immigrants indicate that on arriving in the United States, they encountered considerable indifference to their concerns about the Nazi regime. Novick (1999) asserts that in the postwar years, survivors themselves were silenced both in the United States and in Israel by others reluctant to hear them recount their memories. Currently, scholars, immigrants, refugees, and survivors are reconsidering the purported silences during that period.

13. Liisa Malkki (1995a), in her powerful study of Hutu escaping genocide, finds a complex set of differences in the meanings of national history and identity between those who resettled in an isolated refugee camp and those who resettled in a town. Her work is instructive for her substantive findings, methods, and analysis, and it suggests the importance of resettlement to the meanings of ethnic national identities.

14. This last example suggests the writer was aware that walking was a popular and normal activity, and used that cultural knowledge to cover up the purpose of an extraordinary walk.

15. "Never again," the oft-repeated phrase among Jews in many parts of the world in reference to the Holocaust, is relevant here. My thanks to Sarah Rosenfield for pointing out that this phrase inadvertently proposes the possibility that the Holocaust might happen again but that we need to do everything possible to prevent it.

16. It is also important to recall that within Judaism, biblical texts, customs, liturgy, and laws all emphasize the value of life. When presented with a choice, we should choose life. Human life is sacred. The secular notion that we should go back to "normal" resonates with this principle.

17. The use of the term *pogrom* suggests the importance of comparison again. While Kristallnacht is a specific reference, labeling the event the "November 1938 pogrom" places it in an analytic category with other similar reigns of terror.

18. I thank Ethel Brooks for her suggestion that I consider attacks on civil liberties and the varied meanings of the concept of survivor that follow.

Collective Memory and Cultural Politics: Narrating and Commemorating the Rescue of Jewish Children by Belgian Convents during the Holocaust

SUZANNE VROMEN

Jewish children who were success-fully hidden during the Holocaust to save their lives form a special category of survivors. Because they were young when World War II broke out, their childhood was suddenly and cruelly disrupted as they were torn from the nurturing of their own families. To become the adults they are today, they have had to confront this disruption, make sense of it, ponder how it has affected their lives, and attempt to link their past to their present.

The children were hidden in Gentile families, in orphanages, and in convents. My research explores how Belgian convents were involved in the rescue of Jewish children and how these children interpret today their experiences in religious institutions. By interviewing the hidden children, now grown adults, as they recount their lives during the war, by seeking out nuns and priests who hid and thus enabled them to survive, and by including the women from the resistance who took the children from their parents, escorted them to the convents, and retrieved them after the liberation, three different perspectives on the same series of historical events emerge.

There are cogent reasons to focus on the Belgian stories. About 50 percent of the Jews in Belgium were saved; proportionally many more were saved in Belgium than in neighboring Holland. The subject of hidden children has not been widely studied, so these different perspectives are valuable in themselves. More broadly drawing on sociological perspectives on memory, the research explores the social context in which connections between identity, memory, and personal narratives are made both during the war and in its aftermath. It examines how collective memories emerge, how they are institutionalized, and how gendered memorial trajectories are constructed. It raises the question as to how the politics of commemoration were and are played out in Belgium. While the majority of Jewish children were hidden and saved in Catholic institutions, the official Catholic Church has neither emphasized nor significantly commemorated these deeds for reasons to be discussed later. It is mostly the individuals saved who have chosen to memorialize the rescuers by gathering extensive evidence, often difficult to obtain because of the passage of time. They have presented this evidence to Yad Vashem, the Israeli commemorative institution recognizing the "Righteous among the Nations," and they have undergone Yad Vashem's demanding authenticating and legitimating process. Civil authorities have recognized and memorialized a few outstanding priests who helped the Belgian resistance and saved Jewish children. On the other hand, the politics of commemoration in Belgium are clearly gendered. The role of mothers superior and convent nuns has not been emphasized. Theirs has rather been taken for granted, and seen as an auxiliary role, not an autonomous one. The women have been considered worthy of neither extensive consideration nor focused commemoration.

The research includes lengthy, unstructured interviews with twenty people who had been hidden as children, seven nuns, one priest, the two surviving women members of the resistance who escorted the children from their parents to the convents, the president of the Belgian Association of Hidden Children who was herself a hidden child, various personalities involved in commemorations, and historians unraveling the history of the resistance and the attitude of the Catholic Church during the war. People were eager to talk, and a snowball sample of hidden children emerged easily. The nuns and the priest were reached through the hidden children and through the lists of the Righteous among the Nations kept by the Israeli embassy.

In 1940, on the eve of the Nazi invasion, Belgium was essentially a Catholic country. It counted nearly thirteen thousand priests and fifty thousand nuns, a gender imbalance partially explainable by the more limited opportunities offered to women in the world of that time. The country had many Catholic organizations for adults and for youth. It was proud of its first-rate Catholic university, the University of Leuven, and of an extended network of Catholic elementary and secondary schools through which the majority of Belgian youths received their education. Health care and the care of the elderly were mainly in religious hands. The impact of the church on public life was extensive (Maerten, Selleslagh, and Van den Wijngaert 1999).

During the war, the church was not disrupted by the Nazis; it was left alone, in contrast to other institutions. In fact, the church was the only prewar institution to remain untouched by the Nazi occupation. Therefore, many sought its protection against the terror and the violence unleashed by the Nazis. The higher clergy such as the cardinal and the bishops, with one exception, did not provide this protection; the lower clergy, however, spontaneously extended the help.

The Belgian resistance had different networks. One of the most important was the Front de l'Indépendance (Independence Front, FI), created in 1941, one year after the Nazi invasion, and politically to the left. After the beginning of the deportations in the summer of 1942, the FI encouraged the formation of the Comité de Défense des Juifs (Jewish Defense Committee) with Jewish communists and Zionists. One of its sections was specifically charged with saving Jewish children. This meant finding safe places for the children throughout the country, overseeing their placements and monitoring them on a consistent basis, paying the pensions for the children's upkeep, securing false identity papers, and rationing stamps and clothing. These were the tasks organized and carried out by six women, two of whom are still alive today and agreed to be interviewed. These two, young and non-Jewish, one a schoolteacher and the other a social worker at the time, joined the Comité de Défense des Juifs at great personal risk, specifically to carry out the hiding of Jewish children. It was an extensive and intricate clandestine operation that depended on the cooperation and the silence of many; it resulted in the saving of over three thousand Jewish children. The major safe places for the children were convents, Catholic colleges for boys, and orphanages (most orphanages in Belgium were Catholic).

There is an autobiographical reason for my focus. In 1941, after a year under Nazi occupation, I fled from Belgium with my family and reached what was then the Belgian Congo. There I went to school in a convent because all education in this Belgian colony was in the hands of missionaries at that time. I distinctly remember my initial bewilderment at being plunged suddenly into a Catholic milieu. I also recall how later on I made my peace with the atmosphere of spirituality and the intense socialization that characterize convents. So I asked myself: what was it like for children who did not have the comfort of home and were torn from their parents to enter this strange milieu? My own experience provided me with empathy when I conducted my interviews, as well as with an insider's knowledge and ease.

The Children

Many accounts began with the separation from parents. In some cases parents appealed directly to the resistance, and the decision to bring the children to a convent was taken by members of the Comité de Défense des Juifs. In other cases parents asked for the help of the parish priest in finding a suitable hiding place. According to the historian Maxime Steinberg, the way parents went about finding a hiding place for their children depended on the length of time they had lived in Belgium before the Nazi occupation.[1] Those who had come soon after the rise of Hitler in 1933 had connections with non-Jews through their occupations, their businesses, and the people whose services they used. They appealed to friends and acquaintances to provide a safe haven for their children. It is the newcomers, those who came in the late 1930s, who tended to approach the lower clergy of the Catholic Church, the parish priests, whom they considered sympathetic to their plight.

The children themselves often did not recall how the decision was made, but they did remember the places they were taken to. Some were hidden in only one or two convents, others moved often to escape danger as their hiding place became unsafe due to denunciations or their stay became problematic, and they ended up in a convent. For example, in one case, a farmer's wife requested that the resistance remove a teenage girl hidden on the farm because her husband took too great an interest in her.

Most of my interviewees did not dwell on the emotions of their parents about the separation. The hiding process really began in the third year of Nazi occupation, 1942, when the first round-ups occurred and the wearing of the Star of David was decreed. So the children had already lived a considerable period under stress and threat. For some, therefore, hiding in a convent became a relative alleviation of a situation that had increasingly grown worse.

Going into hiding necessitated a new name. All my interviewees without exception mentioned the French or Flemish names, first names and surnames, drilled into them. Even now one of them said: "I respond to Daniel and to David. Why forget Daniel?" One of the escorts reported that having duly impressed on a six-year-old girl that her name was Annette and not Sarah, they boarded a tram to reach her hiding place. A lady in the tram was enchanted with the child and gushed, "You are such a lovely little girl, what is your name?" The child turned to her escort and asked: "What do I tell her, my real name or my new one?"

According to the latest count, 225 institutions in Belgium hid Jewish children, but the list is incomplete and the exact number remains unknown (Brachfeld 2001). In that list, about three-quarters are Catholic institutions. In this multitude, convents and colleges that harbored the children differed greatly in wealth, size, management, and discipline; they were a kaleidoscope of orders. What did going to a convent mean to these children? The reactions varied. Some reported a sense of security. After the chaotic days they had been living, the convent was a place of refuge, of relative serenity, of order, of structure, and especially of predictability. They could be children again; they could be part of a nonthreatening collectivity, as long as they learned and abided by its rules. Others were appalled by the harshness of collective life, dormitories, and poor food. One boy reported chewing on a piece of meat for so long that it would become gummy, and he could throw it up, making it stick to the ceiling. Some nuns, but not all, were reported as very maternal, especially if the child was young. "There was Madeleine," recalls a man,

she was also a nun. Sister she was called, she was a nurse, and I will not forget her. She loved the children very much. I remember one day I had to undress because I had boils and I was very much ashamed. I was afraid that she should see that I am Jewish, so she told me: you can undress, and you have nothing to fear from me . . . and I adored her. Not only I, all the children.

On the other hand, some nuns were strict disciplinarians and readily meted out punishment. For example, one girl who wet her sheets at night was made to walk during the day with the sheets on her head. Often, but not always, the children were close to the younger nuns and to the novices. The nuns who were hated were recalled by their names without hesitation in the interviews, and in one case qualified as "a camel," a forceful French slang expression that translates as nasty, evil-minded, in short, a "bitch." In another case, a girl who did not clean up properly was treated to the insult of "dirty Jew." The diversity of experiences is vast, yet on the whole the feelings of love and closeness predominate. This is true not only for girls but for boys also, who expressed admiration and closeness to priests. While girls were attached to particular nuns, some also mentioned their love for the priests who came from the outside to the convents to say Mass and

SUZANNE VROMEN

give communion, ritual tasks that the church does not entrust to women even if they have taken the vows.

All children were frequently told to be sure to conform, to do whatever the other children were expected to do, not to stand out, not to draw attention to themselves, in fact, to blend into their new surroundings as unobtrusively as possible. Catholic religious practices presented some challenging problems. For example, what should Jewish children do during Mass when the other children received communion? According to Catholic rules, nonbaptized Jewish children could not receive communion, so this created a dilemma. Depending on the convents, some Jewish children were baptized and had a formal first communion, but others were not. In some cases there were non-Jewish children who had not had their first communion, and in those situations, the Jewish children just blended into the collectivity. According to their own accounts, some children wanted to be baptized. They found their new religion comforting, warm, hopeful, in fact, an oasis of spirituality in a world gone mad and rendered incomprehensible. They cherished crosses, rosaries, prayer books, holy images, and sought their mothers in the Virgin Mary. They prayed to her with devotion for the return and the safety of their families. They embraced the rituals with little difficulty and found their solace in them. One woman reported that her parents wrote from their hiding place, "you should be ashamed to want to be baptized while your family is suffering so much." One man noted that he and his mother both attended catechism and were baptized. Another interviewee remembered that her mother shed silent tears when told that she had been baptized. The children were in fact responsive to the powerful emotional appeal of the Catholic religion; they also wanted to be like all the others around them: belonging, accepted, embraced.

This did not necessarily mean that they gave up whatever forms of Judaism they had been exposed to and had absorbed before the German occupation. Some recited Jewish prayers under their blankets at night, or spoke in their sleep in Yiddish and were warned about it. The children were aware of the problem of detection. One boy, newly arrived in a college under the name of Timmermans, a common Belgian name, entered the crowded dining room and heard himself hailed by a student who knew him from his previous school: "Hey Tabakman, what are you doing here?" The encounter had no consequences for him, and none of the interviewees reported being aware of denunciations. Neither did they comment on friendships with Gentile children. In one case, one of the non-

Jewish pupils became a nun, and when my interviewee visits the sisters who saved her, she has a special visit with the one she knew as a little girl.

On the whole, the children reported a heartfelt emotional acceptance of the church doctrines. This was particularly true, but not only, for the younger children. But what happened at the end of the war? One particular account seems remarkable. After telling me how he embraced the Catholic religion with great devotion, and how he enjoyed helping to serve the Mass and singing in the choir as an appreciated choirboy, my survivor calmly told me, "I evacuated all this in about six months." The choice of words was quite striking in this case. This easy flipping of identity was far from common; it represents one extreme of a continuum that stretches wide and ends with those who responded totally to this intense resocialization by remaining practicing Catholics to this day. Anecdotes are appropriate here. When one interviewee came to meet her mother just returned from Auschwitz, her first words to her mother were: "Now you come with me to the chapel to thank the Virgin Mary for saving you." And for the first and the last time in her life, this mother went to the chapel. One man, interviewed in Israel, still heatedly recalled:

As a reward I received a card of the Virgin Mary, and on the other side they wrote a commendation for being an outstanding pupil. After the Liberation I returned to Brussels and right away hung up the card in my aunt's home. My aunt said to me: what are you doing, we are Jews here, what the Virgin Mary! I felt terribly offended, insulted, she hurt me, she wounded me. It is a pity that the card is lost, it would have been a memento!

It is possible to theorize this adoption of a new identity as a form of "passing." However, one would have to refine the concept before applying it. The children did not select to pass; there was an imposition on them, there was no free selection here of one identity over another. Neither, at the onset, was this passing expected to be permanent. Some saw it as a survival strategy, as a mask to be discarded after it ceased to be useful, others were more deeply affected.

Were the children entirely isolated in the convents? The situation varied. Some children never saw their parents again. For them, the period after the liberation proved the hardest. They waited and hoped, and for some the closure of mourning never happened. Others received news from their parents, and some even visits. These visits could be dangerous. In one convent near Louvain/Leuven, where many Jewish children were hidden, mothers would come for short visits, traveling by trams. The Nazis did not appear in the convent to search and confront, nor were the nuns aware of any formal denunciations. However, on returning by tramway, the visiting mothers were denounced and policemen came on board to check papers and identity cards and to arrest. One mother calmly succeeded in getting off the streetcar, and quickly went back to the convent in order to alert the remaining visitors to the dangers that awaited them.

The hidden children who had parents that came back from the concentration camps found themselves in a difficult situation. Faced by parents who had suffered indescribable horrors and who were often broken in body and spirit, the children's stories did not merit attention. "We were told: you are lucky" some surviving children explained to me, which prevented them from narrating their hidden lives and expressing their wartime feelings. In a wider context, the hidden children ranked lowest in the poignant hierarchy of victimization dominated by concentration camp survivors, and their personal wartime experiences were seen as socially inconsequential and unworthy of concern. In 1980, however, an amateur filmmaker, Myriam Abramowicz, living in the United States but born in Belgium to a formerly hidden family, made a documentary on the Belgian resistance networks and on the individuals who saved both adults and children. The film was entitled *As If It Were Yesterday*. It undoubtedly had a resonance and an influence. In the aftermath of the documentary, Abramowicz also initiated the idea for an international conference on hidden children. Surviving hidden children had no formal status, no institutional representation, and no public voice until the "First International Gathering of Children Hidden during World War II" conference of 1991 in New York City, almost half a century after the end of the war. As a result of this conference, numerous hidden children associations were formed throughout the world to create a forum that articulated and legitimized their experiences. In Belgium, the government granted to hidden children the moral statute of war victims only a few years ago; it has now granted them the right to minimal material claims.

The emergence of the concept of the hidden child and the structures of memory it has given rise to exemplify what French sociologist Maurice Halbwachs (1980) meant by collective memory. It encompasses individual memories and transforms them into a totality, providing a site for a rhetoric of survivorship and agency.

After the war, to what extent did the children maintain contact with those who hid them? Was any gratitude shown, and if so, in what way? The parents wanted the children to forget as quickly as possible their Catholic socialization.

Since some of the children had been enveloped in an intense and deeply satisfying spirituality, parents had to undertake a powerful resocialization process in which there was immense relief but little room for immediate gratitude. It was as if a bad dream, rather a harrowing nightmare, had to be quickly forgotten, and a new life forged as fast as possible. These new beginnings did not prove easy. Property, means of livelihood, and lives had been lost. In reconstructing their families, parents reached out to the difficult present and to a hopeful future; they had no place for the past. In a process of normalizing Jewish families, there was no room for relationships with nuns, as maternal as they might have been. In one account, a young woman tried to sneak out Sundays to Mass only to be followed by her widowed mother, who ripped her prayer book to shreds and hauled her home. The young woman then wrote to the nuns who had hidden her that she wanted to convert and become one of them. She received no reply, and thus the relationship ended. Other parents were more prudent and understanding, and the resocialization process lasted longer.

Parents scrutinized whether the motivations for hiding the children were mainly economic. Parents and the resistance paid monthly sums for the upkeep of the children. The resistance had obtained money through donations, as well as illegally from the Belgian government in London through the connivance of local banks. When parents were deported and the payments stopped, the resistance often paid the necessary pension. Convents were not necessarily similar to each other. Some were quite wealthy, the Sisters of Charity of Ghent, for example, others, like the Sisters of Saint Vincent of Paul, were so poor that they had to beg food from the farmers. Orphanages were particularly destitute. Clearly, hiding children offered a way of increasing income. Yet many convents did not choose this way to increase their income, so there was something special about those who elected to do so, and to run risks. The financial motive was sometimes invoked as the sole reason for saving children, and in some sense, that exonerated both parents and children from having to feel grateful. It was only about twenty years after the war that some hidden children renewed their relationships with the clerics who had saved them and began to manifest their gratitude. I interviewed a hidden child who periodically returns to the convent where she was hidden, laden with presents. Hidden children have seen to it that nuns, priests, and lay people are recognized as Righteous among the Nations and given a medal from Yad Vashem. It is a long and cumbersome procedure that demands a lot of perseverance. Those who have been so honored have been immensely proud of it.

The children who remained Catholic after the war talked of the immense attraction of the Catholic religion. One of them felt the need to justify himself by emphasizing that nobody in his family had come back from deportation. The priest who had helped to hide him during the war was the figure who anchored him. All complained with particular bitterness about being treated as renegades and being much despised by the Jewish community. They also showed me both directly and indirectly how they considered their former Jewish identity as stigmatizing. For example, a fervent practicing Catholic brought up the fact that she has never been able to tell any of her five children that she was born Jewish.

The narratives of the children testify to the powerful appeal of Catholic socialization in the convents, which may be defined as total institutions. These narratives also illustrate the flipping of identities required during the war. They show the adaptability of children to extraordinary circumstances and indicate that identity may be more malleable than commonly expected.

One major gender difference exists in the accounts. Most of the men emphasized the quality of their education. They had no need to catch up to their peers after the end of the war, they did not lose any school years, and their educational track had not been disrupted. If they had been orphaned, they were housed in Jewish institutions after the war, and if they were bright and studious, they received scholarships to university. By contrast, some of the women spoke of a minimal convent education. They learned to sew and to embroider, and after the war they had some catching up to do. Even when they were bright and studious, the Jewish institutions directed them to nursing, office work, and elementary school teaching. I detected quite a bit of bitterness for the paths not taken and the opportunities not offered. The women, by now of retirement age, did not consider their lives a failure, at least within the limits of the interviews, yet viewing their past from the perspective of the present, they judged harshly the stereotypical gender blinders worn by those who had the power to steer them to adulthood.

Nuns and Priests

They are elderly, yet those that I succeeded in finding and interviewing remain clear-minded and have vivid memories of their involvement in the rescue of Jewish children and of the dangers to which these children were exposed.

Who took the decision to accept and hide Jewish children in the convents? It was a decision taken by mothers superior, heads of the convents, when parents, the resistance, and parish priests approached them. There is no evidence of a centralized resolution initiated at the level of cardinals or bishops, with one exception: in the province of Liège, the French-speaking southern part of the country, Bishop Louis-Joseph Kerkhofs clearly took the initiative to extend help and shelter to Jews. Much credit for saving the children goes to individual spontaneous decisions of the lower clergy, whose members did not wait for any encouragement likely to emanate from the higher echelons of the church hierarchy (Maerten, Selleslagh, and Van den Wijngaert 1999).

Often it was only a small circle around the mother superior who knew that some of the children were Jewish. One nun, when asked who took the responsibility to hide a Jewish girl, answered unequivocally: "It was Mother Bernadette. She was courageous, a great woman, really a great lady. . . . She took the whole responsibility. She told us that we could not know anything." The decision making of mothers superior is firmly corroborated by another interviewee from another convent: "It was Mother Cécile who took the responsibility," in this case to give refuge to more than sixty Jewish children at different times during the last three years of the Nazi occupation. A few nuns knew about it because "they had to work with the complicity of the municipality to obtain ration cards for the children whose names had been changed, . . . but everything was done discreetly." On the whole, however, the strategy was to have as few nuns as possible privy to the situation. "We did not know what went on specifically outside our wall. I shudder still to think of that. . . . We did not know the danger these children faced," a nun recalled with great feeling. The one priest I interviewed was told by his superior that one student in his class in a well-known Catholic college was Jewish. After the war, he found out that there were two Jewish boys in two other classes, but he never knew it during the war as such. His hidden youngster became a well-known lawyer and jurist. In 1993, this lawyer began the proceedings to have his teacher declared a Righteous among the Nations. At the end of our interview, the priest brought out his medal and proudly showed it to me. He then eagerly described how he was invited to the celebrations in Israel on the occasion of the fiftieth anniversary of Israel's independence.

I sometimes raised the issue of baptism with my interviewees, and at other times they brought it up spontaneously. Many asserted forcefully that there was no coercion toward baptism. On the contrary, they argued, the clergy resisted appeals by children to be baptized and thus to conform to all Catholic practices. The way the denials were expressed clearly indicated that this was an issue brought out frequently and for which a standard answer had been formulated. An anecdote reported by one nun, however, reveals the ambiguity:

Mother Bernadette told the little girl called Rosette from the beginning to behave like everybody else, and at communion time Rosette walked forward . . . oh, you have to understand how it was fifty years ago . . . I would say that the presence of Jesus in the consecrated wafer was nearly seen materially. . . . Bernadette then said: my God I have forgotten to tell her, and she took the girl's arm quietly and led her away. Rosette was then baptized in secret so that she could take communion; this had really little to do with faith, it was a way to save her, . . . to save a human life. At night, she would say her Jewish prayer in her bed . . . the poor little thing.

The subject has caused much tension and reveals itself as a murky and difficult area to clarify. If baptism had been coerced, then the motivation for hiding Jewish children might well be interpreted as instrumental: it would lose its quality of a spontaneous humanitarian act and become merely the stepping stone to conversion. Some of the hidden children that I interviewed attested to the nuns' resistance to their appeals for baptism. Some nuns claimed that they needed parental permission before they could baptize the children. As it was difficult and even dangerous to try to reach parents in hiding, permission could not be obtained, and the matter could be postponed. Nevertheless, there is some evidence of widespread baptism. The irony is that baptism per se did not preserve the life of Jews. For the Nazis, the rationale for the extermination of Jews was fueled by a racial ideology: religion, and therefore conversion, was irrelevant. Faced by this savage onslaught, any strategy of survival was seen as better than none, and baptism, signifying conversion, was considered a resource for claiming and seeking the protection of Catholic clergy and institutions. In a certain sense, it created the illusion of an entitlement. For the nuns, hiding nonbaptized Jewish children presented a double predicament. Allowing the children to take the consecrated host without baptism would amount to blasphemy, but if these children did not participate in important Catholic rituals, their hidden identity could be compromised. So baptism could be justified for tactical reasons in order to complete the cover-up.

We had long conversations about the logistics of running the convents, and evidence of the moral authority of mothers superior abounded. There were numerous links to the resistance. A famous event acquired mythical proportions: In a convent in a Brussels suburb, fifteen Jewish girls in hiding were denounced.

The Gestapo came to arrest them. The head of the convent, Sister Marie Aurélie, talked the Nazis into postponing the arrest for a day so that she could prepare the children for their departure and pack their belongings. When the Gestapo departed, the sister alerted the resistance. They came to whisk the children away, staging the flight to appear as though it had been accomplished by force. They bound and gagged the nuns, cut the telephone lines, and created a disorderly scene to indicate the use of violence. By the time the Gestapo came the next day, the girls had been safely dispersed in hiding places throughout Brussels. After the war, many people claimed that they had been part of this audacious rescue mission. One of my interviewees, the woman in charge of dispersing the children, felt the need to record the event, stating the names of "those who did it." A photograph of Sister Marie Aurélie is displayed in the Jewish Museum of Deportation and Resistance. While some heads of convents have been recognized in addition to Sister Marie Aurélie, priests on the whole have received markedly more recognition and commemoration. They were visible agents in resistance groups; some created their own resistance networks. Many sheltered Jews in their parish individual residences in addition to monasteries, and undertook to disperse them when needed. These priests were actors in the public world. By contrast, nuns were limited to their narrower world—the walls of the convents restricted their field of action.

How isolated were the convents from life around them? It varied. In one convent, the Germans requisitioned one wing for their headquarters. In the remaining two wings, Jewish children were hidden. In a way, the proximity of the enemy may have provided a blanket of security. In other cases, convents employed outside workers, making secrecy essential. The small number of people aware of the situation allowed the maintenance of this secrecy. Still in other cases, the convent was mostly self-sufficient with little outside contact. Some convents and colleges hid not only Jewish children but also adults, parachutists rescued from Allied planes, people from the resistance who had been denounced, and those who had been called up for work in Germany but had refused to go. A formerly hidden child recalled that when he was assigned a new room in his Catholic college, he was soon ordered to take off his heavy shoes with protective metal plates when he entered his room. He was not given an explanation, only an order. After the war, he found out that his room was above a cellar in which three parachutists were hidden. His heavy shoes had frightened them into thinking that these were Gestapo boots.

SUZANNE VROMEN

When I asked a nun whether she was frightened, she misunderstood my question. I had meant afraid of the Germans. But she responded by telling me in great detail about the Allied bombings that took place after the debarkation of Allied troops. One bomb fell on a shelter, and a nun was killed together with the two small children she had on her lap. There were many mentions of Allied bombings, sometimes bombings by mistake. One of my interviewees described in detail how each evening she prepared the small boys for the possibility that they would have to go down into the cellar. In her own words: "When they had to go down in the cellar each had slippers and a washcloth ready near his bed.... Sometimes we watched through the windows as the flying bombs passed us on their way to Germany, they passed us.... I believed really that guardian angels were everywhere. One hopes and believes that God's goodness will save these children." That fear of the Germans was not predominant in the mind of some of my interviewees is understandable in the context of German policy in Belgium. The church had a tacit agreement for the maintenance of the status quo. The convents were not risking the lives of their members when they hid Jewish children; but discovery would mean certain death for the children.

Some convents housed German sisters. One in particular, Sister Rodriguez, seems to have been an imposing figure. She lived in the convent that partially served as German headquarters. When the convent was displeased in some way, Sister Rodriguez was sent as emissary of complaints, and she was clearly respected. Apparently, she also helped people outside the convent in their negotiations with the German authorities. An Irish nun also lived in that convent, and she was required to show herself to the authorities every six months to attest that she had not fled to England. It was the formidable Sister Rodriguez who accompanied her for these visits. In another convent, four German nuns served the same function of negotiators; not only were they prized for their fluency in German and ability to intervene, but "they were also such superb cooks."

Children in convents went to classes, but they also helped to run the convents. In a large convent near Louvain/Leuven, classes in French were held in one part of the convent, while classes in Flemish took place in another part. The children had kitchen chores—the peeling of potatoes is mentioned nearly iconically—and they also had cleaning duties. They related particularly well to novices who were younger than the nuns. The nuns who were in charge of dorms were the ones more likely to know which children were Jewish. Food was scarce, though with the connivance of some local authorities, ration stamps were obtained for the children with false names. Some nuns went begging in the surrounding farms. "Imagine," said one, "we asked for potatoes, and they gave us beans! Nevertheless I thanked them. In the evening a cart with a horse would come to haul what we had collected during the day." When one convent celebrated its fiftieth-year jubilee in 1943, a nun recalled: "We ripped up suits, and sewed them up again so that each little boy was outfitted with a sailor suit." The occasion was commemorated in remarkable photographs.

I asked all my informants why the church had not officially recognized what the convents had done during the war. Why, for instance, were there no plaques on convents in which Jewish children had been hidden? The response was often an astonished one, as if the question had never occurred to anyone. But the response of the priest, given quite rapidly, was that to celebrate what had been done would show the lower clergy at its best and shame the higher clergy. This is of course not the whole answer, but it does underscore the fact that the lower clergy, or at least part of it, filled the moral vacuum left by the Catholic Church hierarchy through its failure to speak out publicly against the persecutions of Jews and to organize their protection.

My interviewees highlighted the central role of mothers superior, something the historical record has failed to articulate sufficiently. These formidable women who embraced the rescue mission belong perhaps in the tradition of decisive medieval abbesses.

The Escorts

As mentioned previously, one part of the Comité de Défense des Juifs was specifically concerned with saving Jewish children by placing them with families and in institutions. I interviewed the two surviving women from the resistance who took the children from their parents and brought them to safe hiding places. One of them was a major figure in the network. She had invented an intricate system of notebooks to keep track of the children's real names, false names, parental homes, and hiding addresses. These notebooks were each hidden in separate places and were never found by the Germans; they served to trace the children after the liberation. The women were keenly aware of the trauma the parents suffered in separating themselves from their children, sometimes very young. One remembered taking a seven-day-old baby. After the war, she made great efforts to track her down and eventually succeeded. They taught the children their new names and their new behavior; they visited the hiding places in order to see that the children were well cared for. They did not locate the hiding places; these were negotiated by a non-Jewish member of the Committee for the Defense of Jews, Brigitte Moons. Supposedly, Moons had a letter from the cardinal of Belgium, the head of the Catholic Church, asking Catholic institutions to give her all necessary help. This letter may or may not be mythical. Nobody alive today has seen it, and historians are inclined to deny that it ever existed. My interviewees, with one exception, do not know of any instance of refusal to accept Jewish children; historians report a very few. After the liberation, the escorts were also the persons particularly aware of the difficulty of tearing the children once more from environments in which they had been protected, had thrived, and had been cherished. On the whole, the problem applies much more to children who had been hidden in families than in institutions.

Asked whether they knew fear, one related that she did not show it and, being young, had felt rather fearless. She was nearly caught once while delivering a false identity card, and a second time while carrying a large sum of money meant to pay for the children's upkeep. She was also not too cautious. She once wore a summer dress adorned with large Ps given to her because her real name was Paule. One of her colleagues remarked that it was a strange dress for a person known as Solange, her war pseudonym. One escort has remained in close contact with many children she saved, and her own children have also done so. They form her vast extended family. A documentary entitled *Un simple maillon* [*Just a Link*] has recently been made about her war activities and has been shown on Belgian television.

It is evident that women would be the escorts of choice. They were seen as naturally maternal by gender and training, and parents would trust them. They were also somewhat less likely than men to attract attention and be required to produce their identity papers. By the force of circumstances, they were particularly well placed to play an important part in the children's rescue, and most important, they were devoted to it at great risk to themselves.

Conclusion

The Belgian resistance movement early on organized a special section entirely devoted to the rescue of children, and it drew on Catholic institutions as an important resource for its efforts. As a Catholic country, Belgium had a widely established network of parishes and convents. Part of the lower clergy played an important role in the resistance to Nazi occupation. However, no overall comprehensive assessment of the contribution of Catholic institutions to the rescue of Jewish children has ever been drawn, nor have the voices of the nuns and priests involved in the rescue been heard clearly enough. What has been particularly ignored, as noted above, is the role of mothers superior in whose hands lay the final decision to hide Jewish children.

The research relies mainly on interviews in order to discover how people today make sense of their past during the Holocaust years and how they link their individual experiences to the social context. It also asks how their past has become part of their present. This exploration of the relationships between identity, memory, and personal narratives is rooted in the sociology of memory. The detailed anecdotal reporting of personal incidents is meant to lead into a more abstract discussion of general conditions and experiences.

Testimony derives from the Latin word for "witness," in the sense of seeing and awareness. As James Young (1988) has argued, to testify is therefore to make knowledge both about oneself and about one's world. The link between testimony and knowledge is related to the construction of identity. Testimony is a means through which the individual comes to know herself or himself; interviewer and interviewee generate a shared project.

The Holocaust violently overthrew conventional social relations and cultural practices, producing a profound sense of disorientation for individuals, a disjunction between worlds. In testifying about their experiences, the hidden children recreate themselves and establish threads of continuity between who they were before the war and who they have become subsequently. The narratives also commemorate parents, both those who did and those who did not survive.

Lawrence Langer (1995) has argued that survivors live inevitably with a fractured self. For him, the process of testifying does not imply the attribution of meaning to experience. Retelling is simply a process of reliving. This argument replays the discussion between the philosopher Henri Bergson and the sociologist Maurice Halbwachs in the first quarter of the twentieth century, at the time when Halbwachs was developing his concept of collective memory. Bergson argued that memory is a simple repository of past experiences that remembering activates. For Halbwachs, however, in his concern to show the social aspect of memory, remembering is a reflexive activity shaped by concerns with the present (Vromen 1986). Langer takes a Bergsonian position: when victims talk, they are not engaged in the process of reflection. No meaning can be wrung from their experiences, no sense can be made of them. The memories are repositories for pain and suffering. However, disagreeing with Langer, one can argue that testimony is integral to the construction and maintenance of self and identity. Testimony allows for the restoration of continuity, an essential element of individual and social life. In telling stories, survivors structure and give significance to experience, fusing past and present. Langer's argument is articulated on the basis of his analysis of testimonies from camp survivors, testimonies that rank highest in and dominate the hierarchy of victimization alluded to in the previous discussion of survivors. But testimonies have more than one dimension. Those testimonies that are not descriptive of the ultimate evil of the camps may not necessarily reveal a damaged fractured self, but on the contrary, may uncover an awareness that seeks the continuity and maintenance of self and identity in reflection. Furthermore, survival seems to inspire narratives seeking to provide a legacy for the next generations.

From another perspective, testimonies allow us to see the kind of impact that historical events have on witnesses. For example, when asked about fear, as discussed above, a nun responded by remembering her fear of bombardments. That event was the one uppermost in her mind, not the fear of the detection of hidden children.

Commemoration is another broad sociological issue that my research raises. As Eviatar Zerubavel (1996) has argued, remembering is regulated by social rules that define what we should remember and what we can forget. As members of mnemonic communities, we have a collective memory, which means a shared past, jointly remembered and commemorated. Who, what, why, when, and how we commemorate is affected by the groups we belong to. Robin Wagner-Pacifici (1996) has added that memories are never formless, that they are "shared significance embodied in form" (301–21). This description exactly fits Yad Vashem, the remembrance institution of Israel, which honors the Righteous among the Nations and rewards them with plaques and medals. Some hidden children have gone through a lengthy and arduous process of providing evidence to obtain these plaques and medals for those who saved them. Some are discouraged by the obstacles. The recognition is only granted to individuals, not to institutions. So while the convents do not qualify, individual mothers superior do. Much time has passed, however, and mothers superior, who generally were the oldest members of their convents, have died. In addition, as institutions that advocate humility and as gendered institutions, convents are not well placed for commemorative recognition. As one of the nuns I interviewed reported, when it was suggested to her mother superior that she deserved recognition, she responded that she had done only what was to be expected, and that was enough.

The list of the Belgian Righteous among the Nations recognized by Yad Vashem up until October 2000 published by Sylvain Brachfeld includes the names of 1,299 individuals, and by January 1, 2006, the Yad Vashem Web site listed a total of 1,414 (Brachfeld 2001:201–12).[2] On this list, one finds forty-six nuns and fifty-two priests (including Protestant pastors). As Brachfeld and Dr. Mordecai Paldiel, director of the Department of the Righteous among the Nations at Yad Vashem, wisely provide the year of recognition for each individual, when we compare nuns and priests, two very different trajectories of memorial recognition emerge. Before 1992, seven nuns were recognized, and thirty-nine in 1992 and after. For the men, the opposite holds true. Among the priests, thirty-two were recognized before 1992 but only twenty since then. Looking at it another way, fifteen percent of the nuns honored were recognized prior to 1992; in contrast, sixty percent of the priests received the award during that period. This shows clearly that the role of the priests in the saving of Jewish children had been very visible; they were active in the resistance and in the public world in general. As a result, they received recognition relatively early, rewarding their preeminence and importance. The mothers superior and the sisters remained quasi-invisible until the hidden children gained status and definition and were empowered to shape their collective memory. Under the impetus of the 1991 International Gathering of Hidden Children, the women clergy slowly emerged out of the shadows as children they had hidden mobilized to gather evidence for their recognition. A portion received their awards posthumously.

There is another aspect to commemoration, one in which political and religious aspects are connected. As stated previously, it was undoubtedly the lower clergy of the Catholic Church that acted to save the children. How can this be explained? When I began my study, I knew that the Catholic Church is a hierarchical institution. Though matters of dogma are centralized, I also knew that bishops and cardinals make autonomous decisions. In spite of the pope's passive attitude during the Holocaust, I fully expected to find directives to rescue Jewish children emanating from the higher echelons of the Belgian Catholic Church. I was naive and wrong. The church remained just as silent as the Vatican. The matter of the church's official position is greatly debated in Belgian post-Holocaust historiography (see Maerten, Selleslagh, and Van den Wijngaert 1999). I went to Belgium to find out how, in the post-Holocaust era, the Catholic

Church has formally commemorated the rescue of Jewish children by Belgian convents. I did not find such a commemoration; my interviewees were astonished when I asked the question. As mentioned previously, one priest argued that commemoration would shame the high clergy. Another possible answer I was given stated that immediately after the war, the church in Belgium was engaged in anti-Soviet politics; the Cold War became a more important concern than the recognition of the fight against fascism. Finally, I would argue that as convents are gendered institutions and women occupy a relatively low position in the Catholic Church hierarchy, there was little incentive to underscore the important role of mothers superior. While there were a few formal recognitions of the contributions of individual priests to resistance and rescue, mostly civil recognitions, the church was not ready to see medieval abbesses in these formidable women who embraced the mission to rescue.

In conclusion, this research sheds light on a relatively little-known series of historical events that happened during the Holocaust. More important perhaps, it illustrates some of the sociological processes through which memories are constructed, institutionalized, and gendered.

Notes

A greatly expanded version of the material in this essay is to be published as a book by Oxford University Press.

1. Maxime Steinberg, interview by the author, Brussels, April 2000.
2. See the Yad Vashem Web site: (http://www1.yadvashem.org/righteous/index_righteous.html, accessed September 21, 2006) for more information. After several personal communications, on December 12, 2004 Mordecai Paldiel kindly provided the names of the Righteous honored from 2000 to 2004. Helen Potezman from the Israeli embassy in Brussels kindly provided a list that clearly showed honored members of the clergy (personal communication, December 16, 2004, April 12, 2005, and July 6, 2006). *The Encyclopedia of the Righteous Among the Nations: Rescuers of Jews during the Holocaust–Belgium* can be consulted for the names until the end of 1999.

Holocaust Testimony: Producing
Post-memories, Producing Identities

DIANE L. WOLF

The past dozen years have seen a burst of Holocaust testimonials—both in written and oral forms—in great part due to survivors' reaching the end of their lives and feeling a sense of obligation to record these histories (Bartov 1993). Although many survivors recount that they felt that no one wanted to hear their stories after the war, there is now a great demand for them.[1] After living with their stories for fifty years, it is not uncommon for Holocaust survivors to decide to finally speak in reaction to the denials of Holocaust revisionists, or after seeing a film such as Steven Spielberg's *Schindler's List*. Many spoke for the first time about their experiences to those videotaping for Spielberg's Shoah Visual History Foundation (VHF), which fulfilled its goal by recording more than fifty thousand interviews with Holocaust survivors. Clearly, one of the main purposes of producing Holocaust testimonials is to ensure that the past is not forgotten, thereby creating a collective memory that will contribute to the perpetuation of Jewish identity. The other purpose, many feel, is to learn from history, so that such discrimination and murder never occur again.

Survivor stories provide rich possibilities for contemporary analysis. Such testimonies can be seen as transnational narratives par excellence; they speak of cultural multiplicity (Foster 1995), of fluid and multiple selves (Langer 1995), of a dispersed sense of self (Gallant and Cross 1992), of identity, of the creation of doubly or multidiasporic existences, and of negotiation among the languages of emotion (often Yiddish), of schooling (Hebrew), of nation (e.g., Polish), of the wartime experience (German), and of their new home (e.g., English). Due to these experiences, Holocaust testimonies are both homeless and global (Suleiman 1996), both about dislocation and transnational existences. Holocaust testimonials remain, however, surprisingly overlooked and underanalyzed by sociologists and other social scientists.[2]

The purposes of this article are threefold. First, based on a survivor's testimonial I took as an oral history, I will explore how a displaced and stateless Jewish survivor, Jake Geldwert, made his way in post-Holocaust Europe and North America, with particular attention to his emigration decision and his resultant relationship to home and the diaspora. Second, I will explore the linkages between Holocaust testimonials, post-memory, and the construction of Jewish identities in the third generation and beyond. In this sense, my essay deals with not only the politics of memory but also the politics of Jewish identity. One major subtext driving this work is to connect the richness of Jewish post–World War II refugee experiences with contemporary sociological and interdisciplinary discourses concerning immigrants, refugees, and diasporas as part of a broader effort to counter "sociological silences" (Bauman 1991:3; Kaufman 1996:6) about the Holocaust.

Steven Spielberg's pet multimillion–dollar project, VHF, has gathered more than fifty thousand videotaped interviews with Holocaust survivors worldwide. These interviews are currently being indexed and will become electronically available in the future. Indeed, in another fifteen to twenty years, when all survivors have died, the VHF will likely be the most accessible data bank containing Holocaust testimonies for the education of future generations. This essay will illuminate differences in approach, representation, and in the creation of post-memory by comparing the videotape of Jake Geldwert done by volunteers from the Spielberg project with the oral history I conducted with him. I will argue that the theory and methods underlying Spielberg's VHF project will contribute to the creation of a partial and simplistic Jewish post-memory and Jewish identity, reflecting more of a Hollywood ending than the complexities confronted by these survivors. In this way, I will link Holocaust testimonials with the production of memory and Jewish identity.

Memories

Collective memory refers to the "common shared awareness of the presence of the past in contemporary consciousness" (Stier 1996:1). In her book on the politics of remembering, Sturken (1997) argues that "memory establishes life's continuity; it gives meaning to the present . . . memory provides the very core of identity" (1). Although no monolithic "Jewish" collective memory exists (Aschheim 1997), contemporary researchers suggest that the Holocaust comprises one of the most important bases of American and Israeli Jewish identity. Goldberg (1995) pushes this argument further, pointing to what he terms a "Holocaust cult," which has made the Holocaust into a Jewish "civil religion." Certainly the very popular March of the Living both reflects and contributes to that process (Stier 1996). One ramification of centering Jewish identity in the Holocaust is to perpetuate the notion of victimhood. This became evident to me in the spring of 2004, when several Jewish American seniors in my seminar on American-Jewish identities and communities were convinced that anti-Semitism was rampant and another Holocaust was just around the corner. These fears seem paradoxical given that American Jews have never been as successful, as free from anti-Semitism, and as powerful an ethnic group as they are in the contemporary United States (Biale 1986).

Cultural and collective memory does not simply occur; it is a social construction. Linenthal (1995) provides an unusual view onto the politics of producing Holocaust memory in his book documenting the creation of the United States Holocaust Memorial Museum in Washington. Contentious and divisive debates on the museum's initial committee focused on who should be represented in the museum (i.e., which groups) and how they should be represented. These debates, however, can also be seen as metadiscussions about who and what counts as Jewish cultural memory (Sturken 1997) and how Jewish identity gets shaped. Indeed, the production of a kind of cultural memory is pivotal in creating and perpetuating links for the third generation and beyond, with an imagined home and imagined community, and with a sense of Jewish identity. An important question thus becomes, as survivors die and the past "passes from living memory to history" (Patrick Hutton qtd. in Young 1997:49), how this past is remembered and what impact this past has on contemporary and future Jewish identities.

The Role of Testimonials: Witnesses as Political Actors

Testimonials have proven an effective vehicle for Holocaust survivors to make their pasts public and to transmit a particular slice of Jewish history. As holds true of the Latin American *testimonio* (Latina Feminist Group 2001), testimonials tell the story of oppression as a necessary and political act for the teller because they reveal injustices. Thus giving testimony constitutes a form of remembering (Langer 1991) that goes beyond the individual, inscribing the memory in history. At the same time, creating testimony may become a form of restitution, of bringing some order, mastery, and some relief "to the unmastered portion" (Hartman 1992:324).

As the Holocaust survivor Saul Friedländer (1992) points out, given that the Nazis "invested considerable effort not only in camouflage but in effacement of all traces of their deeds, the obligation to bear witness and record this past seems even more compelling" (3). Indeed, more contemporary historical revisionists and Holocaust deniers catalyzed many survivors to finally recount their histories.

For Jews in general and Holocaust survivors specifically, the importance of bearing witness can be traced back to biblical roots. According to Jewish law, a witness must report an unjust event once she or he has seen it, thereby making "more witnesses by informing others of events" (Young 1988:18). In his book on Jewish memory, Yerushalmi (1996) notes that the command "to remember" (*zakhar*) is used 169 times in the Hebrew Bible (5). Ritual retelling such as the Passover seder provide a cultural basis for retelling the experiences of the Holocaust, thus the injunction to remember in addition to the responsibility of reporting injustice may help explain the proliferation of Holocaust testimonials.

Clearly, many Jews experienced transformations in a similar manner under Nazi rule—for example, boycotts of Jewish stores, taunts, ghettoization, train rides to concentration camps, the camp experience, death marches—but due to various configurations of family history, age, gender, class, life-cycle state, nationality, culture, and the availability of family members, all of these stories have their own particularities, and they were experienced and processed differently. What varies is not so much what happened to each and every Jew, but *"how victims and survivors have grasped and related their experiences"* (Young 1997: 56). What thus seems important in these testimonials is not only what happened during the war but also how subjects came to understand their lives and create meaning and a new life after the war. The ways in which Holocaust survivors' lives have been reconfigured in a post-Holocaust world—as displaced persons, as refugees, and transnational subjects, most of them in diasporic settings far from their native homes—reflects these intrinsic differences.

Jake's Narrative

Typically, both ethnographers—anthropologists and sociologists alike—and some historians utilize oral histories as a method. While it is not possible to broadly generalize from one case, certain arguments and themes emerged in my work that prove highly relevant for the construction of Jewish memory and identity.

I first met Jake in his and his wife's corner grocery store in Ithaca in 1980 as I was preparing to go to Java to do fieldwork. Never having taken a course on how to pursue fieldwork, something I now teach with great pleasure, I wanted to "practice" doing an oral history with someone from my own cultural background before trying to do so in a foreign language. A professor of anthropology at Cornell had gotten me in touch with Jake, and I was immediately taken with his story and his cheerful personality, particularly in light of what he had been through. I visited weekly for some months, taking his oral history, which I then presented at a course at the YIVO Institute for Jewish Research in New York City. We maintained contact over the years by correspondence, phone, and an occasional visit to Ithaca. In 1996, I returned to Ithaca in order to redo Jake's oral history, this time more professionally (Wolf 2002).

PREWAR AND WARTIME

Jake was born Jakob (pronounced "Yakov," but called in Yiddish "Yankel") in 1921 in Osweicim, Poland, a city later to be renamed by the Germans with a word that became the time-space symbol of the Third Reich's terror—Auschwitz. He was born into a very religious Hasidic family of solid middle-class status, with five children, when Osweicim was approximately 80 percent Jewish. His life followed a path typical of a young male destined to follow in his father's and grandfathers' footsteps—he went to Polish public school from age six to ten, attending Jewish school in the afternoon, and then at age eleven was sent to Krakow to live with his paternal grandparents and to attend heder (a Jewish school for males) full-time. In 1936, at age fifteen, he was also sent to a school to learn the leatherwork trade, so that he could support a family once married.

As a religious Jew, Jake was raised to think of himself and other Jews outside of Palestine as living in exile: "All Hasidim felt themselves to be exiled; you were always a stranger in the land." Home was *eretz Yisroel*, the land of Israel, then Palestine, and the biblical image indicated that when the *moshiach* (messiah) came, all Jews would return there. While a religious and textual notion of a true home elsewhere existed for Jake and other Hasidim, Osweicim and Krakow also signified home, consisting of a large extended family embedded in a strong and religiously and politically diverse Jewish community. For Jake and those around him, the Jewish religion and family life were interdependent, constituting the raison d'être of their lives.

When the Germans invaded and enforced registration and identification cards, Jake's family resisted and did not register him and his next youngest brother, instead obtaining fake identification cards for the two. They had realized that young Jewish men who were registered had been called away by the Nazis to work elsewhere and either did not return, or in the case of their neighbor, were returned in an urn for which the family was forced to pay. The two brothers were able to hide successfully in the family's house and cellar, remaining undetected during several house-to-house searches. In April 1941, Osweicim was made *Judenrein* (free of Jews), and Jake's family (his parents, siblings, and maternal grandparents) was sent to the Sosnowiec ghetto. He and his next youngest brother remained hidden inside their house in the Sosnowiec ghetto for over one and a half years, studying Talmud.

In August 1942, obeying German orders, his family and all other remaining Jews in Sosnowiec reported to a soccer field while Jake and his brother hid in the cellar. A day or two later, on a Friday night when the entire family remained at the stadium, he despaired: "I did my prayers, *lecha-dodi* and the *kabbalat shabbat*, I was crying, tears, I'd never cried in my life like this here, because I was alone, I was the oldest one at home. I'm alone. . . . Where am I going to get something to eat? I was in such a desperate situation." His father and maternal grandfather both escaped and eventually returned back to Sosnowiec, and his sisters were also sent home as part of an agreement that the Nazis would release fifty children from the stadium. His grandmother, mother, and baby brother did not return. In early 1943, all Jews in Sosnowiec were sent to Srodula, where Jake and his brother successfully hid for another three months, until Jake, at age twenty-two, was caught by the police as he went outside to use the outhouse. As he later found out, his brother was caught shortly thereafter.

After being caught, Jake was sent to a labor camp, Sachenheim, in Upper Silesia in Poland, then under the administration of the Third Reich, where he was a slave laborer for I. G. Farben for one year. Prisoners in that labor camp were allowed to wear civilian clothes and keep their prayer books; indeed, Jake received a package from his father with work shoes, matzo for Passover, and a prayer book with a special prayer taped inside that his father instructed him to say daily.[3] After one year, Jake was sent to an ss camp, Blechammer, where all personal items were taken from him, and he was given his first of two tattooed numbers: 184685. He met up with his brother in that camp, and they stayed together until after liberation.

After nine months in Blechammer, in January 1945, Jake and five thousand others were sent on a death march for about two weeks in the brutal cold of winter wearing one layer of clothing and a thin blanket. During the march, they received neither food nor water, but were forced to survive on whatever grass or roots they could forage themselves. Jake and his brother were among the approximately two thousand or so who survived, but he suffered frostbitten toes. The march ended up in the camp Gross Rosen, in Lower Silesia, where they stayed for a short period, after which they were sent to Buchenwald in Germany.

In February 1945, Jake and his brother were sent to a camp called Zweiberger in the Harz mountains in Germany, where Jake labored in Hermann Goering Werke for almost two months, under conditions he feels he could not have survived for long. They worked in a mountain carved out by prisoners in which the V-1 and V-2 rockets were made: "Hell was in there. Every time you got in there, screaming and yelling, 'faster, faster.'" His job consisted of digging into the mountain to make tiles for the walls of the mountain, which meant carrying concrete pieces of twenty-five kilos, sometimes up a ladder, and subsisting on a subminimal diet and poor health. In addition, he and others had to carry the dead out, those who died during the job or during the night. One morning, the prisoners noticed that the ss were gone and cautiously ventured out of their barracks, an act that one day earlier would have meant severe punishment or death on the spot. In April 1945, wearing striped prisoners' garb, twenty-four-year-old Jake was near starvation and almost toothless—but free.

In this brief summary, I have skipped over descriptions of beatings, cruelty, starvation, illness, injuries, resilience, of Jake's risking disease while caring for an ill friend who died, of Jake's watching others be killed or drop dead, of resistance, of inhumane acts that defy description, and of a few acts of courage by some Germans who tried to help. However, I am being brief in order to include a focus on the postwar period to examine how such displacement led to particular decisions and a long-term multidiasporic life.

AFTER THE WAR

In the several months following the war, Jake, his brother, and some friends lived as squatters in an ex-Nazi's house in Halberstadt, Germany, slowly repairing their bodies, eating many meals daily, regaining weight, and searching for their families. Jake's photo ID card from that time as a DP (displaced person) shows a handsome, healthy young man. Jake found out from other survivors and eyewitnesses that his grandmother, mother, and baby brother had been sent from the stadium in Sosnowiec on a train to Auschwitz and were never heard from again. He does not know how long they survived there, but from what we know now, the elderly and women with small children were sent directly to the gas chambers. He heard later from someone who had been in the same ghetto as the rest of his family that his father, grandfather, and two sisters hid in a bunker but were eventually found by the Germans. He never learned exactly how they met their end, but simply said, "You can imagine what happened." Thus Jake's liberation and searching for his family confronted him with some harsh realities: most of his immediate family had been killed. Jews who returned to Poland were often met with contempt if not outright hostility and violence there, that is, with pogroms and murder. Clearly, home and family as he knew them had disappeared. Thus, although Jake was free from the threat of Nazi violence, he was simultaneously a citizen of nowhere, a displaced person. Indeed, the only form of identification that exists on his DP identity card besides his photo is the concentration camp number tattooed on his forearm, a reminder that all remnants from the past were in his memory or embodied in other ways.

All survivors at the time were searching for their families, and in confronting the aloneness of their condition, made close connections with other survivors. Many married other survivors during this period and had children. The kinds of ties created between survivors after the war became a kind of surrogate for family ties; these were friendships that lasted until death. Jake met his future wife Shayne (later renamed Jeannette) immediately after the war. She was part of a group of women liberated from Auschwitz-Birkenau searching for their family members who had heard that there were some young men in Halberstadt. She had hoped to find some of her five brothers among them. The group of women, along with Jake, his brother, and friends moved to Bergen-Belsen in July 1945, a former concentration camp that had been turned into a DP camp. Jake and Jeannette married nine months later and had a son a year and a half after that. Those years were spent searching for family members, trying to survive on rations and the black market, and trying to heal the emotional and physical damage done.

In 1948, Jake's brother left for Palestine (Israel), but the British then sent him to Cyprus. Unlike Jake who had a surviving brother and a few other family members (e.g., an aunt, an uncle, and two cousins), Jeannette was the sole survivor of her natal and extended family in Poland. Jeannette's only living relative in the entire world was an aunt who had emigrated to Canada before the war, and Jeannette set about finding her in hopes of reconnecting with kin. Although Jake would have preferred to go to Palestine with his brother, Jeannette's desire to be reunited with her one blood relative made their decision. Jake said that Jeannette "felt very strongly that 'this would be my mother.'" Eventually, her aunt in Rochester, New York, sponsored them, and in April 1949, the three emigrated to the United States.

Welcome to America

After a week or so visiting Jeannette's aunt in Rochester, the family moved to Ithaca, where they lived in a tiny apartment connected to a store, and Jake went to work for Jeannette's cousin (the aunt's son) in his grocery store. Barely able to speak English, Jake was asked to perform all kinds of tasks, from stacking cans and unloading deliveries to sweeping the store. After two weeks, they

put me in front of the cash register to take in money. I didn't even know the money yet! You know, like somebody came in and said, "Here's a nickel and two dimes and says, "Give me two bits back." And I looked around, I said "What's two bits?" I finally found out that two bits is a quarter. I made errors but they probably didn't know it. I found out afterwards, you know like "oh, it's not eighty-one cents, it's eighteen cents. [Laughs].

I was supposed to work from 7:30am to about 5pm or 6pm every day with one afternoon off, after 2pm on Mondays. Thursday, I came in, the first Thursday [sighs], I said, [in anticipation of the Sabbath on Friday] "it's Shabbes, Shabbes, I'm not going to work." [In a voice imitating their surprise and anger:] "What? Everybody works, look at the stores here, all the Jews work who have stores; nobody closes." So she [the cousin] sends after Jeannette's uncle to come to talk to me. And here I was already moved in to Ithaca, "Where am I gonna go? Even if I go to New York, I don't know anybody, where am I gonna go? What am I gonna do?" So I had no choice, you know, I had to work on Shabbes.

For those who observe Rosh Hashanah (Jewish New Year) and Yom Kippur (Day of Atonement), this is a time to pray and be with family. On their first Yom Kippur in Ithaca, approximately six months after their arrival, Jake, Jeanette, and baby Joe went to

Kol Nidre at the shul [synagogue]. We came out from shul and said, "Let's go over to Marion and Nate's," the cousins in Ithaca. . . . We walked there, with the baby on the hand in the dark to a bad part of town. We got there to their house and they weren't home! They weren't there! They went to Elmira, to her brother and we didn't know that. They had their own family; she [the aunt] didn't think about us the way we thought about them. Like the boy is more in love with the girl than the girl with the boy. It was a disappointment; there was a lot of disappointment.

Although Jeannette had hoped that her aunt would be a second mother to her, "her aunt had her own children and was a mother to her own children."

WORKING FOR FAMILY

When he first started his job, Jake returned to the store in the evenings simply to hear people speak English so that he could learn the language. "So while I came to the store after supper to listen how people speak English, they made me do things up, up until ten thirty at night. Every night. After I had started doing it, they wanted me to come every night. So that's when I came early in the morning until night. I worked about ninety-three hours." The minimum wage was $0.75 an hour at the time, which would have brought Jake a weekly wage of $70; instead, he made half that amount, $37.

Jake's hard work and excellent memory made him an indispensable part of the store:

I knew every price; I marked it and I put it on shelves and sometimes at night when I came home, I couldn't feel my fingers because of everything what I was doing. . . . Sometimes a price falls off or something like this here so they'll come ask, "Nate, what is the price?" He had to go take the book to find out what it is. But it got so that he didn't have to look at the book for the price. He called, "Jake, what's the price?" I already knew it by heart. I knew every single thing in the store.

In the store, Jake worked under abusive conditions:

She [the cousin's wife] was [lowering his voice to a whisper] just like a Gestapo or something. They used to come in about 9:30, 10:00am. When we opened up the store, we had to have already the displays made—meat display out, we had to take out every morning I had to take out all the displays and clean everything meanwhile. So when she came in about 9:30, she expected everything to be right. But what happened, sometimes a delivery came. Nobody wanted to go, to take in the delivery. Why? Because they knew that it takes a half hour and she comes in here in the store, she wants to have everything done. So I said, "To heck with it [laughs], I'll do it." And when she came in at 9:30, she sees the case is not made, she screams [imitating angry voice] "What are you guys doing in here!?" She didn't know that you had something else to do. So that's the way how she was.

As his English improved, Jake found out that in a nearby air force base, other immigrants were making fifty to sixty dollars weekly for half the amount of time he worked. After his daughter was born, he asked for more money and received $55 a week; after two years of working at highly exploitative wages, he finally got a raise: "If you didn't scream about something, they'd never give you any more." Even though his wages improved, working conditions did not.

A lot of times she used to come in and get, you know, get mad or something. Once, I remembered, she used to buy turkeys after the season. And she used to sell the turkeys to the fraternity houses, and you could sell all year long. Once she bought turkeys and the freezer, the freezer was packed with turkeys. You opened up the door, it was packed. So she needed something, we opened up the door and there were about a hundred boxes of turkeys. So I go in, I go in, I knew where this stuff is. And I start taking out about fifty or sixty boxes of turkeys, 'til I get to this here. And, one of the customers was waiting over there. And, so finally, she comes out here, and she says [angrily], "Uh, how come it takes you so long? You, you—." So I said, "If you wouldn't buy that many turkeys [laughs], it wouldn't have taken me so long." And she said [angrily], "You gonna teach me how to run my business? You gonna tell me, eh?" She starts yelling at me. I was taking off my apron—I was gonna go, she goes and grabs me, "Jake, Jake, Jake," starts kissing me, "Don't go, I have two kids to go to college." She only paid four hundred dollars for [laughs] help. . . . So, I went back [chuckles]. She didn't let me out [chuckles]. And that happened several times. She started kissing me, you know.

One day, in 1962, after Jake had worked for the couple for thirteen years,

after *Yom Kippur*, I come to the store, the butcher doesn't show up. So if nobody's here, Jake is gonna be the butcher too. So, I started doing it. And, she starts talking to me, telling me what she did yesterday [on Yom Kippur]: "Gertrude Berg from Binghamton came to visit me yesterday morning. I was fasting, too, I only had a cup of coffee in the morning." [laughs] That's what she said. And, I knew, eh, it's not right [that she didn't really fast on Yom Kippur] so I didn't say nothing, but she knew I didn't approve. So, she got mad. And she starts, you know, screaming at me, you know, "Why did, why it takes you so long to cut the pork chops. You cut the pork chops just like a carpenter." And all this here, and she walks by, trying to, you know, rile me up, to, to make me mad. And I was already mad [chuckles], but I didn't want to start a fight. I didn't start a fight, I didn't want to. So, I kept going, I kept quiet, I figured in another five, ten minutes, she'll calm down. But she didn't. She kept going on like this here. So finally, she tells me to bring out the kosher salami, she's gonna help me 'cause we had all those orders, you know. So, I came out, because I was doing something else and I throw the salami at her, "Here you are—have it" and I go and take off my apron.

A customer, there was a customer over there, he said, "Jake, I don't blame you!" And I took off my apron and that was it. So finally I quit. I quit [sighs] so that was one day. I was home, at night Nate comes over and asks me to come back. And I said to Jeannette, "No way. I want out—even if I have to eat a piece of dry bread—I'm not going back anymore." Always, you know, I try to quit a few times, but I didn't go up, but this time I went out, and no matter what—. Then, he [Nate] comes to me and tries to offer me a partnership. So I said, "Thank you. [laughs] We don't want it."

ON HIS OWN

After quitting, Jake went job hunting: "So, I started looking around. I didn't know how to drive a car yet at that time. And I started looking, I go to, wherever I go to for jobs, I can't find a job, [whispering] and I see it's bad, I can't find a job, you know . . . and I didn't have any money, what to eat, what to feed my family." Jake was unemployed for a short but stressful period and felt disappointed that no one in the Jewish community tried to help him during that time. He ended up working in another grocery store for some months, and shortly thereafter, he bought his own.

When Jake bought the store in Ithaca later in 1962, his entire family began working there. But

even when I opened up the store, I kept feeling that "this is not what I want. I don't want the kids to get into this kind of business. I'll build up the store as much as I can and then get out and go to Israel." I thought this when I had the store. I wanted to sell it in the 70s and maybe had a buyer but he didn't buy it. I would've sold it because I wanted to go to Israel. We even looked at apartments there.

I asked him why he and Jeannette did not move to Israel when they sold the store in 1982 and their children were already grown. He explained that it was too late by then because his brother had died in the meantime, so "we forgot about it. Now it's too late; we can't; it's too much at our ages." Thus they had missed their chance in 1949 to emigrate to Israel, and by the time family and finances made it possible once again, their primary reason for moving, Jake's brother, had died.

JAKE'S REFLECTIONS ON FAMILY

In retrospect, Jake is aware of other missed opportunities in terms of family relationships.

This is the trouble, because I was working that long, I didn't have time [for the family]. [Imitating his son speaking in reference to Jake:] "When I was playing ball, he never came to see me playing ball." I still remember the one day I made that effort to go see [Joe play ball] . . . until I got there the ball game was over. This was the one time I was gone over there, you know, I get over there, there's the whistle; it's all over.

This incident occurred because while Jake was supposed to finish work by 2 p.m. on Mondays, his employers never let him leave until 3 p.m. or 3:30 p.m., always finding one more thing for him to do.

Because I was working that long, with my son, I didn't get the chance to teach him anything [in terms of Jewish education]. I didn't get the chance. When he was small, I was all the time in the store. When he got bigger, I had a business. I didn't come from the business till 10:30 at night, until I was catching up, it was 11:30pm. Six o'clock in the morning, I had to get up and go work again. Somehow, my life was like this here, that I couldn't do things what I usually I would have done. . . . Well, maybe it had to be like this, and maybe, I don't know why, why I came here to Ithaca in the first place.

As I asked Jake to reflect on how his relations with his children and grand-children might have been affected by his experiences, he explained by way of a parable: "I was mostly brought up with my grandfather. He went to the *mikvah* [ritual bath], I went with him to the *mikvah*. And we went to the rabbis, I went with him. . . . Every night, when he comes, you know, I went to bed, he had to go tuck in my feet so they won't be cold. We didn't hug. We didn't kiss, because it's not our style, it's not our custom to do this here."

Retired since 1982, Jake now lives an active life, praying daily with an Ortho-dox group at the Young Israel house on the Cornell campus, and more recently with a Lubavitcher rebbe. In December 2003, he had triple bypass surgery, and at eighty-five he is still going strong. He and his wife see their children and grand-children whenever possible; in 2004, their first great-grandchild was born in Israel, an event Jeannette found to be near miraculous after having been in a camp. Yet Jake still feels himself "to be a stranger" living in the United States. Had Hitler never come and Jake had continued the life he was brought up to lead in Poland, he imagines that today he would "probably be a Jew with a nice, long white beard [chuckles] with probably six or eight children [chuckles]. And many grandchildren. And great-grandchildren." Thus his image of home revolves around the interdependency of religion and family, conjuring up memories of home as he knew it in Poland.

Analysis of Family, Home, and Diaspora

In this section, I turn to a sociological analysis of the themes of family, home, and diaspora as evoked in Jake's narrative. Given their orthodox backgrounds, Jake and Jeannette found it unimaginable that fellow Jews would force Jake to work on a holy day, the Sabbath, denying him the weekly rest, prayer, and family time they felt was sacrosanct. And that it was *family*, the only kin Jeannette had left in the world, who forced this on Jake, and therefore his entire family, after the Shoah, shook their very core. Jake's wife described this sense of treachery and subversion to me more graphically: "We came from the ovens to work on *Shabbes?* We came for this?"

This transgression made Jake and Jeannette realize early on that they had erred in choosing to emigrate to the United States over Israel, but they had few resources and nowhere else to go. The constraints Jake confronted often overwhelmed his ability to make meaningful choices. Under such conditions, "agency" becomes little more than reacting to circumstances beyond one's control. In other words, we should take care not to romanticize notions of human agency given that most immigrants, refugees, and transnational subjects confront debilitating and overwhelming constraints.

Jake and Jeannette had to confront their intense sense of aloneness in the diaspora during their first high holidays in Ithaca when they walked to her family's house and found that the cousins had been invited by other family members also related to Jeannette. Of course, the painful point was that Jake and Jeannette had not also received an invitation and were not treated as family. Ironically, the pair made the decision to emigrate to the United States so that Jeannette could join her one remaining family member and reconstitute a notion of home, family, and belonging. Instead, the decision resulted in the exact opposite—Jeannette's pain of her orphaned state and her sense of displacement in a diasporic place far from home both intensified.

In some sense, the exploitative behavior of Jeannette's relatives seems extraordinarily cruel in light of what Jake and Jeannette had just lived through. Furthermore, it also seems very likely that Jake tolerated a high degree of exploitation for thirteen years not only because he felt obligated to his wife's relatives for sponsoring them as stateless refugees but also because the concentration camp experience had raised his level of tolerance for exploitation. During his camp years, he had worked at many jobs, including slave labor for the large industrial firm I. G. Farben and building German war rockets. Jake and his fellow inmates quickly learned that survival was based on working hard and not complaining. In other words, Jeannette's relatives were perhaps able to exploit Jake to such a high degree because of what the Nazis had ingrained in him.

This aspect of Jake's narrative provides an excellent example of why it is important to explore, rather than make assumptions about, the "natural" altruism of kin in general, and after the Holocaust in particular. Many people have responded to my presentation of Jake's story with more examples of Jewish relatives exploiting a refugee relative from Hitler's Europe. This resonates with scholarly research on contemporary (post-1965) migrants, refugees, and transmigrants who work in exploitative conditions for kin or coethnics in ethnic enclaves in the United States and elsewhere (Bonacich 1994; Guarnizo 1996). Such research challenges romantic assumptions about the receiving family of immigrants, about coethnic solidarity, and about family in general. This particular case suggests that the kind of exploitative relationships extant between coethnics and kin among Jews from previous immigration waves to the United States (e.g., in sweatshops) were repeated after the Holocaust. This dynamic has not received attention in the literature.[4]

Due to the above-average demands at the workplace, Jake ended up having little time with his children, and he reflected on his regrets, particularly as it affected his relationship with his son. While Jake's relationship with his grandfather was close, had daily signs of affection, and completely reflected Jewish learning and practices, his relationship with his son was shaped by the demands of making a living in a foreign culture and a secular society. That chasm speaks of lost possibilities and distance from the one unit that had been the center of Jake's life. This distance results mostly from his diasporic condition because had he and Jeannette emigrated to Israel, their family life and family relations would have been vastly different. Indeed, his image of what his life would be like today had they gone to Israel is centered on the interdependency of family and religious life, much like the prewar life he experienced in Poland.

Jake reiterated his sense of diasporic life outside of Israel: "In World War I, Jews got killed for Germany . . . what good did their medals do later? Jews who were Polish soldiers in World War I were treated like dirt later. You give your life for that country and you're still a stranger . . . you never know in America either." Among the Cambodian Americans she interviewed, Katharya Um (1990) also found a persistent sense of insecurity in that America offered them both sanctuary *and* marginality.

In terms of Jake's relationship with Israel, he maintains close connections with his family there and has visited many times; indeed, he continues to visit to attend weddings and bar mitzvahs, most recently his granddaughter's wedding. He no longer needs to send his family money, but instead sends money to literally hundreds of charities. He has returned to Poland twice since the war, once with his daughter and once with his grandson, to show them his "roots." He does not, however, maintain any other connection with Poland.

Although he has certain transnational ties with Israel, Jake's ties with Poland can be seen more as an emotional transnationalism. Jake's identity is made more complex by being multilocalized within multiple frames of reference, as he lives a kind of doubly diasporic existence. This case aptly illustrates Guarnizo's (1996) contention that "transnationalism, contrary to certain idealized visions," is not necessarily a "socially liberating" force (310). The current academic enthusiasm for all things transnational may neglect its potentially destabilizing impact on family, gender, and class relations. The more or less voluntary emigration Jake and his family undertook after the war as transnational subjects did not end up freeing them; quite the opposite.

The Jewish experience in Nazi Europe might be compared with the multi-diasporic experiences of other middlemen minorities such as the Indians in Uganda and the Chinese in Vietnam, both of whom were expelled and became "twice migrants" (Bhachu 1985). Postwar Jews such as Jake, however, were "twice refugees" if not "thrice refugees," having lost their rights and been forced from home (Poland) to concentration camps in Poland and Germany, and then, at the war's end, as stateless subjects, going to the United States or elsewhere. These multiple and forced movements added to the experiences of genocide and exile underscore the greater complexities refugees confront when compared with other immigrants.

Narratives, Post-memory, and Jewish Identity

To return to one of the goals of this article, then, we must ask: what are the implications of Jake's narrative for the creation of Jewish collective memory and the construction of a post-Holocaust Jewish identity? As we consider post-Holocaust generations, it is useful to further differentiate memory. *Post-memory*, a concept developed by Marianne Hirsch (1997) in her discussion of children of Holocaust survivors, is experienced by those with a generational and historical distance from the Holocaust. Post-memory is a very "powerful and very particular form of memory precisely because its connection to its object or source is mediated not through recollection but through an imaginative investment and creation. Post-memory characterizes the experience of those who grow up dominated by narratives that preceded their birth, whose own belated stories are evacuated by the stories of the previous generation, shaped by traumatic events that can be neither fully understood nor re-created" (Hirsch 1997:22). Here I am utilizing the notion of post-memory somewhat more broadly to refer to third-generation Jews whose notions of the Holocaust are mediated through the memories of others and through the production of Jewish collective memory. For the third generation, it is mostly parents, grandparents, Sunday school, Jewish summer camp and perhaps a trip to Israel that created its sense of Jewish collective memory, but these Jews have not necessarily known a survivor, and none of them are children of survivors.

THE CREATION OF POST-MEMORY

Earlier in 1996, the same year I interviewed Jake for his oral history, volunteers from Steven Spielberg's Shoah Visual History Foundation also took Jake's testimonial. The availability of two different testimonials from the same person offers a unique opportunity to contemplate how they might contribute to very different kinds of post-memory and Jewish identity. I also had the opportunity to visit the VHF in 1997, where I interviewed the person who oversees the training of interviewers and the interviews themselves. In general, the VHF wants interviews to have a 20 percent focus on the prewar period, 60 percent on the war, and 20 percent on liberation. The ten-hour oral history I did with Jake spends approximately half the time on wartime experiences, while the other half is divided between prewar and postwar life, making the division closer to 25 percent, 50 percent, 25 percent.

The two-and-a-half-hour VHF videotape mainly focuses on Jake's wartime experiences, in keeping with the project's goals. His postwar existence, however, is given much less time and attention. Toward the end of the interview, Jake states: "I worked in a grocery store for Jeannette's cousin for thirteen years and that's it, until the end of 1962, and a few months later, I opened up my business by myself." The VHF videotape ends with Jake showing the photos of his two children and six grandchildren and reciting their names. If possible, the VHF asks the children and grandchildren to be present for those final frames.

The oral history I took includes aspects not covered by the VHF video that occurred during Jake's postwar life in the United States—extreme exploitation, exploitation by kin, the prevention of pursuing a religious life by kin, all in addition to successful adaptation, irony, discontent, sadness, and possibilities lost. It is of course very positive that Jake and Jeannette were able to have two children who are now successful professionals, and many grandchildren who are doing well, but the nature and texture of some of those relationships are problematic. None of that nuance appears in the VHF tape. Jake and Jeannette survived, worked hard, and succeeded economically in the United States. However, Jake's statement in the VHF video—that he worked for thirteen years for Jeannette's cousin, then opened his own store, and "that's it"—obfuscates the harsh life imposed on him by kin for thirteen years and the mistake the couple felt they made by emigrating to Ithaca, if not to the United States. Thus the VHF tape obscures much of the ambivalence, alienation, loneliness, and discomfort Jake and Jeannette experienced for many years after their arrival.

The narrative I presented unsettles a binary opposition between Jews as victims and Nazis as perpetrators because it is clear that Jake was also deeply exploited by other Jews after the war. Indeed, it was Jewish kin who took advantage of his vulnerability and marginality and prevented him from developing the religious Jewish life he wished to observe with his family. Thus the comforting notion of an extended Jewish family that a viewer of Jake's VHF video might receive is imploded by Jake's depiction, in the longer narrative, of how he and Jeannette were abandoned, exploited, and kept from their religious practices by kin. Finally, the success story transmitted in the VHF video about how he became a self-employed store owner is overshadowed in the longer narrative by his sense of having made a serious error in emigrating to the United States and, as a result, always feeling displaced. In the longer narrative, both the United States and Jewish kin are presented as less of a safe refuge, somewhat blurring and perhaps muddying the redemptive quality in the video.

I would like to suggest that the VHF's greater emphasis on the wartime experience creates a clearer division between right and wrong, between victims and perpetrators, and offers a more linear view: from obliteration to regeneration, from destruction to redemption, and from destitution to success. Simply put, the message from the VHF video is that Jews were victims whose entire families were destroyed yet, despite Hitler, they managed to overcome the past and create a new generation of Jews.[5] However, Jake's narrative makes clear that while the war may have officially ended in 1945, its effects bore down on him for years after.

For my current research, I interviewed a substantial number of survivors who had been hidden as children in the Netherlands during the occupation and the war.[6] The striking aspect of their particular experience is that most of them saw the postwar period as much more traumatic than the occupation and war. Many reiterated to me, "My war began after the war." As parents returned to children who did not know them, children were sometimes traumatically separated from the family who had hidden them as their biological families reformed. Family life never returned to "normal," and many suffered from the separation. However, those interviewed by the VHF project were asked mainly about their wartime hiding, and again their postwar experiences were skimmed over. One interviewee explained when speaking about her experience with the VHF interview: "I felt I didn't have enough chance to speak about today. . . . I wanted to talk about how the war affected me today, but they wouldn't let me."

In the decades to come, after all survivors have died and can no longer present their stories to classrooms, they will still speak posthumously through such videos, instilling a notion of history in the minds of young people. The VHF's focus on the wartime experience of Jake and fifty thousand other Holocaust survivors will deeply affect the future of Jewish cultural memory, post-memory, and the shape of Jewish identity. Although Spielberg's Shoah project is laudable and the VHF's wartime focus understandable, both unwittingly end up decontextualizing and simplifying the lives of survivors. These testimonials provide partial and truncated views of the individuals meant to be honored. In this way, the project will create Jewish post-memories focused on romanticized notions of Jewish prewar life, followed by Jewish persecution and death, and then redemption. The way that survivors are represented will contribute to an identity built on a simplistic view of Jewish life and Jewish victimhood.

A crucial issue concerning these testimonies is how the Holocaust is defined and what gets included under its rubric. The VHF focuses its notion of the Shoah on the period of Nazi rule. While this is understandable, it is also very limiting. A broader approach, as defined by many survivors, demonstrates that the postwar period remains inextricably linked to the war. The postwar period defined how Jews lived and delineates the complexities and the challenges they confronted. Thus I would argue that in order to fully understand the war, one must include and examine the postwar period as well.

In its push for an enormous sample, the VHF structured its interviews in a formulaic manner and ended up truncating and simplifying the lives it attempts

DIANE L. WOLF

to capture and portray. As important, interviewers were volunteers rather than trained professionals who often did not have sufficient experience or were not grounded in history. I do not question the well-meaning intent of Spielberg, the VHF staff, or the interviewers; however, in their rush to interview such an unusually large number of people, they have sacrificed quantity for quality in many instances, and, as a result, a deep understanding for a simpler approach.

SOCIOLOGY AND TESTIMONY

What can we gain from a sociological analysis of survivor testimony? How can our understanding of Holocaust survivors be enriched, and how might sociology gain from such an analysis? A more sociological approach has pointed to several important threads in the one particular testimony under discussion here, threads that undoubtedly exists in other testimonials as well. First, by engaging with the concepts of diaspora and home, we saw that the Jewish experience during and after the Holocaust was one of expulsions, involuntary transnational movements, statelessness, and postwar immigration. Like other refugees, Jewish survivors did not move simply from one point to another but had to endure multiple movements and few choices in the end. Jake's emigration to the United States was voluntary, but it did not involve many options. Once in the country, he had a doubly diasporic experience: he was still in the diaspora in relation to Israel, but now also in relation to Poland.

Although a transnational framework does apply to his case and those of most other Holocaust survivors, the discourse of transnationalism is perhaps overly sanguine. It unwittingly presumes that transnationalism embodies somewhat liberatory behaviors and imbues considerable agency to those involved. The term *transnational actor*, for example, exudes a much more active and positive image than the term *refugee*, which implies being acted on. However, a greater focus on Jake's postwar life illuminated how he acted and reacted with greatly limited and highly constrained agency. His and his family's well-being lay in the hands of relatives who mistreated him. He had the desire to leave, but not the ability to do so. For this transnational actor, there were no choices and no real way to exert his agency; perhaps the term *transnational refugee* more precisely expresses the statelessness and dependency he and other refugees experience.

A broader definition of the Holocaust (and of genocide in general), coupled with a critical analytical approach, has opened up questions about how Holocaust testimonies will create post-memory and future Jewish identities. The trauma and tragedy of the Shoah is likely to continue shaping a substantial portion of contemporary and future Jewish post-memory. For example, the highly staged manner in which the March of the Living contrasts the anti-Semitic Poles who murdered millions of Jews with Israel as the Jewish homeland, creating a dichotomous framework consistent with Jewish victimization by non-Jews and Jewish redemption among other Jews (Stier 1996). The way in which the VHF project is structured creates a similarly dichotomous view. Yet this constitutes only part of the story and omits other traumas, tragedies, and misfortunes after the war, including possible mistreatment by other Jews. Indeed, it is in the behavior of Jake's relatives after the war where we can observe less fettered agency. As ethnic identities become more simplified and symbolic over time, and more distant from the immigrant experience (Waters 1990), the VHF will abet a post-memory and feed the resultant sense of Jewish identity with a simplified and superficial version of the Shoah and its effects.

Conclusions

The VHF approach understandably emphasizes the war, but it obfuscates problematic arenas in which Jews exert both agency and power or sites such as the family in which conflicts tend to exist. Furthermore, undercurrents of survivors' post-Holocaust sense of displacement, marginality, or political involvement are swept away by an emphasis on Jewish regeneration. The VHF interviews are choreographed to produce a feel-good Hollywood ending. In that sense, recording survivors' testimonials is political, not only as an act of witnessing and as a way to rebut Holocaust deniers but also in its very form and content. Indeed, it is imperative to critically consider the broader social, cultural, and political ramifications of the particular narrative style adopted by the Shoah Visual History Foundation for the future production of post-memory and its contribution to the creation of Jewish identities. I have attempted to present a more holistic portrait of a post-Holocaust life that reflects tremendous adaptation, disappointment, hard work, sacrifice, achievement, and loss, while also acknowledging ambivalence, conflict, and power. It is a critical analysis of this mélange of marginality despite success, of displacement despite prosperity, and of the dialectic between home and Home that has the potential to contribute further to immigration and diaspora studies and, at the same time, to a more nuanced and complex Jewish identity.

DIANE L. WOLF

Notes

The present article is a substantially revised version of Wolf 2002b.

1. There are many Holocaust oral history projects in the United States—in San Francisco, at Yale University, at the United States Holocaust Memorial Museum, and at Steven Spielberg's Shoah Visual History Foundation, to name but a few—based on taped interviews. In addition, there are collected volumes of survivors' lives (e.g., Blum et al. 1991; Hass 1996; Helmreich 1992; Linden 1993; White 1988; Wolman 1996) and written personal memoirs that may have been done in conjunction with a writer/editor (e.g., Appleman-Jurman 1988; Friedländer 1979; Isaacman 1984; Jackson 1980; Weiss Halivni 1996; Zilversmit 1995; Zuckerman 1993).

2. The few sociologists who have focused on Holocaust testimonials have analyzed them for the ways in which they might inform notions of ethnicity (Climo 1990), for the relationship between human agency and social structures (Berger 1995), and for feminist epistemology (Linden 1993). Psychologists have tended to focus on survivor adaptation. Most studies find that survivors' experiences have long-lasting negative effects on their emotional state and ability to function (Chodoff 1980; Dimsdale 1980; Eitinger 1964, 1980; Krystal 1968; Luchterhand 1980; Niederland 1964). A few have focused on the very successful adaptation of Holocaust survivors (Hass 1996; White 1988), challenging notions of Jewish passivity and pathology. The sociologist Helmreich (1992) studied the traits of "successful survivors" (267).

3. This was the will from the Rambam (Moses Maimonides) to his son, which Jake's father told him to say daily so that he would survive.

4. American Jews tend to focus on exogenous factors when thinking about the United States and the Holocaust, such as the American government's knowledge of concentration camps or immigration quotas.

5. Suzanne Vromen, a contributor to this volume, was interviewed by the VHF and has written about that experience in an as-yet-unpublished essay. She underscores the formulaic nature of the interview, which left her unable to explain important parts of her life during the prewar and wartime period. The interviewer was so focused on following the interview questions that she missed important aspects of the interviewee's life.

6. My findings are published in *Beyond Anne Frank: Hidden Children and Postwar Families in Holland* (University of California Press, 2007).

Survivor Testimonies, Holocaust Memoirs:
Violence in Latin America

IRINA CARLOTA SILBER

During ethnographic research in El Salvador in the aftermath of a violent civil war, a Jesuit-trained local parish priest explained to me the ways in which contemporary struggles for justice and peace were rendered meaningful through a painful history lived in memory. He commented about the experiences of communities in former conflict zones characterized by shared though diverse experiences of popular organizing, armed combat, displacement, and violence:

The postwar is a hard, difficult time. It is like trying to find one's lost voice. It is about trying to make the connection between 1979 and 1997 . . . the Chalateco and Salvadoran peasants, they like to live in the present, and do not want to remember the past, because of the pain. And we have to understand that as well. The anguish, the sadness, so much that was lived . . . but historical memory gives us meaning. It helps us put our feet on the ground.[1]

Statements such as these index Judith Gerson's call for comparative understandings of the Holocaust and post-Holocaust life. Specifically, recent scholarship on the legacies of violence, the search for justice, and the role of individual and collective memory in Latin America provide an interesting comparative lens for the kinds of issues raised in part 3 of the current volume. In my commentary on its three insightful articles, I will concentrate on themes of the aftermath of violence through a discussion of narratives, memory, and displacement, and the challenges of rebuilding lives that break apart homogenized assumptions of prototypical survivors across time and space. To do so, I will also provide examples from my own work on materially and discursively marginalized communities in El Salvador. My aim is to address not only social theory but also to raise questions around engaged methodology, and ultimately pedagogy, for researchers working on issues of political, religious, cultural, structural, and gendered violence.

Memory and Displaced Survivors

As the pieces under discussion here eloquently demonstrate, the category of survivor and the role of bearing witness are fraught positionings. Gerson, Suzanne Vromen, and Diane Wolf clearly target representations of prototypical Holocaust survivors, as well as conceptions of a hierarchy of victimization or suffering. Their work suggests the importance of taking into account people's lived experience, self-identification, and contexts through time, ultimately breaking apart essentialized notions of survivors, a monolithic Jewish community, and the role of memory more generally. In doing so, they underscore inadvertently silenced prewar, wartime, and postwar stories.

Gerson provides an analysis of Jewish immigrants who fled Germany between 1933 and 1941 and settled in New York City by 1945. Her focus shifts attention to an understudied population, time, and genre—unpublished memoirs. While significantly different than Wolf's exploration of more political testimonies, and Vromen's presentation of hidden Jewish children in Belgian convents, Gerson's work addresses the relationship between displacement and memory, which the authors variously assert proves central to the périodized study of pre- to post-Holocaust life. Here the work of Liisa Malkki (1995a) on genocide in Burundi, in particular her theorizing on refugees, displacement, and deterritorialization, is fruitful as she examines the local logics of constructing history in two different contexts of exile. These are issues also at the heart of many discussions on the aftermath of violence throughout Latin America that seek to understand and theorize particular practices and discourses within a framework that emphasizes the tensions between global and local processes and between structure and agency.

While Vromen and Wolf concentrate on oral testimonies, Gerson discusses written narratives in her urgent call to make useful and appropriate sociological comparisons. In particular, her focus on landscape in memory resonates with the lived experiences of many Salvadoran residents I worked with in a former conflict zone in the department of Chalatenango. I often listened to the ways in which particular places held multiple meanings for residents. A mango tree, the curve of a mountain, a fork in the road, a church, a school yard—these locations erupted with stories of death, disappearances, escapes, births on the run, neighbors betraying neighbors, and ambushes. Importantly, the separation between social and natural landscape is quite blurred.

In the memoirs that Gerson discusses, immigrants, too, reflect on a rural place from their newly acquired urban space. Indeed, a significant body of literature explores the relationship between narrative, the social and political uses of oral history, and the cultural construction of place (Basso 1996; Borneman 1993; Bruner and Gorfain 1984; Nash 1979; Rappaport 1990, 1994; Tonkin 1992). Stories shape and are shaped by society. These narratives and their contexts, coconstructed by speakers and audience (Duranti and Brennis 1986; Goodwin 1986; Ochs and Capps 1996), can inform analyses of the meanings and practices of social memory. What I emphasize in my own work are the differences in a postwar call to remember the past. These are differences according to gender, generation, wartime experiences, and postwar locations that are refracted through people's narrative recollections. As Cole (1998) reminds us in her work on colonial memories in Madagascar, memories are not "equally salient all of the time, and . . . the process of remembering and forgetting is tied to the very flow of social life and local people's attempts to control it" (627).

An interesting comparative direction may be one that focuses on parallel German Jewish migratory populations during this same period throughout the Americas (e.g., in Argentina, Uruguay, and Brazil). Also of interest may be comparing genres, such as family letters and diaries. In a recent piece, Karen Armstrong (2000) discusses issues of migration, violence, and remembrance through the exchange of letters between female kin in wartime Finland. She explores the merging of personal experiences with collective experience in Finnish history as a regional identification is constructed over a national war story. Reading with attention to gender is also important. While the narratives in Gerson's analysis often feature the voices of male migrants, Armstrong's data suggests that the domestic basis for political memory may offer an interesting point of comparison. In the Finish case, the letters are archived, read, and interpreted by subsequent generations. One could ask if the memoirs Gerson discusses are read, who reads them, in what context, and hence what politics of memory do they construct?

Testimonies, Witnessing, and the
Pursuit of an Engaged Scholarship

Many human rights activists, scholars of violence, and students of the Holocaust share a common interest in the pursuit of social justice built on documenting atrocities, expressed in the urgent call of "never again." In Latin America, this call for uncovering the truth, of *nunca más*, flows from Argentina to Guatemala, evidenced in the work of truth commissions, of forensic anthropologists recovering clandestine graves, and of local and international peace, development, community, and human rights organizations. Men, women, and children survivors' eyewitness accounts or testimonies have proven central to unmasking official histories of violence, providing sociological descriptions of brutality and constructing accounts that aim to hold the material and intellectual authors of violence accountable in a context of widespread amnesty for human rights abuses. As Sanford's *Buried Secrets* (2003) meticulously details through the collection of over four hundred testimonies, archival research, and forensic work, Mayan widows of massacre victims in Guatemala publicly call for the exhumation of clandestine graves by forensic anthropologists so the truth can be told and to chart a path toward not only national justice but also communal healing in a context in which violence forced on these communities has implicated everyone. In another example, Marguerite Feitlowitz (1998) describes the legacies of the Dirty War in Argentina through an analysis of a "lexicon of terror." Like Wolf, she pursues repeated interviews with those who survived torture and looks specifically at language, asking what words those who were disappeared cannot tolerate. She also raises the critical issue of remembering and forgetting. One of the protagonists of the book poignantly expresses this balancing act of memory, leaving us with more questions than answers. Mario says, "A lot of things you'd like to forget . . . but there's the imperative to remember. A lot of things you do forget, and that's a torment too. Is forgetting a sin or salvation? Neither? Both?" (Feitlowitz 1998:76). As Wolf suggests in her analysis of three versions of one man's life history, these testimonies do the work of memorializing and commemorating alongside the later construction of commemorative sites.

Wolf poignantly makes the connection between narratives of the Holocaust and *testimonios* as a genre. The structure is that of a life story, orally produced, typically audiotaped, transcribed, most often decontextualized, and often translated into English. Some scholars suggest that testimonios "rewrite and retell . . .

[the] correct Latin American history and reality from the people's perspective" (Gugelberger and Kearney 1991:11). However, the testimonio must be understood in terms of its production, consumption, circulation, and representation. For instance, Rigoberta Menchú's (1984) now famous and contested testimony can be seen as a performative event told in a politically violent and dangerous time. Other testimonios, like that of Salvadoran activist María Teresa Tula (1994), have been performed for Congress or told to the Immigration and Naturalization Service (INS),[2] and many have been circulated through solidarity movements. They are produced for and consumed by a U.S. population—generally a white, educated, middle-class audience—in order to solicit aid in fighting human rights abuses, and they are used by grassroots activists as political tools (Stephen 1994).

Today, some scholars critique these types of stories as they question their empirical truth. The debates they generate often decontextualize the larger narrative event, as well as the performative context. As a result, these debates produce political implications, some intended, others not. For example, in the anthropologist David Stoll's (1999) work, Menchú was forced to (re)legitimize herself in the world media as her Nobel Peace Prize was contested on the front pages of leading newspapers such as the *New York Times*.[3] Critically, as Wolf beautifully lays out for us in her rich case study of Jake Geldwert's testimony across three different moments, a problem with this genre is its tendency to homogenize and romanticize "the people" and "the people's voices" and to silence gender differences.

And like Wolf, I believe it is important to ask questions regarding the circulation and representations of these varied life histories, and in particular attend to the narrative trajectories that extend beyond the recounting of violence. Wolf marks the importance of focusing on her subject's postmigration stories. In doing so, her work breaks new ground as it writes against a romance of the prewar past and post-Holocaust survival. A critical direction for comparative work is a focus on the relationship between kin in migration stories. Wolf illustrates how in Geldwert's case, a pattern of exploitation by kin created material limitations for agentive moves and a great deal of suffering. A further comparative direction would be one that focuses on region. For example, what does postgenocidal migration in Ithaca, New York, look like when compared to Orthodox and ultra Orthodox Jewish migration to Brooklyn, where a religious enclave community flourishes (see Fader 2006). In my case I ask, with the transitions away from military rule and toward peace and democratic efforts, what happens to this

IRINA CARLOTA SILBER

narrative genre? Are testimonios transitional? Do they lose their meaning and strength and stop being "ideological weapons" precisely because the revolution is over, though social injustice is not (Beverley and Zimmerman 1990:206–7)? What do stories of personal, familial, and communal violence do outside of the solidarity movement in the context of reconstruction? I suggest that to answer these questions, understanding the context of tellings and retellings is critical. For example, much of my fieldwork in a former conflict zone and site of popular organizing in El Salvador involved listening to war stories of which I was both the intended and unintended audience. On one occasion, after hearing the story of a young mother brutally killed by her neighbors and paramilitary forces, Chavela, the narrator, said, "*Uno como ya lo vivió en carne propia, le da corazón duro. Ya lo vivió. Pero esa gente que viene, lloran cuanda se cuenta eso*" (Since we've lived it in our own flesh and blood, our heart gets hard. You've already lived it. But those people [internationals] who come here, they cry when we tell them this [story]).

In accord with Susan Gal's (1991) insistence that the ethnographic interview constitutes a linguistic practice in which the relationship between silence, speech, gender, and power must be taken into account, and where researchers must also be aware of and theorize their role in eliciting narratives and seek to find "conditions under which informants can talk" (191), a central aspect of pursuing this kind of research (for many) is the role of bearing witness. Wolf's work also provides an entrance into contested discussions of witnessing, as well as the limitations of communicating pain and suffering. She suggests that hearers become witnesses. As an international listener, I believe one of my obligations is to document the stories as they carry on the sacrifices of the dead for the living. Indeed, as Feitlowitz asserts, "among the most powerful connections forged by testimony are those that reunite the living" (1998:17). I also must theorize or interpret (for at least an academic audience) what these stories of past atrocities do. Did Chavela tell her story for my consumption and socialization as I fit the known category of *internacional*? Did she think I should have cried?

And it is to the coconstructed nature of the narratives Wolf discusses that I now turn. While she addresses the politics of her own location, an interesting issue to consider may be the role of an unintended audience. In several places, Wolf hints at the role Jeannette, Jake Geldwert's wife, has in shaping her husband's stories. Moreover, because my own research has pointed to questions of the socialization of the next generation of Salvadorans by those who are still healing from more than a decade of military repression, I wonder about the couple's children and grandchildren. While Wolf shows us Geldwert's series of contextually defined regrets in raising his children in terms of religiosity, it would be interesting to know the ways in which his narratives intersect with those of his kin, to learn what gets told across generations. Perhaps a multigenerational oral history project may provide a vehicle to contest what Wolf aptly identifies in Steven Spielberg's Shoah Visual History Foundation project as the creation of a post-memory focusing on Jewish persecution and ultimately feeding into the construction of Jewish victims.

Hidden Children, Disappeared Children

The essays in this section reflect a concern with narrative, language, and positioned interpretations. Like Wolf's and Gerson's work, Vromen's article provides us with an understudied dimension of the Holocaust that seeks to write against notions of prototypical survivors and to give voice to the range of experiences that she marks as historically silenced. Her focus on the various actors (the children, parents, clergy, resistance members), and their recollections, involved in hiding children in convents throughout Belgium has both theoretical and methodological implications. Indeed, in anthropology there has been a recent turn to attend to the agency of children and childhood itself. Work on children and political violence may prove an interesting direction for further comparisons as it underscores how children are makers of history and culture, not just receptacles of adult society. As Coles (1986) has observed, children do have a political life. Vromen begins to shed light on this as she discusses former hidden children's desire to inscribe the Gentiles who aided them into a history through commemoration. In doing so, Vromen is careful to not represent a story of resilience against all odds, but one in which identities are fluid and contested.

I think here of the critical work done by the search for disappeared children in El Salvador. La Asociación Pro-Búsqueda de Niñas y Niños Desaparecidos has found over 170 children systematically separated from their families in counterinsurgency campaigns during the war (Asociación Pro-Búsqueda de Niñas y Niños Desaparecidos 2001). In some cases, children were placed in orphanages after massacres, in other instances, they were adopted by military and elite Salvadoran families, and in many cases, they were adopted internationally (e.g., by families in the United States, Australia, or Italy). The work of reuniting these children, now teenagers and young adults, with their biological families is perhaps the most hopeful locus for reconciliation in El Salvador. As one of the founders of this organization explains, "What is important for these youth is to find a way to make peace with the past so that it stop weighing upon the present with all of its weight" (Asociación Pro-Búsqueda de Niñas y Niños Desaparecidos 2001:259). As a found adolescent girl articulates it, "I feel as though only someone who has lived what I have lived will understand me and I will understand that person as well. I know that we speak the same language. It gives us strength to share our history" (qtd. in Asociación Pro-Búsqueda de Niñas y Niños Desaparecidos 2001:286–87). In Vromen's work, it would be interesting to hear some of the (retrospective) voices of the children and of the clergy, for example.

Finally, Vromen's piece lends itself well to comparative and historical work on the role of the church in Latin America as it points to the importance of looking at hierarchy and gender. For example, much has been written on the workings of liberation theology and its support for progressive social movements as evidenced in the training of lay catechists priests and its emphasis on the preferential option for the poor.

From Scholarship to Pedagogy

In these essays we see a powerful call for stories, for the contextualized words of variously positioned survivors of the Holocaust. The scholarship of Gerson, Wolf, and Vromen decenters a master narrative of the Holocaust and of post-Holocaust Jewish life. Through the lived experiences of actors, this work links up to larger theoretical issues—including that on diaspora, the politics of memory, and the terrain of social justice. The significance of these theoretical issues also has practical implications for our pedagogy. For example, in my teaching of both political violence and social movements in Latin America, the Holocaust comes up in interesting and important ways. When I assign texts by Primo Levi, such as *Survival in Auschwitz* (Primo [1958] 1996) in conjunction with ethnographies of political violence in Guatemala, Argentina, and other countries, the Holocaust stands as the marker of suffering and the model for the search for justice. At times, this creates a problematic attempt to hierarchize atrocity and crimes against humanity. Undergraduate students in particular often enter social science courses with knowledge on the Holocaust made available to them through popular culture representations of this time period. Simultaneously, their awareness of post-Holocaust life, of the Jewish diaspora through time, and of contemporary and global instances of genocide and political violence often remain quite limited. A volume such as the present one both amplifies our understanding of the historical period of World War II and broadens the comparative questions we can ask. Moreover, it fits well with an engaged research practice attentive to degrees of agency and suffering as it asks readers to witness experiences and agendas that typically fall outside of metanarratives (Silber 2004).

Notes

1. Interview by the author, October 1997. All unmarked translations from Spanish to English throughout the essay are mine.
2. In March 2003, the U.S. Immigration and Naturalization Service (INS) became part of the Department of Homeland Security (DHS) as the U.S. Citizenship and Immigration Services (USCIS).
3. For an excellent volume that presents multiple perspectives on this debate see *The Risoberta Menchu Controversy*, edited by Arturo Arias (Minneapolis: University of Minnesota Press, 2001).

Historicizing and Locating Testimonies

ETHEL BROOKS

What are the social meanings and implications of memories, histories, and testimonies about the Holocaust within and for a post-Holocaust era? How do understandings that have particular familial, local, national, and cultural inflections locally and nationally get picked up and interpreted within the realm of the global? What is gained and what is lost in transnational, cross-cultural circulations of images, representations, histories, memories, and testimonies? What role does capitalist modernity—read often as globalization—and its reproduction as U.S.-centrism play in forming representations of the Holocaust and of post-Holocaust lives? What role does it play in forming those of other types of oppression, violence, and loss? Of other genocides? Of the lives people lead in their aftermath? Can we theorize the role that production and consumption practices at once local, national, transnational, and global play in shaping our notions of memory, history, testimony, and their meanings over time? How are memories and representations of the Holocaust and of post-Holocaust life particularly gendered, classed, raced, and nation-based?

The three articles that I address in this commentary—"*In Cuba I Was a German Shepherd*: Questions of Comparison and Generalizability in Holocaust Memoirs" by Judith M. Gerson, "Collective Memory and Cultural Politics: Narrating and Commemorating the Rescue of Jewish Children by Belgian Convents during the Holocaust" by Suzanne Vromen, and "Holocaust Testimony: Producing Post-memories, Producing Identities" by Diane L. Wolf—consider these and other questions important both for a scholarly exploration of the Holocaust and post-Holocaust life and for studies of globalization, the use of memory and testimony, gender studies, nationalism, and the meanings of citizenship. All shed light on various aspects of history, memory, and testimony; all explore alternative ways of representing histories of the Holocaust; and all are in conversation with each other about immigration, identity, and the role of the everyday in a sociology of the Holocaust and the post-Holocaust period.

The authors open up Holocaust research temporally, in their look at the post-Holocaust era, spatially, in their focus on areas outside of Germany, and conceptually, by asking questions that are comparative in nature, in intriguing ways. My own research looks at the current antisweatshop movement and at transnational campaigns for worker's rights through their effects on the shop floors and neighborhoods that are their focus. In my work, based on fieldwork among mostly women garment workers in Bangladesh, El Salvador, and New York City, I explore the ways in which local meanings and testimonies of work, everyday life, and of exploitation and oppression get reproduced and translated in the realm of the transnational. Questions of representation, of Otherness, class, ethnicity, gender, of local relations, and of citizenship come up against and are worked through the dominance of consumption paradigms, corporate media, and the discourse of the global. One of the most salient questions that has emerged from my work, and that can be asked in studies of the Holocaust and of post-Holocaust life, is: What relation do global circulations of stories, images, and histories have to everyday relations—in homes, workplaces, and communities—in struggles for social justice and in reclaiming the agency of the garment workers, of Holocaust survivors, of immigrants, and of those who hear these stories and experience the testimonies secondhand, as history?

Memories, Stories, and Commodities

In order to consider this question, I think the work of Paul Gilroy (1993) in *The Black Atlantic* might prove helpful. Gilroy argues that there existed within the abolitionist movement an intellectual division of labor, with sympathetic "white commentators who articulated the metaphysical core of simple, factual slave narratives," and that, with the work of Frederick Douglass and others, "a new discursive economy emerges with the refusal to subordinate the particularity of the slave experience to the totalizing power of universal reason held exclusively by white hands, pens, or publishing houses" (69). In my own work, and in the work of the authors in these pages, we see scholarship that takes such divisions of labor into consideration, that provides a critique of the class, ethnic, and gendered dimensions of narrative control and the circulation of testimony, and looks at how the relations among publishing houses, movie studios, museums, and other media outlets influence the ways in which representations—of slavery, exploitation on the shop floor, and the Holocaust and post-Holocaust life—are carried out.

This exploration leads also to other questions that the scholars in this section are attempting to address. What effects does the push to consume history, memory, and culture—as an aspect of U.S. hegemony and globalization—have on representations of people, of suffering, and of trauma? Borrowing from Gayatri Spivak (1988), we might ask what kinds of epistemic violence are enacted in the attempt to bring to the foreground a true subaltern narrative that would help scholars and others who have not lived through the Holocaust to "know" the experience? Who controls the circulation of memory? Who is in a privileged position to disseminate it? Finally, who is in the position to claim agency? The authors in this section point to ways in which these questions can be answered, from Gerson's consideration of the uses of comparison and generalizability to Vromen's study of hidden children in Belgian convents to Wolf's exploration of familial practices and the problematics of family unification for survivors.

Gerson's work addresses a number of difficult issues such as transnationality, immigration, and the legacies of war and regimes of terror. In her look at people's memoirs of migration, and by taking seriously their own self-conception as immigrants, refugees, or survivors, she emphasizes the importance of the every-day and of people's lives in examining the meaning of "big" issues. In this way, Gerson is salvaging kinds of histories that often remain untold in the historiography of the Holocaust. The pre-1941 immigrants often differentiate among those who are immigrants, meaning those who arrived before 1941, refugees, those who arrived after 1941, and survivors, those who lived through the concentration camps. As Gerson points out: "If immigrants respect the suffering of survivors, the term of current use in this period of significant public acknowledgment of the Holocaust, and survivors remain comparatively silent about their traumas, immigrants may find it difficult to speak, thereby inadvertently contributing to their own invisibility" (Gerson this volume: 119).

By bringing forth these narratives, and rendering their writers more visible, Gerson is able to document some of the everyday aspects of the terror of Nazism and the Holocaust that came before the implementation of the Final Solution. She is also able to highlight the agency, alongside the legacies of Nazi terror, of the people at the center of her analysis. Furthermore, Gerson reminds us that not only do the memoir writers she looks at use comparison as a way of understanding their own life experiences; but those very experiences can in some ways serve as bases for comparison for phenomena seen as emblematic of the current period of globalization and empire, such as multisited migration, transnational subjectivity, and an understanding of how people deal with terror and other kinds of trauma.

Vromen's research weaves together a number of complex narratives that shed new light on our understanding of the Holocaust and post-Holocaust life. In her piece, Vromen looks at the experiences of nuns and other clergy, hidden children, and the resistance fighters who hid them in Belgian convents over the course of the war. She discusses the feelings of security experienced by the hidden children, felt in contrast to the chaos of their lives before their removal from home, and the conflicts that often occurred at the end of the war with their families over religious practice. In this way, Vromen opens up the traditional periodization of the Holocaust in order to explore it as part of life histories that encompass questions of daily routine, religious practice, and familial relations.

Vromen points to the agency of the lower clergy in her study, looking at the "logistics of running the convents," at who knew that the children were Jewish, and at the everyday heroism practiced in sheltering the children from persecution and death. Vromen's analysis would benefit from the insights put forth in Danielle Juteau's (1999) analysis of the role of nuns in the constitution of the gendered nation. This might help shed some light on one question that Vromen asked her informants, namely, "why the Church had not officially recognized what the convents had done during the war. Why, for instance, were there no plaques on convents where Jewish children had been hidden?"

By pairing Vromen's work with the other articles in this section, a number of potentially fruitful questions arise: Who were the children? Were they from Belgian Jewish families, or was Belgium one of their sites of migration since the rise of the Nazis? For the time during and after the war, Vromen gives us a view of the conflicts and confusion around the children's religious attitudes, but given the work of Gerson, Wolf, and others in this volume, it would be interesting to consider their feelings of national and family affiliation during and after their years spent in Belgian convents. Where did they go afterwards? All in all, Vromen's work opens up some fascinating questions for further scholarship on the role of religion in the resistance movement, on subaltern agential practices in the Holocaust and their implications for post-Holocaust life, and on questions of gender and nationalism in the study of the Holocaust, resistance, and subjectivity.

Wolf's work points us to the importance of narratives, testimonies, and everyday lives as lived during and after the Holocaust. Wolf's article analyzes the testimonies of a Holocaust survivor over the course of several years, someone whose ethnography she had taken in 1980 in preparation for carrying out fieldwork in Java among a different population with different life stories and histories. When she interviewed him again in 1996, the survivor, Jake Geldwert, had told his story publicly only very recently, when it was videotaped for the archives of Steven Spielberg's Shoah Visual History Foundation (VHF). In her discussion of Geldwert's migration decisions, his family memories before the war, his relations after the war, and of the ways in which his testimonies changed in their retelling, Wolf is doing the important work of recovering the subaltern subject-effect by showing how Geldwert's testimonies serve to disrupt and complicate the accepted pattern of testimonials in the Holocaust literature.

Wolf, in her telling of her subject's story, situates it, giving it a richer and more contradictory context in relation to his family, work, decisions, and his feelings about his past and present. This is a very different mode of storytelling and analysis than that pursued by the VHF: Wolf also covers Geldwert's postwar life in the United States, from, in her words, "extreme exploitation, exploitation by kin, the prevention of pursuing a religious life by kin, all in addition to successful adaptation, irony, discontent, sadness and possibilities lost" (Wolf this volume: 171). The Spielberg project focuses on Geldwert's life during the war, and, as Wolf puts it, "creates a clearer division between right and wrong, between victims and perpetrators, and offers a more linear view: from obliteration to regeneration, from destruction to redemption, and from destitution to success" (Wolf this volume: 171). Through Wolf's analysis, we can better understand the implications of the project that creates the Spielbergian progress narrative and put forth a critique of the politics of dissemination, periodization, family and gender relations, and the complexities of immigration and assimilation. Furthermore, Wolf's discussion of Geldwert's story and its Spielbergization problematizes the importance and meaning of memory—what kind, to whom, and in which period —and its legacies in the practice of sociology, historiography, and in the creation of a collective notion of "what happened." Finally, by highlighting the importance of testimonials to Holocaust histories, and pointing out the equally central role of *testimonios* in Latin American histories of terror, disappearances, suffering, and genocide, Wolf also shows us a way to compare without trivializing.

Testimony, Agency, and Modernity

In my work, I find that narratives and testimonios by garment workers—a term borrowed rhetorically from wartime testimonios as a way to talk about suffering—shift depending on audience, repetition, and context. The shaping and recounting of testimony is also a product of the agency of the person making the testimony, though structured, among other things, by narrative conventions and by the kinds of questions asked of the teller. Often, the women garment workers I spoke to talked about how they knew which narratives of their lives and experiences were expected at which time. Is it possible to discern the audience(s) of memory at particular times, in particular situations and spaces? What happens when the audiences have not participated in the shaping of collective memory? When the receivers of history are part of global circuits, transnational audiences, and the effects of commodity culture? Conversely, how are the national, the transnational, and the global brought into, and how do they influence, the particular memories of, for example, the hidden children several decades later? In what ways do hegemonic national or globalized and commodified representations of the Holocaust inform these local memories? What informs social and family memories? Is there a split between global representations and the work of individual and collective memory making? Is there something about this particular moment in history that has made projects such as the VHF, or the Holocaust memorials and museums throughout the world, possible?

Wolf's and others' scholarship mark an important shift that focuses on the sociology of both the Holocaust and of post-Holocaust lives precisely because, as their work shows, it points to an examination of individual agency, the negotiation of collective memory making, and the importance of the everyday and everyday people. I wonder if it would be useful to extend that analysis to explore more fully the gendered, sexualized, and classed effects of the disruptions experienced by pre-1941 immigrants, survivors, hidden children, and, perhaps, the clergy discussed by Vromen and the disruptions experienced by other victims of the Holocaust, such as the Roma, among other communities. Both Wolf's and Gerson's work offers important steps toward thinking about the ways in which memory is worked through local, national, and international contexts and the politics of memory in a larger sociological context.

Currency, Periodization, and Other Histories

By maintaining the categories of *survivor, victim,* and *perpetrator,* and by bounding the history of the Holocaust so as not to include post-Holocaust life and lives, we constitute the Holocaust as what Timothy Mitchell (2000) calls the "constitutive outside of modernity" (15–16)—modernity's contained Other. The three authors in this section shed light on the ways in which family, everyday life, and meaning have been maintained, negotiated, called into question, and have sometimes fallen apart in light of Holocaust and post-Holocaust trauma, loss, disruption, and survival.

A sociological examination of the Holocaust and of post-Holocaust life proves especially hopeful if it leads to a recognition of the plight of Turkish Germans, Roma, or Palestinians in the current period, and to an expansion of mourning, remembrance, and the celebration of survival that could be embraced by people the world over. Such recognition and remembrance would, in some ways, defy the logic of capital accumulation, commodification, and the violence of the nation-state to bring us to a common place. Sociological explorations in the manner of those performed by Gerson, Vromen, and Wolf could provide answers to the current decontextualization and dehistoricization of the Holocaust, and the common erasure of post-Holocaust life, through transnational capital circulations. This work could potentially bring the histories of the Holocaust, of its survivors, and of its effects on events, places, and people in other times and places to the forefront in order to help us understand, and avoid, racialized and sexualized national persecution, as well as the othering of Jews, Muslims, Roma, queer people, women, blacks, and of any other groups not assimilated into a hegemonic model of whiteness, patriarchy, and heteronormativity. This could also lead scholars to explore more fully whether the racist stereotypes that condemned Jews and Gypsies in the Holocaust are now being reconfigured in ways that help us turn a blind, or perhaps weary, eye to genocides in Bosnia, Rwanda, Guatemala, against Muslims in India, and against Roma in many parts of present-day Europe.

The treatment of memories, histories, memoirs, and post-memory by Gerson, Vromen, and Wolf help to point us in the right direction in order to take on the difficult propositions outlined above, and to begin to answer some pressing, often problematic, questions. Poststructuralist theorists such as Gayatri Spivak or Jacques Derrida warn us that the apparent seamlessness of memories as histories would call for the act of deconstruction in order to examine the politics and meanings of precisely those seams and gaps that a historical or collective memory narrative would conceal. In my own work, I explore the ways in which oppression and various historical phenomena can have different meanings and effects at any particular time or location, depending on everyday practice, representation, and struggle. By thinking through how various meanings, epistemological legacies, and everyday practices inflect our understanding of the Holocaust and of post-Holocaust life, the authors in this section have pushed us to consider these phenomena sociologically, so that they resonate more clearly historically, narratively, and for our understanding of collective memory and people's experiences of the everyday.

IMMIGRATION AND TRANSNATIONAL PRACTICES

In "Immigration and Transnational Practices," part 4 of the current collection, the contributions cover decidedly different Jewish immigration streams—one due to Hitler's ascendancy, another due to the push to remove Jews from the former Soviet Union, and one forming a new category of Jewish transnationals who operate in multiple sites within the global economy. Rhonda Levine's essay, drawn from her book *Class, Networks, and Identity: Replanting Jewish Lives from Nazi Germany to Rural New York* (2001) complements Judith Gerson's previous article on German Jewish refugees. Using a political economy approach, Levine demonstrates how rural German Jews moved to rural New York in the 1930s and within a relatively short span of time took over the cattle-dealing business, as well as milk production. It is very much an untold story about another kind of German Jewry—the approximately 20 percent of rural petit bourgeois German Jews who lived and worked in small agrarian villages before Hitler's rise to power. Concentrating on their resettlement in the United States, Levine finds that these refugees managed to maintain their previous occupation, something few immigrants experienced then or even now. The enclave they established in central New York provided the socioeconomic infrastructure that shaped their lives and their work, and sustained their collective identities as German Jews. At the same time, Levine is careful to point out that ethnic networks are not necessarily a panacea and can also create problematic and highly exploitative work environments for coethnics (also see Wolf in this volume).

Kathie Friedman's research on Jews from the former Soviet Union (FSU) analyzes the identity strategies that both first and second generations utilize once in the United States. While mainstream research on American Jews measures identity in static terms, Friedman explores the more complex and nuanced aspects of Russian Jewish American identities. Russian Jewish immigrants tend to see their nationality as Jewish but their culture and faith as a choice (Gold 1995a). Most arrived in the United States with little interest in the Jewish religion. Friedman's research deepens our understanding of the new second generation by illuminating how a group seen as white and European actually consists of those struggling with their identities within American discourses of diversity and multiculturalism. Furthermore, this new addition to American Jewry identifies little with American Jews, and that clearly poses some challenges to any notion of a collective American Jewish voice. Friedman points to an important paradox relevant for other immigrant and refugee groups: how does one deal with a homeland identity when the homeland has vanished in political and juridical terms and a new homeland has been reconstructed? Her chapter constitutes no less than a call for comparative work in immigration studies and the new second generation.

Steven Gold's essay on post-Holocaust Jewish immigration focuses on the shift from mainly refugee status before and immediately after the war to the contemporary phenomenon of transnationalism. In other words, Gold distinguishes between the Jewish immigrants discussed in Judith Gerson's, Diane Wolf's, and Rhonda Levine's contributions—who fled to the United States as refugees or as displaced persons—and contemporary Jewish immigrants who live as transnationals gliding through the global economy. In the 1980s, at the height of Jewish immigration from the Soviet Union, there was pressure for them to settle in Israel. Yet many of these Jews then left Israel to come to the United States. Gold points out that there has been a shift in the general Israeli view of Israelis who emigrate, from condemnation to understanding. Due to a number of domestic and global factors, highly educated Israelis (including Jews from the former Soviet Union) may leave for the United States, where they are now welcomed. Indeed, with no clear resolution in sight between Israel and the Palestinians, emigration has become more inviting to Israelis. Contemporary Jews are more transnational in their orientation and practices than were their ancestors, which suggests less uniformity in identities.

Richard Alba articulates the significance of these essays to immigration research, centering on the question of the paradigmatic status of Jewish immigration. His particular interest lies in the processes of incorporation, and he interprets the authors' emphases on the characteristics of immigrant groups as a corrective to traditional immigration research that stressed the features of receiving communities. In Levine's study of cattle dealers, Alba notes the importance of human capital resources, an inability to plan their migration, relatively large numbers of middle-aged (rather than younger) immigrants, and dense racial-ethnic immigrant networks in a region in which dairy farming was declining as explanatory of the cattle dealers' success. Years later, their children left their families' farms, seeking their livelihoods elsewhere, thereby breaking the link between ethnic entrepreneurship and ethnic preservation.

By contrast, Gold's study of contemporary Israeli immigrants draws Alba's attention to the importance of transnationalism and diasporic identities. Faced with choices about where to immigrate and armed with expanded knowledge about those locations, immigrants now rationally assess their options about where to live and recognize that their migration decisions may not be permanent. Citing Gold's finding that contemporary Jewish immigrants rely less on settlement agencies and social networks than their earlier counterparts, Alba stresses the significance of these data and interprets their implications in terms of greater autonomy and individual control over resettlement and identity redefinition. Although Jews were among the early transnational groups with diasporic identities (rather than nationally circumscribed ones), Alba argues that they remain distinct from contemporary transnationals because they are unlikely to return home or sustain ties to their homelands. Alba wonders if the consequences of transnationalism affect only first-generation immigrants and if their children's and grandchildren's identities are influenced by groups closer to them. This generational divide is evident as well among the children of immigrants in Friedman's study of nominally Jewish immigrants from the former Soviet Union. Young 1.5 and second-generation immigrants select from locally available resources in American culture and their memories of Russia filtered through their parents to define themselves—a process Alba interprets as commensurate with American individualism. When read together, the main chapters in this section lead Alba to conclude that Jews may not be the exceptional ethnic group sociologists have assumed. Despite a unique integration of religion and ethnicity, a diasporic consciousness, and a history of survival, Jews also embody the very patterns visible among other immigrant groups on resettlement.

Yen Espiritu situates the foregoing articles in the larger literatures on immigration, which until recently had maintained rather limited understandings of immigrants' modes of incorporation. Previous theories of assimilation, the melting pot, and cultural pluralism all stress immigrant adaptation and native-born reactions. More recently, scholars have opened up these discussions, concentrating on appropriately more complex ideas of circuits and networks, suggesting that immigrants transform the places in which they settle, bringing with them a range of transnational resources. She reminds us that Jewish immigrants are "twice-minorities" and frequently "twice-immigrants," having been excluded in their homelands and again on resettlement, often having resettled in new lands more than once. As such, Jewish immigrants are comparable to other twice-minorities and twice-immigrants, and it remains for future researchers to consider the questions emanating from a historical comparative approach. Espiritu suggests one approach to this comparison as she considers the racial middleness of American Jews and Asian Americans, both intermediate groups. The double vision that derives from being in a structurally liminal position and attendant associations with a "model minority" speak to important research questions concerning the links between racial and immigrant statuses within a particular racial/ethnic formation of sending and receiving nations and local milieus.

In the Land of Milk and Cows:
Rural German Jewish Refugees and
Post-Holocaust Adaptation

RHONDA F. LEVINE

This article shows how post-Holocaust studies can be informed by sociology and in turn can contribute to debates in sociology concerning immigrant adaptation in the United States. It does so through a brief presentation of my detailed case study of a little-known group of rural German Jewish refugees from Nazi Germany who were able to rebuild their lives in rural south-central New York between the late 1930s and 1980, maintaining a Jewish identity while residing in small towns and villages with very few Jews. The essay explains how the changing structure of the milk industry made it possible for these refugees to use their business skills and ethnic network connections to resume the profession of cattle dealing that their families had practiced for generations in rural Germany, far from the urban centers in which better-known German Jews had briefly flourished as scholars and bankers (Levine 2001).

The study makes use of what is called the extended case method. Unlike traditional case studies, which tend not to be based on theoretical concerns, or else focus on testing a specific theory-derived hypothesis, the extended case method draws on an existing theory to frame the particular case and then uses the results of the study to reconstruct the theory. The method is useful for examining how particular social situations are shaped by external forces, and in turn shape them. That is, it attempts to connect the microworld of the individual, family, or group with the macroworld of the social structure (Burawoy 1991). More graphically, it is a way to look at the intersection of biography and history

(Mills 1959). Based on this method, my study of how German Jewish cattle dealers successfully transplanted their lives into rural south-central New York suggests that a theory emphasizing the interactions among three factors—the economic opportunity structure at the time of immigration, the immigrants' class-based resources, and the nature of the immigrants' ethnic networks—can explain the patterns of adaptation, mobility, and identity formation that have been found for a wide range of immigrant and refugee groups.

This particular extended case study uses two methods for collecting and analyzing data. The first method is ethnographic in nature. Unstructured interviews with elderly German Jews who left Germany in the late 1930s and their adult children provide rich data on how their lives unfolded in both Germany and the United States. Over forty unstructured interviews were conducted that lasted from one and a half to over two hours. Approximately twenty additional interviews were conducted for a shorter time and were structured around specific aspects of the interviewees' lives. Several follow-up interviews were also conducted to gain a clearer understanding of specific aspects of the longer, more in-depth interviews, such as the nature of cattle dealing, or to further probe points raised in the initial interview that needed elaboration as the research progressed. The use of unstructured and follow-up interviews allowed me to insert myself in my subjects' world instead of subjecting them to answering a set of standardized questions.

Second, the study uses primary records such as documents in the American Jewish Archives, particularly the records of the Baron de Hirsch Fund and the Jewish Agricultural Society, to provide cross-referencing material to the interviews that better reveal the role of organizations and institutions in the migration and resettlement processes. In addition, a number of primary documents from federal, state, and local government agencies are utilized to grasp the changing nature of the milk and dairy industry in New York and thereby sketch out the contours of the larger political economy in which the German Jewish refugees became embedded.

Several new and interesting findings emerged from the overall study, including the many ways in which Nazism and the migration to the United States altered gender roles and the unique role played by women in managing the transition to the new country, in helping their husbands accumulate capital, and in recreating a German Jewish community and passing on a Jewish identity to their children. The present essay, however, focuses its attention on the factors that account for German Jewish success and eventual dominance in cattle dealing

RHONDA F. LEVINE

in one particular region in New York. That is, it concentrates on the economic adaptations of the men and only secondarily discusses the manner in which ethnic identity was reinforced by occupational concentration. The more complete picture, including the ways in which these families were able to recreate a German Jewish community, maintain their religious identities, and help their children create an American Jewish identity, can be found in my book-length report on the case (Levine 2001).

Cattle Dealing and German Jews

THE POLITICAL ECONOMY OF MILK:
A NEW OPPORTUNITY STRUCTURE

While at one time the number one dairy state in the country, New York was second only to Wisconsin in the production of fluid milk from the 1930s though the 1970s (Conneman 1970). The dairy industry, particularly the fluid milk market, went through considerable changes in this period. Transformations in the milk industry and the consequential transformations in the nature of dairy farming in New York State proved significant for the development of a business opportunity for German Jewish cattle dealers looking to return to their business in the late 1930s and early 1940s.

Simply put, the growth of cities and the expansion of the urban population, particularly the New York metropolitan area, as well as the development of the railroad in the mid-nineteenth century saw the beginning of a fluid milk market. The demand for milk and milk products increased during World War II and brought with it increased production to meet the demand at relatively high prices paid to producers. The end of the war brought temporary milk surpluses shortly offset by population growth and increased urbanization. The growing New York–New Jersey metropolitan market, coupled with large-scale suburbanization in the 1950s and 1960s, led to a decline in local sources of milk. Dairy farms in northern New Jersey and Long Island, and in communities adjacent to New York City, went out of business due to suburbanization and attending higher land values, so milk dealers had to rely on upstate dairy farms as their primary source for fluid milk.

German Jewish cattle dealers therefore had the good fortune to enter the market at a very propitious time. By the 1940s, changes in dairying, specifically the fluid milk industry, were set in motion. With increased competition for milk, dairy farmers wanted to be assured of a good, steady supply of milk to sell.

Although there were cattle dealers operating in the region, the number of farms was plentiful enough to allow for easy entry and provide a decent market for the newcomers. Even with the new opportunities available, native cattle dealers do not seem to have expanded their businesses. For reasons that become apparent in the next section, the German Jews appear to have been better able to take advantage of the new opportunities.

Although many dairy farmers bred their own milk cows, most of them also dealt with cattle dealers. There was always a need for replacement cows, especially better and more productive milk cows. It takes two years for a calf to come of age to lactate, and there was no guarantee that the cow would prove a good milker. In some instances, and depending on the price of feed at any particular time, the cost of maintaining the cow for a two-year period before it milked was higher than the cost to purchase an already milking cow. By the 1940s, with a growing fluid milk market and high prices paid to producers for fluid milk, farmers were induced to improve their efficiency in producing quality milk. Even farmers who bred their own cows in a time of market expansion found themselves in need for more and better milk cows. As dairy farmers faced greater competition and were driven by the market to increase productivity and lower the costs of production, productive cows ("good milkers") offered the key to survival.

CLASS RESOURCES: RAISING CAPITAL, KNOWING COWS, EXTENDING CREDIT

How were German Jewish cattle dealers able to break into the market and eventually dominate cattle dealing in the region? The first answer to this query lies in the class resources the cattle dealers brought from earlier successful careers in Germany, built with the guidance of fathers, uncles, and grandfathers. These resources made it possible for them to accumulate capital and offer multiple services to small farmers. Skill in raising capital constituted one crucial dimension of their class resources. Two other intertwined dimensions also proved critical: they had an incredibly detailed knowledge of cows, as well as an intuitive cultural understanding of the long-term economic value that accrues to all parties through the extension of credit. The knowledge of cows made it possible for them to offer a superior product, and their understanding of credit made it possible for them to help delay the demise of small dairy farms for at least a few decades.

Initial entry into the cattle-dealing business took very little capital investment, but it did take an understanding of capital and the ability to raise it. As one wife of a cattle dealer put it, all that was needed to begin to build accounts was a truck, but a wealth of class knowledge and confidence underlies such a comment. While she worked as a domestic in Poughkeepsie, her husband went to a small nearby town and rented a hotel room, slowly accumulating enough accounts and money to eventually buy a farm and settle permanently in the area. He would travel around in his truck, stopping at farms he would pass on the road, and try to sell the farmer a new milk cow. The dealer would start the business relationship by buying a cow that was no longer milking from the farmer, and then sell that cow to a slaughterhouse as beef. With the money from the sale, he would in turn buy a good milking cow and sell it to a dairy farmer in need of a replacement. Since he did not farm as yet, he would buy and sell cows on the same day. In a relatively short period of time, though, he had enough cash to move from his hotel room, rent a farm, and have his wife join him. Within a year, he bought his own farm and built a prosperous cattle-dealing business, with his wife helping by becoming his bookkeeper.

For other cattle dealers, their wives played a direct role in the accumulation of the necessary capital. Several women contributed economically to their husband's business through the establishment of their own business: operating summer guesthouses. As one son commented, "and actually it was out of necessity more than their love of it because they left [Germany] without anything and they were trying to make something of themselves. . . . Any money they accumulated, they would put in a cookie jar and if my father had to buy a cow, that's how it helped him."

This same son further reflected on how his father began to establish accounts:

People began [in the 1940s] to realize that their livelihood was coming out of the dairy barn. So they began to want better quality cattle. At the same time, they didn't take the animal that wasn't producing well and put it in their freezer. They decided that the animal had some value and my father used to go in and say, "OK, I'll send a cow to you." And he would take a cow there and would take two cows back [cows that were not producing well] and my father would take them to the slaughterhouse and then bring two cows back [to the farmer] and then he would say "OK you owe me." And pretty soon these accounts got bigger and bigger and farms began to grow. . . . the German cattle dealer was there to move the cow in and out of the marketplace.

Although initial entry into the business took little capital investment, cattle dealers had to possess a great deal of business skills that went beyond knowledge of the business itself to include knowledge of milk cows. A cattle dealer, still dealing today, reflected on the unique business skills and knowledge of cows that aided German Jewish cattle dealers in establishing accounts and building a business, and more specifically, being able to compete with the already existing cattle dealers in the area. When asked how he was able to break into the business and if there were many cattle dealers already working in the area, he replied:

Oh yes, There were quite a few of them. There was also a lot of non-Jews dealing at the time. In fact, when I went to my banker who didn't know me from Adam I got the loan—he trusted me somehow. And I said "Now that you got me the farm, now you got to loan me money so I can buy cows and sell cows." He said, "Listen, cow business is maybe 20 dealers in the area and they are all starving to death. How can you deal cows?" I said, "Because I'm a professional." So you go to the farmer—he don't know you. Show the animal. "I guarantee it. It's got to be like I say it is or I pick it up and you don't own it." That's how we started. [We] were more used to it from the old country. In the old country, you had to work very hard because there were so many [cattle dealers] in the business. Aggressive and also pretty smart in their business ways of doing it. And they used the same tactics here. Once you established your name, it was easy. Because the people found out that you were not going to cheat them . . . that you are not going to cheat them and they dealt with you.

He went on to explain how the German Jewish cattle dealers had to prove themselves to the local dairy farmers:

You had to prove yourself. I had a neighbor up here. He wouldn't deal with a Jew . . . he didn't know nothing about Jewish people. And I went in there one day and I said "I'm going to sell you a couple of cows. And you come down and pick them out" and I said "I don't want no money—you milk them a week and if you're satisfied, you pay me. If you are not satisfied, I will come and get them and we're the same friends." And he never dealt with nobody else again.

German Jewish cattle dealers not only knew cows but they were persistent dealers and conducted business in similar ways as they, and the generations of Jewish cattle dealers that preceded them, did in Germany. One non-Jewish dairy farmer remembered how his father and a German Jewish cattle dealer would transact a deal. He said that the cattle dealer would always come by at milking time, because they were sure to find the farmer in the barn, and they would come in and say, "what are you keeping her for?" He explained that his "father liked to wheel and deal as much as [the cattle dealer]." He further stated how he remembers the cattle dealer coming into the barn and that his mother did not like to see him because his father got to talking with the dealer and then the work would not get done. In his words, "They would argue over the price of a cow. And it was like who was going to win, you know? [The cattle dealer] would go out the door, and I would see him going in and out three or four times at one time, you know. They would get mad and [the dealer] would leave and I said to my brother, he would be back. Then he would come back. And they would make a deal." A daughter of a cattle dealer remembers similar scenes when she would sometimes go with her father to sell a cow to a dairy farmer. In her words, "They would talk for hours and argue about cows and they either bought them or they didn't."

Without a doubt, the extension of credit constituted a key element that accounted for German Jewish cattle dealers building accounts and expanding their business. However, the dealer could only extend credit if he had ample capital to cover costs. Much of this capital came from women's economic activities. Not only did the extension of credit allow many small and medium-scale dairy farmers to increase their supply of milk but the cattle dealers, reminiscent of their experience and practice in Germany, oftentimes gave better rates than the banks and in some cases extended credit to farmers who had difficulty receiving a bank loan. Some cattle dealers held mortgages for farmers. They not only sold farmers cows on credit but land too, and even machinery. As a Jewish dairy farmer put it: "In one way, the Jewish cattle dealers were sort of popular. They would finance farmers. Not only for cows, but for farms. Some cattle dealers even financed other cattle dealers to help them get started. But once you were financed, you were dependent on them." Cattle dealers saw it a bit differently. One cattle dealer describes how he started his business, one that became one of the largest cattle-dealing businesses in New York State, in the following way:

The cattle business was 90 percent a credit based business and the farmers we trusted them and they trusted us. Within two months [after I started dealing cattle again since Germany] I had 20 farms that had accounts. And I sold maybe 20 or 30 cows on a note and they were supposed to pay one-third in the milk check. Say they made $1,000 milk check, they paid $333 a month to me. That's how they established credit. That's how they became, most of them, good farmers and after a few years, they owned their own farm. . . . The cows I sold them . . . I looked after the people like I would look after myself. I would never put anything over on anybody. . . . If I didn't look out for my customers I wouldn't have no business.

As it had in Germany, the nature of the cattle-dealing business, especially the extension of credit, lead to ambivalent relationships between farmer and dealer, with the farmer sometimes becoming obligated to the dealer, the dealer needing customers to remain in business, and both trying to get the best deal. And although "deals" generally benefit all parties concerned if they work out, not all exchanges are equal. For example, receiving credit may have helped farmers improve their herd, and even buy land and machinery, but it also meant even greater profits for the cattle dealer. According to one cattle dealer, "there were a few farmers that would isolate the Jewish dealers. They would say 'A Jew came here and I told him I didn't have nothing' that sort of thing. They used to say, 'I Jewed around with the guy for buying a cow.' You ignore it." Other cattle dealers thought there was always a little anti-Semitism at work, but most "had no problem." Cattle dealers recalled comments like "Jew cattle dealers, out to rob you," or "after a farmer would sell a cow to a Jewish dealer another farmer would come along and say, 'oh, you sold that cow much too cheap. You shouldn't deal with that Jew.'"

ETHNIC NETWORKS: MOVING CATTLE
ON SEVERAL ENDS

In addition to their class resources, the German Jewish cattle dealers had another important resource I only mentioned in passing in the previous section: their unique ethnic ties to several ends of the dairy industry. This network consisted of dairies, slaughterhouses, auctions, and cattle breeders. Each of these industries would make a fascinating story in itself, and the overall picture might be a wonderful lesson in political economy, but for the purposes of this study, the network will be discussed from the vantage point of cattle dealing and the success of the German Jewish refugees. Although there were numerous dealers and dairies eager to buy milk in the immediate post–World War II period, farmers did not always have the money to upgrade their herds to produce the milk needed by dairies. Through ethnic connections, German Jewish cattle dealers managed to bring farmer and dairy together, resulting in a profitable situation for the cattle dealer.

Many of the numerous local dairies and dairies located in the metropolitan New York area and northern New Jersey were Jewish owned (Cooperdale, Farmland, Queensfarm, Tuscan, to name a few). With the milk market becoming ever more competitive, the dairies needed the raw material to survive. In some instances, cattle dealers were utilized as brokers for dairies, aiding them in the procurement of the raw material. Dairies in New Jersey and even those located in the New York metropolitan area bought milk primarily from upstate farmers. Due to kin and informal ethnic networks established when initially settling in the Washington Heights area of northern Manhattan, German Jewish cattle dealers were sometimes able to act as agents for the downstate dairies. The cattle dealer would tell farmers interested in increasing their herd that a certain dairy would loan them the money for the new cows if they would promise to sell a specified amount of milk to that particular dairy. In other cases, a dairy would contact lease companies, which would buy the cattle from the cattle dealer, and the dealer would deliver the cows to the farmers.

Unlike previous groups of immigrants, who often relied on formal ethnic networks to aid in establishing themselves in a wide range of business enterprises, German Jewish cattle dealers received little assistance from formal immigrant aid societies. Most of the networks that proved beneficial in their business endeavors were either kin related or formed though informal associations with other co-ethnics. Not only was the cattle dealer able to provide a milking cow, mostly on credit, but he was also able to find the farmer an outlet for the milk and provided a service for the dairy, at the same time, by finding a source for the raw material. This service provided by the cattle dealer enabled smaller dairies and small to medium-size farmers to stay in business perhaps longer than they would otherwise have been able, or to even further expand.

BREEDERS

The successful cattle dealer not only needed to know cows but also needed to know where to obtain cows to bring into the region. Again, ethnic networks come into play. The larger cattle dealers procured milk cows primarily from further upstate New York and Canada, all within a day's driving distance from the eventual buyer, the dairy farmer. For example, one cattle dealer made his upstate connection through a fellow German Jewish immigrant who stayed one summer in the guesthouse operated by the cattle dealer's wife. The guest had moved outside of Rochester and had become a cattle dealer. He rented a barn and bought and sold cattle and became the main supplier for more than one German Jewish cattle dealer. Other cattle dealers in the area had relatives, also in the Rochester area, who became their main suppliers of cattle, which were then sold to dairy farmers in south-central New York.

The more successful cattle dealers forged a Canadian connection. Unlike the United States, Canada operates on a quota system on milk production. In Canada, a quota is fixed, and farmers receive the highest price for meeting the quota. However, if a farmer produced more than the quota, he would not receive the highest price, in effect being fined for going over quota. This resulted in Canadian dairy farmers not wanting to increase production, thus becoming a prime source for productive milk cows. German Jewish cattle dealers, once again through ethnic ties formed when first arriving in the United States and through extended family networks, connected with German Jews outside of Toronto who became their main suppliers of quality milk cows. It did not take long for dairy farmers in south-central New York to realize that German Jewish cattle dealers could provide them with not only credit but also quality cows, thereby increasing their competitive advantage. Moreover, cattle dealers in south-central New York utilized their networks further upstate and in Canada to provide milk cows to cattle dealers closer to the metropolitan New York area. Some German Jewish cattle dealers in south-central New York, therefore, became middlemen for other middlemen.

SLAUGHTERHOUSES AND AUCTIONS

German Jewish cattle dealers also had connections on yet another end of the business, the slaughterhouse. During the 1950s and 1960s, numerous slaughter-houses existed, and many, particularly the larger ones, were Jewish owned. This connection to slaughterhouses provided yet another outlet for farmers to dispose of their unproductive cows. Prior to the 1960s, a time before the big cattle auctions and the increased regulation of the slaughterhouses, cattle dealers were able to buy unproductive cows from the farmers, and then sell the unproductive cow to the slaughterhouse for inexpensive meat. In turn, slaughterhouse owners also provided cattle dealers with potential customers by vouching for the cattle dealers new to the area.

Because of stricter state regulations, many slaughterhouses went out of busi-nesses during the 1960s and 1970s, reducing the total number of outlets for unproductive milk cows. Auctions thus became the primary outlet for selling cows for inexpensive meat. The German Jewish cattle dealers would go to the auctions to either sell unproductive milk cows or even buy a cow to sell to a slaughterhouse. Several German Jewish cattle dealers also owned shares in one auction that was held every week and was one of the larger ones in south-central New York during the 1960s and 1970s.

In a highly competitive market in which farmers were spending most of their time milking and doing basic farmwork, German Jewish cattle dealers could provide quality milk cows on credit, take the unproductive cows off the farmer's hands, and provide an outlet for the farmer's milk if needed. But the cattle dealers had to know cows, and they also needed to keep abreast of various diseases and state laws regulating the movement of cattle. To paraphrase a cattle dealer, they had to be "professional."

Reinforcing Ethnic Identity and Recreating a German Jewish Community: The Social World of Cattle Dealers

The occupational concentration of German Jewish refugees able to reestablish themselves as cattle dealers helped them recreate a German Jewish community and reinforced its members' ethnic identity. It was not the only factor, by any means, but it did have a role.

Although they worked individually, and were often on the road driving from farm to farm, the men did come together while working. For example, German Jewish cattle dealers would sit together and converse in German at cattle auctions. Oftentimes after the auctions, or at certain times during the day when farmers were busy in their fields, some of the German Jewish cattle dealers would meet at a diner to play the German card game skat. As the wife of a cattle dealer put it, "You never told your husband anything you didn't want someone to know or hear about, especially if it were a day he was going to auction. Either at auction or playing cards, all the cattle dealers would gossip. They were worse than the women!"

Most of the German Jewish cattle dealers were members of the New York State Cattle Dealers Association that served as another forum through which German Jewish cattle dealers could share a sense of community. For a period of time, the Cattle Dealers Association would have its yearly meetings at a resort in the Catskills. When the meetings took place at a resort, and especially one that served kosher food, wives would go along, and sometimes the children, for a weekend of activities, a mini vacation. The cattle dealers and their wives recall that the meetings were mainly social; they danced and partied with other German Jewish members.

Some aspects of their occupation, however, had the potential to divide them. Because they competed with each other for accounts, personal rivalries did develop. They therefore had to establish informal rules that would separate their business relationships from their personal, communal relationships. For example, when they visited one another for social purposes, they would not go into the barn. As the son of a cattle dealer explained, since they could instantly recognize the quality of cows, not going into someone's barn was a way to avoid knowing more than one needed to know about the other person's business.

Another cattle dealer said, "We may have been competitors, but we all belonged to the same *shul* [synagogue]." They would sit and pray together in synagogue, and wish each other a good *Shabbas* (Sabbath) or a good *Yom Tov* (holiday). The fact that they were competitors by day and friends by night sometimes proved confusing to their children. One son of a cattle dealer said,

That if there was a Bar Mitzvah or wedding or someone died and you needed ten people for *minyan* [quorum needed for religious service] at the house to sit *Shiva* [period of mourning] for seven nights, it was understood that when I became Bar Mitzvah, my father would go and take me and my brother, whoever's house it was, even if we had been terrible rivals in business and during the day, I mean it was bitter rivalry and [we] wouldn't speak to those people, we went. It was just unquestioned. We changed our clothes no matter what time of night, no matter what had been done, we went. We would go and make sure there was a *minyan* and everyone was friendly and coffee and cake and schmoozing and all that stuff, which was hard for me to deal with. I now somehow understand it, but at the time it was very difficult. It almost seemed that it was a religious obligation. . . . Only with other German Jews. . . . Cause they were out in the country and it was . . . you had to have the *minyan* to sit *Shiva* and say Kaddish. . . . We were supposed to go for these things when they were doing the *minyan* or sitting *Shiva* or whatever.

As the rabbi of the conservative synagogue in Binghamton attested, "The one time I always saw [the German Jews] as a group was if one of them died and there was a funeral, they would all come out."

Meeting at the auction or at the synagogue, cattle dealers would invite other cattle dealers and their wives to their homes for coffee and cake, to socialize and sometimes play cards on either Saturday evenings or Sunday afternoons. For most, Saturday nights became an evening of card playing and eating German pastries. Meeting at a different home each week, Saturday night gatherings became the place where women and men could socialize and share conversation in their native German language. Women would play canasta in one room while the men "would smoke their cigars and play *skat* in another room."

RHONDA F. LEVINE

Immigrant Adaptation and Ethnic Mobility:
Refocusing the Sociological Lens

The foregoing case study shows that post-Holocaust studies can contribute to the ongoing debates over the factors that give rise to immigrant economic adaptation and ethnic mobility in the United States, with a particular focus on why some groups succeed economically and others do not. Whereas the dominant view within the social sciences formerly focused on group characteristics in accounting for differential rates of assimilation and mobility, recent views have shifted the focus to structural factors that contribute to immigrants' opportunities and achievements. These explanations for why some immigrant groups become economically self-sufficient and pass advantages onto their children focus on the creation of immigrant economies, ethnic enclaves, and the availability of business niches (Bonacich 1993; Light et al. 1994; Portes 1992; Sanders and Nee 1992; Waldinger 1994).

According to Gans (1999), much of the research on the adaptation of immigrants has "emphasized microsocial factors, although the study of economic adaptation . . . has brought in macrosocial and macroeconomic issues. This is a constructive trend, for we need to understand how the nature of and changes in the American economy, polity, and society affect immigrant adaptation" (1307). I would go one step further than Gans and emphasize along with Burawoy (1998) that "'structure,' or 'social forces,' really do confine what is possible, although they are themselves continually reconfigured" (15n.8). In other words, structural factors, while different for disparate groups, are always present and set the parameters for outcomes. In any given historical moment, that is, there is a structural configuration that sets limits on what kind of labor is needed and at the same time creates opportunities for immigrants. In the 1890s, for example, unskilled labor was needed in the United States for the emerging industrial economy, and that is the niche filled by the old immigrants. Since the 1970s, on the other hand, two very different kinds of labor have come into demand: technical and professional workers who can carry forward the computer revolution, a niche filled to a large extent by new Asian immigrants, and low-wage workers for the growing service sector. Similarly, but on a much smaller scale, cattle dealers were needed for dairy farmers in New York due to changes in the political economy of milk following World War II.

Although the particular conditions differ, the way that structure constrains the possible remains constant. While it is difficult to generalize about the mobility patterns of different immigrant groups, certain macrostructural factors can be isolated that help to account for relative economic success (Model 1988). Some scholars suggest, for example, that the structure of economic opportunity makes for a significant factor that radically distinguishes the adaptation and mobility patterns of the new from the old immigrants. Although European immigrants may have started in low-paying unskilled jobs, they were not stuck in them, and their children were able to move up the socioeconomic ladder as industry expanded. On the other hand, new immigrants from Asia, Latin America, and the Caribbean face a very different situation. Although they are necessary to an expanding economy, the shift from a manufacturing to a service-based economy means that many immigrants who enter unskilled, low-wage jobs are unable to move out of the bottom. The economy as a whole resembles an hourglass, with ample jobs at the top for those with special skills, a few in the middle, and many poor jobs on the bottom with little hope of moving up (e.g., see Gans 1992; Perlman and Waldinger 1997; Portes and Zhou 1993). Simply put, the new immigrants are entering an economy which does not offer the same opportunities available to earlier immigrants and their offspring.

It is still too early to know definitively if the second generation of the post-1965 immigrants will indeed experience stagnation. After all, southern and eastern European immigrants and many of their children were employed in unskilled and semiskilled factory jobs with little hope of mobility at the time. It was also not predictable if rural German Jewish refugees who first worked at unskilled jobs or as domestics would be able to return to middle-class lives. As Perlman and Waldinger (1997) point out, when compared to the European immigrants of the old migration wave, the immigrant children of the post-1965 immigration in general do not have greater economic disadvantages.

Economic opportunities alone, however, cannot explain differences in adaptation and mobility patterns. The case of rural German Jews suggest that it is not merely the structure of economic opportunity but also class and ethnic factors that prove important in understanding adaptation and mobility patterns. In addition to these factors, scholars of the new immigration also raise the issue of racial differences that may impact processes of adaptation and mobility.

Some scholars argue that European immigrants and their children were more easily acculturated and assimilated into American society, not only because of the expanding industrial economy but also because of their "racial" similarity to native-born Americans. This supposed racial similarity made the process of adaptation easier. The new immigrants are said to be "visibly identifiable and enter a mainly white society still not cured of its racist afflictions" (Perlman and Waldinger 1997). In other words, new immigrants "look different" and thus constitute easy targets of the institutional racism embedded within the very social, economic, and political fabric of the United States.

However, at the time of their immigration, southern and eastern Europeans were also not considered white. Racial definitions for Poles, Italians, and Jews, and even earlier for the Irish, changed to white once they became upwardly mobile. Contrary to those that argue that the old immigrants were upwardly mobile due to their whiteness, evidence suggests that the immigrants only *became* white once they moved up (Brodkin 1998; Jacobson 1998). Race did play a role for the old European immigrants, and certainly race played a role for German Jews in Germany. Whether the new immigrants from Asia and Latin America, in particular, will also go through a whitening process remains an open question. Racial and ethnic boundaries are constantly changing. German Jews went from being defined as an ethnic group, to a racial group, and back to an ethnic group. The same very possibly holds true for the new immigrants as well.

What may be more significant than how a group is racially defined by the outside is what class and racial or ethnic resources the group comes in with. While it is true that the changing political economy of milk in New York created a structure of opportunity for those refugees looking to return to their previous occupation of cattle dealing, it was their class and ethnic resources that enabled them to take advantage of it. German Jewish refugees were able to utilize their unique business skills acquired in Germany to find an economic niche in cattle dealing not because a hostile larger society forced them into an economic sector that serviced an ethnic market, but because of the business opportunity made possible by the changing structure of the dairy industry in New York.

Unlike the situation in some urban areas in which immigrants developed a business niche that serviced primarily the immigrant population, rural German Jewish cattle dealers provided a middleman position within the larger rural economy. Because of the growth and expansion of the fluid milk market and changes in dairy farming, German Jewish cattle dealers did not necessarily have to replace an incumbent native population of cattle dealers. However, German Jewish cattle dealers had an advantage over native cattle dealers, and it is at this point that the literature on ethnic enterprises, ethnic entrepreneurs, and ethnic enclaves can provide some theoretical guidance. German Jewish refugees were not able to bring out material possessions, but they could carry their cultural capital across the Atlantic in terms of both class and ethnic resources. In a similar fashion, many Italian immigrants in the early twentieth century were able to use their fishing skills, especially on the Pacific Coast, and then capitalized on that economic niche to move into the restaurant business. Then, too, Japanese immigrants to California in the late 1800s were able to utilize their experience as small farmers in Japan, playing a significant role as fruit and vegetable farmers in feeding the state's growing population. In their case, however, anti-Asian sentiment in urban areas meant that they did not always go into farming by choice (Tuan 1998).

As others have also shown, immigrant networks constitute important ethnic resources that also can help explain adaptation and mobility patterns (Zhou and Bankston 1998). The case of German Jewish cattle dealers highlights the importance of networks. Familial and ethnically based networks proved crucial for finding first jobs and, later, for resettlement, a point made by numerous researchers of immigration (Baily and Waldinger 1991; Boyd 1989; Hagan 1998). Unlike the situation in urban ethnic enclaves, the cattle dealers did not hire other coethnics, but they did rely on kinship ties to begin the cattle-dealing businesses, with many cattle dealers starting their businesses with other family members or coethnics as partners. Like urban ethnic enterprises and ethnic enclaves, wives and children contributed to the business. In the case of rural German Jews, wives and children helped on the farm, thereby keeping down the overall costs of labor performed by hired help. Moreover, wives started businesses of their own (guesthouses and summer camps) that provided essential capital for their husbands' cattle-dealing operations.

For the German Jewish cattle dealers, these ethnic and extended kin networks also gave them a distinct economic advantage over their competition. In particular, the three-way network that developed for the cattle dealers—with slaughterhouses, suppliers of milk cows, and dairies—helps explain how German Jews came to dominate cattle dealing in south-central New York. For the German Jewish cattle dealers, their unique positioning within a three-way network allowed them to capitalize on the structure of opportunity, especially by bringing the superior breed of Holsteins to south-central dairy farmers. Moreover, their unique business skills allowed them to build accounts with farmers who otherwise would not have been in a position to improve their herds. In this way, the

RHONDA F. LEVINE

microsocial world of the German Jewish cattle dealers also affected the macro-social structure of dairying in New York State, first by bringing in better milkers, and second by enabling small dairy farmers to stay in business. An understanding of the role of networks in conjunction with class resources and structural factors allows for appreciating the important linkage between micro- and macrofactors. Thus Stephen Steinberg's (1989) argument concerning the complex interaction of structural conditions and class resources to explain ethnic mobility is made even more dramatically when networks are taken into account.

Still it is important to note that networks may at times constrain mobility as well, as shown in several cases. While ethnic networks may play a positive role in finding first jobs for immigrants, for example, a study of the Chinese in Chicago found that ethnic obligations may bind immigrants to low-wage work within an ethnic enclave and interfere with future economic opportunities (Li 1977). Mexican immigrant women had strong networks that facilitated immigration and even helped in locating jobs as domestics, for example, but these networks cannot overcome the constraints of larger structural factors. Newly arrived Mexican immigrants in California must sometimes choose to either work as a live-in domestic with little chance of advancement or work as a helper to another domestic worker, and they often remain trapped in a low-paying job (Hondagneu-Sotelo 1994). Similarly, in Houston, social networks tend to channel Mayan immigrant women into private-household domestic work. Long hours of work in isolated residential areas take women out of social contact with others who may be a source of information for more lucrative work (Hagan 1998). In both cases, networks restricted immigrant women into areas that actually limited their opportunities for mobility.

But in keeping with the analysis stressed in this essay, networks alone cannot account for how German Jewish refugees managed to reestablish themselves in the cattle-dealing business and prosper in the process, and networks alone are also unlikely to completely explain the process of adaptation, especially in terms of economic mobility, for other immigrant groups. For example, networks may help to explain why West Indian women are concentrated in domestic work and in health care services in New York City, but once again, structural forces shape their options. With more white women working outside of the home and spending more time developing their careers, domestic help has come into great demand. Moreover, in the case of West Indians, whites moved up in health care services at a time when the demand for services was increasing, leaving a void in lower-level health-related jobs. West Indian women, well trained in their home-lands and speaking English, were able to fill the void. As the demand for health-related services increases, greater opportunities for mobility in the health field are likely to manifest themselves for West Indian women (Kasinitz 1992; Vickerman 1999). The English-speaking West Indians come with skills (class and cultural resources) that enable them to take advantage of the structure of opportunity made known to them through their networks. In this case, we can see once again how structure, class resources, and networks all interact to help explain adaptation and mobility patterns.

Although this article only touches on the point of identity, the fact that cattle dealers and their families were able to create a German Jewish community and retain their Jewish identity in isolated rural towns makes this case relevant to the complex issue of if, when, and how ethnic identity is maintained or reconfigured by different immigrant groups. For the German Jews, their occupational concentration, organizations, and social networks all reinforced a sense of German Jewishness for the immigrant generation. Becoming integrated with their rural communities, as had previous generations of rural Jews in Germany, did not conflict with maintaining a Jewish ethnic identity. The cattle dealers had grown up with the idea of both a national and an ethnoreligious identity, until the two roles came into conflict due to Nazism's use of Jews as scapegoats on the road to power. Thus the maintenance of a German Jewish identity and the ability to raise their children as American Jews did not prove problematic for this particular group (Levine 2001:113–53).

Using a sociological lens that situates post-Holocaust rural German Jewish lives within the larger context of economic and social change without losing sight of the significance of social networks and everyday life shows us how social structure, class, ethnicity, and networks interact to account for immigrant adaptation and mobility patterns.

RHONDA F. LEVINE

Post-Holocaust Jewish Migration:
From Refugees to Transnationals

Since the late 1980s, Jewish migrants to both Israel and the dias-
pora have enjoyed increased options with regard to locations of settlement and
styles of adaptation. Whereas in the past, Jewish migrants were compelled to
accept the identities created for them by resettlement staff in predetermined
points of settlement, they are now increasingly able to act on the basis of their
own desires and interests. The actions of Israeli and diaspora Jewish communal
leaders have influenced this transformation in significant ways. However, the
experience of Jewish migrants is also shaped by the broader political, economic,
and social trends that affect contemporary immigrant and refugee groups more
generally. These include a growing demand for skilled workers, the implementation of human rights movements and multicultural policies that encourage group
self-determination, and the reduced cost of and expanded access to communications and transportation technology.

The enhanced autonomy accessed by Jewish migrants constitutes a positive
development. At the same time, however, it requires Jewish migrants and Jewish
communities to once again confront issues of national affiliation and group
identity that seemed to have been resolved only decades ago by two focal trends
in post-Holocaust Jewish life—the formation of Israel and the increased acceptance of Jewish populations in Western societies. In so doing, Jewish populations
reveal important similarities with other contemporary diasporic and migrant
populations who confront similar quandaries of identification and membership
for many of the same political and economic reasons (Cohen 1989; Gold 1992;

Safran 1999). This article draws on published accounts, fieldwork, and interviews collected with Israeli emigrants and Soviet Jews and their resettlement staff in the United States, France, the United Kingdom, and Israel to explore some of the causes and consequences of the changed context of Jewish migration.[1]

Israel as the Primary Migrant Destination

As recently as the late 1970s and 1980s, a broad consensus in both Israel and diaspora Jewish communities asserted that Israel should be the primary destination and homeland for Jewish migrants. Hebrew terms like *yordim* (those who go down) and *noshrim* (dropouts) stigmatized Israelis or Jews from the former Soviet Union who settled in Europe or North America as "Jewish communal deviants" (Cohen 1986:159). What is more, the denigration of Jewish migrants who chose to settle outside of Israel received substantial endorsement from Jewish populations who are themselves the descendants of earlier migrant flows and residents of the very settings where Israelis and former Soviets hoped to live (Markowitz 1988; Shokeid 1988).

CONDEMNATION OF ISRAELI EMIGRATION

The most vilified of Jewish migrants have been those leaving Israel. In contrast to the Hebrew term *aliyah*, which refers to Jews' move from the diaspora to the higher place of Israel, *yeridah* describes the stigmatized downward path of Israelis who descend from the Promised Land into the diaspora. Emigrants are the yordim. From the Zionist point of view, Jewish migrants who do not have the Jewish state as their destination threaten the assertion that Israel constitutes the best place for Jews to live. And practically, Jews are needed to populate the Jewish state and ensure its military, economic, and demographic viability in a hostile world region: "There is an implication that the citizen who has left Israel is guilty of a subtle form of betrayal of the shared obligation to protect the land of Israel" (Linn and Barkan-Ascher 1996:7). While emigration has been condemned since at least 1948, during the 1970s, Israeli politicians such as the prime minister Yitzhak Rabin were especially vitriolic on this issue, calling Israeli emigrants "moral lepers," "the fallen among the weaklings," and "the dregs of the earth" (qtd. in Ritterband 1986:113; Kimhi 1990). In order to discourage further emigration and impede the settlement of those abroad, from the early 1970s until the late 1980s, the Israeli consulate in New York "repeatedly urged the [Jewish] Federation to provide no special services to Israelis" (Cohen 1986:159; see also Tugend

1989). As recently as 1989, an opinion piece in the *Jerusalem Post* described Israeli emigrants as bearing "The Mark of Cain" and asserted "as every *yored* knows only too well, he has simply deserted, abandoned the defense of his country and the shared responsibility for it" (Zvielli 1989).

If Israelis have been hostile to the emigration of their compatriots, Jewish communities outside of Israel have been ambivalent about Israeli newcomers. Following the lead of the Israeli government (which wanted to discourage settlement), diaspora communities offered little of the support that they have customarily extended to other immigrant Jews (Gold and Phillips 1996). In her report titled *The Israeli Corner of the American Jewish Community*, Sherry Rosen (1993) asserted that the communal response has been to approach Israeli émigrés as "anything but Jewish settlers seeking to build new lives for themselves and their families in the United States" (2). During the Immigration Reform and Control Act (IRCA) amnesty for undocumented migrants enacted in the mid-1980s, Israeli emigrants in the United States who felt rebuffed by Jewish agencies were sometimes forced to rely on Catholic organizations to assist them in normalizing their residency status. In the following quote, an employee from a New York agency working with Israeli emigrants describes the climate of hostility toward such migrants during the 1970s and 1980s: "I wouldn't call it [American Jews' attitude toward immigrants] hostility, but I would say that there was a real discomfort. For the Americans, it wasn't an individual thing but a global phenomenon that is, 'How could they come here? They belong *there*. I mean, they're beautiful Israeli Sabras [Jews born in Israel]. Sabras belong in Israel, and you know, we help them and they could fight in the wars. That was the American perception."

DIASPORA-TO-DIASPORA MIGRANTS

While Soviet, Iranian, and other Jewish migrants have been officially resettled in diaspora Jewish communities, their presence, too, caused considerable consternation because they were rejecting Israel as a homeland. According to the journalist J. J. Goldberg, "The first [American] Soviet Jewry activists in the 1960s hardly intended their work to result in Jewish immigration to the United States. The movement was from the start a Zionist enterprise, conceived by Israelis and driven by activists who wanted the world's second largest Jewish community 'repatriated'—brought en masse 'back' to Israel, their ancestral homeland" (Goldberg 1996:180). From the late 1960s until the mid-1970s, the majority of Soviet

Jews granted exit visas did settle in Israel. However, between 1976 and 1989, at least half opted instead to dwell in the United States, and by the late 1980s, less than 10 percent each year chose the Jewish state.

Along with this rise in immigration came increased pressure from certain segments of the world Jewish community to resettle Soviet Jews exclusively in Israel rather than the United States or elsewhere (Gold 1995a; Orleck 1999). Soviet Jews who opted for other destinations were labeled noshrim and were subject to inferior treatment by resettlement agencies in Europe. For example, it was the standard practice of Jewish immigrant aid agencies to provide émigrés who chose Israel with rapid resettlement, while those who migrated to the United States had to languish for weeks or months before placement (Panish 1981; Woo 1989). Former Soviets who left Israel for other settings were eligible for few, if any, resettlement benefits.

Proponents of settlement in Israel demanded that the United States deny Soviet Jews group-level refugee status as a way to increase the movement to Israel. They had considerable success. In late 1989, the Bush administration revoked Soviet Jews' universal refugee status, instead only providing it on a case-by-case basis, favoring those with relatives in the United States (Tress 1991; Ungar 1989; Woo 1989). By the 1990s, Israel received far more Soviet Jewish arrivals than the United States, although the numbers entering both countries were enormous (Gold 1994a).

Paternalistic Acculturation to the Host Society

Whether they settled in Tel Aviv, Toronto, or Los Angeles, Jewish migrants of an earlier era were expected to cooperate with the religious, economic, political, cultural, and national agendas created for them by their host communities. For those settling in the Jewish state, this involved the replacement of diaspora Jewish identities with Israeli ones. Boas Evron (1995) summarizes the rationale: "For a nation to be created, the Jews must undergo a mental and social transformation and establish a society that is in diametrical opposition to the concepts and values of the Jewish caste community" in the diaspora (105). A mere two years after Israel's independence, the nation's first prime minister, David Ben Gurion, described how diaspora Jews would be transformed into Israelis: "The transformation of this human dust into a successful nation . . . is not an easy task . . . we need to resort to enormous educational and moral efforts, accompanied by genuine, deep and pure love of these forsaken brothers . . . in order to imprint in these incoming and defeatious diasporas the values of our proud culture, language and creativity" (Ben Gurion 1964:34; also qtd. in Yiftachel 1998:41). Re-counting the practice of this theory, the Israeli anthropologist Moshe Shokeid (1998) wrote, "all immigrants were expected sooner or later, to shed their separate ethnic cultures and embrace 'Israeli culture'" (235).

Reflecting a similar tendency in American resettlement programs, during the 1970s and 1980s, several articles in the *Journal of Jewish Communal Service* pro-vided resettlement staff with hints on how to bring Soviet émigrés into the American Jewish community. For example, one article asserted: "It is absolutely essential to exploit ESL [English as a second language] classes . . . where they are actually a captive audience . . . for inculcating Jewish attitudes and values . . . to foster a positive Jewish self-concept while developing Jewish cognition, Jewish language expression and Jewish life skills" (Schiff 1980:45–49). Another essay urged resettlement staff "to create a Jewish need in him [the Soviet émigré] just as we would with a child, while at the same time understanding that he is no child" (Goldberg 1981:161).

Precisely because of Soviet Jewish émigrés' close ties to American Jews (who often share Russian or Eastern European origins and have been crusading for the Soviets' right to emigrate since the 1960s), Soviet Jews were given little oppor-tunity to express their own political, cultural, and religious identities in the United States. Several émigrés, including the following resident of Oakland, California, described how American Jews often questioned their Jewishness: "I remember, even when I didn't know the language so well, I could hear the question 'How do you know you are a Jew if you didn't do this and you didn't know that?' And 'why didn't they go to Israel?'"

Host-country Jews, primed by decades of anti-Soviet/Russian propaganda and having heard numerous tales about religion-seeking Soviet Jewish refuse-niks, were unprepared to acknowledge that most Soviet Jews identified with their country of origin. By and large, however, émigrés do prize the Russian language, culture, and landscape, enjoy aspects of the Russian lifestyle, and take pride in the accomplishments of the former USSR—and accordingly, seek to retain a Russian identity in the United States, Canada, or Israel (Siegel 1998). Host-country Jews often assumed that the Soviets would happily give up their inured perspectives for host-society ideologies, forms of Judaism, and styles of commu-nity membership. When émigrés were reluctant to do so, host-country Jews repudiated them: "As American Jews found some of the ways that Soviet Jews act to be alien, they came to label these behaviors and the individuals associated with them not 'Jewish' but 'Russian'" (Markowitz 1988:84).

Some Israelis had similar reactions to the Russians and Ethiopians resettled in the Jewish state, with factions even questioning their Jewishness and demanding conversions (Ben-Ezer 1994; Siegel 1998). Describing another point of settlement for Jewish migrants, Cohen and Gold (1996) report that Toronto Jews describe Israeli emigrants via the same stereotypes that Canadian Gentiles use to portray Jewish Canadians: loud, dishonest, arrogant, and rude. (Israelis respond by depicting Jewish Canadians with the identical platitudes that Canadian Jews attribute to their non-Jewish neighbors: formal, lazy, naive, and beer-drinking.)

Grateful for the generosity of their coethnic hosts, Jewish migrants nevertheless resented the paternalistic treatment they received (Gold 1992; Howe 1976). However, lacking resources, it often took them decades or even generations to either create their own institutions or be accepted as equals by the established community. The following quote from a Soviet Jewish activist interviewed in Los Angeles during the 1980s reflects this:

The reason we came here is because 20 years ago, people like you just shouted in the streets, "let our people go." But here we are, we are already considering ourselves like Americans. Not just immigrants, but already Americans with good experience. A position of irony is that we still treated as boys and girls. We are not even close to policy making in this country. The whole decisions are made without us. They just use us as bait for raising money. So what's going on right now, its a process of recognition of the Soviet Jews as a power. And I'm doing a lot of things in this matter just to help establish ourself as a real strength.

In sum, while Jewish refugees from the diaspora have received significant assistance from Jewish hosts in Israel and the diaspora, their resettlement has often been paternalistic in nature. In contrast, Israeli emigration has been condemned. Prior to the 1980s, few benefits were extended to assist emigrants' resettlement.

Jewish Migrants' New Status

Since the late 1980s, Jewish migrants have been able to maintain a level of autonomy that significantly surpassed that of the recent past. Israel began to treat its own emigrants in a more benign manner, and in accordance with this evolving Israeli policy toward expatriates, Jewish communities in settlement countries have established outreach programs for recently arrived Israelis. At the same time, new Jewish immigrants in both Israel and diaspora communities have been more able to shape the conditions and nature of their adaptation according to their own preferences, as opposed to those of their hosts.

With regard to Israeli emigrants, the new perspective can often be traced to Israeli policy. In the late 1980s, the Israeli government encouraged its consular officials to initiate the development of relations between Israeli immigrants and host-society Jewish institutions. During a 1989 trip to Los Angeles, the Israeli absorption minister Yitzhak Peretz claimed that Israel should change its attitude toward émigrés if they cannot be convinced to return. "Israelis," he said, "should be encouraged to be part of the Jewish community and become integrated because it offers them, and particularly their children, some chance of retaining their Jewish identity" (Tugend 1989). In 1991, Prime Minister Yitzhak Rabin recanted his famous condemnation of Israeli émigrés in an interview in the Israeli-American newspaper *Hadashot* saying, "What I said then doesn't apply today . . . the Israelis living abroad are an integral part of the Jewish community and there is no point in talking about ostracism" (Rosen 1993:3). Finally, "because of the importance it attaches to the re-emigration of Israelis to Israel" (*For Those Returning Home* 1995) in 1992, the Israeli government took responsibility for so-called re-aliyah and offered a package of benefits including cash assistance, low-cost air fair, the suspension of import duties, education, assistance in finding jobs and housing, financial aid for school tuition, and a reduction in military duty for Israelis and their family members who return.

Denial and outrage were the initial reactions of many diaspora Jews to the Israelis in their midst (Cohen 1986). However, on seeing coreligionists in need, realizing the human and financial resources available within the émigré community, and heeding Israel's call to assist emigrants, segments of host populations began to acknowledge both the existence of the Israeli migrant community and the importance of outreach to them. In the words of the employee of a New York Jewish agency:

As an American Jew, for me, I had already begun to realize "Why can't they live here? They're perfectly entitled to live here." It was funny. My personal thinking was parallel to some extent to what I saw happening around. And now, we have a lot of young Israeli families, some of whom I have been involved with since their little one was in nursery school and now they're in the Israeli Hebrew School and a lot of them started their own businesses and many of them have Green Cards and it's accepted that this is where they want to be.

Since the early 1990s, major Jewish communities (Paris, London, Toronto, New York, Los Angeles, Chicago, south Florida, and the San Francisco Bay Area) have created various endeavors to aid and incorporate Israelis. These include social activities, secular, Israeli-style education programs, and Israeli divisions of community, social, and philanthropic organizations (Gold 1994c; Shokeid 1998; Uriely 1994). Moreover, recent Jewish population studies in New York (1991, 2002), Los Angeles (1997), the United Kingdom (1998), and South Africa (1993) all enumerate Israelis, their presence one of the few positive tendencies in a general trend of shrinking Jewish demographics (Dubb 1994; Herman 1998; Horowitz 1993; Schmool and Cohen 1998). Faced with an aging native Jewish population, the settlement of numbers of energetic, family-oriented, and Jewishly identified Israelis are increasingly seen as a valuable asset to established Jewish communities. The Israeli presence is especially appreciated in older urban neighborhoods, where large numbers of local Jews have recently left for more family-friendly suburban locations or retirement communities (Waterman 1997). Finally, Israeli emigrants have created a variety of businesses, organizations, social activities, and other programs to assist in their own adaptation (Gold 1994a).

Similarly, by the late 1980s, official acknowledgment was given to the fact that most Soviet Jews in the United States were not interested in becoming religiously active in the manner planned by their hosts (Orleck 1999). Initial hopes for rapid religious assimilation were replaced by a more realistic acknowledgment of Soviet émigrés' secular and ethnic rather than religious identification (Carp 1990). This encouraged resettlement agencies to assist Soviet Jews in ways that they desired rather than subjecting them to religious indoctrination. An American rabbi who worked with Soviet Jews reflected on this realization: "One of the disappointments that many rabbis felt was that most of the Soviet Jews did not find a need to express their Jewishness. We should have understood this, because they come from a secular, atheistic country, but it was difficult to accept" (Barber 1987:41).

Social workers engaged in resettlement were among the first to apprehend that émigrés' most immediate interests involved achieving economic stability and ensuring secure careers for their children, not studying Hebrew or going to temple (Zahler 1989). Noting their clients' resistance to religious indoctrination, many resettlement workers downplayed the role of religion in resettlement. A Southern California social worker commented:

And for our lay people, if our board people were really to hear that . . . [Soviet Jews came to the United States for other than religious reasons] I don't think that they would be really thrilled. I think they really think they rescued them . . . they think about it in terms of the refusenik. But I tell you, as far as I'm concerned, it doesn't really bother me. They are people, they want to restore their lives, they want to live in the United States. You can't work in this business and sit in judgment of people.

Most recently, Jewish scholars and community activists have recognized that while Soviet Jews, Israelis, and other Jewish migrants frequently express their Jewishness in ways at variance with the local Jewish population, they often have a stronger Jewish identity and more extensive Jewish social ties than do American Jews (Gold 1994c; Herman 2000; Ritterband 1997).

Just as former Soviets have been able to alter the tone of resettlement programs in the United States, they have also moved Israel toward multiculturalism. The size, educational achievements, and ideological orientation of the Soviet Jewish aliyah has made them the first group to successfully retain their own culture in the face of established Israeli social forms. Writing in the preface of Dina Siegel's book on Russian Jews in Israel, the Israeli anthropologist Emanuel Marx (1998) asserts: "The Russian immigrants have been the first group to withstand the efforts of the state to absorb them culturally. Its bureaucratic agencies have been unable to tame and subdue the new citizens, to strip them of their native culture and mould them into standard Israelis. . . . The overall result was that, for the first time, Israel began to move toward greater cultural and ethnic pluralism" (ix).

Most recently, the economic decline of 2000–2002, coupled with the hostile environment associated with the al-Aqsa Intifada has once again made emigration an important topic within Israeli society. While emigration still has many opponents in both Israel and abroad, several respondents and newspaper reports suggest that a considerable fraction of the Israeli population is now more tolerant of emigration than ever before. According to a recent article in an Israeli newspaper, "it is also clear that the Israelis who are leaving the country have liberated themselves from the stigma of being a yored . . . that was once derisively hurled at emigrants. In a world where flights out of the country are available and cheap, and moving from one land to another for employment is a routine matter, leaving is not necessarily forever" (Shavit 2001). A survey on emigration conducted by Israel's *Ha'aretz* magazine during 2001 found that only 37 percent of respondents had a negative opinion of emigrants. Sixteen percent had a positive reaction, while 43 percent were indifferent (Shavit 2001).

Why More Alternatives for Today's Jewish Migrants?

In the section that follows, I trace some of the reasons for Jewish migrants' increased ability to determine the nature and location of their resettlement. These include issues specific to Jews and Israel, such as the economic and demographic growth that occurred in the country during the 1990s, as well as trends impacting migrants in general—an increased demand for skilled labor, the expansion of human rights regimes, easy access to low-cost and high-speed technology for travel and communication, and a tendency toward multiculturalism in Western societies (Levitt 2001).

A MORE SECURE ISRAEL

Israel's recent attitude toward Israeli emigrants and Jewish migrants developed in a context of unprecedented demographic and economic growth and significant improvements in Israel's political situation. In 1989—the time of the last major spike of antiemigrant editorializing in Israeli newspapers—Israel was suffering economic stagnation, had a rate of inflation near 20 percent, an ongoing fear of war, and an inability to retain many of its best and brightest (Maoz and Temkin 1989). However, a mere decade later, Israel had signed the 1993 Oslo Peace Accords with the Palestinians and seen a relaxation of the Arab economic embargo. In addition, due to the massive Soviet aliyah, the Jewish state's population had increased by close to 20 percent—almost 1 million persons, many of whom were highly educated. Its inflation rate was below 3 percent, and it had the greatest number of engineers per capita in the world (almost double that of the second-ranking United States).

Moreover, during the 1980s, Israel's economy was plagued by stagflation, and its major export was citrus. By 2000, Israel had become a center of high technology and was seen as among the world's top growth economies (Hiltzik 2000). As such, it could offer its more affluent citizens a standard of material life equal to that of the industrialized West (Hiltzik 2000; Trofimov 1995). These political, economic, and demographic developments transformed Israeli society, making it better able to tolerate demographic losses to emigration and the diaspora resettlement of Jewish migrants. Further, Israel's recent economic transformation make it ever more in need of a globalized workforce—including the overseas involvement of Israelis in venture capital markets—to facilitate the continued growth of its economy (Lipkis 1991).

AN EMPHASIS ON SAVING JEWS

Another reason for Jewish migrants' recently enhanced status can be traced to Jews' growing concern with saving oppressed coethnics. While there has been wide awareness of the Holocaust since the 1940s, several writers have noted that the meaning of the event, and the related goal of protecting Jews, has been an

issue of special interest in diaspora communities since the late 1960s (Segev 1993).
One writer attributes the increased attention to the publication of *While Six
Million Died: A Chronicle of American Apathy* by Arthur D. Morse in 1968:
"Remembering the Holocaust became a central driving theme in Jewish community activity. . . . Learning the lessons of the Holocaust, ensuring that it would
never again happen, ending the decades of silence that had followed the events
themselves—these became the watchwords of the American Jewish community"
(Goldberg 1996:145). Similarly, Rabbi Arthur Hertzberg (1989) asserts that in
the 1970s, avoidance of the Holocaust was recanted, and its lessons summoned to
remind increasingly secure and complacent American Jews of the dangers of anti-
Semitism. The Shoah's impact was emphasized in books, Jewish studies courses,
and elsewhere, and found its expression in the slogan "never again": "American
Jews would define themselves by fighting their enemies and clinging to each
other" (Hertzberg 1989:382). The recent growth in Holocaust-themed museums,
books, films, and cultural programs suggests the gravity of this movement
(Seidler-Feller 1991). Accordingly, oppressed Jews became the target of intense
campaigns by Israel, by diaspora Jews, by Western nations, and by human rights
groups. Since the 1980s, such campaigns have been devoted to opening opportunities for emigration among subjugated Jewish communities in the Soviet
Union, Eastern Europe, Iran, Syria, Ethiopia, Bosnia, and other locations.

HUMAN RIGHTS AND REFUGEE MOVEMENTS

Another base for Jewish migrants' enhanced autonomy has been the growth of
movements to assist migrants and refugees in general. In the post–World War II
era, Western countries have been involved in a variety of programs to resettle
forced migrants and refugees. While highly selective, and subject to political
agendas, "many liberal states adhere" to "a partial global refugee regime" (Faist
2000:75; see also Salomon 1991). The refugee aid movement has been supported
by a wide range of interest groups ranging from idealistic reformers to religious
communities to governments seeking to discredit their geopolitical opponents
(Churgin 1996). The topic of Jewish migration is often cited as a motivating force
behind this movement, even as it seeks to ensure rights for various populations—
because of the terrible price paid as a result of the world's refusal to offer safe
havens to Jewish refugees during World War II (Faist 2000; Salomon 1991).

The demand for Soviet Jews' free emigration benefited greatly from the Cold
War politics of the 1970s and 1980s because the image of millions of religion-

seeking Jews being held against their will behind the so-called iron curtain provided a powerful indictment of the Soviet Union. From the late 1960s through the mid-1980s, various reports regarding the fate of refuseniks—Soviet Jews who had applied to emigrate to Israel but were not permitted to do so—appeared with regularity in the Jewish and mainstream media. The plight of Soviet Jews was linked to that of other groups seeking to escape communist regimes—including Cubans and Southeast Asians—and incorporated into the Refugee Act of 1980 and other laws facilitating the resettlement of refugees in the United States.

While the most extensive efforts have been directed toward refugees, there has also been a wide range of activities to enhance the rights of immigrants generally (Faist 2000; Soysal 1994). What has been called the rights revolution has resulted in a widespread acceptance of groups' self-determination and inclusion (Bauböck 1996). The "continual invocation of human rights establishes and advances universal contiguities and thus legitimates claims for rights and identities of 'persons,' from within or without national limits" (Soysal 1994:7). Moreover, according to human rights doctrine, populations defined by ethnicity, nationality, language, religion, or other factors are entitled to resist both national exclusion and assimilation. If they are compelled to do so in one state, they may be eligible for refuge and assistance in another.

EVOLVING RELATIONS BETWEEN ISRAEL AND THE DIASPORA

The increased willingness of Western Jewish communities to resettle Jewish migrants is clearly related to an evolving relationship between Israel and the diaspora. The state of interdependence between the two has been long acknowledged (Evron 1995). In recent decades, divergence accelerated as a more confident and powerful Israel sought to express its own prerogatives free from diaspora influence, while diaspora Jews increasingly focused on local concerns, experienced mixed feelings toward an Orthodox, Likud-led, and affluent Israel, and began to question Zionist assertions about the inevitably degrading nature of Jewish life in the diaspora (Becker 2001; Biale 1986; Cohen 1991; Hertzberg 1989; Shain 2000). According to the sociologist Steven M. Cohen, "Policymakers in American Jewish life and Israeli need to confront . . . the fact that Israel and American Jewry have been parting company politically, culturally and religiously" (qtd. in Hertzberg 1989:385).

While they commonly support Israel, Western diaspora communities are

STEVEN J. GOLD

generally patriotic and satisfied with life where they are (Bershtel and Graubard 1992; Wolitz 1991). They enjoy high levels of education, affluence, and political influence (Cohen 1999; Gold 1999; Gold and Phillips 1996; Hyman 1998; Lipset 1990; Pollins 1984; Schmool and Cohen 1998; Waterman and Kosmin 1986). David Biale (1986) writes that in the view of some American Jews, "the success of the American Jewish community is cause for celebration in virtually messianic terms: as opposed to all other Jewish communities, the Jews of America no longer live in exile. . . . For those who subscribe to this position, the ethos of America and the essence of Judaism have become virtually identical" (198).

Further, for many diaspora Jews, the appeal of Israel is not as strong as it once was. Since the 1980s, Jewish communal surveys have found that young diaspora Jews are less inspired by Israel than was the case during an earlier period. Differences concerning political ideologies and religious doctrine are among the major sources of contention (Cohen 1991; Tobin, Tobin and Troderman 1995). A small but influential movement—both in Israel and abroad—questions Zionism altogether (Azria 1998; Boyarin and Boyarin 1993; Finkielkraut 1994; Safran 1999). According to Avi Becker (2001), the director of the International Affairs of the World Jewish Congress, "the new generation of Israeli politicians and intellectuals have had trouble accepting the phenomenon of successful and flourishing Jewish life in the diaspora, especially in the US. This fact does not jibe with the Zionist ideology of the 'negation of the diaspora' nor with the image of the diaspora Jew these Israelis are familiar with and about which they studied in school."

One result of their differing views is that Israel and diaspora Jewish communities have come to develop contrasting perspectives on Jewish emigration. This has been most evident with regard to Soviet Jewry: "Most American Jews had been fighting for their Soviet brethren out of a belief that human beings had a natural, God-given right to live wherever they chose" (Goldberg 1996:185). This position contrasted dramatically with that of Israel, which emphasized "the God-given right of Jews to live in Israel" (Goldberg 1996:185). Accordingly, "when the American Jews' notion of free choice became enshrined in a federal law formalizing the flow of Soviet Jews to America, Israelis went on the warpath. The chairman of the Jewish Agency [the Israeli organization overseeing Jewish migration to Israel] . . . issued thunderous warnings that the American Jewish community was joining the crusade against Zionism" (Goldberg 1996:185). Greater conflicts were avoided because so many Jews left the former Soviet Union that both Israel and the United States were able to host a large number ("Number of Arrivals by Origin" 2001).

As a consequence of both Jewish migrants' and host communities' support for settlement outside of Israel, Israel's ability to control the process dwindled, and a new compromise emerged. While Israel and many of its supporters abroad would prefer the settlement of migrants in the Jewish state, they realize the futility of efforts to ban human movement. Instead, they have deployed a policy of selective cooperation and outreach.

JEWISH MIGRANTS' HIGH LEVELS OF SKILL AND WESTERN CULTURAL COMPETENCE

While issues internal to the Jewish community have shaped opportunities available to Jewish migrants, so have broader economic, social, and political trends. Jewish migrants have long been noted for their high levels of education and skill (Gold and Phillips 1996; Joseph 1914; Steinberg 1989). Yet until the 1960s, such skills were not generally regarded by countries of settlement as having overwhelming value. Instead, prejudice reigned. Jews and other ethnically stigmatized migrants were often seen as undesirables rather than as economic assets. For example, during World War II, when asked how many Jews should be admitted to Canada, one of the country's chief bureaucrats replied "None is too many" (Abella and Troper 1982 qtd. in Plaut 1996:24). Similarly, in the late 1940s and 1950s, The Displaced Persons Act—legislation invented by the American Jewish Committee to rescue Jewish Holocaust victims—was ultimately enacted with several revisions intended to exclude Jews.[2] Of the 365,000 arrivals the law ultimately permitted, only 16 percent were Jews. Far more entrants were Nazi collaborators from Baltic nations fleeing the advancing Soviet army: "In effect, a plan hatched by the American Jewish Committee to rescue Jewish Holocaust survivors ended up doing more for the Nazis' henchmen than for their victims" (Goldberg 1996:128–29).

However, by the 1970s, prejudice was less of an obstacle to the entrance of skilled immigrants. Instead, Jews and other groups previously subject to racial or ethnic discrimination were increasingly seen as valuable workers, especially if they were both skilled and immersed in Western culture (Gold 2000; Lipset 1990). According to Castles and Miller (1998:92), Findlay (1995), and Findlay and Li (1998), highly skilled migrants are much sought after, even in countries where there is growing hostility to immigration. The economist George Borjas (1996) describes a world market for highly skilled workers in which various countries compete for the most desirable migrants. Governments, business interests, educational institutions, and organizations in various locations understand the value of what Nonini and Ong (1997) call "transnational functionaries associated with the globalization of capitalist production" (10) to the furtherance of political and economic integration and capital growth. Because a large fraction of contemporary Jewish migrants are both skilled and cosmopolitan, they are in the position to choose among countries of settlement and can consequently often avoid less desirable locations. Contemporary Jewish migrants often pursue transnational lives to realize these possibilities.

Available evidence suggests that the skills and educational levels of contemporary Jewish emigrants are very high. Israeli emigrants are far more educated and skilled than Israelis generally, and among the very most highly educated of all arrivals in their countries of settlement (Toren 1980). Yinon Cohen (1996) determined that "regardless of the data and methodology used, Israeli Jewish immigrants in the United States were found to be more educated and to hold higher status occupations than both US and Israeli populations" (78). Census data from the United Kingdom reveal that Israeli emigrants in Britain are also marked by high levels of education and occupational prestige: "The Israeli-born form a skilled professional work-force, 56 percent were in professional, management or technical occupations" (Schmool and Cohen 1998:30).

Soviet, Iranian, and South African Jewish migrants are also noted for their high levels of education, skill, entrepreneurial experience, and in some cases, access to capital (Feher 1998; Gold 1999). For example, Soviet Jews have a higher level of education than the U.S. population as a whole. More than 27 percent of those over age twenty-five are college graduates. A large fraction, including both men and women, are trained in sought-after scientific and technical fields, and over 20 percent of those aged sixteen and over are employed as professionals in the United States (Gold 1995a; Portes and Rumbaut 1996).[3] About 50 percent of Iranian Jews in Los Angeles have four years of college. Over 80 percent work as entrepreneurs, and they tend to live in the city's (ergo the nation's) most affluent neighborhoods (Kelley and Friedlander 1993).

SETTLEMENT IS NOT ALWAYS PERMANENT

Another reason for Jewish migrants' increased self-determination can be traced to new understandings about the relationship between location, identification, and settlement. While commonsense thinking and popular ideology assume migration as a permanent move, the actions of contemporary Jewish migrants suggest that it is not. This is especially the case with regard to Israeli emigrants, who have the option to return home. Many studies of Israeli emigration report that Jewish migrants—including those who have spent a decade or more in the host society—continue to "sit on their suitcases" and refer to their imminent return to Israel. Migrants do this in order to emphasize their identity as Israelis, while denying their status as yordim, stigmatized migrants (Mittelberg and Waters 1992; Shokeid 1988; Uriely 1994). Several of my respondents did just this. Ilan, a London restaurateur, told us, "I make a living here—I don't really live here." When the investigator asked: "Do you feel any change in your identity? Do you feel more or less Israeli or Jewish since you came here? Do you feel English?", Ilan responded: "No change at all. I'm an Israeli and I will go back to Israel. I do not see myself living here, and we made no such decisions to stay here. We have no plans to emigrate. It's a rolling snowball. We will go back eventually. When I'm 40 years old—I'll go back home."

Such sentiments are often put into action. Data suggest that a significant fraction of Israeli emigrants eventually return (Chabin 1997; Cohen 1996; *For those Returning Home* 1995). In fact, Israeli demographers assert that the "failure to consider Israeli's high rates of return migration" is a major reason for the controversy surrounding Israeli emigration (Cohen and Haberfeld 1997:200). Since migration is not always permanent, the presence of Israelis and others does not prove as threatening as it might be. In fact, former Israelis are much more likely to make aliyah than other segments of diaspora Jewry, a fact not missed by Israeli officials, who have altered policy toward emigrants to encourage return (*For those Returning Home* 1995). Both economic realities and national policy now tolerate and even encourage transnationalism among Israeli emigrants. Jewish migrants draw on multiculturalism and diversity to choose patterns of adaptation in host societies.

As is the case in most Western countries, Israel and major centers of diaspora Judaism have been powerfully influenced by identity politics and multiculturalism. Rejecting their assimilationist traditions—whereby elites sought to impose identities and ways of life on migrants—these settings now increasingly tolerate the maintenance of diverse identities by immigrant and ethnic groups. Describing the situation in Israel, Moshe Shokeid (1998) asserts that expressions of ethnic culture that would have been considered unpatriotic in previous decades

STEVEN J. GOLD

are now accepted as expressions of Israeliness: "Ethnic jokes and manners considered 'diasporic' lost most of their humiliating consequences long ago. They have actually become part of Israeli culture" (240).

Movements to maintain subgroup identities, which have a long, if obscured, tradition in Jewish history, have multiple impacts on contemporary Jewish migrants (Goldstein 1995; Howe 1976). First, they often reinforce migrants' belief in the value of their own cultural, linguistic, and religious traditions and provide a vocabulary for articulating such values and identities in the public sphere. For example, Israelis, Jews from the former Soviet Union (FSU), and to some extent Iranians understand Jewishness in large part as a *nationality*, which stands in considerable contrast to American Jews' identity, increasingly seen as a *religious* persuasion (Gold 1999; Kelley and Friedlander 1993). Accordingly, they seek to maintain their own outlooks rather than accepting dominant perspectives in points of settlement. A Soviet Jewish activist in San Francisco describes how Russian and American notions of Jewishness differ:

I want the American community to understand who we are, because I feel personally a lot of our problems and a lot of our, you know, negative feelings toward each other is because people don't understand each other. . . . First of all, we are not like your grandparents, people from Sholom Aleichem. We are educated, professional people. If you talk about the community in general, it's a non-religious community and that's it. Because we don't have religious ground. You have to form this ground first, but I don't think this will be an overnight thing. Right now, I try really to impress to American community, for us, Jewishness is non-religious.

Multiculturalism and Jewish diversity further alter the experience of Jewish migrants by challenging singular definitions of Jewish identity and practice. Because there are so many ways of expressing one's Jewish identity in both Israel and diaspora communities, even if migrants wanted to conform to the "mainstream," they would have a very hard time doing so. Illustrating this propensity is the fact that when Jewish immigrants—including Israelis, Soviets, and Iranians—seek to become Jewishly active in diaspora communities, a large fraction do so through involvement in the immigrant outreach activities of the ultra Orthodox Chabad movement, seen as marginal by many diaspora Jews and their communal organizations (Gold 1995a; Hertzberg 1989; Shokeid 1998).

Reflecting their cultural and linguistic preferences, recent Jewish migrants in both Israel and abroad often create their own social, economic, religious, and cultural activities, some of which have limited contact with those of the larger Jewish community (Frankentel 1998; Gold 1992; Kelley and Friedlander 1993; Markowitz 1993; Sabar 2000; Siegel 1999). Migrants' reluctance to affiliate with their proximal hosts can provoke resentment among the host communities. A Los Angeles communal professional complained about Israelis' self-segregation: "I've come into contact with many Israelis for years. Some were here for a long time and they didn't want to have anything to do with anybody else. They wanted to have a little Israel you know, a junior Tel Aviv here, a Ramat Gan. And they wanted to associate with nobody else but Israelis and have their kids hang out with nobody else but Israelis and they didn't want to integrate with the other American Jews." Similarly, in their book on Iranians in Los Angeles, Kelley and Friedlander (1993) point out that while Iranian Jews live and work near hundreds of thousands of coreligionists, "on the whole, the Iranian Jews have kept to themselves, preferring the familiarity of their own social networks and Persian cultural traditions" (102).

While emigrants' expressions of alienation and distance from the host community are common, they are hardly universal. A number of Jewish migrants feel relatively satisfied with their new homes. Such is the case for David—a Los Angeles entrepreneur and communal activist. Successful in unifying Israeli emigrants and native-born Jews, he believes that Israelis need to join the American Jewish community:

The Israelis have to come into the Jewish community. Take for example my own family. I don't see that just because somebody's grandmother left the same village in Poland that my grandmother lived in 80 years ago and came to New York, and my relatives came to Israel, that I'm that different from that person. I mean, all Israelis somewhere harbor the hope that they will go back to Israel. But the truth is that all of them are here temporarily, and then they die. And that's the reality. I've been here eighteen years, I would like to go back, I don't know if I will. You have your businesses, people have families. You know, they cannot just pick up and leave. And they have gotten used to the way of life here and that's their reality. So these two communities need each other. I think that instead of having their divisive or divided Jewish community, we need to have one strong united community.

Finally, sources of difference beyond national origins can also shape complex reactions to national identification and settlement within Jewish populations. For example, a growing body of research demonstrates that reactions to migration and settlement are gendered (Hondagneu-Sotelo 1994; Pessar 1999). Studies of Jewish immigration confirm this finding, showing that Israeli, Russian, and Iranian women and men have distinct evaluations of life in the country of origin and host society. Frequent international travel is often provoked by couples' efforts to stay together, or if they fail to do so, is instigated by their divorces (Dallalfar 1994; Gold 1995a).

In sum, Jewish migrants have diverse reactions to their host societies and to local Jewish communities within them. These diverse beliefs shape their patterns of adaptation, concepts of homeland, their national and religious identities, and their plans about settlement, future migration, or return to the country of origin.

Conclusions

Observers have noted a growing diversity among Jewish communities in both Israel and the diaspora (Friedman 2000; Goldscheider 1996; Sobel 1986). In each of these settings, increasing polarization occurs along lines of ideology, class, religion, gender roles, and other factors. The elevated autonomy available to migrants is a product of these tendencies. At the same time, migrants' disparate and often transnationally focused patterns of life further contribute the diversity present within Jewish populations (Gold 1992, 1994b, 1994c; Orleck 1999; Sabar 2000; Shokeid 1988; Uriely 1995).

This suggests a trend toward less geographical unity among Jews. Simultaneously, however, while there is less uniformity, there is also evidence of new, often international, forms of interconnection and cooperation. One example of this trend is that diaspora residents (including former Israelis) are increasingly involved in Israeli politics. It is common for them to fly to Israel to participate in demonstrations and elections (Broder 1999; Radler 2001). For their part, Israelis increasingly travel to diaspora locations to accomplish goals associated with religion, politics, family, business, and other purposes (Orleck 1999). Yossi Shain (2000) demonstrates that segments of the American Jewish community increasingly seek to make Israeli Jewish identity compatible with their own American values. These tendencies toward diversity and border crossing among Jewish interest groups are likely to lead to further internationalization and network formation within the world Jewish community. As the French sociologist Reginé Azria contends, more than ever, emigration and travel now form accepted features of Jewish reality: "Thus, today, some Jews are simultaneously Israeli Jews and diaspora Jews without being concerned about either this or which passport they carry. They travel around the world simply because they feel like it, or because they need to for professional, academic, family or vacation purposes" (Azria 1998:24).

Jews reveal similarities to other skilled migrants in terms of their transnational networks, occupations, and settlement patterns. Moreover, like other migrants, Israeli and diaspora Jews have to deal with political and identificational involvement in multiple nation-states. Also like other migrant and diasporic populations —such as Chinese, South Asians, Koreans, Middle Easterners, and Filipinos—the group features sizable class, gender/family, and ideological differences between the country of origin and migrant populations (Castles and Miller 1998).

Like other transnational populations, Jews are finding that nation building and solidarity no longer revolve around a single location. Their challenge is to create a model of nationality, homeland, and peoplehood capable of unifying a dispersed population. This quest is long-standing in Jewish history. However, the contemporary context both demands new understandings of identity and offers new possibilities. Reflecting on the ongoing transformation of Jewish identity, Etan Levine (1983) contended that with the creation of the Jewish state, "the existential Jewish question is not only how to sanctify a moment in time, but how to sanctify a point in space as well" (7). However, only twenty-three years later, given the increased number of Jewish migrants, their enhanced self-determination (in terms of both culture and location of settlement), and the impact of evolving relations between Israel and the diaspora, Jews can no longer focus on a singular, geographically delimited location in space to resolve this dilemma. Interdependent Jewish communities now exist both within and beyond Israel, and individuals, ideas, and resources continually oscillate between them. While many Jews hoped that the creation of Israel would resolve questions of their national identity, current patterns of Jewish migration demonstrate that the controversy endures. As the Israeli political scientist Gabriel Sheffer (1998) asserts in his article on the Israeli diaspora, "Decades after Israel's independence it is still not clear which is the dominant component in world Jewry" (10).

Notes

1. Data for this article were collected through the ethnographic study of Soviet Jewish and Israeli immigrant communities. With both groups, interviews and participant observation focused on premigration life, motives for emigration, patterns of social and economic adaptation, religious, ethnic, and national identity, and plans with regard to settlement or return. Research on Soviet Jews was conducted between 1982 and 1994,

STEVEN J. GOLD

primarily in the San Francisco Bay Area and in Los Angeles. I conducted in-depth interviews with sixty-eight émigrés and twenty-five nonrefugee service providers. I also did extensive participant observation as a volunteer English teacher in émigré homes, businesses, and other settings. Finally, I worked for two years as a resettlement worker and several years as a board member in agencies that served Soviet Jewish immigrants (Gold 1992; 1995a). To learn about the experience of Israeli immigrants, I worked in conjunction with five Hebrew-speaking women research assistants to collect several forms of data between June 1991 and July 2000. A major source were 194 in-depth interviews (conducted in both Hebrew and English) with Israeli immigrants and others knowledgeable about their community in the Los Angeles area. We also interviewed fifty Israeli emigrants in London, fourteen in Paris, and thirty returned emigrants in Israel. Additional interviews were collected in suburban Detroit and New York City. Referrals to Israeli respondents were obtained from a variety of sources including Jewish communal agencies, the Israeli consulates (Los Angeles and New York), representatives of various Israeli associations, research assistants' acquaintances, and snowball referrals. To facilitate rapports and openness, we did not use a formal interview schedule. However, questions were selected from prepared lists of interview issues (Gold 1994c). In addition to in-depth interviews, we also conducted participant-observation research at a variety of religious and secular community activities and in other settings.

2. For example, the legislation included a preference for farmers in order to reduce the number of largely urban Jews who would be eligible to enter the United States (Goldberg 1996:128).

3. These figures include non-Jews because the census does not collect religious information. However, if data were specific to Jews, educational and occupational profiles would likely be even higher (Gold 1994c).

"On Halloween We Dressed Up Like KGB Agents": Reimagining Soviet Jewish Refugee Identities in the United States

KATHIE FRIEDMAN

The concept of transnationalism has recently become for sociologists of immigration a type of compass that directs questions, explanation, and method. A parallel theoretical consequence of intensifying globalization is the rebirth and widespread application of the term *diaspora*, once reserved as a descriptor for the dispersion of the Jewish people. Discussions about the forms, extent, and consequences of transnational and diasporic practices of immigrants and their children have added important new global dimensions to the narrow debates over assimilation, modes of incorporation, and multiculturalism in the United States, promising a more holistic approach, more depth, and some unexpected comparisons (Basch, Glick Schiller, and Szanton Blanc 1994; Clifford 1994; Cohen 1997; Espiritu and Tran 2002; Smith and Guarnizo 1998; Van Hear 1998; Wahlbeck 2002; Wolf 1997). The present interest in transnational communities and diasporas thus raises the question of what a transnational or diasporic identity is, and how it might be experienced. What is the subjectivity or self-understanding of a transnational subject? What is the process by which that self-understanding is constructed, and in what terms? Finally, what are the implications, social and sociological, of analyzing transnational identities?

These conceptual advances and new questions have scarcely touched the study of recent Jewish migrations. The indifference of sociologists to the study of former Soviet Jewish refugee families after more than three decades of their migration, compared to analyses of Latin American, Caribbean, and Asian immigrants, is puzzling, even troubling.[1] This essay proposes to close this lacuna to a limited extent by examining the transnational process of collective and personal identity construction on the part of former Soviet Jewish refugees and their children in the United States. It advances a limited explanation for the relative absence of Jews within transnational studies, applies a process- and relation-centered approach to analyze how Jewish refugees and their children understand their multilayered and fluid sense of ethnic affiliations, and concludes with a suggestion about the broader conceptual insights and implications that might follow from the inclusion of new Jewish refugees in global migration studies.

I argue that the making of identities by former Soviet Jewish refugees and their children in the United States is a transnational process. Refugee diasporas are, however, distinct from other transnational networks, particularly in the extent to which they are defined and collectively self-represented by a history of prior minority status, victimization, and forced displacement (Cohen 1997; Safran 1991). In the words of Jonathan Boyarin, "Jewish experience often entails 'multiple experiences of rediasporization, which do not necessarily succeed each other in historical memory but echo back and forth'" (qtd. in Clifford 1994:305). Building on the insights of transnationalism, I start by contextualizing former Soviet Jewish refugee identities at home in the multinational USSR, and then examine how these were transformed during the journey to the United States. In the still-evolving process of resettling, I explore how the meanings and lessons of past collective group identifications and family memories may be evoked or reworked as boundaries are negotiated with the institutions of the new host society, the American Jewish coethnic community, and ethnic Others in the multicultural United States.

Data for this study is drawn from in-depth interviews of first- and 1.5-generation former Soviet Jewish immigrants in Seattle, conducted between 1998 and 2001.[2] Knowledge about refugee identities generated through intensive life-history interviewing, in contrast to reliance on more generalizable survey data, is indispensable. It offers space for refugees to represent themselves and may thus generate new research questions from outside the well-trodden models; it evidences the simultaneous presence of multiple perspectives and ambivalent, even contradictory experiences; and it provides a much-needed humanism in refugee research to supplement the more structural and policy-driven studies.

Wandering Jews: From Scholarly Desert
to Strategic Research Site

Though the more than four hundred thousand Soviet Jews who immigrated to the United States between 1965 and 1999 are a numerically small group when placed in the context of the post-1965 migrations of Latin Americans and Asians,[3] they and particularly their children have conceptual significance well beyond their numbers. So what may account for the relative invisibility of new Jewish immigrants and their children in this rapidly proliferating transnational migration literature? One part of the answer lies in the underlying assumptions and motives driving research on the new, post-1965 immigration to the United States. Another rests on presumptions about Jews and former Soviet citizens. The remaining piece of the invisibility puzzle exposes some of the shortcomings of recent applications of transnational and diasporic analysis.

Questions of immigrant or ethnic economic mobility, political behavior, and cultural adjustment dominate much of today's sociological research, mirroring the interests and fears of native-born Americans, much as they have since the analysis of the last great wave prior to World War I. Put bluntly, many present-day social scientists wonder about the extent to which nonwhite, non-European immigrants can adapt and contribute to U.S. society. Given this as the underlying concern, new Jewish immigrant invisibility stems from the group's characterization by both sociologists and Jewish American institutions as unproblematically white, European, modern in religious practice, highly educated, highly skilled, and family-centered. At the same time, a notion of Jewish exceptionalism pervades U.S. assimilation studies in other ways: Jews are represented as the classic outsider, neither a purely ethnic nor religious category, unassimilated yet successful.

Despite decades of useful constructivist thinking among social scientists, new Soviet Jewish refugees and their children are nonetheless grouped with American Jews and presumed to be part of the same internally homogeneous and externally bounded "Jewish people." Yet significant intragroup differences characterize both immigrant waves. Central European coreligionists of the pre–World War I period, together with many native-born Americans, viewed Eastern European Jewish immigrants as not-quite-white or not-yet-white (Brodkin 1998; Friedman-Kasaba 1996; Jacobson 1998). First-generation Soviet Jews I interviewed identified "Russians" as non-Jewish, whereas "Georgian" Jews were portrayed as "believers"

KATHIE FRIEDMAN

(religiously observant), "traditional," clannish, and "uneducated." In the words of a St. Petersburg Jew, "Georgians wouldn't know if it was Hebrew or Russian you were speaking." On the other hand, "Jews" (particularly those from Moscow or St. Petersburg) were characterized as "cosmopolitans" and "intelligentsia." Once, when I questioned one of my Saint Petersburg informants about what made her Jewish, she replied nervously, "writing a dissertation."

This essay questions ethnic affiliations after ethnic unmixing in the former Soviet Union without taking groups for granted, or presuming group affiliation, the object of the analysis. The former Soviet Union, a complex multiethnic, multinational, multiracial, multiclass, and multireligious society, unraveled along equally complex lines. Following political collapse in 1991, its splintering into increasing numbers of economically and otherwise untenable ethnonational fragments, and widespread often again forced population movements from one newly nationalized fragment to another, nothing seems more problematic than to assume any sort of homogeneous, bounded, fixed, or stable identity for Soviet Jewish refugees.

Despite the centrality of globalization in our understanding of today's world, immigration scholarship still tends to be too centered on the perspective of the host society, on the problem of adjusting immigrants to a single, bounded nation-state, and relatively disinterested in the internal identity work of transnational immigrants or the transformations immigrants effect on their host society. The two important critical perspectives in the field of immigration—transnational and diaspora studies—both tend to uncritically reify transnational communities and ethnic groups, treating them as if they were themselves actors in world affairs or relatively stable, discrete, internally unified and externally bounded units, simply linked via material practices that cross nation-state lines. Though early practitioners of transnational studies forewarned that "by applying a label [transnational] we risk recreating a bounded, classless reification similar to the very construct of 'ethnic group' and nation" (Basch, Glick Schiller, and Szanton Blanc 1994:290), a decade later sympathetic scholars nonetheless admit that "transnational studies have their own contradictions that may reintroduce methodological nationalism in other guises" (Wimmer and Glick Schiller 2003:576).

Diaspora studies similarly presume the stability, internal coherence, and unity of a deterritorialized civilization or "people." In this case, the emphasis lies on the boundary between "the Jewish people," wherever and whenever one finds them, in contrast to all of the "others." Rogers Brubaker (2002) describes this as "the tendency to represent the social and cultural world as a multichrome mosaic of monochromatic ethnic, racial, or cultural blocs" (164). Diaspora studies, by overlooking the significance of intradiaspora differences (e.g., the distinction between those diasporans who have lived in their homeland and those who identify with a homeland they have only dreamed of or heard about, as well as divisions based on class, region, language, gender, politics, etc.) takes for granted that ethnicity *should* feel binding and *should* predispose people to form group allegiances. This compounds the problem of understanding the variability of ethnic identification, how and when ethnic affiliations are produced, become salient, are reproduced, or transformed. Similarly, interactions across ethnic boundaries that impinge on notions of self-contained diasporas or transnational communities (e.g., assimilation) tend to be minimized. These assumptions explain little about how the world of ethnic identification works and leave unanswered questions that go to the root of the concern about ethnic identity: the motives for ethnic conflict, cooperation, and refugee flight. Projects of establishing ethnic identity may be more or less successful, may produce optional, rather loose and situational identities, "or may create identities which deeply enough shape actors' self-understandings and understandings of how the world itself is organized that they feel compulsory and are powerful variables in social analysis" (Calhoun 2003:561).

In this essay I apply a process- and relation-centered approach to the project of evolving transnational identities among Jewish refugee families from the former Soviet Union (FSU) in the United States. The process of social identity construction is fluid, interactive, and dynamic, yet neither immigrants nor their children are entirely free to choose the identities they want, or to attach their own meanings to these identities. The adoption (subversion, evasion, transformation, or rejection) of group identities, affiliations, and allegiances reflects how an individual thinks about himself or herself in the context of the historical and symbolic meanings attached to any particular identity. It represents as well the ways individuals negotiate their identities in the face of myriad power relations and social institutions, including family life, that shape possibilities and behaviors.

Understanding ethnic self-identification, unmixing, and remixing requires understanding the role of narratives in creating ethnic group identities. Families are a particularly powerful locus and preserver of narrative memories (schools, ethnic associations, states and their organizational components are others), as elders tell stories to younger people replete with historical heroes and villains, as well as the meaning and purpose of group identity. For the children of immigrants, who did not make the decision to uproot and transplant themselves, the question of identity appears particularly vexing, with important consequences for their futures, as well as for the host society's. Growing up partly in the United States and partly outside, the 1.5 and second generation respond to their immigrant parents' ideas and attitudes, but they also construct and manage their identity trajectories on the basis of their own experiences and stereotypes of America's multiple ethnic Others. This study of FSU Jewish refugees demonstrates how social institutions interact with individual experiences and narrative memories to produce varying perceptions and performances of ethnic allegiance. It seeks to understand the ways people combine and deploy their own home-country memories, post-memories, and more official diasporic and coethnic narratives of collective destiny with their everyday interactions both to construct affiliations and to create external boundaries between themselves and others.

One objective in taking this approach to the study of self-identification is to demonstrate how Soviet *Jewish* migration can be sociologically comparable to some other refugee migrations, rather than it being so anomalous and exceptional as to remain excluded from analysis. Shining a sociological spotlight on the perceptions and affiliations of minority-group refugees and their children who escaped a complex multiethnically disintegrating system for a multicultural society that includes coethnics of previous migration waves raises new questions and can result in new conceptual insights. What is the homeland identity of a refugee whose country of origin has vanished in political-juridical terms? Where do refugees return to, literally or symbolically, when "new homelands" in which they have never lived are constructed on the physical territory in which they did live? To whom may we usefully compare these twice or thrice displaced refugees and their children? The case of former Soviet Jewish refugees and their children is treated here as a strategic research site for its potential to extend transnational and diaspora studies, as well as to elucidate social processes and concepts that may be generalized beyond this particular case.

The First Refugee Generation: Transnational Families and the Production of Identities

Because international migration directly exposes and challenges presumed categories of social and political identification, it offers a window to explore how individuals perceive and construct their identities. In a context that offers both possibilities and constraints, refugees perceive their identities in the light of selective memory, past experience, present interactions, and future aspirations for their children. In this section, I explore how one transnational Soviet Jewish refugee family understands its ethnic, racial, national, and religious identities as it crosses international borders and resettles in the United States and Israel.[4]

SVETLANA'S FAMILY: A TALE OF MIXING, UNMIXING, AND REDIASPORIZATION

Whether a refugee was from birth designated Jewish on his or her internal Soviet passport, or chose the Jewish nationality at age sixteen as the child of a "mixed nationality" marriage,[5] he or she experienced a physically and psychologically difficult period of internal exile, displacement, or estrangement from their home country prior to crossing an international border (e.g., loss of livelihood, educational prospects, and sometimes homes and friends). Despite this, when I asked Svetlana to tell me when she first started to consider emigration as an option for herself and her family, without blinking an eye she launched into a lengthy and detailed three-generation family history of transnational migration. What was important to Svetlana was the knowledge that her family had only been in the Soviet Union for a relatively short time, historically speaking. Her Jewish grandparents were originally German and Romanian, and she had grown up with stories about having family members everywhere, including California and New York. Remembering this legacy of migration seemed to provide her with some sense of family continuity across shifts in space. Perhaps the thought of being part of a larger ethnic diaspora even offered some solace or comfort. In addition to diasporic cultural memories (Laguerre 1998), Svetlana was able to draw on a bit of the cultural capital, that is, the migratory know-how accumulated within the diaspora. Access to knowledge of how to go about migration, how to deal with brokers and bureaucrats, how to utilize preexisting contacts in receiving countries, or how to develop them helped transform Svetlana from a potential refugee into an actual one (Van Hear 1998).

This part of Svetlana's story demonstrates the multilayered and situational or contingent nature of ethnic/national/religious self-identification. Further along in her tale, she betrays also what she perceives as a lesson about the sticky or essentially unchanging nature of Jewish identity. Svetlana's mother is half-Russian, that is, her grandfather was Russian Orthodox and her grandmother Jewish. At age sixteen, her mother chose the non-Jewish "Russian" nationality designation for her internal passport, as did the vast majority of children in

KATHIE FRIEDMAN

mixed Jewish-Russian families during that time. Svetlana, however, recalled for me with pride a story her mother often told to her during her childhood about the moment during World War II when she assumed her true Jewish identity. As it was told, Svetlana's mother, then age eight, repeated some anti-Semitic remarks she had overheard to a Jewish neighbor, who rebuked the young girl, took her in hand, and taught her Jewish culture and the Yiddish language. In fact, when I interviewed Svetlana's mother, at the time visiting from her new home in Israel, she offered me the choice of a conversation in Russian, Hebrew, or Yiddish. Svetlana helped translate some of her mother's Russian into English for me, while I translated some of her mother's Hebrew and Yiddish into English for Svetlana. Svetlana took her mother's story as a lesson not to hide her authentic nationality, and thus as the child of a mixed marriage herself, she assumed a Jewish internal passport identity in the 1970s, against her mother's and grandmother's strong fears.

From Svetlana and her mother I learned about the ways transit camps, refugee centers, and resettlement agencies organize individuals into more manageable, less messy identity categories before they reach their destination. With anger as palpable as if the events I recount in the following had just transpired, Svetlana recalled for me her encounter with resettlement authorities in the late 1980s. While in transit to the United States, she related how a Hebrew Immigrant Aid Society (HIAS) worker in Rome had challenged her Jewish identity. My outspoken informant identified herself to this resettlement worker as Jewish by nationality (her USSR passport identity), but not Jewish in terms of her faith or spirituality. "Faith," she explained to me, "does not mean the same thing as nationality. Nationality is a blood thing, a given. My nationality is Jewish. But religion is about culture . . . and culture is a matter of choice." When, as she put it, she was "too honest" with the HIAS caseworker about the precise nature of her beliefs, she was informed, "under our laws you aren't Jews, so we can't help you." Svetlana's identity had never been challenged like this. She became frightened that her honesty would put herself, her husband (Muslim, atheist, artist, from the northern Caucausus), and their three small children (one just born in transit) "on the streets of Italy" without food. Her voice, strong with strong emotion, continued, "My religion is my personal choice. But I'm born a Jew and I will die a Jew!" Ultimately, Svetlana was turned away from HIAS. She eventually located another resettlement agency in Rome, the Tolstoy Foundation, who according to its mission statement helps resettle "Russian Jews, primarily those in mixed marriages," and other immigrant nationalities. Ironically, Svetlana's mother, with her non-Jewish identity stamped on her internal passport, found herself and the rest of the family assisted by HIAS in migrating to Israel in 1990, while the self-identified Jewish daughter found herself in Salt Lake City, (a node for the Tolstoy Foundation) with her Jewishness an object of suspicion. Ethnic and friendship networks permitted her to make a secondary migration to Washington State. Because parents, children, and grandchildren may have selected different nationalities for the internal passport depending on the political climate of the moment, they may have been resettled in different countries. Some were only accepted in Israel, while others found themselves denied admission to Israel but allowed into Canada, Australia, Germany, or the United States. Thus the notorious Soviet internal passport may have paradoxically assisted in the re-diasporization of Jews, and in the development of a new, more complex transnational Jewish community.

As I was preparing to leave Svetlana's home one evening following an interview session with her and her mother visiting from Israel, two of her young sons plopped themselves against the kitchen table and demanded to know what the three of us had been talking about. "About how we are Jews," Svetlana replied. The kids looked stunned. "No, we're not," they chimed in unison. Their mother looked embarrassed and responded, "Yes, you are and so am I and so is your grandmother." In an annoyed voice, the oldest said, "No, we're American." Svetlana turned to me and attempted to explain that after being beaten up in pre-school for being "Russian," her boys wanted to be known as "American." Then she sighed, looked outside the window at the worn housing in the neighborhood, and muttered under her breath, "That's why we have to move away from all these Russians." Svetlana feared that if she did not move her family into a middle-class Jewish neighborhood, and if her sons did not adopt Jewish identities, they would continue to be stigmatized as lower-class Russians, and likely adopt tough Russian personas in response. When her teenage daughter fell into the wrong crowd, Svetlana resorted to a traditional strategy of transnational families: she sent her to live and finish school with relatives in Israel.

At the same time, Russianness continues to loom large in Svetlana's life in both negative and positive ways. One afternoon when I was interviewing Svetlana at work, a Russian colleague burst in (a non-Jewish former political dissident) waving an anti-Semitic pamphlet circulating in the Seattle Russian-speaking community. Svetlana sighed, "What we left, we came to." Yet the Russian language persists as a positive dimension of her identity. To paraphrase her, "being separated from the mother tongue [from American English] keeps you at a distance from the host society—and this is negative—but being a Russian speaker in the United States gives you a height from which you can feel superior to them [to monolingual English speakers]." The last time I saw Svetlana, she handed me her crisp new business card: she was starting to edit a local Russian-language magazine.

The story of Svetlana's family's migration underlines, first, the multiple layered and contradictory interpretations of transnational or diasporic group belonging—Russianness and Jewishness—held by refugees themselves and by resettlement authorities. These have not fared well in translation. Contradictory interpretations include understanding identity as a "racial" blood-related or biological identity, as nationality, as a matter of personal spiritual beliefs, and as a set of shared transgenerational and transnational cultural symbols and practices. Moreover, these are not always and everywhere held to be mutually exclusive. Second, Svetlana's family's experiences highlight the almost literal renegotiation and reorganization of identities on the journey, between the gatekeepers and institutions who control the means of exit and entry, on the one hand, and those who desire admission based on what they perceive as their group-based rights. How Svetlana's children, and other members of the 1.5 and second generation, understand themselves in relation to multiple Others in American society and also transnationally is the subject of the following section.

The 1.5 Generation: Establishing Cultural Bridges and Transnational Identities

For children of former Soviet Jewish refugees who did not themselves make the decision to migrate, the question of self-identification proves particularly challenging. In their early twenties at the time of their interviews, they carry their own young memories of cross-national relationships and ethnic unraveling in the former Soviet Union, as well as selective memories and beliefs handed down from other family members and the symbols and myths of a collective destiny for the diaspora. But they experience themselves and their futures based equally on interactions with multiple ethnic Others in their neighborhoods and schools in the United States.

IDENTITY AND MEMORIES OF LEAVING

What children of refugees remember about their departure, what they have been told by parents and grandparents, and how they integrate this information into their everyday lives in the United States has an important impact on the development of their self-identities. Although all immigrants and refugees faced profound structural constraints in departing, journeying, seeking admission, and resettling, children faced the additional dilemma of being displaced presumably for their own good but without their participation in the decision making. Bella was brought to the United States, her parents told her, "for the kids' futures, to avoid army service for my [younger] brother, and because of anti-Semitism" right after her fourteenth birthday. She was forbidden from telling any of her classmates or friends that she was leaving. "Peoples' [refugees'] experiences really depend on what age they were when they came to the U.S. [It's] really important," she instructed me in heavily accented English. "How can we just take off?!" she recalls wondering at the time. "I didn't make the decision myself."

Igor came to the United States when he was ten years old. He was told "to escape anti-Semitism, to start a new life, [because] the place was falling apart, for the typical American dream." Most of his relatives ended up in Israel, but his parents told him they wanted better economic opportunities for him and his brother. Similarly, Lara arrived in the United States when she was ten, yet most of her relatives and family's friends emigrated to Israel.

Max, who migrated when he was twelve, proudly celebrated his ten-year anniversary in the United States a week before our interview.

If you're Jewish going to Israel is very easy. Coming to America without relatives, which was our situation, is like winning the lottery. So, I think that I'm probably not going to win the lottery again in my life, this is it, you know? I think this is the greatest thing to happen to me so far in my life, and I mean it has a lot to do with my parents, how hard my parents have worked at this.

Rina (Irina), who was only three years old when she came to the United States, confessed, "You know, I have no memories of Russia. I sometimes try so hard . . . I have little memory spurts of different things but . . . I don't know for sure." When I asked what she remembered her parents telling her about their reasons for leaving, she looked relieved and launched into the story her mother told her: "It's actually an interesting story. My Dad's sister decided that she was going to come. She's like, you know, 'we should go to America. There's so many great opportunities.' She's the one that kind of got the ball rolling for my parents."

Age at the time of migration has an important impact on the project of establishing collective identities. Bella felt torn from beloved classmates at a fragile moment in her personal development, and she continues to feel disempowered in most areas of life by her heavily accented English, while Rina's grammar and hand-me-down memories mark her as more second generation. A strong and persistent motif among all respondents was the debt they owed their parents for taking them out of the FSU and to the United States, a clear demonstration of the impact parents' memories, stories, and aspirations have on childrens' identities. Yet these young adults also granted Israel an important place in their ethnic self-understanding. Spontaneously and without the least bit of prompting, Igor, Lara, and Max each felt called on to defend at great length their family's decision to *not* settle in Israel, indicating they were well aware of the expectation placed on Jews in the diaspora.

IDENTITIES AND MEMORIES OF ARRIVAL: ENCOUNTERS BETWEEN SOVIET JEWS AND THE INSTITUTIONS OF JEWISH AMERICA

Children of Soviet Jewish refugees remember their early years in the United States as laced with economic hardship and cultural misunderstanding. They associate much of both with the mainstream or established Jewish American community organizations that helped to sponsor them and subsidize their initial years. As a result, they evidence some inherited as well as directly experienced ambivalence toward mainstream Jewish Americans, hindering a close identification. The young adults I interviewed are seriously working out how they fit into Jewish America, balancing their own interactions and goals in the United States against their immigrant parents' experiences of being uncomfortably Jewish in two places. As they have all found out, parents and children together, being Jewish in the former Soviet Union means something entirely different than in the United States.

Each respondent started life in the United States in a Jewish American parochial school. Their early education was subsidized in part or in whole by various Jewish community institutions. Besides the utter shock of having to learn Hebrew before they learned English, each also contrasted the humiliating poverty of their early years with the wealth of the Jewish American community.

Bella characterized her nationality as Jewish, following the Soviet pattern. She had no religious upbringing as a young girl:

I went for one semester to the Jewish [middle school]. I had different classes, but I had to learn Hebrew, and I didn't even know English yet! Everyone else was really wealthy. Something I wasn't used to. I used to notice the parents' cars while I took a school bus.

When I had the choice of going to the Jewish [high school] I didn't consider it for a minute . . . too expensive . . . too strange to be immersed in religious upbringing.

Max attended a Jewish middle school for three years.

I was Jewish, but I was Russian. There were quite a few Russian kids there at the time and the [other] kids weren't always that friendly. They would pick on us. I got a sense of [being] treated second-rate, and I think it was probably understood that we weren't paying the full fees for the school. . . . This whole Orthodox Jewish aspect and learning all about the dietary laws and all these other customs . . . it was quite overwhelming. Prayer in the morning and prayer after eating, and not understanding English so well, and then having Hebrew thrown at you.

It was pretty difficult being poor at that school. . . . We'd get clothes donations from people at our synagogue, and there were a couple of situations where kids would recognize clothes of their friends that I was wearing, and I was quite embarrassed about that. . . . The way you dress is really different in Russia. I remember coming over here and I have three of the same shirts. My mom bought three of them because they are really good shirts and I'll wear them all the time and people thought I was wearing the same shirt all the time because nobody buys three things of the same over here.

Igor went to a Jewish middle school for three years, all subsidized. After his father worked out a complicated plan to obtain a subsidy to the Jewish high school, Igor refused to attend. "I said I wanted to go to a public school. . . . All my friends were going to public school. And I wanted to meet other people."

Both Rina and Max expressed a sort of self-deprecating humor about learning to be Jewish American. Their stories centered on the New Year's tree, an important symbol of identity clash and shift for all informants. Rina remembered that when her family first arrived,

We got a New Year's tree, decorated like a Christmas tree . . . I remember the *Chabad* [ultra Orthodox denomination] rabbis coming over to our house, just to see how we were doing and everything, and they walk in and we have this Christmas tree. And they're like, "oh, my god," you know, "what's going on?!" And my mom's trying to explain to them that it's not. . . . It's a New Year's tree. Like she didn't understand why they were so awed by it. And I remember we got presents, and they were just awed at that. My mom, she was like offering them, like oh, my gosh, "can I offer you some food?" And she's serving them pork and they didn't know, and these rabbis are looking at her like "are these people really Jewish or what's the deal?" But that was the only year, the first year we came, well the first or second year . . . and then after that they learned that it was not something that Jewish people do here, so we never had it again.

Max and his family started lighting Chanukah candles only after arriving in the United States. Before they immigrated, they had never celebrated any Jewish holidays, only birthdays, national holidays, and on New Year's Eve they would put up a big tree with presents underneath.

When we came here we stopped doing that. . . . We never did that here, and the explanation I got from my parents is that we were sponsored by a synagogue. What if someone from synagogue walks in around Christmas time, or New Year's time? They're only six days apart, and they see the tree. What are they going to think? So now we light Hanukah candles. . . . Some of our Russian friends, they put up trees, [those] who weren't necessarily sponsored by someone [a synagogue]. They were brought here by their relatives. I don't know . . . I like Hanukah candles better, anyways.

Against the mixed backdrop of gratitude and resentment in initial encounter stories with Jewish American institutions, these young people struggle with ways to incorporate Jewish identity and Jewish religious practice into their lives. For the past five or six years, Rina has led her family's Passover seder (a ritual holiday dinner) because, as she told me, her parents did not know how to practice Judaism. "It always makes me so mad because my family's just not used to doing it, they're like, 'why do we have to read this?' . . . My dream would be for it to be like the real thing."

Igor wrestled with his parents over wearing a *kippah* (a skullcap worn by Orthodox or Conservative Jewish males). "I made a decision to wear a *kippah* all the time. I told my parents. Their reaction was 'What?! Are you crazy?!'" His father argued that while Igor should not hide his Jewish identity, he "shouldn't jump out and flash it" either. This was the beginning of a lengthy debate between father and son that eventually widened to include Igor's friends and a local rabbi.

I tell my dad it's illegal in the U.S. to discriminate. It's not Russia. I've never heard of a Jew being beaten up here. But he makes a good point that I agree with. He said that racist people are better at hiding it now. He said "if you apply to medical school with a *kippah*, they'll find some reason to reject you." I had to concede that point and agree with him. Black people can't escape racism, but with you, you're given the option to wear it or not. I made him a deal. I'll wear it on the holidays . . . about two weeks a year, a compromise. . . .

My friend also decided to just wear it on the holidays. It's just not worth risking it. . . . If I was more established, they couldn't hurt me as much. Maybe it's a decision for later in life.

These young adults are also thinking about who they would like to form more permanent attachments and families with. Jewish identity is part of those reflections. Again, their own experiences and interactions are weighed against the strong debt they feel to their parents, particularly in light of the stories they have been told about their extended families' past hardships as a minority in the USSR. Against the backdrop of transmitted memories of Jewish victimization during the Holocaust and subsequent waves of anti-Semitism in the Soviet Union, all respondents expressed the wish to behave according to their parents' desires—that is, to marry a Jewish person. Rina claimed:

I'd say it's very important to me to marry someone who is Jewish. . . . My parents came here not only for a better life for us, but to be able to practice our Judaism, and even if they don't say it outright, my mom's told me stories. . . . My grandparents are Holocaust survivors. My parents experienced a lot of anti-Semitism in Russia. I just feel like what a waste if I were just to give that up . . . I know it would just crush my grandparents especially if I didn't marry someone Jewish.

Igor's mother was very direct with him about her expectations. "It's a big thing with my Mom. She says 'You should marry Jewish.' She insists I marry a Jew. . . . When my brother objected to this, my mother simply could not believe him. She excommunicated him. She said 'If you want to marry a *shiksa* [pejorative expression for non-Jewish woman], then you are not Jewish. . . . I do hang out with non-Jewish girls, but I made up my mind. I want to marry Jewish." Lara, who describes herself as "Americanized to the extreme," is "much more comfortable dating just Americans." At the same time, she makes clear that "I've just picked one side which is very hard for me because . . . I realize that if I marry an American I will always be missing an aspect." Bella explains she has not dated much, and she feels this is due to her strong accent.

MULTICULTURAL INTERACTIONS:
PREJUDICE ACROSS BORDERS

Probably all Soviet Jewish refugees mention anti-Semitism as a motive for their emigration, and my 1.5- and second-generation respondents were no exception. Although Bella had introduced anti-Semitism as one of her parents' reasons for leaving, she immediately followed this up with some clarification, and disagreement with that picture based on her own memories. "They faced anti-Semitism not because of religion. But because of our name. *I* never faced any anti-Semitism, not with my friends. There were only one or two Jewish kids in my class at school, but I didn't really know them." Max's experience was different. He learned under some duress that he was Jewish when he was in the second grade in Russia.

My parents started telling me, told me that I was Jewish when I started getting pushed around a little bit. Somehow the other kids found out that I was. And so, they had to explain to me what was this whole Jewish thing, because I thought "well, if I live in Russia, I must be Russian." That was basically the assumption I had, and I must have been nine when I found out that I was, we were different. So it was kind of hard to understand at first . . . but I eventually figured it out, started reading books about the Six Day War in Israel and about Israel and things like that, and I kind of . . . I had a pretty strong sense of Jewish identity I would say at that point . . . between nine and twelve.

Igor's experience in the FSU was similar. "When I was in the third grade in Russia in our school we all had to answer the question in class 'What is your nationality?' I knew the stigma of Jew, so I didn't say anything." Igor, who came to the interview wearing a necklace with his name in Hebrew letters, is now in the position of trying out various identity strategies to cope with anti-Russian prejudice in the United States.

Most people noticed the weird name [Igor] and guess what it is, and say things. Most people make the Rocky and Bullwinkle reference. They ask "do you have a girlfriend named Natasha?" I consider it purely a joke. I say "no." Or they ask that James Bond question. When the character in the film says "I'm invincible." They ask me to do it . . . I smile. I realize it's my thing. It's my Forrest . . . you know in the film "Forrest Gump". . . when they shout at him, "run Forrest run." This is my Forrest.

In the United States, Bella has been frequently bothered with anti-Russian stereotypes about heavy vodka drinking, sex trafficking, and mail-order brides, wives who come to the United States to just stay home and have lots of kids, and the criminal underground. Once a professor accused her and another student in the class of cheating on an exam. "I went to see [him] and the chair of the department, and I broke down crying about this accusation of cheating. I think [he] thought because we were from a communist country that we thought it was okay [to cheat]." Bella attributes this harassment to her strongly Russian-accented English. Like Bella, Lara addresses her multilayered and shifting identity partly through the prism of English proficiency. But for her, the outcome is different, as is her self-identification strategy.

I try to speak Russian as much as I can *now*. Earlier on, it was like, I don't wanna speak Russian. Especially when I was very young I was ashamed of it. I didn't want people to know I was different. . . . If I don't tell anyone that I'm Russian, they don't really know. They just assume I'm American. . . . You know if we were in a store, I would try to get my parents to speak English. I don't recall this—having a feeling of being very embarrassed—but my parents tell me about it. You know I can understand that I didn't. When you first make such a move, and then trying to adapt to a new culture, you don't want to stand out by any means. And then when you're growing up, you get to a certain point where you want to stand out, you want to be different, and the fact that you can speak another language and are from another culture is fascinating to other people.

When I first came here, in fourth grade, I experienced more discrimination than I do, or than I have in the past. You know when I first came here, I didn't understand what this meant when all the little kids called me a Russian spy. . . . And you know in Russia you were taught to take care of your own problems so I hit a boy who called me that, and then I ended up getting in trouble, and my parents said, you know, it was okay, you did the right thing, because he never called me that again. . . . Once I started speaking English that went away. Once in a while I'll hear a comment about an immigrant, just someone immigrating, and usually the comment is if someone doesn't know that I'm an immigrant. And someone will say like, "oh they should go back to their own country," you know, something like that. They don't realize what they're saying is affecting someone standing around them. Very rarely do I encounter it. And to tell you the truth, the majority of the time, if someone does know I'm from another country, it interests them a lot, and I get a lot of questions, and I always get "oh, that's amazing, that's wonderful, you speak such good English, tell me about it." . . . I never get negative responses. . . . I get a lot of "where are you from?" because people assume I'm from another country because of my physical characteristics. But I never get—if I say guess—never have I gotten Russia. I've gotten Italy a lot, I've gotten Spain, I've gotten Israel, and I've gotten Greece. I've even gotten Persia. Not once have I gotten Russia.

Respondents' comments are marked by the absence of much discussion of anti-Semitism in the United States. Only Max went on at some length about a non-Jewish fraternity brother who constantly teased and quizzed him about being Jewish, yet he ended his story with the remark, "But for the most part, he's not bad. I don't really feel anti-Semitism." I was rather astounded by Igor's response to my unusually direct probe: "Have you heard or experienced anti-Semitism here?" His response: "Only in-group remarks with Jewish friends." While each of the young adults has faced hurtful remarks, stereotypes, and prejudice, these have mostly been about their accents and their immigrant or Russian origins. None seem to have injured the economic or social mobility chances of these students or recent graduates, all of whom now have good jobs or good job prospects.

WHERE IS HOME? BUILDING CULTURAL BRIDGES AND TRANSNATIONAL DIASPORAN IDENTITIES

How the children of Soviet Jews understand and represent their identities in relation to other Jews in a multisited diaspora and to different Others opens an important window on their process of establishing transnational diasporan identities.

Though the idea of returning or at least traveling to "the homeland" is central to Jewish thought and to conceptualizations of transnationalism and the diaspora, the relationship to ancestral homeland is problematic for children of Soviet Jewish refugees. First, where do they locate their ancestral homeland? Second, how intense is the imperative to return? Third, under what circumstances is the obligation to return evoked?

Not one of the young adults I interviewed had ever been back to the FSU. None had close family members still living there. Rather, family and friends were dispersed among the United States, Israel, Canada, Germany, and Australia. Returning "home" to Russia, the Ukraine, or Moldova is not something they consider given the circumstances under which they departed, recurring waves of anti-Semitism, a deteriorating economic picture, and an unpredictable political situation. Though Israel constitutes a central theme in their migration stories, none consider it their homeland or part of the future they envision for themselves. None are fluent in Hebrew, and none evidenced interest in becoming more fluent in the language or more conversant with Israeli culture. Each had extended family members in Israel and had visited them once or twice. These are all characteristics of the relationship that many fourth-generation American Jews maintain with Israel. The major difference is that when in Israel, these young people spoke Russian and moved solely within Russian Israeli circles.

Young adult children of Soviet Jewish refugees consider the United States home, but that also makes for a problematic notion. In the United States, Igor prefers life in the Russian Jewish enclave of Brighton Beach, Brooklyn, with "the raw people," people who are polite and yet will tell you the truth without sugarcoating it. He referred to himself as "a hybrid," someone who applies Russian values to an American life. Elaborating further, he identifies as

Jewish first, American second. If I had to specify, and Americans always want you to do that a lot, I would say I'm a Bessarabian Jew. . . . But mostly I identify as American Jewish. . . . I never say I'm Russian. . . . In the Jewish community [in the United States] I'm referred to as Russian. . . . Jokingly, I guess you could say I'm Ashkenazi, but that's not a term I would use to label myself. It's an American category that I learned here. To me, I'm Jewish first.

Sensitive to ethnic stereotyping, he vehemently resists the notion of making friends on the basis of religion or ethnicity. "My best friend is the only immigrant in the mix. I hang out with mostly Americans. It depends on having the same interests."

Bella claims, "I don't feel that I belong to one or another world," emphasizing her strong accent. She portrays American Jews as "more religious" and "stick[ing] to their own people, and socializing [exclusively] with other Jewish families"—in other words, everything she is not and does not do. When I asked about her own friends, she responded, "They are from St. Petersburg. Well, I am not sure where they are from. I think they are from Armenia. They're not Jewish, so we don't have this in common. Maybe they are mixed. . . . My friends are non-Jews, but it's about what we have in common, not religion." Lara identifies herself as a hyphenated Russian-Jewish-American, and includes among her closest friends some "whites," some "Asians," some "African Americans" . . . but there are no "Russians." For Lara, "American as a word encompasses being a multitude of things. You know you can be American and be five different things at once. I struggle with that a lot. I am very Americanized, to the full extent, but I'm also European."

Max self-identifies as an American Jew who comes from Russia. And although Rina has spent all of her growing-up years in the United States, she identifies as Russian Jewish because, as she puts it, she "grew up in the culture."

I knew that I was a little different. I just knew growing up because my mom would always be like when I came home from school and I needed help and she's like "oh my god, in Russia we did this in like the first grade. I can't believe you're in the fourth grade and they're only starting to teach you this" kind of thing. . . . And for as long as I can remember when I was little and we'd sit down and we'd do the traditional vodka toast. . . . It's just so prevalent, and no matter what we'd have a toast for those of us who are not with us, people that are deceased, and God Bless America, and those were our two toasts as long as I can remember.

Part of the project of self-identification for children of Soviet Jewish refugees involves developing a knowledge and perception of prejudice and discrimination in the United States, its effects and subtleties, many of which their parents are not aware. For this they draw as much on their actual and inherited memories of minority status in the FSU and their own encounters with American Jews and ethnic Others at arrival as on any multicultural knowledge gained in the United States. Bella ended a rambling description of her fears of African American men with a revealing insight: "I went to Renton by bus, by the end of the bus ride we were the only white girls, and felt like minorities for the first time. Now I know how *they* felt." Pausing, she recalled the anti-Russian remarks directed against her by a former professor and sighed, "So, it's hard when you feel yourself holding stereotypes."

The children of former Soviet Jews do not simply assimilate, or incorporate into one or another preexisting segment of multicultural America. They are uncomfortable and wary of the available options—mainstream Jewish American, Israeli, Russian, Soviet Jewish like their parents, white American—all mutually exclusive identities. Their identities are multilayered. Their in-betweenness in their own families and coethnic communities, and their status as a rediasporized transnational minority encourages them to become cultural bridge builders. This was very much on the mind of one young man who described for me his work in a university organization that promoted Arab-Israeli coexistence. The forces of acculturation do not only act on them but they also interpret, react, and correct misperceptions as they work to define their identities. Part of making their way in the United States involves the work of cultural interpretation and translation, of building cultural bridges between their families, coethnic communities, and other communities.

If Bella could teach others about her refugee experience, she would want them "to have more patience with people, use less stereotypes." Rina, focused on family memories of poverty at arrival, says that her migration experience made her an advocate for people who have less. Igor states that being a Soviet Jewish refugee has given him a "different point of reference." He "would want people to know and appreciate the variety, to know the differences." Because of his immigration, Max reflected that he "finds it easier to relate to people 'cause I try to look for things, the commonalities I have with them . . . because people often have things in common they don't see." The worst thing, Max thinks, is for immigrants to "seclude themselves to their own ethnic group." "There's more out there, and there's no reason to limit yourself," he argues. Though Lara wants her future children to be immersed in Russian culture, she adds, "it won't just be with Russian, it will be with maybe other cultures as well."

The children of Soviet Jewish refugees have made their experiences as a rediasporized transnational minority central to the project of self-identification in the United States. Their world is a place in which identities are not mutually exclusive, but rather multilayered and hybrid. Rina laughed as she described how she and her brother playfully dressed as the goblins of the Soviet past for an American holiday in clothes worn by their refugee parents when they fled. "I don't know if they [my parents] still have the fur coats [they brought with them from the Soviet Union], but I know they have the fur hats. I was like 'you can't get rid of the fur hat!!' And my brother was like . . . we used them on Halloween, you know, KGB agent. Kind of funny."

They still struggle with how and where to fit Russianness, Europeanness, Jewishness, and Americanness into their lives, recognizing some dimensions to be more or less flexible and optional, while others feel more compulsory. All expressed gratitude to parents who taught them the important life lesson of how to triumph over adversity, and in return they feel they owe their families a great deal, both in terms of succeeding materially and of staying within certain bounds of Jewishness. Yet at the same time, they have absorbed aspects of the American discourse of multiculturalism, and their own experiences as transnational diasporans have given them a flexibility and openness that their parents may not have foreseen and may not appreciate. All have close friends who are neither Jewish nor Russian; all either work or go to school in mostly non-Jewish and non-Russian environments; all have dated non-Jews and non-Russians. Against the admonitions of parents, the prescribed coethnic diasporic ideal, and the fairly uniform plan of each to marry someone Jewish, is the more likely outcome that this group of 1.5-and second-generation Soviet Jews will continue to intermarry at rates comparable to both the previous Soviet Jewish and the current American Jewish trajectories. In other words, they will continue to introduce additional diversity into an already heterogeneous and transnational diaspora.

Conclusions

The insights of recent transnational and diaspora theories have been difficult to apply to a minority refugee population flung not only across space but along historical time. These concepts have not translated easily to a twice or thrice displaced population that hardly constitutes a bounded homogeneous group, identifying as one "people" in some instances but not in others, or holding connections and attachments more symbolic than literal, though no less powerful. Social scientists frequently analyze Jews as an exceptional group or exclude them from analytic comparison as altogether too anomalous. This essay has aimed to demonstrate that the theories and the case of former Soviet Jewish refugee identities each benefit by being brought to bear on the other.

I have argued that the insights of transnational and diaspora theories are weakened by their tendencies toward "groupism" and methodological nationalism. However, the case of former Soviet Jewish minority refugees and their children, caught up in the unraveling of a complexly multinational state, displaced, and forced to rejoin other Jews in a multisited diaspora or in Israel, compels us to recognize the significance of intragroup diversity. Transnational encounters and interactions between American Jews, Israelis, and Soviet Jewish refugee families are as productive of new identities as intergroup relations with non-Jewish Others.

What does a transnational identity look like for former Soviet Jewish refugees and their children? How is it experienced? What processes and relations evoke strong collective transnational identifications, and when do efforts to create group cohesion fail? Are there other comparable cases of transnational diasporan minorities?

The first-generation refugee parents I interviewed grew up during a time in which they believed—on the basis of their parents' stories about persecution in the Soviet Union before and during World War II, coupled with their own experiences—that it was dangerous to identify or be identified as Jewish in the Soviet Union, so most distanced themselves from Jewishness in public and private life. Many intermarried and adopted identities based on Soviet constraints and opportunities. Yet claiming Jewishness in the American way was their only ticket to the United States. This was the cause of much confusion and frustration on the journey and during the initial years of their resettlement by Jewish institutions. Some parents still fear their children will face hostility and discrimination if they are "too obviously Jewish" in the United States, yet based on a sense of historical debt, symbolic attachment, and home-country stereotypes of Jewish success, they prefer their children to marry Jews and become Jewish-Americans. Refugee parents distance themselves from Russianness in the United States, their perspective based on their own experiences and memories of

Russian and Soviet anti-Semitism. Yet all identify strongly with the Russian language, with Russian literature, and with Russian culture.

Children of Soviet Jewish refugees, subject to the reverberating echo of past persecutions and migrations in their extended families, their own mixed memories of cross-national interactions in the FSU, and encounters with Jewish Americans and Other Americans, have made the work of transnational bridge building central to their project of self-identification in the United States. Their in-between status in families who are often intermarried in faith or nationality terms, their sense of a class divide between their families and American Jews, and their lack of experience with Judaism has sensitized them to prejudice in the United States and predisposed them toward an identification based on bridging cultures at home and in their diverse communities. Rather than incorporating into a segment of American society, the identities they make are multilayered and hybrid. Jewish American projects to evoke and produce strong coethnic affiliation based primarily on religious teaching and practice, or identification with an undifferentiated attachment to Hebrew-speaking Israel, have generally failed. On the other hand, extended family narratives about both the Holocaust and successive waves of hardship for the Jewish minority in the Soviet Union recalled in the context of parents' references to their recent sacrifices for the children, as well as their own firsthand experiences of displacement, stir up the stronger, more compulsory sense of Jewish peoplehood.

The case of Soviet Jewish refugees has important implications for researchers in global migration and ethnicity, especially for those concerned with other refugee diasporas, or with ethnic minorities who were transnational before their most recent migration (e.g., twice-displaced Lebanese Palestinians in Detroit; East African Sikhs in London; Chinese Vietnamese in San Francisco; Indonesian Armenians in the Netherlands; Azerbaijani Meskhetian Turks in Seattle, etc.). Comparisons between groups can be valuable, particularly for discerning generalizable social patterns from unique features.

What this case of Soviet Jewish refugee family identities highlights is the importance of explaining, rather than presuming, group belonging. Diasporan belonging or ethnic solidarity is something that must be produced, transmitted, and reproduced. Families, ethnic institutions, schools, and states produce (or not) varying degrees of belonging through everyday interactions, as well as in references to symbolic attachments. This article has argued that efforts to produce strong ethnic group identification and cohesion are sometimes successful, sometimes not; some elements of ethnic belonging are made to feel relatively sticky across place and time, and nearly compulsory, whereas others are treated as more optional, more flexible, and fluid. The Soviet Jewish refugee case is most instructive in this regard because it highlights the general significance of intragroup (rather than intergroup) encounters in accounting for the ebb and flow and varying degree of ethnic group affiliations. In these times, researchers need to be armed with better tools to understand how strong group affiliations are made and transmitted, how projects aimed at creating strong ethnic group allegiance sometimes fail, and how new kinds of transnational hybrid identities are created.

Notes

1. One notable exception is the sociologist Steven J. Gold's (1995) study of first generation Soviet Jews in California. The anthropologist Fran Markowitz (1993) has analyzed the first generation in New York, as has the historian Annelise Orleck (1999). The sociologists Phil Kasinitz, Mary Waters, and John Mollenkopf added the children of former Soviet Jewish refugees to their study of the immigrant second generation in New York after receiving support from the United Jewish Appeal Federation and affiliated organizations (see Kasinitz et al. 2002). A current project to study the immigrant second generation in Los Angeles now also includes a small component on the children of Soviet Jewish refugees (see Rumbaut et al. 2002).

2. The empirical work reported on in this article derives from four in-depth interviews with first-generation refugees and five interviews with the 1.5 or second generation, all conducted in Seattle. Pseudonyms are used to protect the anonymity of all informants. One key informant, Svetlana, was interviewed in four sessions, each two to four hours long. Otherwise, informants were only interviewed once in sessions lasting 2 to 4 hours each. Quotes and excerpts from interviews are based directly on transcripts. Despite the qualitative depth of the interviews, the sample size and nonrandom sampling method do not allow for wide generalization.

3. See the Hebrew Immigrant Aid Society (HIAS) arrival statistics for 1954–79 and 1970–99.

4. Some of the empirical work reported on in this section is discussed in Friedman 2000. There, I contrast the ways a Jewish refugee and a non-Jewish political dissident experienced the challenges of ethnic classification and self-identification.

5. The 1979 Soviet census reported that 47 percent of Russian Jews lived in mixed-nationality or mixed-faith households (see Brym 1994; Chlenov 1994; Ryvkina 1998).

The Paradigmatic Status of Jewish Immigration

RICHARD ALBA

An issue that never loses its salience in the study of immigration concerns how newly arriving individuals and groups insert themselves into the society of reception, becoming a part of it and occupying a social location recognized by others native to the society as well as by themselves. In contemporary social science lingo, this is identified as the process of "incorporation," and our current understanding emphasizes the "context of reception," primarily characteristics of the receiving society and community, as governing the process (Portes and Rumbaut 1996). The articles by Friedman, Levine, and Gold help to right the balance by underscoring the roles of the immigrant group itself, including its human capital, in the broad sense of its learned capabilities (such as cattle trading) and its ethnic solidarity; and the agency of its individual members, who craft social identities out of a palette of materials provided by the receiving context and reworked memories of the society of origin.

Levine's story of German Jewish cattle dealers is remarkable, not only in shedding light on a little-known, and surprising, aspect of the Jewish immigration experience but also in demonstrating that under some circumstances, immigrants are able to recreate a substantial facsimile of the world they left. Moreover, it indicates the limits of the common wisdom that refugees—who, unlike economic immigrants, are not able to plan their immigration and frequently enough emigrate when they are middle-aged and thus not able to adapt easily to a new labor market—are generally quite disadvantaged in the society of reception.

Levine's compelling analysis suggests that a fortuitous confluence of structural changes in the economy of milk and the arrival of German Jews with extensive experience in cattle dealing and a willingness to work hard at deal making is one key to understanding this unusual story. Like many immigrants, the German Jews refused to take the preexisting economic relationships for granted; perhaps they did not even see the links between farmers and native livestock brokers. In addition, the solidarity exhibited by the refugees—who, though forced to compete with one another in the marketplace, recognized the crucial bonds of ethnicity and religion that linked them—provides a second key. Undoubtedly, the recreation of a lost world at a particular site in the new society was no accident produced by the simultaneous discovery of an opportunity independently by a number of immigrants. Rather, it was a network-driven phenomenon in which the early arrivals to central New York's dairy areas informed friends and relatives of the good prospects to be found there. The motivation was, of course, to regenerate a community that shared powerful meanings that would be lost if only ego-centered economic interests predominated. The symbol for this was the *minyan*, the minimum number of participants necessary to create a valid religious witness to critical life passages and events.

One might ask at this point how such a significant number of cattle dealers were able to escape the Third Reich. One suspects that their affluence in Germany provided them with the means to depart in a timely manner, that is, before the authorities in Germany and the countries of refuge closed the exits (see Klemperer 1998). Yet the very nature of their trade, with its requirement of investments in land and livestock, might easily have kept them rooted in their German milieus until it was too late. Certainly, they suffered from severe economic discrimination in Nazi Germany, but so did other Jews (see Levine 2001:37–55).

But the American environment also had its effects, especially on the next generation, whether born in the United States or in Germany (and then immigrating as children). The German Jewish cattle dealers of central New York were by and large a one-generation phenomenon, despite the traditions of the trade that had reigned in their families for generations in Europe. Even though these traditions crossed the Atlantic more or less intact, they failed to cross into the second generation in the U.S. context. The opportunities in the mainstream economy and society were, despite anti-Semitism, sufficiently available to the 1.5 and second generations that their members could risk leaving the small world of upstate New York. This is an old story and belies the common portrait of ethnic entrepreneurialism as a shelter for preserving ethnicity.

The immigration analyzed by Levine belongs, in a common view, to a past era. The new era, which began in the late 1960s in the United States, features a possibly novel set of dynamics, including transnationalism, the subject of Steven Gold's essay, whose subtitle, "From Refugees to Transnationals," marks the separation from the world of immigrant possibilities described by Levine. Transnationalism, linked to globalization, arises in large part from the greater ease of travel and communication across borders; it signals a loss by states of a measure of control over immigration and, concomitantly, an increase in the options for immigrants, who can more easily reverse their immigration by a return home or can leapfrog from one receiving nation to another.

As Gold's essay demonstrates in the case of Israeli immigrants, the role of utilitarian calculus in migrant decisions seems to be increasing as immigrants and potential immigrants have more choices to consider. In the United States, the economist George Borjas (1999) has warned that American immigration policy must recognize that the United States now participates in an international marketplace for immigrants and thus competes against other potential destination countries. In Israel, one response to this recognition has been to diminish the stigma formerly attached to those Jews who, given the choice, opt for a destination other than Israel or, even worse, emigrate from it. The new transnational possibilities imply that migrant settlement is no longer tantamount to putting down permanent roots, but may be followed by another migration, from which Israel may benefit. Perhaps there is also growing acceptance of these migrants in the communities of the diaspora, such as in the United States, because of anxieties about the declining size (in the United States, this is certainly true in a relative sense and may also be true in an absolute one) and weakening power of Jewish identity as a result of assimilation (Goldscheider 2003 gives one view of the demography).

Gold makes a potentially profound point in suggesting that contemporary Jewish immigrants are less dependent on settlement agencies than were those of the past. That immigration is a deeply social process because immigrants lack detailed knowledge about the destination and thus depend on the assistance of social networks at every stage of the process is one of the field's axiomatic truths. But many contemporary immigrants, possessing high levels of human capital, have sophistication about relocation that the immigrants of past eras lacked; they are no longer like the immigrants of the early twentieth century who arrived with destinations or family names pinned to their clothing. Potentially, they may have less need of social networks and settlement agencies to negotiate the difficulties of the immigration process (which is not to say that they have no need of assistance). In principle, this should give immigrants more choice over the contexts in which they settle and, by implication, more control over their identity options, which are shaped in part by these contexts.

Identities are, in fact, a major motif of the transnational account of immigration, which holds that a hallmark of the transnational era is the emergence of new forms of identity that transcend national settings: immigrants may recognize themselves as part of a diaspora rather than of a nationally bounded ethnic group. If the transnational account is true, and the research evidence so far indicates that it applies to some fraction of contemporary immigrants but leaves considerable uncertainty about how large that fraction is, then immigrants in general may be becoming more like Jewish immigrants. Jews were one of the early transnational populations, but their transnationalism proved complex. Unlike some other turn-of-the-century immigrant groups—such as the southern Italians, who mostly intended to return eventually to their Mezzogiorno home villages—Jews were usually not interested in maintaining permanent connections to the countries from which they immigrated. They learned English and naturalized as U.S. citizens more quickly than most other groups. But they did have a consciousness of forming part of a diaspora that the Italians and most other groups did not have. The experience of being an excluded minority in Eastern European societies helped to prepare Jewish immigrants to become an unusually solidary ethnic minority in the United States. Moreover, Zionism created for some of them an ethnic identification with events occurring outside the United States (though, in this respect, they resembled the Irish). The refugee immigration of the 1930s and 1940s brought some highly educated immigrants who retained a strong interest in the German-language culture. Contemporary transnationalism has, in other words, some precursors in the earlier eras of Jewish immigration to the United States.

A large question hovers over contemporary transnationalism: what are its chances of surviving the transition to the second and third generations? In other words, transnationalism perhaps affects the options of the immigrants, but not those of their children, likely to grow up in settled circumstances in a specific national context. Here is where the role of the resettlement agencies may reassert itself, and the concept of "proximate others," as the already extant ethnic category to which a new group will be "assimilated" in the eyes of a society's natives, becomes relevant (Mittelberg and Waters 1992). The proximate others for Soviet Jews are still determined in significant part by settlement agencies. As Philip Kasinitz and his coauthors describe in an unpublished paper, in New York they may be Orthodox Jews, and the youthful 1.5 and second generations may attend yeshivas and end up becoming far more Jewish in a religious sense than they would have been had they stayed in Russia.

This brings me to Kathie Friedman's article, which demonstrates that for the 1.5 and second generations, a range of identity options exist. In evaluating this portrait, one should keep in mind, however, that the immigration under examination is very recent—the great majority, I assume, is within ten to fifteen years of departure from the Soviet Union or its successor states. This point particularly bears on the relative significance of American and Soviet "materials" for identity construction.

Nevertheless, what Friedman's work also reveals is a process of "relocalization" (a term I borrow from Aristide Zolberg). This is not to deny that contemporary youth of immigrant origins appear to have more identity options than would have been the case for their equivalents a century ago (one should, of course, recognize that the options of a century ago have been simplified in our accounts of them and were undoubtedly more complex than we typically acknowledge). This much one can chalk up to multiculturalism. However, these options appear to be framed by two sets of parameters: one, the available identities in the proximate American environment, including that of Jewish Americans; and, two, the memories, however altered by the migration of experience of migration, of Russia. The clever title—"On Halloween We Dressed Up Like KGB Agents"—signals the possibilities that emerge from the fusion of these elements. To be sure, the essay gives evidence that at least among young people, the elements are melded in personal ways by members of the 1.5 and second generations, but this is appropriate in a society that places such emphasis on individualism and individual choice (Gans 1988). Whether identities will subsequently be channeled along a few specific lines remains to be seen.

Friedman's portrait, admittedly limited by the small number of cases involved, proves very suggestive in another way: the transnational horizons to be glimpsed among immigrants are not evident in the young members of the next generation. Instead, the impression we get from her contribution to this volume is that the youth's identity choices—whether to wear a *kippah* to school, what music to listen to, and how to think about the prickly, ambiguous connection to Russia—

are ones that make sense in their U.S. contexts. She observes that although Israel had been a possible destination at the moment of immigration and, unlike Russia, remains a place to visit, the United States means home for the young adults of the 1.5 and second generations. She writes, "they experience themselves and their futures based equally on interactions with multiethnic Others in their neighborhoods and schools in the United States" (Friedman this volume: 245).

Jews have often been treated by sociologists as a unique ethnic group on the American landscape, for they exhibit a combination of some uncommon features, such as the interpenetration of religious and ethnic elements and a tradition of diasporic consciousness and of survival as an ethnic minority. But the surge of intermarriage since the 1950s demonstrates that they are buffeted by the same societal forces as other ethnic groups—indeed, they could be considered the acid test of them. This set of essays continues in this latter vein, showing that Jews very much exemplify patterns visible in immigration and its settlement aftermath more generally.

Circuits and Networks:
The Case of the Jewish Diaspora

YEN LE ESPIRITU

Much of the published work in the field of U.S. immigration studies narrowly emphasizes the immigrants' "modes of incorporation" (Portes and Rumbaut 1996). The dominant theories in the field of U.S. immigration studies —theories of assimilation (including segmented assimilation), of amalgamation, of the so-called melting pot, and of cultural pluralism—have focused on immigrant cultural and economic adaptation and incorporation and on responses by native-born Americans to the influx. In the past decade, reflecting the current saliency of transnational processes, scholars have shifted from the dualism inherent in the classic models of migration—the assumption that migrants move through bipolar spaces in a progressive time frame—to nonbinary theoretical perspectives not predicated on modernist assumptions about time and space. Recent writings on diaspora, the transnational community, transmigrants, the deterritorialized nation-state, and transnational grassroots politics have challenged our notions of *place*, reminding us to think about places not only as specific geographical and physical sites but also as circuits and networks (Clifford 1994; Basch, Glick Schiller, and Szanton Blanc 1994; Espiritu 2003; Levitt 2001). Focusing on circuits and networks, the essays by Kathie Friedman, Rhonda Levine, and Steve Gold in this section confirm that like most immigrants, Jewish immigrants do not merely insert or incorporate themselves into existing spaces in the United States; they also transform those spaces and create new ones, often by drawing on and extending their transnational resources and networks.

Twice-Minorities: Multiple Routings

Most U.S. immigration studies treat newcomers as if they were all first-time migrants who confront minority status and become "ethnics" or "minorities" only in the United States. The long-term Jewish diaspora that crisscrosses multiple countries over time reminds us that many immigrants live transnational lives before they ever arrive in the United States. All three essays in this section emphasize the transnational patterns of Jewish life: Levine relates the experiences of New York's Jewish refugees who first lived as persecuted minorities in Germany; Friedman focuses on the identity strategies of Jews who have migrated to Seattle from the Soviet Union; and Gold traces the routes of Jewish migration through the United States, France, England, and Israel. The Jewish diaspora thus raises important questions for the field of U.S. immigration studies: When does migration begin? When does transnationalism begin? What are the global-historical processes that produce massive and multiple displacements and movements of refugees to the United States and elsewhere? All three questions push U.S. immigration scholars away from a U.S.-centric perspective that focuses only on the migrants' modes of incorporation and toward a critical transnational perspective that takes seriously the experiences that migrants had *prior* to their arrival in the United States.

What most Jews faced prior to immigrating to the United States is the shared experience of an excluded minority in many European countries and elsewhere. In the United States, these Jewish immigrants constitute the "twice-minorities" because of their minority status in both their old and new countries.[1] Whereas many immigrants confront minority status for the first time in the United States, the twice-minorities had already adjusted to and organized around this marginalized status. Becoming a solidarist ethnic group constitutes a central part of this adjustment. As an example, the Jewish community in Poland displayed their ethnic solidarity when they demanded successfully from the Versailles Peace Conference the right to be regarded as a minority people: to establish their own law courts, to occupy seats in municipal councils and the national parliament, and to use their own language; in sum, to maintain themselves in Poland not only as Poles but also as Jews (Hendricks 1923). It is thus not surprising that in his discussion of nationality in American life, Oscar Handlin (1961) reports that "some groups were already aware of their identity at arrival, as were the Jews of the seventeenth and eighteenth century" (225). In his contribution, Steven Gold likewise mentions the strong ethnic identity of the Soviet Jews in Israel, noting in particular their refusal to be stripped of their culture and molded into standard Israelis.

The Jewish experiences are thus instructive for our understanding of more recent cases of twice-minorities including the Chinese from Vietnam, the Indian Sikhs from East Africa, and numerous other diasporic religio-ethnic minorities resettling in various countries around the world. Because of their previous experiences as ethnic minorities in Vietnam, the Chinese Vietnamese arrived in the United States and other resettlement countries with an established community infrastructure. As Lewis Stern (1985) reports, the Chinese population that survived the 1960s and 1970s under the government of the Republic of Vietnam "had accumulated a long history of self-rule and organization through durable and independent institutions" and "was experienced in contending with political maneuvers . . . intent on breaking the Chinese community's economic power" (25). In the new country, the Chinese Vietnamese reestablished these communication networks and reproduced their ethnic institutions. In her study of Vietnamese refugees in Australia, Nancy Viviani (1984) reports that the Chinese Vietnamese "are long practised in minority status and its implications, and unlike the Vietnamese have few group identity problems" (264–65) In other words, when Chinese Vietnamese arrive in Australia, they already "belong" to an ethnic community. As a consequence, Chinese Vietnamese networks develop rapidly and are often built on previous links in Vietnam or in refugee camps (Viviani 1984). In the same way, in a study of African Sikhs who migrated from India to Africa and then to Britain, Parminder Bhachu (1985) reports that their common experiences in East Africa have given them skills they are able to utilize in the establishment of communities in the United Kingdom.

The available case studies suggest that since the "twice migrants" (Bhachu 1985) and the "twice-minorities" (Espiritu 1989) were already part of an established community before resettlement in the United States (or another country), they have been able to reproduce community ties and to establish ethnic institutions rapidly on arrival. Their skills have helped them to establish themselves much more rapidly than direct migrants who lack the same expertise, linguistic facility, and communications network to develop community structures at the same pace.[2] The ethnic solidarity of these twice-minorities can manifest in powerful economic institutions, as in the case of the Chinese Vietnamese in California who have developed successful business enclaves in Los Angeles and Orange counties.[3] The Chinese Vietnamese success is also due in large part to their ability to tap into ethnic Chinese networks across Southeast Asia in Singapore, Taiwan, Hong Kong, Malaysia, the Philippines, and in Vietnam (Stern 1985). These case studies suggest that the relative economic success of Jewish immigrants in the United States is due not only to their human capital, their willingness to work hard, and the structure of economic opportunity in the host society but also to the resources and networks accumulated through their multiple cycles of displacement and resettlement.

Home, Memory Work, and Generation

Kathie Friedman's article is a rich and suggestive piece on the multilayered world of first- and second-generation Soviet Jews in the United States as they juggle to fit Russianness and Jewishness into their American lives. Like most other refugees, Soviet Jewish refugees and their children do not or cannot maintain real ties with their home country. Friedman explains that this is due in large part to the recurring waves of anti-Semitism in the former Soviet Union, to the country's unpredictable political situation, and to the dispersal of family and friends once there to the United States, Israel, Canada, Germany, and Australia. At the same time, Friedman reports that their emotional ties to home remain deep as "all identify strongly with the Russian language, with Russian literature, and with Russian culture." Friedman's findings thus suggest that home is not only a physical place that immigrants and refugees return to for temporary and intermittent visits but also a concept and a desire—a place they visit through the imagination. Hamid Naficy (1999) defines home in the following way: "*Home* is anyplace; it is temporary and it is moveable; it can be built, rebuilt, and carried in memory and by acts of imagination" (6). In other words, the process of migration, especially for refugees, encompasses not only a *literal* but also a *symbolic* transnationalism or imagined returns to one's home (Espiritu 2003). As suggested in Friedman's interview data, the practice of symbolic transnationalism is often most evident—and most poignant—in the lives of the second generation. How do these U.S.-born young people who have never been "home" imagine the homeland? And how do they recall that which is somewhere else, that which was perhaps never known? (Espiritu 2003).

According to Friedman, a key part of the Soviet Jewish struggles is the knowledge and perception of anti-Semitic prejudice and discrimination in both Russia and the United States. And yet, these narratives, told by both the immigrant parents and their children, are marked by a silence on the issue of the Holocaust. How identity is experienced and transmitted to the next generation after collective cultural trauma is a key question that links the Jewish experience to that of war refugees worldwide. Scholars of war memory have repeatedly shown that memory activities are never politically disinterested, but are always already mediated and shaped by relations of power (Fujitani, White, and Yoneyama 2001; Tai 2001). For example, in the United States, the highly controversial Vietnam War Memorial, commissioned to commemorate and memorialize U.S. soldiers who fought in Vietnam, must necessarily "forget" the Vietnamese and "re-member" the American veterans as the primary victims of the war (Sturken 1997). As Burchardt (1993) reminds us, the process of generational transmission of war and genocide memory is even more complex and difficult, as the second generation struggles between honoring the survivors' memory and constructing its own relation to this legacy. Marianne Hirsch (1996) has called the second generation's "memory" of war "post-memory": "the experience of being separated in time and space from the war being remembered, yet of living with the eyewitness memory" (649). As an example, the identity strategies and practices of the Vietnamese American second generation are mediated by their own post-memory of the Vietnam War, by their parents' direct experience with the war, and by the politics of war commemoration practiced by both Vietnam and the United States. It behooves scholars of the Holocaust and of post-Holocaust life to record the memory work performed by the post-Holocaust generations as they variously sustain, erase, and/or transform memories of the genocide for specific present and future purposes. In a recent essay on the politics of post-Holocaust memory, Diane Wolf cautions Holocaust scholars not to manipulate this history so that Jews appear as solely victims (Wolf 2002).

Jewish Americans, Racial Middleness, and Double Vision

The history of Jews in the United States is one of "racial middleness": of marginality in relation to whiteness, and of whiteness and belonging with regard to blackness (Brodkin 1998:2). According to Karen Brodkin (1998), Jews' racial assignment in the United States changed from the not-white side of the American racial binary during the late nineteenth century and the early twentieth to the white side after World War II. The GI Bill benefits and the Federal Housing Administration (FHA) and Veterans Administration (VA) low–down payment, low-interest, long-term mortgage loans were crucial to the postwar whitening of

Jewish (and other eastern and southern European) men. These benefits provided Jewish Americans, who long faced anti-immigrant, racist, and anti-Semitic barriers in the United States, with new educational, occupational, and residential opportunities that proved crucial for their mass entry into a middle-class, professional, home-owning suburban lifestyle during the postwar years.[4] Indeed, the relative economic success and social integration of the Jewish refugees in the United States documented in the three articles in this section can be attributed in large part to the post–World War II whitening of Jewish Americans. As an example, Friedman reports that although young Soviet Jews endured occasional anti-Russian or anti-Semitic remarks, "none seems to have injured the economic or social mobility chances of these students or recent graduates, all of whom now have good jobs or good job prospects."

In many ways, American Jews' racial middleness is similar to the racial positioning of Asian Americans, another intermediate group.[5] During the years before World War II, white Americans declared Asian immigrants "aliens ineligible to citizenship." As unassimilable aliens, Asian Americans embodied for many other Americans the "yellow peril"—the threat that Asians would one day unite and conquer the world. This threat included military invasion and foreign trade from Asia, competition to white labor from Asian workers, the alleged moral degeneracy of Asian people, and the potential miscegenation between whites and Asians (Wu 1982:1). In contrast, the contemporary model-minority stereotype proclaims Asian Americans to be the minority whose success affirms the status quo. Yet while Asian Americans are lauded for their alleged successes, they continue to face white racism in the political, economic, and social arenas, as well as white resentment and violence for being "too successful." In this sense, as Gary Okihiro (1994) argues, both the yellow-peril and model-minority concepts prove anti-Asian: even as the model minority blunts the threat of the yellow peril, if taken too far, the model minority becomes once again the yellow peril (142).

Karen Brodkin (1998) suggests that American Jews' racial middleness gives many Jews a kind of double vision: an ability to see beyond the two-tiered racial order. This double vision, Brodkin argues, enables many American Jews to invest in social justice and to disinvest in whiteness. In the same way, many Asian American scholars, activists, and advocates have urged Asian Americans to resist the lure of the model-minority myth and to refuse the status of a racial "buffer zone" between blacks and whites (Kim 2000–2001:35). These clarion calls to action suggest that the kind of double vision that comes from racial middleness can potentially lead to antiracist struggles taking place across racial lines as American Jews and other racial intermediate groups declare in no uncertain terms: "We will not be used" (Matsuda 1993).

Notes

1. The term *twice-minorities* is used here for easy reference; it does not exclude the possibility that groups can and do become minorities more than twice (see Espiritu 1989).

2. It is true that some first-time minorities also possess organizational skills on arrival. For example, Korean immigrants bring with them their religious organizations. However, these social institutions served a limited role in the home country (e.g., to perform religious functions); as such, they differ from the ethnic institutions of the twice-minorities. In the new country, these organizations have to be realigned and expanded to serve the multiple organizational needs of the emergent ethnic community. This realignment is necessary because of the constraints imposed on the immigrant group by the new society.

3. The Vietnamese American community often boasts about the prominent presence of Little Saigon in Orange County. However, while most of the residents and shoppers are ethnic Vietnamese, it has been estimated that Chinese Vietnamese own most of the ethnic businesses.

4. This whitening process, however, was accompanied by the intensification of racial segregation, institutional discrimination, and urban neglect directed against African Americans and other groups of color.

5. I will not tackle in this commentary the larger and more complicated question of whether or not Asian Americans have gone or will go through a whitening process.

COLLECTIVE ACTION, COLLECTIVE GUILT, COLLECTIVE MEMORY

Our final section, "Collective Action, Collective Guilt, Collective Memory," begins with Rachel Einwohner's study of the Warsaw Ghetto uprising in 1943. Although the Warsaw Ghetto is widely understood as the paramount example of Jewish resistance, Einwohner argues its uniqueness does not preclude the need to consider how the uprising compares to other forms of collective action. Using the analytic tools of social movement research, Einwohner finds that ghetto fighters were more likely to be younger people better able to withstand the deprivations of ghetto life. Often they were also friends and/or knew each other as activists from earlier political groups. Friendship ties enabled resistance fighters to recruit new members and nourish their own commitments to the resistance. Though women were as likely as men to serve as combatants, other work of the resistance required that people pass as Aryans, and passing was a gendered act. Unlike the bodies of Jewish men, the bodies of Jewish women were not marked by the ritual practices of circumcision. Jewish women became more suitable couriers since they were deemed less threatening. Einwohner concludes that the Warsaw Ghetto uprising was unique in some respects and yet at the same time embodied some of the same characteristics as other forms of collective action. The availability of young resistance fighters, their proximity to one another, and socially constructed definitions of identity all contribute to our understanding of the uprising as a social movement.

Jeffrey Olick shifts our focus to questions of cultural memory, specifically to how guilt, responsibility, and perpetration were constructed in the Federal Republic of Germany. He argues that we need more knowledge of the perpetrators —particularly at the intersection of political interests, nationalism, and German collective identity—for a more thorough understanding of the Holocaust. If we are to begin to understand how justice came to be defined in the postwar years and nation-states rebuilt, it is important to consider how perpetrators and bystanders were defined, and individual and collective guilt assessed. During the war and in the decades that followed, considerable public discussion centered around what has come to be known as "the other Germany" issue. Were Hitler and National Socialism the essential definition of German history and the German people, representing a long-standing pathology within German culture? Or conversely, was there no meaningful relationship between the German people and the Third Reich since the German people were effectively held hostage by the Nazis, leaving the treasures of German culture—including Beethoven, Bach, Kant, and Goethe—categorically separate.

Daniel Levy and Natan Sznaider's contribution focuses on the transformation of Holocaust memory from specific local and national memories to cosmopolitan memory and thus evokes the themes of memory and sense of place in tandem. The authors compare the remembrance of the Holocaust in Germany, Israel, and the United States in the period immediately following the war, the 1960s, the 1980s, and the 1990s, which they understand as serving different purposes and having distinct meanings in each national context. Whereas in Israel, memory of the Holocaust was summoned by the Arab-Israeli conflict, in Germany it was tied to militarism and anti-immigration efforts, and in the United States it was linked to other human rights violations. With the end of the Cold War, Levy and Sznaider argue, once widely shared moral values and interests were no longer relevant, a reordering of values in which the Holocaust played a pivotal role occurred. They demonstrate that through the interplay between local and global forces a cosmopolitan understanding of the Holocaust has developed. Now dislocated in both time and space, the memory of the Holocaust has become a moral touchstone of good and evil and constitutes the standard reference point for a wide range of past injustices. Cosmopolitan memory of the Holocaust complements national memories, and its significance is mirrored in the numerous institutional initiatives around human rights protection.

Martin Oppenheimer begins his commentary reminding us that not only has sociology done little work on the Holocaust but it has for the most part also avoided the extensive study of communism, fascism, and nuclear war as well. The question that remains for Oppenheimer is whether sociologists have anything to say about the Holocaust that would make the incomprehensible comprehensible. He uses a sociology-of-knowledge approach to provide some tentative explanations for the dearth of Holocaust research in sociology and to explore why the research that exists takes the forms it does. Oppenheimer first considers the consequences of the academic marketplace that legitimates and rewards some research projects while marginalizing and devaluing others. Subjects such as the Holocaust stand outside a paradigmatic definition of the discipline and are thus more likely the object of description rather than of analysis (see Williams this volume). Moreover, Oppenheimer understands that most academicians want to feel included in the academy, and that Holocaust study would mark them as outsiders. In addition, Holocaust research, Oppenheimer argues, is apt to be controversial and hence a risky career-building strategy; moreover it leaves one vulnerable to charges of perpetuating the Holocaust industry (see Finkelstein 2000). Furthermore, research on such large subjects is often ill suited for journal articles, the publication format generally favored in the social sciences. Oppenheimer also deems the lack of extensive foreign language training among U.S. researchers a decided disadvantage when dealing with sources in languages other than English, and he attributes the relatively large number of writings on the Holocaust by refugee scholars as reflecting this imbalance in language abilities. What about the research that does exist? It focuses on Holocaust discourse and meta-analyses about the Holocaust, but it does not deal directly with the roots of Nazism or the genocide. Yet Oppenheimer understands that this emphasis on discourse, narrative, and cultural studies is not limited to either Holocaust studies or to sociology, but instead represents a shift that transcends subject matter and discipline.

Issues of power, knowledge, and the politics of representation are central to recent discussions of violence and its representation, and these literatures frame Leela Fernandes's readings of the above essays. Fernandes asks how we can study violence and represent it without generating new forms of what Spivak (1988) has called "epistemic violence," which further debases the victims studied. Can we understand and depict the materiality of violence without getting trapped in a spiral of postmodern relativism, modernist constraints of social science objectivity, and the pitfalls of popular spectacle? Fernandes urges scholars not to get caught up in vexed debates over which representations are better or more real than others, but instead to consider the "power effects of representation" that account for both the narrative form as well as the context of its reception. Attention to the audience suggests the importance of location and the variability of value over time and space. Fernandes demonstrates that narratives of violence are alternately implicated in the specific localities of nation-states, while they also transverse national boundaries, generating a global or cosmopolitan narrative. The centrality of the Holocaust to campaigns for universal human rights suggests a need, moreover, to understand the ways gender, race, and nation are invoked in discussions of violence, genocide, and victimhood. Most of the writing on violence has focused on the subjectivity of its victims, and Fernandes argues we know considerably less about the subjectivity of perpetrators and bystanders. Questions of subjectivity become a means through which Fernandes considers a larger set of ethical issues that surround the representation of those who witness or survive, as well as of those who participate, direct, or condone violence. Ultimately, Fernandes argues that if we are serious about representing the sacredness of the Holocaust, we need to articulate a set of ethical practices that would alter predominant discursive practices and methodological assumptions not only in sociology but in the social sciences and several interdisciplinary areas of inquiry as well.

Availability, Proximity, and Identity in the Warsaw Ghetto Uprising: Adding a Sociological Lens to Studies of Jewish Resistance

RACHEL L. EINWOHNER

One common misperception about the Holocaust is that Jewish victims were largely passive in the face of Nazi aggression, going to their slaughter "like sheep." In response to such claims, a vast scholarship on Jewish resistance has emerged (see Grubsztein 1971; Marrus 1989). However, most studies of Jewish resistance during the Holocaust have consisted of either historical accounts or personal memoirs. Notably absent are any analyses that make use of sociological concepts or research findings.

As the other articles in this volume illustrate, the discipline of sociology has a great deal to offer our understanding of the Holocaust and of post-Holocaust Jewish life. My contribution toward a sociology of the Holocaust is to use research findings from the field of social movements to present a more distinctly sociological analysis of Jewish resistance. In fact, I argue that a sociological lens proves particularly useful for illuminating the dynamics of Jewish resistance, especially the participation in collective resistance. My discussion focuses on the Warsaw Ghetto uprising of 1943, the best-known and perhaps most revered instance of Jewish resistance during the Holocaust. I pose two questions about this case: who participated in the uprising, and what was the motive for their actions? In doing so, I hope to illustrate just one of the ways that the discipline of sociology can contribute to academic analyses of the Holocaust.

While my primary goal is to show how sociological concepts illuminate certain aspects of the Warsaw Ghetto uprising, a secondary goal is to address the uniqueness of the Holocaust and its appropriateness as a topic of sociological inquiry. Whereas some scholars have argued that the uniqueness of the Holocaust renders it incomparable to other phenomena (see Gerson this volume), I take the opposite approach, arguing that Holocaust studies can contribute to a general body of knowledge about a host of similar cases—here, other cases of protest and resistance. I address these issues in the conclusion of this essay.

Case Selection and Data

Jewish resistance during the Holocaust took a number of different forms. Individually, Jews resisted by defying Nazi edicts, going into hiding, passing as Aryans, and sabotaging factory products and other goods earmarked for the Nazi war machine (Appleman-Jurman 1988; Gutman 1994; Melson 2000; Szpilman 1999; Vromen this volume); collectively, Jews staged mass uprisings and escapes in a number of ghettos and concentration camps, and they also joined partisans and other underground networks across Europe (Bauer 1989; Grubsztein 1971; Marrus 1989; Tec 1993; Werner 1992). With this wide a range of activities, illustrations from a single case can hardly shed light on all the analytically important aspects of Jewish resistance. While my discussion is necessarily limited to the specifics of one case, I suggest that the Warsaw Ghetto uprising stands as a useful site of inquiry for several reasons. First, it is the best-known example of Jewish resistance and is often pointed to as a symbol of a wider variety of acts of resistance during the Holocaust. Armed resistance in the Warsaw Ghetto also had a far-reaching impact, inspiring resistance in other ghettos and camps (Kermish 1971; Kurzman 1993); in fact, Modigliani and Rochat (1995) refer to the Warsaw case as the paradigmatic case of Jewish resistance. Second, the Warsaw Ghetto uprising is the best-documented case of collective Jewish resistance during the Holocaust. A vast array of primary data recovered from portions of the Oneg Shabbat archives,[1] along with a number of additional diaries and memoirs written by ghetto residents, have been used by historians and other scholars to produce a number of secondary sources that describe both life in the ghetto and the resistance that emerged there.

This article forms part of a larger research project that makes use of secondary sources, as well as primary data from published diaries and memoirs written by ghetto residents and other written material preserved from the ghetto, to analyze the dynamics of resistance in the Warsaw Ghetto (see Einwohner 2003). The

RACHEL L. EINWOHNER

primary data sources, not all of which are cited here, are listed in the appendix of my earlier work, while secondary sources are found under the references. My goal in this essay is not to provide a detailed historical account of the Warsaw Ghetto uprising (for such accounts, see Ainsztein 1979; Gutman 1982, 1994; Kurzman 1993). Instead, I use qualitative descriptions of ghetto life to illustrate the distinctly social and sociological aspects of the uprising, especially as these help explain individual participation in the resistance.

Concepts from the Field of Social Movements:
Availability, Proximity, and Identity

A great deal of empirical research in the field of social movements has focused on questions of movement participation: what draws people into social movements, and what keeps them committed to their cause? Three distinct concepts that have emerged from this research prove particularly relevant to understanding participation in the Warsaw Ghetto uprising: individuals' *availability* for activism; their *proximity* to activism through membership in activist networks; and *identity* processes that compel activism.

McAdam's (1988) research on the civil rights movement reveals that "biographical availability" helps explain social movement participation. Individuals who wished to participate in what became known as Freedom Summer, a civil rights campaign devoted to voter registration and education for African Americans in Mississippi in the summer of 1964, had to undergo a formal application process. McAdam shows that most of the applicants were white, affluent college students whose class background afforded them the ability to devote a summer to unpaid activist work. Further, since applicants under the age of twenty-one required parental permission to travel to Mississippi, and parents were less willing to allow daughters than sons to participate in high-risk activism, those applicants who actually participated in Freedom Summer were more likely to be male and were slightly older than the no-shows. Thus age, class, and gender rendered certain individuals more available than others for activism. Other research has also found that social movement participation is shaped by systems of difference such as race, class, and gender; for instance, gendered divisions of labor were evident in the civil rights movement (Barnett 1993; Evans 1980; Robnett 1997), and women predominate in certain movements such as the animal rights movement (Einwohner 1999; Groves 2001; Jasper and Nelkin 1992), the peace movement (Marullo 1991), and the toxic waste movement (Krauss 1993). In short, this body of research has found that individuals' various social statuses shape their ability to participate in social movements.

Another robust finding about social movement participation is what McAdam refers to as "social proximity," or the network and organizational ties that draw an individual into activism. For example, Freedom Summer participants were more likely than the no-shows to be part of friendship networks with other participants, and they were also more likely to have been previously active in political organizations. Additional research on the civil rights movement (McAdam 1982; Morris 1984), as well as the women's movement (Buechler 1990; Evans 1980; McAdam 1988; Taylor 1989; Whittier 1995) and animal rights movement (Jasper and Poulsen 1995), has also demonstrated that preexisting networks, either formal or informal, serve as "mobilizing structures" (McAdam, McCarthy, and Zald 1996) through which individuals become involved in social movements (see also Snow, Zurcher, and Ekland-Olson 1980).

Finally, an extensive literature on identity and social movements has examined the identity processes involved in social movement participation. Based on the insights of new social movement theory (Melucci 1989, 1996), which argues that collective action both forges and is based on participants' shared sense of identity, scholars have described how collective identity acts as a selective incentive for movement participation (Friedman and McAdam 1992) and sustains activists' commitment to a cause (Hirsch 1990; Neuhouser 1998; Taylor 1989; Taylor and Whittier 1992, 1995; Whittier 1995). In fact, this research suggests that collective action is not possible without collective identity, or "the shared definition of a group that results from members' common interests, experiences, and solidarity" (Taylor and Whittier 1992:105); a strong sense of "we" is a necessary component of collective action frames or the subjective assessments that make activism possible (Gamson 1992). Some scholars go so far as to suggest that collective action is the enactment of identity in that individuals participate in protest because doing so is a reflection of who and what they understand themselves to be (Calhoun 1991, 1994; Melucci 1995; Neuhouser 1998).

By pointing to individuals' social statuses, participation in networks, and shared sense of "we" as factors that explain social movement participation, the concepts of availability, proximity, and identity offer a distinctly sociological account of the dynamics of collective action. In what follows, I demonstrate how these concepts also help explain collective resistance in the Warsaw Ghetto, thereby adding a sociological lens to studies of Jewish resistance.

The Emergence of Armed Resistance in the Warsaw Ghetto

Soon after invading Poland in September 1939, Germans began to ghettoize Polish Jews throughout the Nazi-occupied areas, deporting them from the countryside to reside in crowded, walled-off sections of the major cities. In the Warsaw Ghetto, which was established in the fall of 1940, five hundred thousand Jews were forcibly confined to a 1.36–square mile section of the city's Jewish quarter (Gutman 1982, 1994; Kurzman 1993). The first year of the ghetto was characterized by great suffering; insufficient food rations (estimated at less than three hundred calories per day) and crowded conditions created widespread hunger and disease (Kurzman 1993). The memoirs of David Wdowinski (1985), a ghetto resident and member of one of the two fighting organizations that emerged there, note that "obtaining food was the all pervasive occupation. We used to run from place to place, store to store, trying to buy food, when we still had some money . . . later all food was smuggled into the ghetto and for it one had to pay a king's ransom" (28–29). Warsaw Jews also suffered from the Nazis' repressive edicts, beatings and other physical abuses, and roundups for forced labor (Gutman 1982, 1994).

Interestingly, however, collective resistance did not occur until January 1943, more than two years after the ghetto was sealed. Simply put, Warsaw Jews saw no need for resistance at first. With no knowledge of Hitler's Final Solution, which had not yet been enacted in the early years of the ghetto, Warsaw Jews had every reason to believe that they would survive as long as they managed to obtain adequate food and shelter. In fact, many Ghetto residents believed that Germany would eventually lose the war and that life would return to normal. Describing the mood in the ghetto in the spring of 1942, Wdowinski (1985) wrote: "In spite of the very frequent but sporadic acts of terror that were visited upon the Ghetto by the Germans and their Jewish henchmen; in spite of the corpses left in the streets after each such brutal attack, and the panic that was spread amongst the population, many still believed that things will get better and they will be left alive" (60–61). Thus despite emerging calls for resistance from some segments of the ghetto population—notably, young activists from a variety of political movements—many in the Warsaw Ghetto felt that collective resistance was either unnecessary or unnecessarily risky. For example, on April 25, 1942, the ghetto resident Chaim Kaplan (1999) wrote the following in his diary, in reference to a rumored Polish rebellion: "What a rebellion that would be! Hundreds of victims would be sacrificed on its altar—in vain . . . the Nazis, of course, will put down any sign of a civilian rebellion and inevitably there will be innocents who, eager for the prestige attached to such a nationalist action, will be caught in the net of revolutionary propaganda" (317–18).

Such feelings persisted throughout the spring and summer. Even when the inevitable occurred—mass deportations of Jews from Warsaw to the death camp Treblinka, beginning in July 1942—few in the ghetto supported the idea of resistance. At a meeting held a few days after the roundups began, community leaders still downplayed the need for resistance, claiming that the entire ghetto could not be liquidated. Describing the meeting in her memoirs, the ghetto resident Vladka Meed (1979) wrote:

Once again the question of armed resistance arose, and again it failed to gain unanimous support. The Jewish leaders did not want to assume the responsibility of risking the lives of those who still hoped to survive. The prevailing opinion still was that no more than, say, 60,000 or 70,000 people would be deported and that the rest would survive. Under the circumstances, how could anyone find it in his heart to jeopardize the lives of the entire Warsaw ghetto for the sake of active resistance? . . . The will to live blotted out the appalling reality. "To fight the Germans is simply courting death," became the conventional wisdom. Having endured so much, were we now to invite immolation? Life had to go on, no matter the cost. The illusion that one was bound to survive drowned out voices of warning. (69–70)

However, as the daily deportations—involving thousands of people each day—continued throughout the summer of 1942, Warsaw Jews were eventually forced to accept the reality that the Germans intended to liquidate the entire ghetto. With this recognition, a new mood took hold: since death was inevitable, it was better to die while fighting than to allow oneself to be murdered (Cochavi 1995; Einwohner 2003; Gutman 1982, 1994). By the end of that summer, two fighting organizations—the Jewish Fighting Organization (Żydowska Organizacja Bojowa), known by its acronym żob, and the Jewish Military Union (Żydowski Zwiazek Wojskowy), or żzw—emerged and began planning for armed resistance.

Who Resisted? Availability and Proximity

Although the residents of the Warsaw Ghetto all eventually came to embrace the idea of resistance, it is notable that those who both made the initial call for armed resistance and who planned and fought in the uprising were young activists from a variety of preexisting political organizations. The concepts of availability and proximity therefore help explain who resisted. First, as seasoned political activists hailing from organizations such as HaShomer Hatza'ir (The Young Guard) and HeHalutz Hatza'ir (The Young Pioneer) as well as a variety of socialist and other workers' organizations such as the Bund, these young people already possessed the organizational skills and political orientation necessary for participation in collective action.[2] For example, ŻOB commander Mordechai Anielewicz came from HaShomer HaTza'ir, and Yitzhak Zuckerman and his wife, Tsivia Lubetkin, were members of HeHalutz (see Zuckerman 1993:xvii–xviii for a description of the various youth organizations from which the ŻOB and ŻZW were staffed). Further, the friendship ties among many of these youth helped recruit new members and sustain their commitment to collective resistance. For instance, Vladka Meed, a Bundist who became a ŻOB courier, was recruited for such work through her friendship ties with fellow Bundist Abrasha Blum (Meed 1979:73). The ŻOB fighter Simha Rotem also had prewar ties to fellow activist Rivka Pasmanik (Rotem 1994:17).

Not only did organizational ties help recruit members for the ŻOB and ŻZW but the friendships among the fighters helped them survive the adverse conditions in the ghetto. In his memoirs, ŻOB fighter Tuvia Borzykowski (1976) described the ghetto residents during the first few days of the mass deportations in July 1942 as "broken people, deprived of all human feelings. They accepted everything, did not even hesitate to step over dead bodies, and all eyes expressed the same self-evident truth: 'We'll all end up as soap.' . . . People had already lost the natural family feelings, the normal attitude towards wife and child, the attachment to home" (18). However, he and his comrades had a different perspective:

Like the others we felt the approach of death—but we did not passively wait for death to come. The Halutz movement whose members lived communal lives, was in a different moral and spiritual state from the rest of the ghetto. Here was a social life, here people lived with problems of the community and the nation. . . . Communal life made it easier to bear the burden of loneliness which weighed so heavily on all the other Jews. Old ties of comradeship and preparations for fighting the enemy strengthened our spirits. (Borzykowski 1976:19)

The ghetto fighters' previous activist experience also made them more available for participation in the uprising. Though diverse, the various political ideologies represented among these ghetto youth—a vast spectrum from right to left, including Zionism, socialism, and communism—predisposed these young people toward collective action. This was especially true of the right-wing Revisionist Betarim youth of the żzw, whose militaristic orientations made their participation in fighting units a logical choice (Wdowinski 1985). Furthermore, the fighters' youth rendered them available for activism. For instance, without families to care for, they could devote their energies to resistance (Gutman 1989b). Perhaps more important, the ghetto youth were some of the only people remaining in the ghetto who could assume a leadership role since many seasoned political leaders had fled Warsaw soon after the German invasion (Gutman 1989b). Finally, as young, relatively strong people, this segment of the population was better able to survive the harsh ghetto conditions. Some of the activist youth even spent important periods of time away from the ghetto, having been sent by their various organizations either to work farms or to safe places in other cities, which further preserved their physical strength and ability to participate in the resistance (Zuckerman 1993). For example, Simha Rotem (1994) spent time at a cooperative work farm (a Zionist-led kibbutz) in 1942, along with other żob fighters from Dror and Akiba (16).

Lastly, gender shaped participation in the uprising as well. Young men and women were actually equally likely to participate in combat, and they were also lauded equally for their bravery on the battlefield. The memoirs of Jack Klajman (2000), who was a ten-year-old boy in Warsaw in 1941, mention a young female fighter:

So many courageous young people were taking part in the uprising—women as well as men. I remember one of the people who dropped into our hideout was a woman who seemed particularly stoic. She was proudly wearing a German helmet. I asked her where she got it. "This is a souvenir of a stinking Nazi I killed," she said. "I grabbed his gun and his helmet." I asked her if I could kiss her on her cheek for her bravery. Laughing, she granted me permission. I grasped her hand and told her I hoped she would survive the war and save that helmet to show her grandchildren one day. I could see the tears forming in her eyes. "I don't think so," she said. "I don't think I will ever see that day. I'm ready to die any time, at any moment, and I'm happy that I was able to be a part of this movement to take revenge on the Nazis." I knew they were preparing for another attack so I wished her well and told her to come back in one piece. She never returned. (70–71)

Yet while men and women were equally likely to participate in combat, other resistance activities were gendered. Notably, women were more likely to work as couriers, performing the all-important tasks of transporting messages, documents, money, and arms between the ghetto and the "Aryan side." These jobs required individuals who looked "good" (i.e., non-Semitic) and who could speak flawless, unaccented Polish. However, since such work could only be undertaken by individuals who could pass physically as non-Jews, and since Jewish men's circumcised penises were clear indications of their identity, women were better suited to such tasks. The ŻOB leader Yitzhak Zuckerman (1993) wrote in his memoirs, "The girls [couriers] were invaluable and their sacrifice was infinite. Without them, it would definitely have been impossible to maintain the Movement throughout the German occupation zone. All of them and every individual according to her ability risked her life and demonstrated unimaginable loyalty. . . . Apparently, what sustained them was a great ideal, as well as the extraordinary friendship within the Movement" (129). Similarly, Syrkin (1948) describes one of the female couriers:

Renya, because of her typically Polish appearance, was particularly useful for the job of smuggling arms. With a kerchief over her head and a basket on her arm, she was a pretty peasant girl going to market, and no S.S. man who tried to flirt with the attractive blond girl was likely to dream that she was a Jewess carrying a pistol concealed somewhere on her person or under the vegetables in the basket. The methods of concealment were of the crudest. Even a single weapon would have been too bulky to escape notice were a search instituted. The important thing was to avoid being searched. That was why the first requisite for smuggling arms was a disarming presence. This set a premium on young girls of "Aryan" appearance. German soldiers and guards, imbued with the notion that a Jew was someone who resembled a Streicher caricature, found it hard to believe that a girl who looked so much like the "Gretchen" of his dreams could belong to the proscribed race. Even in the case of a sudden street search, it would generally be a cursory affair if the girl's false papers seemed to be in order and her manner confident. (199)

Thus prevailing assumptions about race and gender—that is, that Jews were readily identifiable, and that women did not pose political threats to the Germans—as well as the unmarked nature of Jewish women's bodies made Jewish women more available for certain types of participation in the ghetto revolt.

Motives for Resistance: Identity and Honor

As stated earlier, research on social movements places an importance on identity processes in explaining why individuals stage collective resistance. The Warsaw

Ghetto uprising provides an excellent example of the power of collective identity in this regard.

It is important to note that the members of the ŻOB and ŻZW held no illusions about their ability to beat the Germans and achieve safe passage out of the ghetto. Instead of protecting their own lives, the ghetto fighters sought to protect the honor of the Jewish people by dying on the battlefield instead of in the gas chambers (Cochavi 1995; Gutman 1982, 1994). As ŻOB fighter Hirsch Berlinski wrote in his diary,

In one way or another, deportation means annihilation. It is therefore better to die with dignity and not like hunted animals. There is no other way out, all that remains to us is to fight. Even if we are capable of putting up a fight that will only resemble real fighting, it will still be better than a passive acceptance of slaughter. . . . By acting in this manner we shall show the world that we stood up to the enemy, that we did not go passively to our slaughter. (Qtd. in Ainsztein 1979:36–37)

Similarly, ŻOB fighters posted flyers saying "To fight, to die, for the honor of our people!" throughout the ghetto, and ŻOB leader Yitzhak Zuckerman, whose non-Semitic features allowed him to work on the Aryan side procuring arms and false documents, issued the following manifesto to Warsaw Poles during the fighting in April 1943:

Poles, citizens, soldiers of Freedom! Through the din of German cannons destroying the homes of our mothers, wives and children; through the noise of their machine guns, seized by us in the fight against the cowardly German police and ss men; through the smoke of the ghetto that was set on fire, and the blood of its mercilessly murdered defenders, we, the slaves of the ghetto, convey heartfelt greeting to you. . . . Every doorstep in the ghetto has become a stronghold and shall remain a fortress until the end. All of us will probably perish in the fight, but we shall never surrender. We, as well as you, are burning with the desire to punish the enemy for all his crimes, with a desire for vengeance. It is a fight for our freedom, as well as yours; for our human dignity and national honor, as well as yours. (Qtd. in Kurzman 1993:198).

Thus a strong sense of Jewish identity among the fighters, as well as a fierce desire to put forth an image of Jews as strong and honorable, was what motivated the resistance.

Ironically, while their fight was motivated by a strong sense of collective identity, staging resistance required many of the ghetto fighters to go to great lengths to mask the very identity they cherished so much. This was especially true of the couriers and other activists who worked on the Aryan side of the ghetto walls. The memoirs of Adina Szwajger (1990), a Ghetto physician who also smuggled documents for the ŻOB, describe how the Polish family harboring her on the Aryan side gave her a fur collar to sew into her coat to help her hide the fact that she was Jewish; since Nazi edicts forced all Jews to turn their furs and other valuables over to the Germans, people without fur collars were easily identified as Jews. Even the most subtle displays of emotion could bespeak one's Jewish identity. Szwajger notes that it was important for her to be with another young woman at all times when in public: "If one of us went out alone, she might forget herself, and have 'sad eyes,' eyes that betrayed the pain within" (1990:83). Similarly, Vladka Meed (1979), another ŻOB courier, wrote,

The so-called "Aryans" had to blend with their surroundings, adopt Polish customs, habits, and mannerisms, celebrate Christian religious holidays, and of course, go to church. They had to watch their every movement, lest it betray nervousness or un-familiarity with the routine and weigh their every word, lest it betray a Jewish accent. Nevertheless, there were always trivial but telltale signs that could not be controlled, and these could betray one's identity. . . . The eyes were a special danger sign. A careworn face might be transformed by a smile; an accent could be controlled, church customs and prayers could be learnt, but the eyes. . . . How could one hide the mute melancholy, the haunted look of fear? (194)

Hiding one's identity was also made more difficult by the presence of blackmailers, or *shmaltsovniks*, who extorted fees from Jews in hiding in exchange for not turning them in to the SS. The ŻOB fighter Tuvia Borzykowski (1976) wrote, "Though I too have an 'Aryan' appearance, I did not have the necessary self-assurance one needs in order to move freely under the eyes of passersby. I constantly thought that among them were individuals whose sole reason for walking in the street was to detect Jews and hand them over to the Germans" (115).

Participation in the uprising even required that Jews hide their identity from fellow Jews at times. The memoirs of the ŻOB fighter Simha Rotem (1994), also known as "Kazik," who had Aryan features, describe his participation in an "expropriation," one process by which the ghetto fighters procured the money needed to buy weapons:

One of us knocked on the door and when it opened we burst in, identified the man of the house, stood facing him in a "persuasive" movement, and announced, "We've come to get your contribution for the ŻOB." The Jew refused. I put the barrel of my revolver near him;

he froze and didn't utter a sound. Then Hanoch [Gutman] ordered, "Kazik, kill him!" When he called me "Kazik," I was to understand that I had to appear as Kazik, that is, as a Pole. I assumed a strange expression, rolled my eyes, puffed up my chest, grabbed the Jew by the collar, and dragged him into a corner of the room. "Listen, with me you don't play games!" I told him. When he heard the name "Kazik," he understood he was dealing with a Gentile, and you didn't get smart with a Gentile, especially not in those days. He broke down, asked for a brief delay, went to a hiding place, pulled out some money, and reluctantly gave us his "contribution." . . . These actions weren't exactly my pride and joy. Naturally, I preferred to work against the Germans, but circumstances dictated our methods. (28–29)

Thus it was not only the ghetto fighters' sense of identity as Jews but also others' assumptions about the markers of Jewish identity that facilitated resistance.

Summary and Conclusion

An examination of participation in the Warsaw Ghetto uprising reveals some of the sociological aspects of Jewish resistance during the Holocaust. Data from both primary and secondary sources show that not everyone in the ghetto was equally likely to participate in the uprising, or even to advocate resistance; on the contrary, the ghetto fighters were mostly young men and women who—by virtue of their previous activism, ties of friendship, and their abilities to endure the conditions in the ghetto—were both "biographically available" and "socially proximate" to the organizations that planned the armed resistance. Further, their resistance was motivated not by a desire to survive, but by one to shape the lasting image of Jews among the non-Jewish world. As Klajman (2000) notes, "We knew from the start that we were no match for the Germans, but to die in battle gave some meaning to inevitable death. They could kill us but they could never take our accomplishments away from the history books" (81).

Applying the concepts of availability, proximity, and identity to this case shows that a sociological lens proves useful for illuminating aspects of Jewish resistance during the Holocaust. That is not to say, of course, that sociological analyses are superior to other disciplinary examinations, or that they alone provide the best insight into the Holocaust; for instance, this essay has obviously relied on historical accounts. Nonetheless, asking questions that pertain to core sociological concepts of identity and difference, as I have done here, help further our understanding of the Warsaw Ghetto uprising. More broadly, I suggest that the benefits of sociological examinations of the Holocaust include an expansion

RACHEL L. EINWOHNER

of research questions and analytic concepts that can shed additional light on the Holocaust and its effects.

Such applications have implications for the uniqueness of the Holocaust as a phenomenon, however. As Gerson's contribution to this volume suggests, questions of comparison and generalizability complicate sociological analyses of the Holocaust; while some scholars argue that the Holocaust was a unique event, standard sociological methods require that the Holocaust be seen not as unique, but as a case from which generalizable findings may be drawn. By using research findings from the field of social movements—most of which are based on protest in the contemporary United States—to analyze the Warsaw Ghetto uprising, I have implicitly argued that the uprising is just one among many cases of collective action, and that it operates in ways that resemble other cases. Clearly, though, the Warsaw Ghetto uprising is also different from other cases of collective action, in analytically meaningful ways. Perhaps most important, the fact that the uprising took place in the context of genocide—where Warsaw Jews faced a certain death, regardless of their decision to resist—sets this case apart from most other cases of collective action that have received attention from sociologists (Einwohner 2003). Yet the unique characteristics of this case need not preclude its use as a focus of sociological inquiry. On the contrary, analyses of extreme or supposedly deviant cases can be quite useful toward the development of sociological theory, either by expanding theories or by identifying their scope conditions. That availability, proximity, and identity help explain participation in collective action under conditions of genocide points to the robustness of these findings across a wide variety of protest settings, and serves as an important test of social movement theory. Thus not only can sociological research illuminate aspects of the Holocaust but studies of the Holocaust can make contributions to the discipline of sociology as well.

Notes

This research was supported by a School of Liberal Arts Dean's Incentive Grant, a Library Scholar's Grant, and a Purdue Research Foundation (PRF) Summer Grant, all from Purdue University. I am especially thankful to Richard Williams for his comments on earlier drafts.

1. These archives were organized by Emmanuel Ringelblum, a historian and ghetto resident, and contained underground newspapers, letters, and diaries, as well as reports on ghetto life that were researched and written by Ringelblum and his assistants. Since Nazi decrees forbade political meetings in the ghetto, Ringelblum and his archive workers met on Saturdays and used the words *Oneg Shabbat* as a code term for their activities (Gutman 1989a; Kermish 1986). *Oneg Shabbat*—literally "joy of the Sabbath"—refers to

small celebrations held in conjunction with the Sabbath. Ringelblum and his colleagues used this term because they often met on Saturdays, the day of the Jewish Sabbath.

2. *HeHalutz* is an umbrella term for the broader movement comprised of Zionist youth movements like HaShomer HaTza'ir and HeHalutz HaTza'ir. See Zuckerman 1993: xvii–xviii.

The Agonies of Defeat: "Other Germanies" and the Problem of Collective Guilt

JEFFREY K. OLICK

In 1986, the conservative German historian Andreas Hillgruber (1986) published a small book called *Two Kinds of Destruction: The Shattering of the German Reich and the End of the European Jews*. The book's first part provided a substantial and passionate account of the German army on the Eastern Front in the winter of 1944–45; the second part was a much shorter, dryer report of the "end" of the Jews in the same period. Hillgruber explained the difference in his treatments as appropriate to what he saw as the natural sympathies of a German historian with the terrible plight of Hitler's soldiers rather than with the Jews. The repugnance of this assertion was obvious to critics, though as we will see, it was not wholly unprecedented.

Another anecdote reinforces the point: In 1955, members of the reconstituted Frankfurt Institute for Social Research published the results of a study they had conducted in Germany in 1950 into the persistence of fascist attitudes in the German population (Pollock 1955). Dissatisfied with opinion polls, which showed a remarkable turnaround in German political culture, the Frankfurters used an aggressive strategy to "provoke" what they referred to as "nonpublic opinion," the deeper yet truer indications of the persistence of fascist sympathies. In a highly critical review, however, the conservative psychologist Peter Hofstätter (1957) charged the Frankfurters with expecting too much of Germans, who bore the burdens of the atrocities committed in their names; the Germans, Hofstätter seemed to be saying, carried a very great weight indeed, and the Frankfurters were adding to their suffering inappropriately by expecting too much. In turn, Theodor Adorno (who had been the leading intellectual force behind the study and whose interpretive essay formed a major section of the report) fired back that Hofstätter was forgetting that "it is the victims of Auschwitz who had to take its horrors upon themselves, not those who, to their own disgrace and that of their nation, prefer not to admit it" (Adorno 1957:116). Quoting Hofstätter's language, Adorno (1957:105–17) continued, "The 'question of guilt' was 'laden with despair' for the *victims*, not for the *survivors*, and it takes some doing to have blurred this distinction with the existential category of despair, which is not without reason a popular one" (ibid., emphasis added).

It is thus with great care that one approaches German perspectives in the context of an inquiry into the legacies of the Holocaust. On the one hand, one seems to risk a relativization of damages, which has certainly been a common enough trope in German discourse (not least during U.S. president Ronald Reagan's 1985 visit to a military cemetery at Bitburg, during which both Reagan and the West German chancellor Helmut Kohl asserted that all the dead soldiers of World War II were victims equally). On the other hand, as with Adorno, it is also possible to move from describing the discourse of German victimhood to condemning it as despicable self-pitying, in the process bypassing the tasks of sociological analysis, which include explaining the sense of victimhood and the implications of that sense for the reconstruction of German identity.

Nevertheless, it seems to me that we can and must be more differentiating both morally and sociologically. For do we indeed want to deny that Germans were often victims? One thinks not only of the firebombing of Dresden during the war but of widespread rape and starvation at the onset of the occupation. "They reaped what they sowed" is far too convenient and assumes an indefensibly Manichaean worldview in which all Germans were evil perpetrators and the opposing armies purely good. Sociologically, moreover, there were many different attitudes in Germany during the war, many different kinds and degrees of complicity, as well as different responses to the moral and social burdens by Germans in the aftermath. Indeed, insofar as German responses to their moral burdens were highly structured, a sociological rather than philosophical analysis is of primary importance.

Aware of the discomfort of treating so-called perpetrator legacies in the same context as those of the victims—who, *pace* Hillgruber, surely must have *everyone's* sympathies—in this essay I inquire into what I think of as the agonies of German defeat, using the term *agonies* in the classical sense of struggles. How did the Germans define the legacies of perpetration? Among what alternatives did they see themselves forced, and how did they negotiate those symbolic choices? This case of legacies of perpetration, it should be clear, has been consequential not only for Germans but for subsequent cases elsewhere, as well as for our moral and political thinking about political accountability more generally. That thinking—and here I would include cases ranging from how to handle the remnants of repressive regimes in Eastern Europe after the fall of communism to the "de-Baathification" of Iraq—must, it seems to me, be founded on clear sociological knowledge. That knowledge includes an understanding not only of moral gradations of perpetration and victimhood but also of the effects even justified condemnations of perpetrators have on their wider societies.

In the pages that follow, I focus in particular on two agonies that, taken together, illustrate the complexity of the major defensive German trope, that of the "other Germany," which served as the principle alibi for a guilty nation.[1] According to the Israeli journalist Tom Segev (1993), the term *other Germany* was coined by the editors of the newspaper *Ha'aretz*, which used it in 1933 to argue that "all Hitlers in the world cannot eliminate the names Kant, Goethe, and Schiller from German history," thus implying that not everything German was discredited or associable with Nazism. There were, however, two major dimensions to the other Germany trope (17–18). One was the distinction between an other Germany in exile and an other Germany of so-called inner emigrants (intellectual and political figures who stayed in Germany during the Third Reich but whose posture was mainly one of disengagement). The second variety was the distinction between the inner emigrants as representatives of an other Germany in contrast to "ordinary" people, who either more actively supported the regime or whose disengagement was not postured as ironic.

A major locus for the first aspect of the trope was the controversy over whether or not the author Thomas Mann should have returned from exile after the war; a perspicuous example of the second is a debate between the psychoanalyst Carl Jung and the commentator Erich Kästner over Jung's diagnosis of collective guilt. These are, of course, but two examples from a series of public efforts to limn a postwar German identity that would allow Germans to move beyond the unprecedented destruction of life, infrastructure, order, and pride perpetrated in their name without damning themselves forever.

The Mann Affair

Negotiation between the other Germany in exile and the other Germany that had remained took the form of a public debate over the role of Thomas Mann (see especially Glaser 1990; Hermand and Lange 1999; Kurzke 2002; Mann 1999; Sontheimer 2002). One of the most prominent and active German exiles, Mann was perhaps Germany's preeminent man of letters and thus a major propaganda thorn to the Nazis. During the war, Mann published numerous critical essays, delivered important speeches, nurtured contacts with circles close to President Franklin D. Roosevelt, and eventually became an American citizen. At the same time that he served as a leading symbol of the other Germany, however, Mann harbored reservations about that very idea. In August 1943, at a meeting in Los Angeles that Mann attended along with a who's who of famous German exile politicians, writers, artists, and scientists, the National Committee for Free Germany issued a declaration asserting the difference between the Hitler regime and its supporters, on the one hand, and the German people as a whole, on the other. Mann first signed the declaration, but a day later removed his signature, arguing that the declaration sounded too patriotic. This vacillation was emblematic.

The political landscape of German exile in the United States was indeed a complex one. At one extreme were staunch defenders of the so-called other Germany who claimed that the current regime had nothing to do either with the German *Volk* or with German traditions: it was a plague visited on Germany from the outside, the result of flaws that had allowed a small clique of criminals to hold the real Germany hostage. The boundaries of the other Germany, of course, could be drawn with varying extents: it could include only those few who understood the true meaning of Germany and were preserving this sacred essence in the "lifeboat of exile," or it could include virtually the entire people, who, according to the argument, were currently suffering the wildest abuses by a terrorist regime. At the other extreme in the exile community were those who diagnosed deep pathologies in the German tradition itself, and thus rejected the idea of an other Germany as the illegitimate defense of a pathological entity.

Thomas Mann fell into neither of these camps—was neither an attacker of all things German nor a defender of an unsullied other Germany. In a radio broadcast of January 16, 1945, Mann declared, "Let us not speak of guilt. That is a name for the fatal concatenation of consequences of a tragic history, and if it be guilt, it is intermixed with a great deal of guilt belonging to the whole world." In perhaps his most famous speech, at the Library of Congress in May 1945, however, Mann argued that "any attempt to arouse sympathy, to defend and excuse Germany, would certainly be an inappropriate undertaking for one of German birth today" (48). By the same token, "to play the part of judge, to curse and damn his own

people in compliant agreement with the incalculable hatred that they have kin-
dled, to commend himself smugly as 'the good Germany' in contrast to the
wicked, guilty Germany over there with which he has nothing in common,—that
too would hardly befit one of German origin" (Mann 1963:48). Most important
and unusual for one with easy recourse to an identity-saving claim, Mann (1963)
went on to argue that "there are *not* two Germanys [*sic*], a good one and a bad
one, but only one, whose best turned into evil through devilish cunning" (48).

Mann (1963) thus saw the German tradition as a complex contradiction:
"Wicked Germany is merely good Germany gone astray, good Germany in
misfortune, in guilt, in ruin" (64). Indeed, Mann ([1947] 1997) concludes his
great novelistic reflection on National Socialism—*Doctor Faustus*—by arguing
that the great and the horrible are inextricably bound in the German soul:

Our thick-walled torture chamber, into which Germany was transformed by a vile regime
of conspirators sworn to nihilism from the very start, has been burst open, and our
ignominy lies naked before the eyes of the world . . . I repeat, our ignominy. For is it mere
hypochondria to tell oneself that all that is German—even German intellect, German
thought, the German word—shares in the disgrace of these revelations and is plunged into
profoundest doubt?

. . .

Was not this regime, both in word and deed, merely the distorted, vulgarized, debased
realization of a mindset and worldview to which one must attribute a characteristic authenticity and which, not without alarm, a Christianly humane person finds revealed in the traits
of our great men, in the figures of the most imposing embodiments of Germanness? (505–6)[2]

Mann ([1947] 1997) is thus arguing that good Germany and bad Germany are
not alternatives, but mere moments in a dialectic: hence to "proclaim that such a
state was forced upon us as something without roots in our nature as a people,
something totally alien to us . . . would, so it seems to me, be more high-minded
than conscientious" (505–6). No easy defense that National Socialism perverted
the true other Germany, Mann thus argues, is possible.

Despite the subtleties of Mann's arguments, many of his contemporaries
nevertheless read him as an advocate of collective guilt. Clearly, highly differentiated arguments did not work well in this context, despite charges by Germans
against the occupation authorities that their treatment of Germany rested on
insufficiently differentiated understandings. The question was obviously one of
the kind of differentiation.

These reflections burst the bounds of politically engaged belles lettres in August 1945, within the crucible of U.S. reeducation policy. It was in the *Münchner Zeitung* (one of the newspapers published by the Psychological Warfare Division of the U.S. Military Government), as part of an ongoing discussion of German responsibility, that Walter von Molo published a letter of August 8, 1945, to Thomas Mann (see especially Glaser 1990:73–77; Mann 1999:23–36). Von Molo, who had been president of the poetry section of the Prussian Academy of the Arts from 1928 to 1930 and who had remained in Germany during the Third Reich, called on Mann to return to Germany. Mann, who according to von Molo represented the best of the other Germany, was to tend to his compatriots like a "good physician," proving to the world that in its "innermost core" the German people really had nothing in common with the "misdeeds and crimes, the horrible atrocities and lies." In the last analysis, so many had "remained reasonable people" despite the "slogans" and "humiliations" of the occupation,[3] these "Germans who yearned and yearn for the return of that which gave us respect in the counsel of nations." "Please come back soon," von Molo wrote, "and give to these crushed souls consolation through humaneness; revive their faith that justice does exist, that it is indeed wrong to split humanity so cruelly, as has been done here in our recent, gruesome past."[4] Mann represented German humanism, and with him on the scene, no one would be able to deny that this was a core German virtue; Mann was living proof of the difference between regime and *Volk*.

As already clear from Mann's statements at the Library of Congress and the passage from *Doctor Faustus* (which Mann had worked on since 1943 but which was not published until 1947), von Molo's letter was anathema to Mann's argument that Nazi Germany was not something separate from an "inner core" of German identity but a pathological emanation of it. On less of a theoretical and more of a visceral foundation, however, Mann found distasteful the idea that an exile like himself had anything in common with self-styled defenders of German humanism like von Molo who had remained in Germany. Indeed, Mann had specific occasion to respond to that association because of an article following von Molo's by Frank Thiess, a writer who had been editor of the *Berliner Tageblatt* from 1915 to 1919. Thiess's article was titled "The Inner Emigration," thereby coining a term that would appear throughout subsequent discussions (see also Paetel 1946). Thiess claimed a unity of exiles and inner emigrants as representatives of the other Germany, on the basis of which German identity could be rehabilitated, new (old) foundations strengthened, and collective accusations repudiated.

Thiess's argument, however, was not only immodest, it was also supercilious. Responding to the question as to why he had not emigrated, Thiess wrote: "If I were to succeed in surviving this terrible epoch . . . I would gain thereby so much for my intellectual and human development that I would emerge richer in knowledge and experience than I could possibly become by observing the German tragedy from seats in the loges or orchestra stalls of foreign countries." Thiess went so far as to argue that it was more difficult—and thus a more worthy achievement—to preserve one's character in Germany than it was "to send messages to the German people from over there, which fell on deaf ears while we knowledgeable ones always felt ourselves many lengths ahead." Comparing leaving Germany during the Third Reich to leaving one's mother in her sickbed, Thiess nevertheless condescended on behalf of the inner emigrants that they "expect no reward for not having left Germany. It was natural for us that we stayed by it." But he warned Mann and other exiles not to wait so long that they lose their linguistic, and by implication, cultural credibility. Thiess and many others clearly saw themselves as generous, allowing those who abandoned Germany in its time of need to return and participate in the recovery: "That is not to say that I want to rebuke anybody who did leave," Thiess offers backhandedly.

Thiess and von Molo, it is important to note, were not without good reason for their defensiveness. In his wartime speeches, Mann had argued that German intellectuals were partly responsible for the Third Reich since they had failed to resist, especially in the form of a "general strike." In particular, Mann had criticized Ernst Jünger, perhaps the leading conservative writer of the Weimar period, who had been an early enthusiast for National Socialism. Mann charged Jünger with more responsibility for his early flirtations with the Nazis than Jünger and others were prepared to accept after they had withdrawn their support; whether or not Jünger and others had eventually withdrawn their support, their nationalistic "saber rattling" was, for Mann, a serious indictment. For Jünger, in contrast, Mann was a traitor for giving speeches while German cities were going up in flames. In a notorious 1973 interview, Jünger stirred controversy when he criticized Mann for abandoning Germany, fully aware that Mann would have been imprisoned had he stayed: for Jünger, that was a cost Mann should have been willing to bear (Neaman 1999:104–7).

Mann struggled with the issue for many weeks, finally responding to von Molo in October 1945. He gave three reasons for not returning. First, as he had already stated during the war, he was disappointed that Hitler's seizure of power in 1933 had not led to a general strike of all intellectuals. Second, Mann argued that one could not simply forget the horrors of what followed. And third, he had become an American citizen, he admired the United States, and his children had become assimilated there. More emphatically, Mann rejected the charge that he and his coexiles had comfortably observed Germany from afar and thus had not suffered for their views. Thiess and others, Mann argued, did not appreciate the psychic trauma of exile.[5] Mann did not explicitly use Thiess's term *inner emigration* so as not to credit the claim. "I confess," Mann wrote, "I fear . . . that in spite of everything, understanding between one who experienced the witches' Sabbath from outside and you who joined in the dance and served Herr Urian [the name of the devil in Goethe's *Faust*] would be difficult." Mann went so far as to dismiss all intellectual work produced during the Third Reich—the legitimacy claim of the inner emigrants: "It may be superstition, but in my eyes books that were even printed in Germany between 1933 and 1945 are less than worthless and should not be touched [*nicht gut, in die Hand zu nehmen*]. An odor of blood and shame clings to them: They should all be pulped." Despite this indignant rejection, Mann ended the letter by assuring von Molo that he had never stopped seeing himself as a German writer and that he remained true to the German language. More important, he had always sympathized with those condemned by an "undifferenti- ated Anti-Germanism." The positive benefit, for Mann, of not distinguishing a good, other Germany from the bad was that one could, on that basis, reject judgments of Germany as purely bad; the good and the bad together constituted Germany, preventing collectivistic accusations as well as collectivistic defenses. Neither absolute innocence nor absolute guilt made for a justified claim.

As could be expected, Mann's response caused a storm of indignation, and the newspapers were filled in the months that followed with letters and articles addressing Mann's arguments. Mann himself expressed no interest in modifying his position, though very little of the reaction was even remotely sympathetic to him. One of the only examples of public support for Mann came from Hermann Hesse, who had survived the war in Switzerland. Hesse addressed the question of what a "right-minded decent German should have done in the Hitler years." He rejected those responses focused only on the latter years, that is, on what one should have done after 1938 or later. Of those who argued that resistance was

　　　　　　　　　　　　　　　JEFFREY K. OLICK

dangerous, Hesse asked "why they first discovered Hitler in 1933," rather than since at least the Munich putsch (1923); why, instead of supporting the Weimar Republic, they had voted for Hindenburg and Hitler, who were the ones who made it life-threatening "to be a right-minded decent person" (qtd. in Kleßmann 1982:442−44).

Regarding inner emigration, to those who defended their actions in the Third Reich by saying that they had always had one foot in the concentration camp, Hesse quipped that he only trusted "those who had two feet in the camps, not one foot in the camps, the other in the Party." Most important, Hesse rued the fact that of all the people who were writing to him, none admitted to having been a Nazi and to now seeing things differently. Hesse was writing around the same time that leaders of the Evangelical Church in Germany were decrying denazification because it denied people the right to a change of heart, and in response to an argument articulated most forcefully in a widely read article by Eugen Kogon titled "The Right to a Political Mistake." According to Hesse's evidence, no one was acknowledging a change of heart because no one was admitting to having been a Nazi in the first place. For Hesse, the question of political responsibility extended far back into the Weimar Republic, associating early origins and ultimate ends in a more direct fashion than those who focused only on the war did.

Collective Guilt

Whether in the context of the Thomas Mann affair or elsewhere, the central intellectual and cultural issue in postwar Germany seems to have been a cognitive one: What analytical categories were relevant, and who belonged in which ones? What kinds of distinctions were legitimate, which were not? In the Mann affair, the question was whether inner emigrants and exiles together constituted the Other Germany or whether the inner emigrants belonged to the larger culpable mass. Who was guilty? Who was not? What kind(s) of guilt required what kind(s) of responses, and from whom? How widely should the circle of guilt be drawn? These questions proved central to framing how to be German after World War II. These challenges of "boundary work" (Lamont and Fournier 1992), moreover, are constitutive features of reconstruction more generally—that is, moral, in addition to physical and institutional, reconstruction.

The overriding fear of many German commentators, regardless of field, was the possibility of a collective guilt, though what exactly that might mean, we will see, was far from clear. Most German commentators at the time believed that they were being accused of something unbearable, and this perception has remained axiomatic in German public memory—that Germany was indiscriminately and inappropriately charged with collective guilt in the first years of the occupation. This perception is not entirely unreasonable: the original American occupation statute and other official documents often referred to Germany and "the Germans" as a whole; so-called placard actions (in which photographic evidence of camp atrocities was posted in town squares with captions like "The Atrocities: Your Fault!") and documentary films were intended to awaken not only disgust (which they did) but also a sense of responsibility and even guilt (which they usually did not, producing instead more vigorous boundary work: this is the work of monsters, not of us!); denazification formally placed all German adults under suspicion until they could be classified; the so-called Morgenthau plan (calling for the deindustrialization of large parts of Germany) raised the possibility of destroying German political and cultural unity once and for all; Thomas Mann, as we just saw, called for all intellectual works produced in Germany between 1933 and 1945 to be pulped; and public opinion in the United States and Britain remained anti-German, with an expectation of punishment.

By the same token, the occupation authorities were by and large careful, after the first weeks, to avoid vigorous accusations of collective guilt in their official rhetoric. Newspapers sponsored by the United States were careful not to advocate collective guilt, even if their pages did provide a central forum for German and other intellectuals to debate the issues. Extreme ideas (rightly or wrongly) associated with the Morgenthau plan had not carried the day unmodified. While rejecting the inner emigrants, Mann also rejected undifferentiated anti-Germanism. And despite negative opinion polls, Germany's desperate food situation produced a historically unprecedented and extensive response from abroad in the form of care packages and other personal aid. Regarding denazification, it was true that the entire adult population was technically under suspicion; by the same token, the fact that the overwhelming majority were classified as unburdened could have been, but was not, interpreted as a rather generous exculpation.

In what sense, then, was Germany truly accused of collective guilt? In some ways, it does not really matter. There were enough reasons for either interpretation in the early months. The more interesting questions are whether most Germans felt accused, why they felt that way, and how they reacted to their perceptions. Given that evidence for genuine accusations was harder to find after the first postwar months, however, the German reaction to collective guilt theory must be understood as a traumatic memory (Assmann and Frevert 1999); many Germans felt that *they* were victims as much—if not more—than anyone else (Moeller 2001). Indeed, the sense of trauma—an irreparable harm posing challenges to the narrative sense of continuity—is apparent throughout the discourse. As Eugen Kogon, a former Buchenwald inmate and prominent Catholic intellectual, put it in 1946, "While it was still half-dazedly struggling for the first consciousness, a chorus of accusatory voices of repugnance and resentment crashed over the German people. It received nothing else to hear except the thousand-fold cry: You, you alone are at fault! All you Germans are guilty! The heart of the people was confused, in many it hardened" (7). For many official speakers in later decades, the validity of Kogon's perception was taken for granted.

GUILT AND OPPOSITION

Another of the most important intellectual voices of the time was that of Erich Kästner, a world-renowned children's book author both before and after the war, whose books for adults were burned and banned during the Third Reich and who spent the war as an inner emigrant, suffering numerous arrests by the Gestapo. As the war came to an end, Kästner assumed one of the most influential positions in the Allied-sponsored discourse as editor of the feuilleton section of the U.S.-sponsored *Neue Zeitung*. As a victim of the regime, Kästner was particularly struck by any implication of German collective guilt, which he perceived as adding insult to injury. For this reason, Kästner expressed personal relief at the chief prosecutor Robert Jackson's opening remarks at Nuremberg, in which Jackson stated clearly that the whole German people was not accused, that the very fact of the oppressive apparatus of the Nazi state testified to the nonsupport of the German people, and that the Germans themselves had accounts to settle with the defendants.[6] According to Kästner (1998), "The ranks laden with grief, distress, and worry breathed a sigh of relief, because a just thinking man took a remaining burden from them, which they perceived had been unjustly loaded on them. Their burden is still heavy enough. But hope, while still small and timid, patters alongside and helps carry it a bit" (501). For Kästner, this was no mere observation of his compatriots. As we will see shortly, it is clear that he took the accusation—whatever it may have been—quite personally.

For both Kogon and Kästner, and for many others, American reeducation policy was based on an arrogant misunderstanding of German experience and culture and, no matter how it was packaged, revealed a deeply held accusatory attitude. According to Kogon (1946): "To awaken the powers of contemplation in the German world was the task of a far-reaching realpolitik of the Allies. It was included in the program of 'reeducation.' And it stemmed from the thesis of a German collective guilt. The shock of accusation, that they were all complicit [*mitschuldig*], was supposed to bring the Germans to the realization of the true causes of their defeat." Instead, the accusation produced the opposite: "Because of the awful clamor around it and because of its own blindness they [the German people] wanted to hear nothing more of self-examination. The voice of their conscience did not awaken." Finally, "a justified feeling of millions defended itself against the collective accusation, which had a leveling [*egalisierend*] appearance" (Kogon 1946:10). This sense that Allied policy was responsible for whatever "repression" or "silence" about the Nazi past existed was to become a pillar of German leftist critiques in the 1960s.

Kogon, however, was no apologist. In rejecting collective guilt both on principle and for its effects, he warned his compatriots not to use this move as an argument against individual guilt, which many were doing with ever more elaborate schemas. For Kogon, a devout Catholic, guilt was both solely individual and the right of God alone to judge. He duly chastised those who defended Germany with the argument that the Allies were no better and thus in no position to accuse Germany: "Many today in Germany say: Where do the Allies get the right to sit in moral judgment of us? Is their history free from violence and atrocities?" Kogon responds that who is doing the accusing has no bearing on the accuracy of the accusation. To illustrate this, however, he chose a telling analogy: "To this moral question the Bible has already answered, insofar as the prophet named the dictator Nebuchadnezzar the 'servant of God' who was sent by him to lead the people of Israel out of error." According to the analogy, Germans are the people of Israel who erred, and the Allies are Nebuchadnezzar. This is an interesting reversal, consistent with the widespread theory that Germany was the new pariah, just like the Jews. Nevertheless, according to Kogon, whoever examined his own conscience in all honesty did not care where the impulse came from; he made a virtue out of necessity: "The others are servants of God to him, whether just or unjust; he allows them the victor's triumph, even when they have gone the same or similar way that has made him guilty, and does not consider himself the toll collector: 'Lord, I thank you that I am not like that Pharisee over there!'" (8–9).

Kogon's argument, religiously inspired, is that everyone, Germans and Allies, answers to a higher authority: "Most of them [the Germans] sensed that a higher judge would not set them in the same dock with the criminals and activists of the Nazi Party—to say nothing of the countless noble and fearless fighters or at least respectable and effective carriers of the inner opposition against the regime, as of yet so unknown abroad." Again, the implication was that the insult of being charged indiscriminately as a collectivity was responsible for the unwillingness of Germans to face their *individual* guilt: "Had one allowed the yearning expectation of at least half of the German people finally to be freed from the terror of National Socialism, which they could no longer shake off alone, to rise to the heights of true excitement, then the unveiled concentration camps would have become landmarks of German self-reflection, of a deep horror towards the abyss into which the nation had sunk" (Kogon 1946:11). Whether Kogon's optimism was justified about the preparedness of many Germans to engage in this reflection (if only it were not for the insult of reeducation), however, remains an unredeemable counterfactual.

While Kogon's authority rested at least in part on his unassailable credential as a former concentration camp inmate, Kästner's response was somewhat more defensive. Given the discursive context, it is not surprising that this would be so: as we saw, the inner emigration, much to Kästner's dismay and incomprehension, had been impugned by no less a moral authority than Thomas Mann. In many ways, Kästner's attitude was typical of the inner emigration, if not quite as strident as Frank Thiess's. Explaining why he did not emigrate, for instance, Kästner (1959) wrote, "A writer wants to and has to experience how the people to whom he belongs bears fate. To go abroad just then is only justified through acute mortal danger. Otherwise it is his professional duty to accept every risk if by doing so he can remain an eyewitness and someday provide written testimony" (61–65). And this testimony he does indeed provide. For Kästner (1998), the most remarkable accomplishment of the Nazi regime was the reversal of values and the misuse of character they extorted from the population: "For here, in the area of conscience and character, lay the most terrible, the most frightening malediction of those twelve years. The men in power and their party systematically aspired to the biggest, most devilish spiritual corruption of all time. . . . The disorientation [*Ratlosigkeit*] of conscience, that was the worst. The lack of escape out of a muddy labyrinth into which the state had driven a people and at whose exits the executioner stood" (515). Clearly, Kästner saw good Germans like himself as victims of the Nazi state, and he drew a sharp line between regime and

Volk. The perversions of National Socialism, moreover, were no special fault of Germans, "who were not better or worse than other people on earth." The warning is clear: "Whoever did not experience it, whoever was not despairingly caught up in this labyrinth throws the first stone at this people [*Volk*] too easily." As for Thomas Mann, Kästner (1959) had unbounded respect for Mann the writer; for Mann the man, he had none: "It was foolishness to call him. Instead, one should have asked him for goodness sake to stay over there!" (90–92).

DIAGNOSIS AND DENIAL

The full brunt of his scorn, however, Kästner reserved for the Swiss psychoanalyst Carl Jung. Indeed, Jung has served as a mnemonic imago of collective guilt theory: Jung is considered to have introduced the term *collective guilt* into the public discourse (this is unlikely to be true) and to have proffered a most vicious version of the accusation (also, as we will see, not exactly true).[7] This imago is partly due to Kästner's response to him.

With the exception of Sigmund Freud, who had died in 1939, Jung was perhaps the most famous psychiatrist in the world, and he enjoyed an exceptional international reputation for his theory of archetypes and of the collective unconscious, to say nothing of having introduced the terms *complexes* and *free association* into everyday language. Unfortunately, Jung had also flirted with the Nazis in the first half of the 1930s, seeing an opportunity to establish the predominance of his own views against those of his former friend Freud, who was Jewish. Jung collaborated with the psychotherapist Matthias Goering, the brother of Hermann, in the formation of a psychotherapeutic society free of Jewish influence, as well as in the editing of its international journal. In 1933, Jung also gave an interview on Berlin radio in which he seemed to endorse the Führer principle. Indeed, Jung entertained a fascination for the occult dimensions of National Socialism that was more than purely opportunistic; also, it is likely that he personally was not entirely free of anti-Semitic prejudice.[8] So it is not completely incomprehensible why a diagnosis of German collective guilt by Jung would rankle the sensibility of an inner emigrant like Kästner.

In February of 1945, Jung gave an interview to a Zurich newspaper in which he stated that "the popular sentimental distinction between Nazis and opponents of the regime" was psychologically illegitimate. In the interview, Jung referred to the "general psychic inferiority of the Germans" and to a "national inferiority complex," for which, he argued, they had tried "to compensate by megalomania" (Jung 1989:72). Elsewhere, Jung argued that all Germans were

JEFFREY K. OLICK

either actively or passively, consciously or unconsciously, participants in the atrocities, that the collective guilt of the Germans was "for psychologists a fact, and it will be one of the most important tasks of therapy to bring the Germans to recognize this guilt." Jung acknowledged that this might seem unfair, particularly to those Germans who believed themselves to have opposed the regime: "It may be objected that the whole concept of psychological collective guilt is a prejudice and a sweepingly unfair condemnation. Of course it is, but that is precisely what constitutes the irrational nature of collective guilt: it cares nothing for the just and the unjust, it is the dark cloud that rises up from the scene of an un-expiated crime" (Jung 1989:52–53). These statements were reprinted in the *Neue Zeitung* where, again, Kästner was a top editor.

Kästner's response to Jung was withering. Whether or not one accepts Kästner's arguments, one cannot fail to appreciate that this literary master brought to bear here his prodigious talents as a stylist. Throughout, Kästner refers to "the researcher of the soul [*Seelenforscher*] Prof. Dr. C. G. Jung," as if Jung's reputation as an insightful observer were a huge joke, since no one with any insight could possibly have uttered such nonsense as Jung did. For Kästner (1998), however, the issue concerned more than just Jung, who was important not only because of his fame but because his arguments were indicative of an ill wind indeed: "If even one of the most famous judges of the soul in Europe doesn't understand us, one can count on even less understanding from the overseas victors" (520). But this is unfathomable to Kästner, because less understanding seems to him hardly possible.

The real tragedy for Kästner (1998) is that German opponents of the Nazis, who had "for twelve long years resisted the greatest malice," had dared "to count on a bit of consolation and help, encouragement and sympathy. . . . They were, God knows, not proud but tired. A drop of understanding would have been an immeasurable gift for them" (520). Instead, they received the reproach of "the researcher of the soul Prof. Dr. C. G. Jung." For Kästner, "It sounded as if the important man had swallowed the trumpet of final judgment." The result for those such as himself was devastating:

Then the poor, exhausted opponents of the regime sunk into themselves without a word. Granted, they had not been able to overcome the Genghis Kahn of Inn [Hitler was born in Branau am Inn] and his bronzed horde. But they did try to withstand the demons of torture and bloodlust, the furies of the gas chambers and crematoria, the vipers of surveillance, blackmail and dispossession. Not every one of them could be so valiant and incorruptible as the researcher of the soul Prof. Dr. C. G. Jung most certainly would have been if he had been in their position rather than living in Switzerland. . . . So the opponents of the defeated regime silently covered up their pale, tired, starved heads. The "popular sentimental distinction" between them and the Nazis was not permitted. The researcher of the soul Prof. Dr. C. G. Jung was decidedly against it and informed the entire world of his expert opinion.

For Kästner, Germans like himself had a right to expect more than this slap in the face. The charge was even more outrageous because it came from one who himself was not free of guilt. Jung had tried to avoid the charge that such a psychoanalytic diagnosis as his was born of self-righteousness by invoking the New Testament parable "Take the log out of your own eye first, and then you will be able to see and take the speck out of your brother's eye" (Matthew 7:10), saying that "we love the criminal and are ardently interested in him because the devil lets us forget the log in our own eye in the examination of the speck in someone else's" (Jung 1989:52). Kästner (1998) responded: "Too bad that Jung didn't send his log in a special freight train to Germany. The log could have provided many opponents of the regime and their freezing families with a warm oven for months this winter. But unfortunately Jung does not belong to those who make 'that sentimental popular distinction' between opponents and the Nazis. And so he didn't grant us his log" (523–24). Kästner thus argued that any accusation of collective guilt not only made for one further humiliation good Germans like himself had to suffer but that the charge was incomprehensible. In comparison to the religiously inspired Kogon, however, Kästner seemed less concerned with the individual contemplation of guilt. Kästner's evaluation of Nuremberg, for this reason, was resultantly more positive: the big fish are the true criminals. Indeed, he was particularly disgusted with those defendants who, having once claimed to be the masters of German destiny, now claimed to have been caught up in a system beyond their control.[9] Without Kogon's religious devotion, Kästner was less confident of a higher judge, or at least more concerned with the court of public opinion.

One can indeed appreciate Kästner's feeling that accusations of collective guilt did not fairly account for individuals like himself who had never wanted not only the worst outcomes of National Socialism but also its first, more widely praised stirrings. What is more difficult to appreciate is that Kästner deliberately refused to consider Jung's motives and that he misrepresented Jung's argument, in part by responding only to Jung's interview and not to the more considered essay by Jung reprinted in the *Neue Zeitung* from a Zurich newspaper. Jung's argument is in fact not nearly as outrageous as Kästner made it out, though it is rather shrill in places.[10] The crucial questions are thus why Kästner responded as he did, whether Kästner's reaction was representative, and why his reading appears to have stuck in popular memory.

Jung (1989) began by making a crucial distinction between a psychological guilt and a moral or criminal one: "The psychological use of the word 'guilt' should not be confused with guilt in the legal or moral sense. Psychologically, it connotes the irrational presence of a subjective feeling (or conviction) of guilt, or an objective imputation of, or imputed share in, guilt" (51). Jung argued that "guilt can be restricted to the lawbreaker only from the legal, moral, and intellectual points of view, but as a psychic phenomenon it spreads itself over the whole neighborhood. A house, a family, even a village where a murder has been committed feels the psychological guilt and is made to feel it by the outside world" (51). Indeed, Jung warned that "naturally no reasonable and conscientious person will lightly turn collective guilt into individual guilt by holding the individual responsible without giving him a hearing. He will know enough to distinguish between the individually guilty and *the merely collectively guilty*" (53, emphasis added).

This last turn of phrase is perhaps the crux of the dispute: for Kästner and many of his compatriots, collective guilt is in many ways a much more serious matter than mere individual guilt; because the latter (individual guilt) clearly does not affect them, only the former (collective guilt) is a real challenge. For Kästner, however, any imputation of a guilt beyond the criminal risked placing him in community with the Nazis when he and others had already paid a tremendous price to maintain the distinction; he thus felt any imputation of collective guilt—whether an accusation that he shared in this objectively or a diagnosis that he must *feel* guilty for having been present at the scene of the crime—as unacceptable; Kästner denied not only that he was guilty (individually or collectively) but also that he should feel guilty even if he had not done anything punishable. The latter seems to be the implication of Jung's diagnosis of psychological collective guilt.

One explanation of the gulf separating Kästner and Jung comes from the sociologist Ralf Dahrendorf (1967), who attributes the debate over collective guilt to linguistic and cultural differences, emphasizing the different ways different societies draw the boundaries between public and private:

Collective guilt has a very different, much more "external" connotation for Anglo-Saxon ears schooled in public virtues than it has for Germans. "Guilt" (*Schuld*) in German always has an undertone of the irremediable, incapable of being canceled by metaphysical torment; *Kollektivschuld* binds every individual as such for all time. On the other hand, one of the corollaries of collective guilt is the notion of reparations or, more generally, of making up for past failures; what is meant is a collective responsibility that forces those responsible to answer by common effort, that is, in political and economic ways, for the damage they have brought about. Such guilt does not really involve the individual as a person, as a human being—as one would say in the language of private virtues—but in his membership role, thus as a German national. In principle, one can cast off the guilt with the role. (288–89)

Whether it is individual guilt or collective guilt that is "mere" is thus of the essence. While Jung was certainly not the least bit Anglo-Saxon, there may well be something to Dahrendorf's explanation. Again, Kästner felt himself accused personally by collective guilt when Jung claims he did not mean it that way. Just as Jung refused to acknowledge the distinction between Nazis and opponents, Kästner was unable to understand the difference between individual and collective guilt, as Dahrendorf's explanation would predict. Kästner appears to have taken collective guilt as a deeply *private* accusation.

What, then, can be said of Jung's diagnosis? His assessment of German collective guilt draws on his theory of the shadow, his belief that each individual is in some way exactly what that person has no wish to be: "Everyone harbours his 'statistical criminal' in himself, just as he has his own private madman or saint" (Jung 1989:55). An individual is healthy not because he conquers his shadow, but because he understands and has integrated it; the shadow is most dangerous when it remains unconscious. Indeed, this concept of the shadow helps Jung explain National Socialism. Hitler, Jung argued, symbolized something in every individual: "He was the most prodigious personification of all human inferiorities. . . . He represented the shadow, the inferior part of everybody's personality, in an overwhelming degree, and this was another reason why they fell for him" (6). For Jung, National Socialism as a mass movement was an unconscious compensation for the universal chaos of the twentieth century that was "merely" much worse in Germany: "The Germans wanted order, but they made the fatal mistake of choosing the principle victim of disorder and unchecked greed for their leader" (6).

But the shadow also explains Jung's (1989) diagnosis of collective guilt in postwar Germany: "The wickedness of others becomes our own wickedness because it kindles something evil in our own hearts. The murder has been suffered by everyone, and everyone has committed it: lured by fascination of evil,

JEFFREY K. OLICK

we have all made this collective psychic murder possible; and the closer we were to it and the better we could see it, the greater our guilt" (54). Clearly, then, Jung's charge of collective guilt is not meant in any conventional sense. His point is to understand the ways in which one can feel badly for an act that one has not in fact committed, both because no one can honestly claim never to have had a bad motive and because one is always stained by the very proximity to its realization: "Since no man lives within his own psychic sphere like a snail in its shell, separated from everybody else, but is connected with his fellow-men by his unconscious humanity, no crime can ever be what it appears to our consciousness to be: an isolated psychic happening" (53). Collective guilt is thus "a state of magical uncleanliness," but it is also "a very real fact" (Jung 1989:53).

In an essay entitled "Die Schuld und die Schulden" ("The Guilt and the Debts"), Kästner (1998) addressed exactly the same issue that informed Jung's discussion about the feeling of guilt spreading out over a neighborhood: "If I had a brother who had robbed someone, and someone came and said I was guilty, that would be unjust. But if he said that because the thief was my brother I should help the victim get his property or its equivalent back, I would answer without hesitation: 'That I will do.' The guilt I must reject. The debts I would recognize" (502). As Dahrendorf implied, for Kästner a debt is payable, but guilt is permanent.

Kästner, we should recall, was indeed a remarkable individual. Unlike many compatriots who looked away when confronted with Nazi atrocities, Kästner was genuinely struck by the horror of it all. Tasked with reviewing *Die Todesmühlen* (*The Mills of Death*), for instance (an atrocity film about the camps that the Americans forced Germans to watch in exchange for rations), he was baffled by the defenses of his compatriots. And he grew so upset that he was unable to produce his review: "I just can't manage writing a coherent article about this unimaginable, infernal insanity.... What happened in the camps is so terrible that one can neither remain silent nor speak about it. We Germans will certainly never forget how many people were killed in these camps." Nevertheless, consistent with his feeling of victimhood, he added: "And the rest of the world should every now and then remember how many Germans were killed there" (Kästner 1959:64 qtd. in Barnouw 1996:2–3).

One is thus tempted to say that Jung's diagnosis of a *feeling* of collective guilt has some merit, redeeming itself not only in the worst dregs of German society but here in its best representative. This is exactly the kind of defense Jung's theory expects, a "me too" claim of victimhood. Jung's argument certainly takes on a patronizing tone, particularly when he claimed he did not wish to excite the hysteric and, as a physician, was merely telling his patient the hard truth. But instead of examining the argument, Kästner dismissed it from the outset with sarcasm. Instead of engaging with the theory—well rooted in Jung's theoretical system—Kästner attempted to delegitimate it via ad hominem critique: an early Nazi sympathizer himself, Jung had no right to cast the first stone. Of course, if one followed Kogon's Christian ethic of introspection, the origins of the accusation should not matter.

Conclusion

The agonies of German defeat were many, including death, physical injury, psychic trauma, material devastation, and social dislocation. Pointing this out in no way implies a relativization of burdens or necessarily leads one to conflate perpetrator and victim, German and Jew, in a great postmodern hodgepodge of suffering, though such analyses have often been used for that morally and politically suspect purpose. What have interested me, however, are the *moral* agonies of German defeat, in part because these are the agonies that were—and continue to be—the most consequential for Germans. Buildings can be rebuilt and new generations grow out of the rubble, but individual and collective identities depend on early reactions to transformative experiences, as well as a continued engagement with them. If collective responsibility means anything, it is just this: what kinds of answer do people give in the face of moral challenges to their sense of self, both individual and collective.

A common myth about postwar Germany is that Germans were silent or "in denial" about the past. The foregoing pages have demonstrated, however, that at least for public intellectuals, parsing trumps outright denial. There were indeed those who offered halfhearted statements about who knew what and when, or who did not. And such statements did serve their purposes. But how Germans confronted atrocities seems more important than how they denied them. In the critical literature of the 1960s, psychoanalytically influenced thinkers drew an opposition—quite similar to Jung's—between denial and "working through." The foregoing account of the Mann and Jung-Kästner debates, however, has been a sociological and historical investigation of what kinds of working through were possible, rather than a philosophical investigation into what might have been desirable. Given the consistencies of the discourse and the cultural patterning of the agonies, as well as that the interventions presented above were emblematic of the problems faced by the collectivity, it is clear, moreover, that the dimensions of this discourse are social rather than purely psychological.

The way public commentators draw boundaries among perpetrators, victims, and bystanders, between before and after, indeed between good and evil—what many cultural sociologists have recently called boundary work—is thus of vital importance. Understanding the way individuals, whether in public or private, speak on behalf of a morally challenged nation as part of the work of reconstruction is thus to investigate the most important legacy of all: whether memory leads to "next time" or "never again." Following World War I, the memory of destruction stoked new flames through a rhetoric of retrenchment and revenge. Even the deficits of the discourse just outlined, however, point in a different direction.

Notes

1. While more pervasive, claims that "we did not know" were less effective and, because they always begged the question of *what* people did not know (for surely they knew some things), seemed disingenuous and are thus less interesting analytically.

2. A further interesting portion of this passage is Mann's association between the situation of the Germans and that of the Jews: "What will it be like," his narrator asks, "to belong to a nation whose history bore this gruesome fiasco within it, a nation that has driven itself mad, gone psychologically bankrupt, that admittedly despairs of governing itself and thinks it best that it become a colony of foreign powers, a nation that will have to live in isolated confinement, like the Jews of the Ghetto, because the dreadfully swollen hatred all around it will not permit it to step outside its border—a nation that cannot show its face" (Mann ([1947] 1997:505–6). The assertion that Germans were being treated like Jews, or would somehow assume the pariah status of the Jews in the world, was a common trope in the German postwar discourse.

3. It seems strange to lament the slogans and humiliations of the occupation rather than those of the Nazi period.

4. Whether von Molo was referring to the cruel splitting done by the Nazis or currently being done by the Allied occupation authorities through denazification is not entirely clear, through it is more likely the latter. Crucial passages from von Molo's letter, as well as from that of Frank Thiess (discussed below), along with Mann's response, are reprinted in Glaser, *The Rubble Years*, 73–77, among many other places. Mann's complete response is reprinted in Mann, *Fragile Republik*, 23–26.

5. The literature on the exile experience, both autobiographical and scholarly, is extensive. See especially Jay (1990), Coser (1984), Heilbut (1983), Koebner, Sautermeister, and Schneider (1987), Mann and Mann (1939), Reuther (1947), Wiggershaus (1998), and Zuckmayer (1966).

6. "We would also make clear that we have no purpose to incriminate the whole German

people. . . . If the German populace had willingly accepted the Nazi program, no storm troopers would have been needed in the early days of the Party and there would have been no need for concentration camps or the Gestapo. . . . The German, no less than the non-German world, has accounts to settle with these defendants" (qtd. in Taylor 1992: 118).

7. Jürgen Steinle (1995:70) traces earlier uses to the post–World War I era. Other terms, moreover, clearly stand for the same concept.

8. Jung's attitude toward Jews is a much-debated issue in the secondary literature. Understandably, a loyal following minimizes and even denies that Jung was anti-Semitic.

9. In this context, it is important to point out that Kästner's disdain was not for a psychoanalytical approach per se. In an essay entitled "Nuremberg and the Historians" (reprinted in Strich 1989:39–44), Kästner remarked positively on the ideas of the psychoanalyst Alexander Mitscherlich. Mitscherlich argued that a more interesting outcome of Nuremberg would have been to encourage the defendants to undergo psychoanalytical inquiry without overt resistance. Doing so would have produced invaluable knowledge, which could then have been used to prevent future such crimes. Kästner entertained this idea because, consistent with his own view, it drew the circle of guilt narrowly.

10. In fact, Jung justifies his essay by pointing out that "the spoken word very quickly gives rise to legends" (Jung 1989:50).

The Cosmopolitanization of Holocaust Memory: From Jewish to Human Experience

DANIEL LEVY AND NATAN SZNAIDER

This essay explores the nexus of Holocaust representations, globalization, and the formation of what we refer to as cosmopolitan memory cultures. Modernity, one of the primary analytic and normative frameworks for intellectual self-understanding, is itself questioned through memories of the Holocaust. Despite this broad frame of reference, sociological studies of the Holocaust are, for the most part, confined to the parameters of national societies. However, during the past two decades, Holocaust representations have served as a paradigmatic case for the emergence of nation-transcending memories.[1] We trace the historical roots of this transformation and the emergence of cosmopolitan memories through an examination of how the Holocaust has been remembered in Germany, Israel, and the United States. Due to its decontextualization as an abstract representation of good and evil, the Holocaust has emerged as a central political-cultural symbol during the past two decades, and given rise to possible cosmopolitan memoryscapes and new moral-political interdependencies.

In the political cultures of Germany, Israel, and the United States, memories of the Holocaust constitute a prominent theme (Novick 1999; Olick and Levy 1997; Segev 1993). They are expressed in a reciprocal relation of particular and universal forms of memory (Levy 1999). In the past, memories of the Holocaust were organized around a dichotomy of universalism and particularism (Young 1993). Instead of reducing these terms to their ideological assumptions, we treat them as an important object in our investigation. We historicize notions of particularism and universalism, thereby demoralizing them while retaining them as valuable sociological tools. Our primary objective is to disentangle these terms from their conventional either-or perspective and understand them in terms of "as well as" options. Cultural and religious particularism can be justified with universal claims of difference or "contextual universalism" (Beck 2000a) that increasingly accepts transnational connections (such as dual citizenship or bilingualism).

Our concept of cosmopolitanization differs from the Kantian notion of cosmopolitanism and other philosophical variants, which entail a universalistic notion and envision a polis extending around the globe. Such normative concepts are of little use for sociologists looking for global social processes. Conceptually, however, the notion of cosmopolitanization provides us with an analytic prism that captures a key dynamic in the global age, namely, the relationship between the global and the local (or the national, for our purposes). We refer to cosmopolitanization as a process that takes place within national societies. It is the internalization of globalization as global concerns are providing a political and moral frame of reference for people's everyday local experiences (Beck 2002). The Enlightenment understanding of cosmopolitanism was a universalist project, limited to elites and insufficiently responsive to the underlying power relations shaping the diversity, particularity, and history of humanity (Hollinger 2001). The Kantian outlook and the universalism that sustains it predicate equality on sameness. Recent cosmopolitan strands recognize diversity and the quest for particular group identities on sub- and supranational levels as significant features of a globalizing world (Beck 2002; Vertovec and Cohen 2002). In this view, the global and the local are not antithetical categories but are mutually constitutive.

Consequently, speaking about the cosmopolitanization of Holocaust memory does not imply some progressive universalism subject to a unified interpretation. The Holocaust does not become one totalizing signifier containing the same meanings for everyone. Rather, its meanings evolve from the encounter of global interpretations and local sensibilities. The cosmopolitanization of Holocaust memories thus involves the formation of nation-specific and nation-transcending commonalities.

These cosmopolitanized memories refer to concrete social spaces characterized by a high degree of reflexivity and the ongoing encounter with different cultures. In this view, it is no longer the dichotomy, but the mutual constitution of particular and universal conceptions that determine the ways in which the Holocaust can be remembered. Starting from the premise that the global informs the local without replacing it, our argument is that national memories are transformed in the age of globalization rather than erased. Different national memories, in different locations, are subjected to a common patterning. They begin to develop in accord with a common rhythm and periodization. But in each case, the common elements combine with preexisting elements to form something new. In each case, the new, global narrative has to be reconciled with the old, national narratives, and the result is always distinctive.

The Study of Holocaust Representations

Both the historiography and the memorialization of the Holocaust have exploded in the past two decades. But this is not merely a function of the enormity of the event. We would like to argue instead that what has pushed the Holocaust to such prominence in public thinking has been the indispensable role it has served in the transition from nation-centered memories to cosmopolitan memory forms. With the end of the Cold War and in an age of increasing uncertainty, leaders have felt the urgent need for a moral touchstone to call on in mobilizing people. And the Holocaust has become a moral certainty on which action can be based. But the Holocaust is not only a standard by which claims on our conscience can be measured. It is also a moral certainty that stretches across national borders and unites the West. There is a heated debate among theorists about whether the Holocaust is a negative culmination of modernity or a reaction against it (Bauman 1989; Sznaider 2001). That there could be people on both sides of that debate serves as a good indication that our present understanding of the Holocaust no longer fits into the conventional modern framework that privileges the nation-state. It has become a basis of transnational moral claims.

At the same time, we have to emphasize that the central meaning of the Holocaust has differed in every country. With the growth of cosmopolitanism, with the circulation of activists and scholars and media images, there has been a growing cross-fertilization. For this very reason, observers often think that the same symbols have the same meaning wherever they appear. But the fact is that while the Holocaust came to public prominence in the United States, Germany, and Israel at about the same time, it emerged for very different reasons, in very different national contexts, and had very different meanings—in some ways even opposite meanings. A process of glocalization, that is, the encounter of the global and the local (Robertson 1995) paradoxically produced both these differences and the common core that emerged out of them.

Universalism and Particularism:
Cosmopolitanism and the Jewish Experience

What group is most suited to be the carrier of cosmopolitan memories? The social science literature usually concentrates on two groups, the mass media elite and transnational migrant laborers (Castells 1996). In this essay, we examine a group that supports cosmopolitan memories not through its physical presence but rather through its representation as the universal Other. If cosmopolitanism is predicated on identification with the distant other, the significance of the Holocaust is that it allows different nations to have the same Other and the same identification.

Identification with the Jewish victims of the Holocaust allows cosmopolitanism to rise to a new level. Part of the reason is that Jewish experience was the original, paradigmatic case of cosmopolitanism during the first wave of modernity. Jewish existence before the Holocaust, and before the founding of the state of Israel, mixed longing for territorial independence with an attraction and an enmeshment in other cultures. This condition of diaspora did not grow out of Judaism per se, but out of tensions among citizenship, civil society, and cultural identity. European Jews were both a nation *and* cosmopolitan. Jews lived therefore in a tension between universalism and particularism that is increasingly becoming the norm for all nations. Franz Rosenzweig once said that Jews lived in two dimensions, the Now and the Eternal. But this tension between territorial identity (the Now) and deterritorialized existence (the Eternal) is increasingly the destiny—or in modern terms, the danger and opportunity—of all people (Hertzberg 1998).

But how other is this Other, the new hero of universal identity politics? The diaspora never constituted a closed-off sphere. Lived Jewish culture was not only mixed with other cultures but was also itself a mixture of cultures. In a certain sense, its cosmopolitanism lay in "judaizing" the mixture of cultures it absorbed—it gave them a unifying cast without negating them. And this is part of why Jewish culture is so well adopted to be the background model of second-wave modernity. The experience of diaspora, of life in exile, is the clearest example modernity offers of a sustained community life that does not need a territorial container to preserve its history. In Jewish experience, life outside the nation-state is nothing new (Boyarin and Boyarin 1993).

Today, as a century ago, cosmopolitanism is being identified with the heritage of Enlightenment universality and opposed to supposedly authentic national cultures. Elsewhere we have laid out the theoretical shortcoming of this view.[2] The task now is to take these universal and particular schemes of thought and historicize them. We start from the point of view that the universal and the particular exist in a dialectical relation—that every particularization is a particularization of a universal, and that every universal is a universalization of a particular. They do not oppose each other; they define and influence each other. The abstract process is clearly concretized in the history of the memory of the Holocaust. The Holocaust as event was confronted by various forces that sought to universalize it, to particularize it, and to nationalize it. But this memory has continued to exist on a global level. Its strength as a global collective memory has been powered and maintained precisely through the fiery interaction between the local and global.

Iconographic Labor: The Formation of Holocaust Memory

Our analysis of this transformation identifies four crucial time periods during which representations of the Holocaust were recast. We start with the immediate postwar period, followed by the formation of Holocaust awareness since the 1960s, then the subsequent commemorative trend during the 1980s, and conclude our analysis with a look at the 1990s during which we observe the normative and institutional formation of cosmopolitan memories. This periodization reflects the respective developments in the three countries under investigation. However, it also transcends national boundaries and recognizes epochal commonalities, which allow people to identify with cultural representations that originate elsewhere.

The idea of the Holocaust did not spring fully grown from the facts. And yet, surprisingly perhaps, all the facts were there in the beginning. The Nuremberg trials were held in November 1945, less than six months after the invasion of Normandy. There the highest Nazi officials still alive, and under guard, were accused of killing 5.7 million Jews as part of a conscious plan. And then they were hung for it. One cannot seemingly get any clearer than that. But a closer look reveals an epochal change. If one calls up the original court document on the Internet, it is 226 screens long.[3] But only three concern the extermination of the Jews. And that is a fairly graphic representation of how the Holocaust was originally conceived: as one in an almost endless list of Nazi crimes. The case was similar with the famous fragments of film. They were incorporated into newsreels and seen throughout the world even before the trial began (Douglas 1995). So despite the constant assertions to the contrary, the Holocaust was never suppressed. Both the facts and the images were publicized almost immediately. And they registered deeply. But they did not in and of themselves produce the Holocaust because the framework in which the Holocaust could be understood as such first had to be built. The original images and facts affected the world almost exactly the way the images and facts of Rwanda have affected us recently. Everyone was horrified, and then they moved on. The slaughter did not get a name of its own.

The clearest sign that the Holocaust is unique is that it has its own name. There is the Holocaust, and then there are all other massacres. People can argue all they want about how theoretically this is not true, but so long as they use the word—and so long as no other massacre gets its own word—they are designating it as unique in spite of themselves. And the social structure that is language constrains them to do so—if they use another term, they will just have to explain that what they are actually referring to is the Holocaust. The clearest sign that the Holocaust is sacred is that using that word lightly can give offense. All other words that apply to massacres or slaughters appear in the sports and economics pages every day. Hyperbole is the coin of the realm. But if you use *the Holocaust* lightly, you feel it. And if you do not, people will make you feel it. That is what it means to be a sacred word: to be somehow cut off from profane speech, to be surrounded by a charged space.

So the Holocaust is surrounded by taboos, and taboos are the signs of society.[4] They designate its defining beliefs, that is to say, not sharing them means being outside that society. Germany, Israel, and the United States are all different societies with a different set of beliefs that define their members. And yet the Holocaust is a charged word in all of them. But just after it happened, it was a charged word in none of them. It was not even really a word. The Holocaust is now surrounded by taboos in each country, but they are different taboos. The fact that the word has become sacred in this way is a sign that it has a central place in each country's set of principal beliefs—and thus that its meaning in each country must be different. And yet, it is no accident that each country uses the same word: these different national meanings coevolved.

In the following sections, we would like to describe the very different taboos that came to surround the Holocaust in each of these countries and how they express the particularities of each country's individual history. We will also

DANIEL LEVY AND NATAN SZNAIDER

attempt to summarize in passing the very different circumstances under which the Holocaust entered national consciousness in each country—the exact conjuncture in which it changed from a blunt set of facts into a sacred set of images and ideas. There are enormous differences in the meaning of the Holocaust in these three countries, and these differences are expressions of national culture, which is itself an expression of national history. We will then address the extent to which a global meaning of the Holocaust has evolved alongside and in partnership with these national meanings, and demonstrate that the global meaning and the national meanings are two indivisible sides of the same process of cosmopolitanization. And then, returning to our original theme, we will argue that this dual process of particularization and universalization has produced a symbol of transnational solidarity. These cosmopolitan mnemo-scapes do not replace national collective memories but exist as their horizon.

Changing Figurations of Holocaust Memory:
Germany, Israel, and the United States

ISRAEL

Israel was similar to Germany and the United States in that the Holocaust was not officially commemorated until fourteen years after the war (Segev 1993). But differences remain. In the first place, Israelis never ranked the extermination of the Jews as somehow equal with the other crimes the Nazis committed. In the second, Israel is the only country in which the Holocaust constituted a national experience before it became publicly articulated. That is to say, it was an experience that affected a major portion of the population at first or second hand (by 1948 about 350,000 Holocaust survivors had arrived in Israel, constituting almost half of the Jewish population). One could make a reasonable argument that this national experience cried out for symbolic expression and that Israel, ironically enough, might be the one country in the world in which the experience of the Holocaust could actually have been said to have suffered suppression, if by suppression we mean the conscious avoidance of official expression. But even in Israel, conscious collective memory was impossible until the creation of a suitable framework. A framework giving meaning to the Holocaust in present-day Israel was originally inconceivable. Both the original suppression and the current sacred remembrance equally expressed Israel's constitution, its self-understanding, and its place in the world. When all of those changed, so necessarily did Israel's relation to the Holocaust. Both the original and the current understanding are Zionist constructions of the Holocaust. But what changed in the intervening years was Zionism's relationship to religion. Correspondingly, in these early years, there was no impulse to draw parallels between the creation of the state of Israel and the stories of the Bible. In fact, there was an impulse against it. Rather than as the last episode in biblical history, Israel was regarded by its founders as a break and a revolution: as the transformation of premodern Judaism into a normal modern identity. It was thought of as the healing of an incompleteness, as the solution to the problem of the diaspora (Cohen 1999). Religiosity was considered a reflection of the diaspora that would wither with its solution.

Israel today has turned out very different. Religious symbols have gained more legitimacy. In this context, the Zionist meaning of the Holocaust has changed almost into its opposite. It is not, as it was in the beginning, a shameful sign of weakness. It has become instead a sacred memory by taking its place as one more example of the archetypical Jewish story, one more instance in which the enemies of the Jewish people tried to exterminate them and did not quite succeed. And this last story, like the first one, culminates with their delivery into a promised land (Friedländer and Seligman 1994).

The 1960s constitute an important turning point for the reception of the Holocaust in Israel. Together, the Adolf Eichmann trial and the Six-Day War, changed the parameters of self-understanding (Arendt 1963; Segev 1993). We do not have the room here to follow through these developments in all their complexity. But the transformation of Israel from a militantly secular country to a country that increasingly draws on its religious past facilitated the imbuement of the Holocaust with a quasi-religious meaning. This also tied the Holocaust up quite literally with the process of state formation, with the incorporation of new land and new people. The new immigrants from the Middle East brought in a more religious attitude than their European brethren. They also had no personal connection to the Holocaust. Their own experience of a world turned upside down was of Arab countries in which they had lived for centuries suddenly turning anti-Semitic. And this became the bridge between the two points of view, because for European Jews, the story of the Holocaust, even when it was played down, had always been a story of anti-Semitism. So now the Holocaust, by being mapped onto the Arab-Israeli conflict, became a way to bridge the two divergent worldviews: all arrivals were the victims of world anti-Semitism, which

DANIEL LEVY AND NATAN SZNAIDER

had come to a climax, and been solved, with the creation of the state of Israel. And thus anti-Semitism became synonymous with criticism of Israel. But it was arguably the 1967 war that transformed such gestures into a permanent state ideology (Segev 1993). In part, it made it possible, for only thereafter did Israel begin to think of itself as a state that would endure; perhaps that made it possible to stand a contemplation of horror that would have proven demoralizing when people were thinking the state might face destruction at any moment. And in part, it made it necessary. For while its original founders had desired above all for Israel to be a normal state like any other, the retention of the Occupied Territories now made it just as necessary for Israel to be treated as an exception. The 1967 war made Israel into an occupying power. All parties to the conflict realized that the balance of power had changed, that Israel was not going to be pushed into the sea anytime soon. And it is no accident that immediately thereafter the battle transposed to the diplomatic arena. In 1974, Yasser Arafat addressed the United Nations (UN) Assembly. In 1975, the Palestine Liberation Organization (PLO) got observer status. And in the same year, the UN overwhelming passed a resolution that Zionism constituted a form of racism.

This was the international context for why Israeli remembrance of the Holocaust changed from a series of gestures into a central state ideology. It was the only possible refutation of the charge that Israel was racist. And refuting this charge was felt to be vital to the state's existence. Why was Israel not racist when the country engaged in practices that would be considered racist anywhere else? Because it was the victim of racism. In fact, it was the biggest victim of racism in the history of the world. And all it was doing was defending itself, surrounded as it was by enemies that hated it irrationally. And calling it racist was itself a hypocritical act of racism, since the main champions of the slogan were clearly driven by boundless hate, and anyone supporting their slogan was supporting them. This campaign has proven a complete success. Most mainstream thinkers in the West today find it almost impossible to characterize Israeli laws or practices as racist, at least in so many words. If the term crosses their mind, they feel a little electric shock and the immediate need to defend themselves against the charge of anti-Semitism.

THE UNITED STATES

The charge the word *Holocaust* has taken on is a sacred one in the Durkheimian sense: it signifies an agreement that it constitutes a line not to be crossed among people that matter. And if there was one place this gambit succeeded, it was in the United States, which, for the purposes of the UN battle, literally outweighed the rest of the world. Today it is easier to accuse the United States itself of racism in public discourse than to say the same of Israel. This offers a clear illustration of cosmopolitanism. American Jews and Israeli Jews traveled to each other's countries, shared ideas and concerns, and witnessed a common drama in the UN. There is a subtle but crucial difference between the Holocaust as history's worst act of racism (as it was defended in the UN and is understood by non-Jews—i.e., 97 percent of the population—in the United States) and the Holocaust as the culmination of the history of anti-Semitism (as it is understood in Israel). Anti-Semitism only happens to the Jews; racism, thus broadened, can happen to anyone. In Israel, the question was always "why us?" In America, the question in the same debate was "why should we care?" And the answer was because it could happen to anyone—a very good answer to the question of why care, but a very unsatisfying answer to the question why us? Universalization grew naturally out of the needs of the rhetorical context.

There was an additional reason in the fact that race constitutes the central trauma of American history. And racism was the central model of politics in the late 1960s and the early 1970s, when the Holocaust entered American political discourse. Novick (1999) has highlighted the irony that American Jews began claiming that they were the most victimized group in history precisely at the moment when quotas against them had finally been lifted and they were beginning their assimilation into the elite. To this can be added the irony that Israel began to claim its victim status after the 1967 and 1973 wars, precisely at the time it established a military strength sufficient for state survival. But these are not ironies so much as counterreactions. It was precisely Israel's victories on the battlefield that transposed the battle into a diplomatic one in which terms of anathema mattered. And in a similar manner, it was the success of American Jews that put a strain on their political alliance with blacks. It became clear in both contexts that the Holocaust constituted the ultimate riposte to an accusation of racism. But as Jews form only a tiny part of the American population, the meaning of the Holocaust in the United States was not its meaning for the Jews, but the meaning that arose out of the interaction in the public debate—the meaning that answered the question "Why should we care? Why should we remember?" And that was the answer that resonated with racism.

As in the case of Israel, distinctive twists and turns resulted from international position and conjuncture. To defend Israel as vital to U.S. interests during the Cold War meant as well to defend the Cold War. And in the late 1960s and early 1970s in the United States, that meant defending anticommunist interventions around the world, starting foremost with the Vietnam War. But this was not at first obvious. In fact, the opposite seems in retrospect to have been the more natural position: if the Holocaust was something that could happen to anyone, and the lesson was that people should not just stand by and let it happen, then was it not the duty of the United States to stop genocides everywhere? And was it not actually committing genocide from the air? And were not many of its client states doing so on the ground? Was not the legacy of the Holocaust to stop such things?

That became the position of the American left: stop genocides. And it completely opposed the interests of pro-Israel organizations. Out of this debate grew the American idea of the "uniqueness" of the Holocaust (which in Israel had been simply taken for granted). The doctrine was simple: the Holocaust was not simply incomparably worse than any other slaughter; it was simply incomparable. To compare the Holocaust with any other slaughter was to belittle if not deny it. And human rights campaigners who compared events in Guatemala with what happened in Nazi Germany were actually committing a racist act.

In this struggle over the meaning of the Holocaust for the Cold War, the Cold War liberals won, in large part because all the American Jewish organizations sided with them, and with this came the survivors, who testified in public. The debate became charged precisely because it went against the American grain. And the end of the Cold War brought this period of exceptionalism almost immediately to an end. From being against all comparison, the dominant Jewish organizations switched almost immediately to being for all comparisons, to drawing a lesson from the Holocaust that human rights violations everywhere should be wiped out. The twenty-year period from the Cold War's crisis to its end marked an exception in the American view of the Holocaust. And yet it is not an exception that can be merely skipped over. It was the formative period for the concept of the Holocaust and its iconographic status as a form of cosmopolitan memory. And it left lasting marks on an understanding of the Holocaust in both the United States and in the world. If one recalls the Nuremberg indictments that started this section, the American understanding of the Holocaust was originally universalistic: Nazi war crimes happened to 60 million people, among them 6 million Jews. And the original experience of the camps simply reinforced this. The camps the Americans liberated were mixed camps, containing a wide variety of people the Nazis hated, from political prisoners to Gypsies. And so rather than setting off an instant realization that there had been a Holocaust against the Jews, the original experience of opening the camps instead confirmed the Allies in the view that the Jews were one of many groups victimized by the Nazis, the "first among equals."

This has changed in a lasting way, and it parallels the change in the meaning of the pictures. There are at least four ways to universalize the Holocaust: in regards to the victims (was it the Jews plus a supporting cast, or was it lots of people?); in regards to the perpetrators (were the Nazis uniquely evil, or were they only different in efficiency from other mass murderers?); in regard to the future (is the lesson never again to the Jews, or never again to anyone?); and in regard to the subject of memory (i.e., can the United States be the central witness, even though it built no camps and very few of its citizens were victims?). For precisely this last reason, it seems the universal meaning has to dominate in the United States—a particularistic reading would deny it any privileged place. But the result of the particular conjuncture that rendered the Holocaust important in the United States has produced the oddly effective combination that considers the Holocaust unique in the past and universal in the future. That is to say, the Holocaust past is something that happened predominantly to the Jews, while the Holocaust future might happen to anyone. In the United States, that is now so far beyond debate as to be beyond taking offense at. All attempts to memorialize other victims (e.g., homosexuals, leftists, Gypsies) are seen as attempts to garner some of the Jews' reflected glow rather than as an attempt to displace them as the central victims. But as we have just seen, this idea of the past was not a conception given by the facts. It was created by a historical process. And we can see just how dependent this process was on the American national context by comparing it to Germany, where the same conjuncture resulted in almost exactly the opposite.

GERMANY

It is perhaps permissible to skip more quickly over Germany's story on the grounds that its struggles with its Nazi past are generally better known (Diner 2000; Fulbrook 1999; Levy and Sznaider 2005, for some recent examples). We would merely like to emphasize for our purposes here a few elements of its national distinctiveness and their origins in national history and political con-

DANIEL LEVY AND NATAN SZNAIDER

juncture. If Israel was the only country in the world that could possibly be ashamed of the victims, Germany was the only country that could be ashamed of the Nazis. In Israel, shame was a founding emotion transformed during the late 1960s into a sacred memory. In Germany, the passage was almost the opposite. Shame was an emotion created in the late 1960s in the cauldron of the student movement.

For very different reasons, the Federal Republic of Germany, like Israel, originally saw its foundation as a complete break with the past. It was the "successor state" to Nazi Germany, which was portrayed by both Germany and the Allies as a dictatorship from which it had been liberated. Cold War pressures played a big role in this development. But the result was that the Nuremberg trials were widely seen as drawing a line under the past. There had been criminals, yes. But they were no longer in charge. They had been convicted. And the *Wirtschaftswunder* (economic miracle) that ensued allowed the state to paper over most ideological differences.

In 1968, students in many countries in the West saw themselves as completely closed out of a homogenous political elite. And students delighted in denouncing their elders as war criminals. But in Germany, they could prove it. The main thrust of the student movement was that the political elite comprised the direct inheritors of the Nazi legacy, rather than being innocent bystander successors. In this context, the Holocaust became the ultimate proof that the Nazis—and hence the "normal" Germans of the bourgeois sort the students were rebelling against—were uniquely evil. And yet, while it seems so pat, some surprising elements also distinguish the German understanding. Remember that in the United States, an insistence on the uniqueness of the Holocaust was a slogan of pro–Cold War forces. In Germany, on the other hand, it was the mark of anti–Cold War forces. In the United States, an insistence on the comparability of the Holocaust to other mass slaughters has always been an argument of human rights campaigners. In Germany, an insistence on the same comparability has been the staple of right-wing apologists. This provides an excellent example of national meanings transparent to a society's members yet invisible to outsiders unless crossed. Americans took for granted that universalization concerned the future, the identification of new victims with the victims of the Holocaust. Germans took for granted that universalization concerned the past, meant drawing a moral equivalence between the acts of the Nazis and the acts of other regimes. Both are rooted in different senses of shame, and each of them are rooted in a different history, the Germans being ashamed of what they did, and the Americans of what they did not.

The different national perspectives of Israel, Germany, and America led them to think that the Holocaust was centrally connected to completely different phenomena. For Israelis, the Holocaust was immediately evoked by the Arab-Israeli conflict; for Germany, by German militarism or anti-immigrant sentiments; and in the United States, by slaughters or human rights violations occurring on the margins of the Cold War world. And the positions were not reversible. It would never occur to an Israeli that his or her own country's militarism was an expression of the Holocaust. It would never have occurred to a German that human rights violations on the other side of the globe were an expression of the Holocaust. It would never have occurred to an American to think of Arafat or Rabin as a Nazi or a Nazi collaborator. These mutually incomprehensible meanings were what drove the Holocaust deep into people's minds. It made the Holocaust a key word in debates that gripped each nation on an everyday basis for years. But the paradoxical result was for the Holocaust to become more important globally, and for there to emerge a common core of strongly charged shared symbols.

The End of the Cold War and the Emergence of Cosmopolitan Memories

The Cold War was an alliance on the basis of values as much as on the basis of interests. Anticommunism is a value; pro–private property is an interest. Similarly, the decision of each country to enter into the Cold War alliance was a mixture of value and interest. But the same mixture of value and interest lies at the bottom of national loyalty. People feel triumphant or ashamed for their country as if it were a projection of their self at the same time as they stand to gain or lose by its place in the world. The end of the Cold War was thus by definition the beginning of a new world system. When the unifying interest and value of anticommunism vanished, international military cooperation had to be reorganized on a new basis. The attempt to articulate and organize around new values has been a conscious one over the past ten years. And it is no accident that the Holocaust has come to play a major role in that reorganization. It has emerged precisely because of its status as the one unquestioned moral value on which all people can supposedly agree. The end of the Cold War removed the need for the United States to support client states that blatantly violated human rights. This had an almost immediate effect on the discourse of the Holocaust in the country. There was no longer an opposition between the needs of the state and the discourse of human rights.

The Balkan Wars

When a new basis for solidarity is organized, values predominate during the formative period, while interests take over after the association has become normalized. This was certainly the case with the history of the Cold War, and it was true as well of the formation of nation-states. Institutional mediation makes possible this transformation of values into realities. But Western military cooperation during the 1990s has been characterized by a series of ad hoc arrangements; it has clearly not yet arrived at the stage of normalization. Correspondingly, the discussion of common values has played a large role in these mobilizations. The Holocaust has emerged as a central term of agreement not because of unity but because of conflict. Just as in previous forums, the Holocaust has become a trump card of moral debate because there was a debate in which it has proved unanswerable. But just as in those previous forums, this unanswerability has been socially constructed.

The recent histories of Bosnia and Kosovo provide an excellent illustration of this process.[5] The trope that now equates Serbs with Nazis did not spring immediately from the facts. There was unfortunately nothing unusual about the scale of atrocities in Bosnia. Worse went on in many parts of the world during the same period. And the original understanding of the situation was not that one side oppressed another, but that it sprung from the "irrational" and "ancient hatreds" that characterized the Balkans. The lesson of history at the beginning of the 1990s was that the problems were insoluble and intervention was doomed. Slowly over the course of the Bosnian conflicts, the American public came to identify the Serbs with the Nazis. Crucial in this process was an award-winning news photo of a terribly thin old man seen through a fence. In conjunction with Serb "camps," this seemed to have been a turning point. But it did not happen at once. If the power of this idea in the United States can be measured by the country's willingness to act, it did not take hold there until the end of the war. And it never took hold during this period in Israel or Germany.

If Bosnia captured the attention of the West because it was happening in Europe, it was largely ignored by the Israeli public for the same reason, as well as because there were no Jews involved. National perspective begins with the provincialism of local news. But to the extent that Israeli cosmopolitans followed

these events, their perspective was almost exactly the opposite of the one prevalent in the United States. For Israel, the Holocaust is primarily something that
happened once, in the past, to Jews, and countries in Europe are still ranked
according to the role they played then. Croatia and Albania were allies of Nazi
Germany. Both were responsible for atrocities that gave even the Nazis pause,
and the Croatians ran a concentration camp. The Serbs, on the other hand,
heroically opposed the Nazis, refusing to give up even when the odds were
enormously stacked against them. And many of them were slaughtered by the
Nazi-allied Croats or died in the camps. So when, if at all, Israelis understood
the Bosnian conflict in terms of the Holocaust, they saw the colors exactly
reversed: the Serbs were the Jews, surrounded by enemies, and the Croats were
the Nazis.

The German view was sort of a mixture of the two, and different from both.
On the right, there was immediate sympathy for the Croatians, not because of
the Holocaust, but rather in spite of it, that is, on the basis of the cultural
similarities and historical ties that had also underlain the World War II alliance.
Some commentators have argued that the European Union's rush to recognize
Croatia grew out of this same basis, and was the single most important act in
setting off the war. On the left, the Holocaust became an immediate frame of
reference, but it led to exactly the opposite of the American conclusion. Since the
Holocaust was identified in Germany with German militarism, it followed that
German intervention should be opposed, and by analogy so should all interventions by Germany's allies. But when the war in Kosovo happened, the position of
the left in Germany changed 180 degrees. Now suddenly it claimed it was intervening to stop new Auschwitzes. Clearly this had a lot to do with the international pressures and opportunities the war presented, and with the fact that now
the left was in government for the first time in eighteen years. But even in this
drastically changed and globalized form, there was a national distinctiveness to
the German meaning of the Holocaust. The foreign minister Joschka Fischer
emphasized that expulsion of the Albanians itself constituted a form of genocide.
It is described as such in the original genocide conventions. But it also resonated
through the minister's own biography with the history of German expellees—an
issue charged in Germany and all but forgotten outside of it. And of course the
entire debate was filtered through Germany's almost unique fear of its own
military, a fear that can be seen even today in the debate over ending conscription
—which is itself simply the latest ramification of the war in Kosovo.

The war came two days late to Israeli televisions, but this new understanding of the Holocaust challenged their own. Many of the newly immigrated Jews from the former Soviet Union identified with the Serbs. The cosmopolitans identified with NATO. And the right-wingers said, "If you think this is all right, then why can NATO not come and bomb us out of the occupied territory"? But the biggest shock was simply finding out that Israel no longer had a monopoly on interpreting the Holocaust. It had become the world's property—even if, as always, it was immediately translated into national terms for further debate.

Concluding Remarks

We can see how the term *Holocaust* has been turned into a concept that has been dislocated from space and time because it is used—perhaps indiscriminately—to dramatize any injustice, racism, or crime perpetrated in the past. As such, the Holocaust has become a cultural code for the twentieth century as a whole. Conversely, we have to deal with a growing number of localities and allow the universal trope of the Holocaust to catch on to specific local situations with a certain distance form the original event. What has pushed the Holocaust to such prominence in public thinking, then, has been the indispensable role it has served in the transition from the world of classical sovereignty to a new world of interconnectedness. In an age of increasing uncertainty, leaders have felt the urgent need for moral touchstones to call on in mobilizing people. And the Holocaust has become a moral certainty on which action can be based. But the Holocaust is not only a standard by which claims on our conscience can be measured. It is also a moral certainty that stretches across national borders.

The organizing focus of this volume relates as much to the study of the Holocaust as it does to what is referred to as post-Holocaust studies. Our work has focused on the effects and consequences of Holocaust representations on what we call "cosmopolitan memories." Their significance is evidenced, among other things, by the formation of new nation-transcending solidarities that support global norms promoting human rights regimes and other transnational institutions (Archibugi, Held, and Köhler 1998; Levy and Sznaider 2004). An important question in this respect is, of course, to what extent Western Holocaust discourse is promoting or preventing the advancement of memories of other forms of historical injustice, such as slavery and colonization.[6] A large body of literature reveals comparable trends to seek public apologies. Demands for some kind of reparation are by now a pervasive feature in many regions of the world. This further supports our argument that we are witnessing the institutionalization of a global norm. In this view, the territorial confining of memory to nationhood no longer proves adequate. Cosmopolitan memories complement conventional national memories as they are oriented toward nation-transcending symbols and meaning systems such as the declaration of human rights and the stateless concept of crimes against humanity. We have shown here how this type of cosmopolitan memory emerged in conjunction with the rising iconographic status of Holocaust representations. These cosmopolitan memories reflect and shape emergent moral and political interdependencies.

Notes

This text is a revised version of Levy and Sznaider (2002).

1. The classics of sociology are so thoroughly pervaded with a spatially fixed understanding of culture that it is rarely remarked on (Tomlinson 1999). It is a conception that goes back to sociology's birth amid the nineteenth-century formation of nation-states. Ironically, the territorial conception of culture—the idea of culture as rooted—was itself a reaction to the enormous changes going on as that century turned into the twentieth. It was a conscious attempt to provide a solution to the uprooting of local cultures that the formation of nation-states necessarily involved. Sociology understood the new symbols and common values above all as means of integration into a new unity. The triumph of this perspective can be seen in the way the nation-state has ceased to appear as a project and a construct and has become instead widely regarded as something natural, as something that has always existed (Beck 2000b). At the beginning of the twenty-first century, globalization is posing a challenge to this idea that binding history and borders tightly together provides the only possible means of social and symbolic integration.

2. For a detailed critique of the nation-centered collective memory literature, see Levy and Sznaider 2005.

3. The indictment is available as a single text document at www.courttv.com/casefiles/nuremberg/plead.html (accessed August 9, 2006). A hypertext version, along with an archive of related materials, is available at www.yale.edu/lawweb/avalon/imt/proc/count.htm.

4. For a more detailed discussion on the sociological mechanisms of taboos and the particular role of Holocaust representations, see Olick and Levy (1997).

5. A full treatment of the historical processes underlying our theoretical claims is beyond the scope of this essay. For a detailed account see Levy and Sznaider (2005).

6. It is indicative how African American intellectuals draw on the Holocaust metaphor, and how restitutive demands for slavery in particular are modeled after the example of German-Jewish reparations. See Torpey (2006).

The Sociology of Knowledge and the Holocaust: A Critique

MARTIN OPPENHEIMER

There is a general consensus that the social sciences have been woefully remiss with regard to research on and analysis of the Holocaust. Research and writing, especially in terms of major work, is thin. Does sociology in particular have, if not precisely a Jewish problem, a problem dealing with what is one of the defining, most critical historical events of the twentieth century? Judith Gerson and Diane Wolf describe in the introduction to this volume some of the strands of research that do exist. But they are in principle correct: a quick perusal of some of the bibliographies in the essays collected here shows very few references to standard social science literature. Is the topic of the Holocaust simply too big, too complex, too controversial, too unmanageable from the point of view of conventional sociological methodologies? Can it really be that few if any American social scientists have written anything approaching a major, by which I mean macrolevel, work on the Holocaust? But then, only a very few American social scientists have written a major work on communism, or fascism, or nuclear war as well. For that matter, only a few social scientists have dared to tackle one of the hottest issues of the moment—the alleged clash between modernity and fundamentalism.

The first question that arises in this context is "what is there left to say," if indeed anything at all can be "said" in the normal sense of that term. Can sociology contribute anything at all to comprehending the incomprehensible? The Holocaust is of an unprecedented magnitude, and it seems overwhelming. Where does one begin? Where does one end? The contributors to this volume have tried, with some degree of success, to examine small segments of this overwhelmingly difficult subject, but there is still much to be done. Although, admittedly, there is an argument to be made that we know quite too much already, and that it is time to move on.

In this brief essay I will attempt to use the general framework of the sociology of knowledge to advance some tentative ideas as to the reasons for the dearth of research; and more to the point of this volume, why the work that does exist largely takes the form that it does.

The sociology of knowledge can be traced at least as far back as Karl Marx and Friedrich Engels's ([1848] 1964) *Communist Manifesto*. Over the decades, other Marxists ranging from George Plekhanov (1897) to Nikolai Bukharin (1925) have followed in that tradition. In 1931, V. F. Calverton edited a volume in which he contributed the notion of "cultural compulsives" in the context of a debate concerning the nature and origin of marriage. Calverton proposed something that today seems commonplace, especially to cultural studies scholars—that is, that social theories are accepted or rejected not on the basis of accuracy or inaccuracy, but as a response to the cultural milieu. The origins of a theory are less important than its influence and the responses to it, he said. Karl Mannheim popularized this framework as the sociology of knowledge in his much better-known work *Ideology and Utopia* (1936). As Louis Wirth wrote in the preface to the book, Mannheim took on the task of "searching out . . . the motives that lie back of intellectual activity and . . . the manner and the extent to which the thought processes themselves are influenced by the participation of the thinker in the life of society" (1936:xxviii). How do "the interests and purposes of certain social groups come to find expression in certain theories, doctrines, and intellectual movements?" (Wirth 1936:xxviii). This question is no less relevant for studies of the Holocaust, certainly, than it was for studies of the anthropological roots of the modern bourgeois family, theories of literature, historiography, or any other intellectual phenomena.

Scholars do not choose their subjects randomly. People study what they are interested in, which is mediated by what is marketable. If they are rewarded (in the academic marketplace), they will study it further. But the academic marketplace is a territory marked by interests of many kinds, including, as we know, what subjects are considered legitimate to research and what methodologies are deemed legitimate. How legitimacy is defined, by whom, and in response to what interests is of course a very important issue. Perhaps Richard Williams is right in saying that when researchers study "non-paradigmatic" populations, that is, deviants, outsiders, they tend to use descriptive rather than positivistic methodologies, hence limiting their influence within sociology and even, sometimes, excluding themselves from the "territory" of legitimacy (2002: 365). Moreover, grand descriptive and theoretical works are methodological slippery slopes, and they leave scholars vulnerable to career-damaging criticisms. Big subjects are not amenable to publication in journals in the first place. And second, they are likely to be very controversial, very often proffering challenges to dominant paradigms and theories. One thinks of David Abraham's (1981) *The Collapse of the Weimar Republic* and the consequences to his career as a historian because his work challenged the dominant view among American historians about the roots of Nazism. Finally, there is the language problem: how many American researchers study a foreign language, something often necessary to conduct in-depth research on the Holocaust? No wonder the writings of immigrants have in the past played such a pioneering role in this field.

The language problem aside, what kinds of people study the Holocaust? Those most interested in it, clearly, are mostly those of Jewish background. But that tells us nothing. Who studies the Catholic Church, its history, and so on? Mostly those of Catholic background, I would guess. The more interesting observation is that most Jewish social scientists, historians, and the like, do *not* study the Holocaust. They are just as much a part of the academic marketplace as anyone else, hence they face the same legitimacy issues. Furthermore, in all likelihood, having just escaped the ghetto (in the sense of upward mobility into the academy since World War II), they may not want to return to it, that is, risk being locked into Jewish studies or the like, any more than some African American scholars relish being ghettoized into black studies departments. It is also entirely reasonable to assume that not a few feel a sufficiently troubled emotional relationship to the Holocaust that they prefer to stand aside, rather than confront an overwhelming tragedy barely one generation removed. Who needs to shed more tears when other, more immediate issues beckon?

Then there is the rebuke, as Debra Kaufman mentions in her essay in this volume, that those who still at this late date grapple with Holocaust issues are engaged in exploiting the issue for careerist reasons. Not many are prepared to have to expend energy in fending off the charge of being part of what is nowadays regarded as the "Holocaust industry" (Finkelstein 2000). One has only to look at the new memorial constructed in Berlin to realize how this supposed industry has overwhelmed, in the media sense, the simpler, everyday understandings of the Holocaust exemplified by memorials that have been there for quite some time in the neighborhoods in which people actually live. Who really needs a massive architectural project in the center of Berlin? But the smaller memorials do not draw tourists. Surely a reluctance to participate further in the political and commercial manipulation of the Holocaust, no matter the importance of research, is understandable.

So it is logical that émigrés, journalists, and a few political notables rather than the folks who attend the meetings of the American Sociological Association have authored most of the major works on Nazism and/or on the Holocaust in the United States. In contrast to Germany, where so-called fascism research (*Faschismus Forschung*) fills libraries, here there are only a few shelves, even though the topic (not synonymous with the Holocaust, it should be emphasized) is arguably the most researched and theorized political phenomenon of the twentieth century, even including Soviet communism.

What are the important social science books, those we refer to regularly, about fascism, Nazism, or the Holocaust, in English? *Behemoth*, by Franz Neumann ([1944] 1963); *The Origins of Totalitarianism*, by Hannah Arendt (1958); *Why Hitler Came into Power*, a pioneering sociological study, by Theodore Abel ([1938] 1986); *Escape from Freedom*, by Erich Fromm (1941); *The Destruction of the European Jews*, by Raul Hilberg (1961); *From Democracy to Nazism*, by Rudolf Heberle ([1945] 1970)—all of the authors are immigrants. One of the few exceptions is the American-born Richard Hamilton's (1982) *Who Voted for Hitler?* Recent immigrants were also among the earliest writers of social science articles on the Holocaust. Gerth (1940) analyzed the composition and leadership of the Nazi party in the first published sociological article on the topic, and three years later Bettelheim (1943) published what was to become his famous text on concentration camps.

The present volume is intended, in part, to remedy the shortage of academic social science research on the Holocaust. So, going back to a question raised earlier in this essay, what is the nature of this work, and why does it take the form that it does? As the editors point out, "Many chapters focus on the past, and for most of them, memory constitutes a crucial operating principal, while still others consider contemporary Jewish life, practices, and identities. . . . Identity is the current poster child of many disciplines today" (Gerson and Wolf this volume: 31). Identity, memory, discourse, rhetoric, and textual analysis have become privileged as subjects for research, in contrast to the earlier predominance of research

MARTIN OPPENHEIMER

on social structures, the political economy, institutional forces, and more broadly history as a tool for understanding. In a sense what appears to be going on, and by no means only with regard to the Holocaust, or in sociology, is that the very same framework I am using in this essay, the sociology of knowledge—segueing into deconstructionism, and more generally into what is loosely termed cultural studies—has become the predominant paradigm in many disciplines. This essay, almost typically, deals not with the Holocaust, but with Holocaust discourse.

A special issue of the journal *Radical History Review* (Gosse 2003), titled "Terror and History," provides further evidence for the predominance of this approach. Of eighteen essays, the majority involve, at some level, the way terrorism has been socially and politically constructed to serve the interests of ruling classes. The terrorism "narrative," definitions, manipulations, propaganda utilizations are intertwined with and amplify concrete histories, just as the Holocaust "narrative" assumes a place center stage in the present volume.

Cultural studies, in which much of this kind of material finds a theoretical home, has been immensely valuable in demystifying (deconstructing) cultural artifacts, including labels, symbols, definitions, concepts, and especially historical narratives used in the process of domination and oppression, or even just political manipulation. Our understanding of cultural production and distribution, and the institutions that produce culture, counterculture, and alternate culture is very important in any analysis of power systems, as leftist and critical theorists ranging from Antonio Gramsci to Theodor Adorno, Max Horkheimer, and Herbert Marcuse (just to mention a few) long ago told us. These are not "merely" superstructural artifacts, simplistically dependent on economic relations. The way Michal Bodemann (1996c) connects the use of the Holocaust narrative to West German politics, for example, illustrates how intertwined cultural artifacts and political realities can be.

On the other hand, when language, representations, and discourses become dominant, and displace a concern with what some would consider more "real" (perhaps substructural) existence, whether at the macro (institutional) or micro (daily life) level, there is a serious danger that politics becomes dissolved. In the present volume there are, clearly, a number of "real" stories, ranging from Rachel Einwohner's essay on the Warsaw Ghetto to the very real phenomena of hidden children and those who survived by passing. However, the big real stories are scarcely present: (1) the direct exploration of extermination; and (2) the roots of Nazism. It is almost as if the Holocaust appeared like a horseman of the Apocalypse, out of nowhere. The connection between the historical conditions in which Nazism found its roots, the Nazis, and the Holocaust is the larger missing piece. Since it is missing, the connection between the perpetrators, their backers, and the Holocaust also remains absent.

There are several possible responses to this criticism. Much of the literature of concentration and death camps takes agency away from the Jews and depicts them as passive victims. There is a reluctance to contribute further to this image. Yet there exists a considerable literature on Jewish resistance by this time. As for the perpetrators, quite apart from the very old controversy about "who backed Hitler?" (quite a different issue from "who voted for Hitler?" or "who joined the Nazi party?"), there is an increasing amount of material, albeit quite controversial (e.g., Christopher Browning's 1992 *Ordinary Men: Reserve Police Battalion 101*; Daniel Jonah Goldhagen's 1996 *Hitler's Willing Executioners*). There is also a good deal of research on the German resistance. But these very examples demonstrate the risks of attempting to deal with supposedly real events. Examining the social and political construction of events, how they are defined and for what purpose, how they are memorialized, seems somehow less controversial and academically less precarious, especially given the more general popularity of cultural studies in the wider academy. It is also just plain easier and quicker (hence leading more quickly to publication) than spending years in dusty archives.

These are, nevertheless, hardly convincing arguments or even good rationalizations for the absence of the issue of Nazism and its roots from our conversations. If we are to comprehend the Holocaust and, indeed, its aftermath (especially, but by no means only, in Germany), then surely we must comprehend the history that led to it, including the social conditions and social forces that led to the rise of the Nazis and the processes by which they were able to put their grotesque crimes into motion. Recent polls in Germany indicate a continuing strain of anti-Semitism in the population, and a correlation between anti-Semitism and anti-immigrant sentiment. There is considerable evidence that anti-Semitic and racist acts are on the increase in several other European countries. Interethnic violence post-1989 (infamously, in the former Yugoslavia) has overwhelmed the hopefulness that accompanied the fall of the Berlin Wall. Can we not contribute to an understanding of these terrible events by looking not only at the Holocaust and its uses and misuses but also at Nazism and its pre-1933 roots and post-1945 organization? Are these not issues that we need to concern ourselves with in order to try to prevent more disasters?

Violence, Representation, and the Nation

LEELA FERNANDES

In recent years, the social sciences and humanities have witnessed a burgeoning literature that has sought to address the relationship between questions of power, knowledge, and the politics of representation. Interdisciplinary scholarship in fields such as women's studies and postcolonial studies have examined the ways in which strategies of representation are intertwined in broader historical processes and may reproduce or disrupt relations of power based on inequalities such as gender, race, and nation. These questions have been particularly significant when raised in relation to the representation of oppression and violence against various subaltern groups.

Scholars have grappled with two simultaneous and related issues in regard to the study of violence and oppression. On the one hand, research that has been engaged in the study of questions such as ethnic, racial, religious, and gender violence has sought to understand and explain the causes of violence and examine the possibilities of resistance to such structural forms of violence. On the other hand, scholars have grappled with the ways in which such forms of violence can be studied and represented without reproducing a form of epistemic violence (Spivak 1988) against the subordinated social groups studied. In light of such debates, notions of the "real" have become increasingly implicated and unsettled through analyses pointing to ways in which the contingencies of context and social location shape the production and representation of reality in cultural texts such as film, fiction, and ethnography (Hesford and Kozol 2001). However, for scholars informed by such debates yet remaining committed to the writing of histories and ethnographies, an absolute jettison of any notion of the real has produced its own set of problems, such as the pervasiveness of an ungrounded cultural relativism and a potential blindness to the materiality of violence and oppression.

The essays by Rachel Einwohner, Daniel Levy and Natan Sznaider, and Jeffrey Olick taken together raise a set of issues that engage with and contribute in important ways to such questions of violence and representation that scholars have sought to address in comparative contexts. In particular, the essays provide insights that can inform two central themes in the contemporary study of violence and representation. The first theme addresses the ways in which representations of violence may be simultaneously appropriated by nation-states and disruptive of national boundaries in the context of contemporary globalization. The second theme involves the question of violence and subjectivity and the ways in which scholars have cautioned that the representation of violence may involve a form of epistemic violence against subaltern groups depicted as passive victims devoid of agency or the capacity to resist. Through an exploration of these themes, the study of the Holocaust in these essays provides insights that inform debates on the politics of representation, while simultaneously persisting with analyses of the material reality of violence and genocide.

"The Cosmopolitanization of Holocaust Memory" by Levy and Sznaider provides an important discussion of the ways in which the production of a sociocultural memory of the Holocaust is shaped by narratives of the nation-state and of globalization in the post-Holocaust period. The essay contributes to recent interdisciplinary research, which has sought to examine the ways in which public cultural representations both invoke and transcend nation-specific meanings as such representations travel across national boundaries in the context of contemporary globalization. The essay convincingly demonstrates that while meanings of the Holocaust have been contingent on specific national and historical contexts in the cases of Israel, Germany, and the United States, such meanings have also produced a global narrative in which the Holocaust has become a universal symbol of genocide. Global narratives of the Holocaust are thus interwoven with nation-specific meanings.

The essay's analysis engages with a broader debate on the nature of contemporary globalization, one that questions how cultural forms and meanings are shaped by transnational processes of deterritorialization (Appadurai 1996) and territorialized narratives of the modern nation-state. Consider, for instance, a very different context, the case of globalization in contemporary India. Recent research has examined the ways in which meanings of "the global" themselves are often invented and deployed through local cultural and nationalist narratives. Thus the notion that global or cosmopolitan cultural narratives necessarily transcend or destabilize the territorially bound nation-state is one that is placed in question when processes of globalization are examined in specific empirical contexts (Fernandes 2000). As Levy and Sznaider point out in the case of the representation of the Holocaust, new global narratives have to be reconciled with older national narratives in distinctive ways.

The essay further suggests that this interweaving of national and global narratives in the case of the representation of the Holocaust has broader implications for scholars concerned with questions of violence, genocide, and human rights. The authors show that both national and global narratives of the Holocaust have played a central role in shaping discourses around genocide and have helped frame universal claims to human rights. Such processes invoke a broader debate on the question of human rights and the politics of representation. In recent years, for instance, feminist scholars and activists have debated the ways in which movements and claims invoking a language of human rights have invoked subtle yet important strategies of representation. On the one hand, proponents of a human rights approach have pointed to the strategic importance of expanding conceptions of human rights to include gendered violence (Okin 2000). On the other hand, critics have suggested that the language of human rights has often masked subtle national narratives and interests while presenting women largely in Third World contexts as passive, essentialized victims of their cultures (Barlow 2000).

Such debates have focused on the politics of gender and race in discursive strategies that produce categories such as violence, genocide, and victims. However, these debates for the most part have not addressed the significance of representations of the Holocaust in framing the historical development of both national and global debates on human rights. The study of the Holocaust and Holocaust representation stands to present a crucial historical and comparative framework that can inform feminist and postcolonial debates on the issue of human rights.

The interweaving of national and global narratives shapes the politics of representation and the production of sociocultural memory in varying ways and through a wide range of cultural forms such as film, fiction, museums, and oral history. The implications of Holocaust representation, particularly in popular cultural forms such as films (e.g., Steven Spielberg's *Schindler's List*), become contingent on the specificities of the national and transnational contexts in which such forms circulate. In considering the question of the implications of Holocaust representation, one needs to ask to what extent the actual form of representation (a popular culture film versus an in-depth interview) shapes the effects and implications of the cultural memory produced. To what extent is the success of the realist strategies of film and other cultural representations of the Holocaust (e.g., the black-and-white documentary style) a reflection of broader patterns such as the growing consumer demand for "authentic" or real-life stories in the United States? Feminist scholars have critically analyzed the power effects of the consumption of a form of modernist authenticity embedded in the real stories of Third World women in the form of testimonials, autobiographies, and film (Trinh 1991).

These questions point to the much larger issue of how one engages in the representation of the violence of the Holocaust without inadvertently producing a form of epistemic violence through the act of representation, that is, without turning genocide into spectacle (in the case of more popular cultural representations of the Holocaust). The question becomes particularly difficult in the contemporary context of public and media representations in which the visualization of violence has often led to the production of what Rey Chow (1991:84) has called the "surplus value of spectacle."

Such questions have also recently emerged as feminist scholars and activists have struggled with ways to provide the space for women to retell the stories of genocidal rapes in contexts such as Bosnia-Herzegovina and Croatia (Hesford and Kozol 2001). For instance, I have examined the discrepancies of representation of a well-known low-caste woman dacoit, Phoolan Devi (recently murdered in India) by juxtaposing two forms of representation, a film, *Bandit Queen* (1994), popular in both the West and in India, and a transcribed/translated autobiographical account of Phoolan Devi's life (Fernandes 1999). Both the film and the autobiography have circulated transnationally and have claimed to represent the "real" life story of the protagonist. The film in particular has raised difficult ethical questions of representation publicly debated both in India and in Western contexts as it presented graphic scenes of violent rape. In considering these questions, I have argued that rather than revert to a binary approach that either invokes or rejects representations of the real, particularly in the case of representing violence and trauma, we should focus instead on an analysis of such represen-

tations' power effects—effects shaped both by the specific strategies of representation deployed and the specificities of the context in which the representation is
interpreted and received. When viewed from a transnational perspective, the
power effects of representation are not unitary, and they may even prove contradictory. Thus, for instance, *Bandit Queen*'s graphic depictions of rape and violence did manage to disrupt public silences on rape in the Indian context. Yet
they also played into neo-Orientalist stereotypes of Indian men in Western
contexts.

The effects of strategies of representation in regard to stories of trauma and
violence are thus further complicated by the transnational circulation of cultural
forms. At one level, cultural representations and memories travel across national
boundaries. At another level, their meanings are contingent on the local and
national histories of the communities that receive these forms and memories.
The challenge of representing Holocaust memory thus engages with and raises
particularly important issues regarding the politics of representation and the
transnational production and circulation of such representations which prove of
interest to a wide range of intellectual fields: sociology, but also interdisciplinary
studies that focus on questions of identity, culture, and politics.

A central issue arising in discussions of violence and representation concerns
questions of agency and resistance. On the one hand, feminist scholars have
argued that the representation of victims of violence as purely passive and devoid
of agency and the capacity for resistance may hold the danger of enacting a form
of epistemic violence (Mohanty 1991). On the other hand, the case of extreme
forms of violence such as genocide—where structural, state-organized violence
may severely foreclose the possibility for resistance—complicates the picture.
Einwohner's essay makes an important contribution to this debate through an
analysis of organized Jewish resistance that carefully examines the social factors
and conditions conducive to and inhibitive of participation in various forms of
resistance. By examining the ways in which factors such as access to social
networks, gender, and age shaped participation in the Warsaw Ghetto uprising,
the essay stresses the existence of Jewish resistance during the Holocaust without
implicitly representing nonparticipants as passive victims. Thus Einwohner's
sociological perspective engages with and informs broader debates on agency,
resistance, and representation that have shaped interdisciplinary research in
comparative contexts.

In fields such as feminist and postcolonial studies, such debates have for the most part addressed the role and location of victims of violence. While attempts to understand both the nature of violence and the appropriate strategies of representation have been shaped by this focus on victims, the perpetrators of violence have received less attention. Olick's essay makes a substantial contribution in this regard by turning our attention to the role and responsibility of everyday Germans in supporting the Nazi regime and its violence. Such an approach both engages with and substantially reworks the terms of current debates on violence and genocide by shifting our lens to the dailiness of the extant support for genocide and violence.

At a deeper level, the essay asks us to consider the ethical and political implications that arise when the witnesses of violence and genocide come from the dominant social group implicated in the violence, rather than from the victimized group. How, in other words, do we understand the role of violence in constructing the subjectivity of the perpetrators and tacit supporters of such violence? Writing in a different context, Veena Das (2000), in her essay on the effects of widespread violence during the partition between India and Pakistan, writes of the long-standing effects that the act of witnessing violence has for the construction of subjectivity. For the victims, the witnessing of such violence, Das suggests, forms an integral component of the bodily violence itself. She examines the dailiness of these effects for survivors and explores the ways in which they must continually reinhabit the space of injury in the fabric of everyday life.

If the effects of violence permeate the daily life of victims, Olick's essay asks us to confront the ways in which the effects of violence permeate the lives of perpetrators or of those who may have tacitly condoned or benefited from genocide. These issues raise broader questions regarding collective and ethical responsibility for violence and genocide in a range of comparative contexts. Such issues also spark a series of concerns regarding the politics of representation, which, as Olick notes, involve questions such as how to draw boundaries between collective guilt and collective/ethical responsibility, or how to produce narratives on the perpetrators that can address their human suffering while circumventing the moral risks of sympathizing with and inadvertently justifying their actions.

Taken together, the essays in this section inform and in important ways contribute to broader debates on the politics and ethics of representation. It seems that the central challenge is one of producing Holocaust memory and representations that enact a form of witnessing rather than of spectatorship—a difficult project in the context of contemporary processes of cultural commodification, and one further complicated when witnessing is defined in relation to perpetrators, as well as to victims. For scholars, this challenge raises the need to think more seriously about the ethics of representation. The question that I want to end with, then, is one that asks what kinds of ethical practices of representation can be produced when considering the important issues the essays raise about history, memory, and the Holocaust.

Methodological questions in the social sciences have usually tended to focus more on questions of objectivity and scientific rigor rather than on questions regarding the politics of representation. Meanwhile, poststructuralist criticisms have tended to focus more on the power effects of representations. Yet the significance of representing the Holocaust seems to suggest a need for a discussion of a form of ethical action that would need to be embedded in practices of representation. All the essays I discuss here, for instance, touch on the sacredness associated with the Holocaust. Taking seriously this sacredness would require the development of a set of ethical practices that cannot be contained in the narrower preoccupations with objectivity or power that characterize a great deal of the contemporary social sciences. The larger question is thus one that would ask how Holocaust memory and representations would need to transform existing methodological assumptions and discursive practices within the discipline of sociology or the social sciences at large—a question that points to the significance that Holocaust research holds for scholars working in both comparative contexts and interdisciplinary fields of study.

BIBLIOGRAPHY

Abbott, Andrew. 1988. *The System of the Professions: An Essay on the Division of Expert Labor.* Chicago: University of Chicago Press.

Abel, Theodore. [1938] 1986. *Why Hitler Came to Power.* Cambridge, Mass.: Harvard University Press.

Abella, Irving, and Harold Troper. 1982. *None Is Too Many: Canada and the Jews of Europe, 1933–1948.* Toronto: Lester and Orpen Dennys.

Abraham, David. 1981. *The Collapse of the Weimar Republic: Political Economy and Crisis.* Princeton: Princeton University Press.

Adler, H. G. 1994. "A 'Mischling' Attempts to Fight for His Rights." Trans. Jamie Owen Daniel. In *Displacements: Cultural Identities in Question,* ed. A. Bammer, 205–15. Bloomington: Indiana University Press.

Adler, Joseph. 1992. "The Family of Joseph and Marie Adler: Jews in Germany, German Jews in America." Unpublished Manuscript. New York: Leo Baeck Institute.

Adler, Stanislaw. 1982. *In the Warsaw Ghetto: The Memoirs of Stanislaw Adler.* Jerusalem: Yad Vashem.

Adorno, Theodor W. 1957. "Replik zu Peter R. Hofstaeters Kritik des Gruppenexperiments." *Kölner Zeitschrift für Soziologie und Sozialpsychologie* 9:105–17.

Adorno, Theodor W., et al. 1950. *The Authoritarian Personality: Studies in Prejudice.* New York: Harper.

Ainsztein, Reuben. 1979. *The Warsaw Ghetto Revolt.* New York: Holocaust Library.

Alba, Richard. 1990. *Ethnic Identity: The Transformation of White America.* New Haven: Yale University Press.

Alexander, Edward. 1994. *The Holocaust and the War of Ideas.* New Brunswick, N.J.: Transaction.

Alexander, Hanan. 1998. "Literacy, Education and the Good Life." Paper presented at the "Workshop on Language, Culture, and Jewish Identity," December 28, School of Education, Tel Aviv University.

Alexander, Jeffrey C. 2004. "Toward a Theory of Cultural Trauma." In *Cultural Trauma and Collective Identity*, Alexander et al., 6–42. Berkeley: University of California Press.

Alexander, Jeffrey C., et al. 2004. *Cultural Trauma and Collective Identity*. Berkeley: University of California Press.

Anderson, Benedict. 1991. *Imagined Communities: Reflections on the Origin and Spread of Nationalism*. London: Verso.

Anderson, Mark M., ed. 1998. *Hitler's Exiles: Personal Stories of the Flight from Nazi Germany to America*. New York: New Press.

Anheier, Helmut K. 1997. "Studying the Nazi Party: 'Clean Models' versus 'Dirty Hands.'" *American Journal of Sociology* 103:199–209.

Anheier, Helmut K., and Friedhelm Neidhardt. 1998. "The Nazi Party and Its Capital: An Analysis of NSDAP Membership in Munich, 1925–1930." *American Behavioral Scientist* 41:1219–36.

Anheier, Helmut K., Friedhelm Neidhardt, and Wolfgang Vortkamp. 1998. "Movement Cycles and the Nazi Party: Activities of the Munich NSDAP, 1925–1930." *American Behavioral Scientist* 41:1262–81.

Antler, Joyce. 1999. "'Three Thousand Miles Away': The Holocaust in Recent Works for the American Theater." In *The Americanization of the Holocaust*, ed. Hilene Flanzbaum, 125–41. Baltimore: Johns Hopkins University Press.

Appadurai, Arjun. 1996. *Modernity at Large: Cultural Dimensions of Globalization*. Minneapolis: University of Minnesota Press.

Appleman-Jurman, Alicia. 1988. *Alicia: My Story*. New York: Bantam.

Archibugi, Daniele, David Held, and Martin Köhler, eds. 1998. *Re-imagining Political Community: Studies in Cosmopolitan Democracy*. Stanford: Stanford University Press.

Arendt, Hannah. 1943. "We Refugees." *Menorah Journal* 31:69–77.

———. 1958. *The Origins of Totalitarianism*. 2nd English ed. New York: Meridian.

———. 1963. *Eichmann in Jerusalem: A Report on the Banality of Evil*. New York: Viking.

Armstrong, Karen. 2000. "Ambiguity and Remembrance: Individual and Collective Memory in Finland." *American Ethnologist* 27:591–608.

Aschheim, Steven. 1997. "On Saul Friedlander." *History and Memory* 9:11–46.

Associación Pro-Búsqueda de Niñas y Niños Desaparecidos. 2001. *El Día Más Esperado: Buscando a los Niños Desaparecidos*. San Salvador: UCA Editiones de El Salvador.

Assmann, Aleida, and Ute Frevert. 1999. *Geschichtsvergessenheit, Geschichtsversessenheit: Vom Umgang mit deutschen Vergangenheiten nach 1945*. Stuttgart: Deutsche Verlags-Anstalt.

Ault, Brian, and William Brustein. 1998. "Joining the Nazi Party: Explaining the Political Geography of the NSDAP Membership, 1925–1933." *American Behavioral Scientist* 41:1304–23.

Aviv, Caryn, and David Shneer. 2005. *New Jews: The End of the Jewish Diaspora*. New York: New York University Press.

Azria, Régine. 1998. "The Diaspora-Community-Tradition Paradigms of Jewish Identity: A Reappraisal." In *Jewish Survival: The Identity Problem at the Close of the Twentieth Century*, ed. E. Krausz and G. Tulea, 21–32. New Brunswick, N.J.: Transaction.

Bahr, Ehrhard. 1984. "The Anti-Semitism Studies of the Frankfurt School: The Failure of Critical Theory." In *Foundations of the Frankfurt School of Social Research*, ed. Judith Marcus and Zoltán Tar, 311–21. New Brunswick, N.J.: Transaction.

Baily, Thomas, and Roger Waldinger. 1991. "Primary, Secondary, and Enclave Labor Markets: A Training Systems Approach." *American Sociological Review* 56:432–45.

Barany, Zoltan. 2002. *The East European Gypsies: Regime Change, Marginality, and Ethnopolitics.* Cambridge: Cambridge University Press.

Barber, Jennifer. 1987. "The Soviet Jews of Washington Heights." *New York Affairs* 10:34–43.

Barlow, Tani. 2000. "International Feminism of the Future." *Signs* 25:1099–105.

Barnett, Bernice McNair. 1993. "Invisible Southern Black Women Leaders in the Civil Rights Movement." *Gender and Society* 7:162–82.

Barnouw, Dagmar. 1996. *Germany 1945: Views of War and Violence.* Bloomington: Indiana University Press.

Bartov, Omer. 1993. "Intellectuals on Auschwitz: Memory, History, and Truth." *History and Memory* 5:87–129.

Basch, Linda, Nina Glick Schiller, and Cristina Szanton Blanc. 1994. *Nations Unbound: Transnational Projects, Postcolonial Predicaments, and Deterritorialized Nation-States.* Langhorne, PA: Gordon and Breach.

Basso, Keith. 1996. *Wisdom Sits in Places: Landscape and Language among Western Apache.* Albuquerque: University of New Mexico Press.

Bauböck, Ranier. 1996. "Cultural Minority Rights for Immigrants." *International Migration Review* 30:203–50.

Bauer, Yehuda. 1989. "Forms of Jewish Resistance during the Holocaust." In *The Nazi Holocaust: Historical Articles on the Destruction of European Jews*, vol. 7, *Jewish Resistance to the Holocaust*, ed. Michael R. Marrus, 34–48. Westport, Conn.: Meckler.

———. 2001. *Rethinking the Holocaust.* New Haven: Yale University Press.

Baum, Ranier C. 1981. *The Holocaust and the German Elite: Genocide and National Suicide in Germany, 1871–1945.* Totowa, N.J.: Rowman and Littlefield.

Bauman, Janina. 1986. *Winter in the Morning: A Young Girl's Life in the Warsaw Ghetto and Beyond, 1939–1945.* New York: Free Press.

Bauman, Zygmunt. 1989. *Modernity and the Holocaust.* Ithaca: Cornell University Press.

———. 1991. *Modernity and Ambivalence.* Ithaca: Cornell University Press.

———. 2004. "Categorical Murder, or: How to Remember the Holocaust." In *Representing the Holocaust for the 21st century*, ed. Ronit Lentin, 25–40. New York: Berghahn.

Baumel, Judith Tydor. 1998. *Double Jeopardy: Gender and the Holocaust.* London: Vallentine Mitchell.

Baum-Meróm, Gretel, and Rudy Baum. 1996. *Kinder aus gutem Hause: Von Frankfurt am Main nach Israel und Amerika 1913/15–1995.* Ed. Erhard Roy Wiehn. Constance: Hartung-Gorre Verlag.

Beck, Ulrich. 2000a. "The Cosmopolitan Perspective: The Sociology of the Second Age of Modernity." *British Journal of Sociology* 51:79–105.

——. 2000b. *What Is Globalization?* Cambridge: Polity.

——. 2002. "The Cosmopolitan Society and Its Enemies." *Theory, Culture and Society* 19:17–44.

Becker, Avi. 2001. "The Belated Discovery of American Community." *Jerusalem Post,* January 15.

Becker, Carl. 1958. *Modern History: The Rise of a Democratic, Scientific, and Industrialized Civilization.* Morristown, N.J.: Silver Burdett.

Ben Gurion, David. 1964. *Netzah Yisrael.* Tel Aviv: Aynot.

Bendix, Reinhard. 1986. *From Berlin to Berkeley: German-Jewish Identities.* New Brunswick, N.J.: Transaction.

——. 1993. *Unsettled Affinities.* Ed. John Bendix. New Brunswick, N.J.: Transaction.

Ben-Ezer, Gadi. 1994. "Ethiopian Jews Encounter Israel." In *Migration and Identity: International Yearbook of Oral History and Life Stories,* vol. 3, ed. R. Benmayor and A. Skotnes, 101–17. Oxford: Oxford University Press.

Berg, Mary. 1945. *Warsaw Ghetto: A Diary.* New York: L. B. Fischer.

Berger, Ronald. 1995. "Agency, Structure, and Jewish Survival of the Holocaust: A Life History Study." *Sociological Quarterly* 36:15–36.

Berghahn, Marion. 1984. *German-Jewish Refugees in England: The Ambiguities of Assimilation.* New York: St. Martin's.

Berlant, Lauren. 1997. *The Queen of America Goes to Washington City: Essays on Sex and Citizenship.* Durham, N.C.: Duke University Press.

Bernard, Jessie. 1949. *American Community Behavior.* New York: Dryden.

Bernston, Marit A., and Brian Ault. 1998. "Gender and Nazism: Women Joiners of the Pre-1933 Nazi Party." *American Behavioral Scientist* 41:1193–218.

Bershtel, Sara, and Allen Graubard. 1992. *Saving Remnants: Feeling Jewish in America.* Berkeley: University of California Press.

Bettelheim, Bruno. 1943. "Individual and Mass Behavior in Extreme Situations." *Journal of Abnormal and Social Psychology* 38:417–52.

Beverley, John, and Marc Zimmerman. 1990. *Literature and Politics in the Central American Revolutions.* Austin: University of Texas Press.

Bhachu, Parminder. 1985. *Twice Migrants: East African Sikh Settlers in Britain.* London: Tavistock.

Biale, David. 1986. *Power and Powerlessness in Jewish History.* New York: Schocken.

——. 1998. "The Melting Pot and Beyond: Jews and the Politics of American Identity." In *Insider/Outsider: American Jews and Multiculturalism,* ed. David Biale, Michael Galchinsky, and Susannah Heschel. 17–33. Berkeley: University of California Press.

Biale, David, Michael Galchinsky, and Susannah Heschel, eds. 1998. *Insider/Outsider: American Jews and Multiculturalism.* Berkeley: University of California Press.

Bischoping, Katharine, and Andrea Kalmin. 1999. "Public Opinion about Comparisons to the Holocaust." *Public Opinion Quarterly* 63:485–507.

Blum, Johannes. 1993. *Résistance: Père Bruno Reynders, juste des nations.* Brussels: Les Carrefours de La Cité.

Blum, Lenore, et al. 1991. "Tellers and Listeners: The Impact of the Holocaust Narratives." In *The Meaning of the Holocaust in a Changing World*, ed. Peter Hayes. 316–28. Evanston, Ill: Northwestern University Press.

Bodemann, Y. Michal. 1990. "The State in the Construction of Ethnicity and Ideological Labor: The Case of German Jewry." *Critical Sociology* 17:35–46.

——. 1996a. "'How Can One Stand to Live There as a Jew . . . ?': Paradoxes of Jewish Existence in Germany." In *Jews, Germans, Memory: Reconstructions of Jewish Life in Germany*, ed. Bodemann, 19–46. Ann Arbor: University of Michigan Press.

——. 1996b. "Reconstructions of History: From Jewish Memory to Nationalized Commemoration of Kristallnacht in Germany." In *Jews, Germans, Memory: Reconstructions of Jewish Life in Germany*, ed. Bodemann, 179–223. Ann Arbor: University of Michigan Press.

——, ed. 1996c. *Jews, Germans, Memory: Reconstructions of Jewish Life in Germany.* Ann Arbor: University of Michigan Press.

——. 2005. *A Jewish Family in Germany Today: An Intimate Portrait.* Durham, N.C.: Duke University Press.

Bonacich, Edna. 1993. "The Other Side of Ethnic Entrepreneurship: A Dialogue with Waldinger, Aldrich, Ward and Associates." *International Migration Review* 27:685–92.

——. 1994. "Asians in the Los Angeles Garment Industry." In *New Asian Immigration in Los Angeles and Global Restructuring*, ed. P. Ong, E. Bonacich, and L. Cheng, 137–63. Philadelphia: Temple University Press.

Borjas, George 1996. "The New Economics of Immigration: Affluent Americans Gain, Poor Americans Lose." *Atlantic Monthly*, November, 72–80.

——. 1999. *Heaven's Door: Immigration Policy and the American Economy.* Princeton: Princeton University Press.

Borneman, John. 1993. "Uniting the German Nation: Law, Narrative and Historicity." *American Ethnologist* 20:288–311.

Borneman, John, and Jeffrey M. Peck. 1995. *Sojourners: The Return of German Jews and the Question of Identity.* Lincoln: University of Nebraska Press.

Borzykowski, Tuvia. 1976. *Between Tumbling Walls.* Lohamei Hagettaot and Hakibbutz Hameuchad Publishing House.

Boss, Pauline. 1999. *Ambiguous Loss: Learning to Live with Unresolved Grief.* Cambridge, Mass.: Harvard University Press.

Bottomore, T. B. 1984. *The Frankfurt School.* London: Tavistock.

Boyarin, Daniel, and Jonathan Boyarin. 1993. "Diaspora: Generation and the Ground of Jewish Identity." *Critical Inquiry* 19:693–725.

Boyarin, Jonathan, and Daniel Boyarin, eds. 1997. *Jews and Other Differences: The New Jewish Cultural Studies.* Minneapolis: University of Minnesota Press.

——. 2002. *Powers of Diaspora: Two Essays on the Relevance of Jewish Culture.* Minneapolis: University of Minnesota Press.

Boyd, Monica. 1989. "Family and Personal Networks in International Migration: Recent Developments and New Agendas." *International Migration Review* 27:638–70.

Brachfeld, Sylvain. 1989. *Ils n'ont pas eu les gosses: L'histoire de 500 enfants juifs sans parents fichés à la Gestapo et placés pendant l'occupation allemande dans les homes de l'"Associations des juifs de Belgique" (A.J.B.)*. 2d ed. Herzliya, Israel: Institut de recherche sur le judaïsme belge.

——. 2001. *Ils ont survécu: Le sauvetage des Juifs en Belgique occupée*. Brussels: Éditions Racine.

Breines, Paul. 1990. *Tough Jews: Political Fantasies and the Moral Dilemma of American Jewry*. New York: Basic Books.

Breuer, Mordechai. 1992. *Modernity within Tradition: The Social History of Orthodox Jewry in Imperial Germany*. New York: Columbia University Press.

Bridenthal, Renate, Atina Grossman, and Marion Kaplan, eds. 1984. *When Biology Became Destiny: Women in Weimar and Nazi Germany*. New York: Monthly Review Press.

Brin, Rabbi Shlomo. 2002. "'Mi yitein roshi mayim ve'eini mekor di'ah': Yom Hazikaron Lashoah Velagevurah—bein hadat vehamedinah" [Oh That My Head Were Waters, and Mine Eyes a Fountain of Tears': Holocaust Martyrs' and Heroes' Remembrance Day; Between Religion and the State]. *Alon Shvut: Journal of Alumni of Yeshivat Har Etzion* Nissan 5762 [2002] 16:43–48.

Brink, Cornelia. 1998. *Ikonen der Vernichtung: Öffentlicher Gebrauch von Fotografien aus nationalisozialistischen Konzentrationslagern nach 1945*. Berlin: Akademie.

Broder, Jonathan 1999. "Heeding the Call." *Jerusalem Report*, March 29, 34–35.

Brodkin, Karen. 1998. *How Jews Became White Folks and What That Says About Race in America*. New Brunswick, N.J.: Rutgers University Press.

Brown, Wendy. 1995. *States of Injury: Power and Freedom in Late Modernity*. Princeton: Princeton University Press.

Browning, Christopher R. 1992. *Ordinary Men: Reserve Police Battalion 101 and the Final Solution in Poland*. New York: Harper Collins.

Brubaker, Rogers. 2002. "Ethnicity without Groups." *Archives européennes de socologie* 43:163–89.

Bruner, Edward M., and Phyllis Gorfain. 1984. "Dialogic Narration and the Paradoxes of Masada." In *Text, Play, and Story: The Construction and the Reconstruction of Self and Society: 1983 Proceedings of the American Ethnological Society*, ed. Bruner and Stuart Plattner, 56–79. Washington: American Ethnological Society.

Brustein, William. 1998a. *The Logic of Evil: The Social Origins of the Nazi Party, 1925–1933*. New Haven: Yale University Press.

——. 1998b. "The Nazi Party and the German New Middle Class." *American Behavioral Scientist* 41:1237–61.

——. 2003. *Roots of Hate: Anti-Semitism in Europe before the Holocaust*. Cambridge: Cambridge University Press.

Brym, Robert J. 1994. *The Jews of Moscow, Kiev, and Minsk: Identity, Anti-Semitism, Emigration*. New York: New York University Press.

Buckler, Steven. 1996. "Historical Narrative, Identity and the Holocaust." *History of the Human Sciences* 9:1–20.

Buechler, Steven M. 1990. *Women's Movements in the United States*. New Brunswick, N.J.: Rutgers University Press.

Bukharin, Nikolai. 1925. *Historical Materialism: A System of Sociology*. Trans. E. Crawford. New York: International Publishers.

Burawoy, Michael. 1991. "The Extended Case Method." In *Ethnography Unbound: Power and Resistance in the Modern Metropolis*, ed. Buroway, J. Gamson, and A. Burton, 271–87. Berkeley: University of California Press.

———. 1998. "The Extended Case Method." *Sociological Theory* 16:4–33.

Burchardt, N. 1993. "Transgenerational Transmission in the Families of Holocaust Survivors in England." In *Between Generations: Family Models, Myths and Memories*, ed. D. Bertaux and P. Thompson, 121–39. Oxford: Oxford University Press.

Calhoun, Craig. 1991. "The Problem of Identity in Collective Action." In *Macro-Micro Linkages in Sociology*, ed. Joan Huber, 51–75. Newbury Park, CA: Sage.

———. 1994. *Neither Gods nor Emperors: Students and the Struggle for Democracy in China*. Berkeley: University of California Press.

———. 2003. "The Variability of Belonging." *Ethnicities* 3:558–68.

Calverton, V. F. 1931. *The Making of Man: An Outline of Anthropology*. New York: Modern Library.

Caplan, Kimmy. 2002. "The Holocaust in Contemporary Israeli Haredi Popular Religion." *Modern Judaism* 22:142–68.

Carlie, Linda L. 1999. "Cognitive Reconstruction, Hindsight, and Reactions to Victims and Perpetrators." *Personality and Social Psychology Bulletin* 25:966–79.

Carp, Joel M. 1990. "Absorbing Jews Jewishly: Professional Responsibility for Jewishly Absorbing New Immigrants in Their New Communities." *Journal of Jewish Communal Service* 66:366–74.

Castells, Manuel. 1996. *The Rise of the Network Society*. Cambridge: Blackwell.

Castles, Stephen, and Mark J. Miller. 1998. *The Age of Migration: International Population Movements in the Modern World*. 2d ed. New York: Guilford.

Cerulo, Karen A. 1997. "Identity Construction: New Issues, New Directions." *Annual Review of Sociology* 23:385–409.

———, ed. 2002. *Culture in Mind: Towards a Sociology of Culture and Cognition*. New York: Routledge.

Cesarani, David. 2001. "Memory, Representation and Education." In *Remembering for the Future: The Holocaust in an Age of Genocide*, ed. J. K. Roth and E. Maxwell, 231–36. New York: Palgrave.

Chabin, Michele. 1997. "Behind the Headlines: Israelis Living Abroad Wooed to Return by Government Firms." Jewish Telegraphic Agency, www.jta.org (accessed March 2, 1997).

Chai, Avi. 1994. *Jewish Day Schools in the United States*. New York: Avi Chai Foundation.

Chalk, Frank, and Kurt Jonassohn. 1990. *The History and Sociology of Genocide: Analyses and Case Studies*. New Haven: Yale University Press.

Chlenov, Mikhail A. 1994. "Jewish Communities and Jewish Identities in the Former Soviet Union." In *Jewish Identities in the New Europe*, ed. J. Webber, 127–38. London: Littman Library of Jewish Civilization.

Chodoff, Paul. 1980. "Psychotherapy of the Survivor." In *Survivors, Victims, and Perpetrators: Essays on the Nazi Holocaust*, ed. Joel E. Dimsdale, 205–18. Washington: Hemisphere Publishing Corporation.

Chow, Rey. 1991. "Violence in the 'Other' Country." In *Third World Women and the Politics of Feminism*, ed. Chandra Talpade Mohanty, Ann Russo, and Lourdes Torres, 81–100. Bloomington: Indiana University Press.

Churgin, Michael J. 1996. "Mass Exoduses: The Response of the United States." *International Migration Review* 30:310–24.

Clifford, James. 1994. "Diasporas." *Cultural Anthropology* 9:302–38.

——. 1997. *Routes: Travel and Translation in the Late Twentieth Century.* Cambridge, Mass.: Harvard University Press.

Climo, Jacob. 1990. "Transmitting Ethnic Identity through Oral Narratives." *Ethnic Groups* 8:163–70.

Cochavi, Yehoyakim. 1995. "The Motif of 'Honor' in the Call to Rebellion in the Ghetto." In *Zionist Youth Movements during the Shoah*, A. Cohen and Cochavi, 245–54. New York: Peter Lang.

Cohen, Anthony P. 1985. *The Symbolic Construction of Community.* New York: Tavistock.

Cohen, Beth B. 2007. *Cased Closed: Holocaust Survivors in Postwar America.* New Brunswick, N.J.: Rutgers University Press.

Cohen, Malachi Haim. 1999. "Dilemmas of Cosmopolitanism: Karl Popper, Jewish Identity and Central European Culture." *Journal of Modern History* 71:105–49.

Cohen, Rina. 1999. "From Ethnonational Enclave to Diasporic Community: The Mainstreaming of Israeli Jewish Migrants in Toronto." *Diaspora* 8:121–36.

Cohen, Rina, and Gerald Gold. 1996. "Israelis in Toronto: The Myth of Return and the Development of a Distinct Ethnic Community." *Jewish Journal of Sociology* 38:17–26.

Cohen, Robin. 1997. *Global Diasporas: An Introduction.* Seattle: University of Washington Press.

Cohen, Steven M. 1986. "Israeli Émigrés and the New York Federation: A Case Study in Ambivalent Policymaking for 'Jewish Communal Deviants,'" *Contemporary Jewry* 7:155–65.

——. 1991. "Israel in the Jewish Identity of American Jews: A Study in Dualities and Contrasts." In David M. Gordis and Yoav Ben-Horin, eds. *Jewish Identity in America*, 119–35. Los Angeles: Wilstein.

Cohen, Yinon. 1996. "Economic Assimilation in the United States of Arab and Jewish Immigrants from Israel and the Territories." *Israel Studies* 1:75–97.

Cohen, Yinon, and Yitchak Haberfeld. 1997. "The Number of Israeli Immigrants in the United States in 1990." *Demography* 34:199–212.

Cole, Jennifer. 1998. "The Work of Memory in Madagascar." *American Ethnologist* 25:610–33.

Coles, Robert. 1986. *The Political Life of Children*. New York: Atlantic Monthly Press.

Conneman, George J. 1970. *Toward the Year 1985: Milk Production and Consumption*. Ithaca: New York State College of Agriculture, Cornell University.

Coser, Lewis A. 1984. *Refugee Scholars in America: Their Impact and Their Experiences*. New Haven: Yale University Press.

Cuddihy, John Murray. [1974] 1987. "Jews, Blacks, and the Cold War at the Top: Malamud's *The Tenants* and the Status Politics of Subcultures." In *The Ordeal of Civility: Freud, Marx, Levi-Strauss, and the Jewish Struggle with Modernity*, 203–24. Boston: Beacon.

Czerniakow, Adam. 1979. *The Warsaw Diary of Adam Czerniakow: Prelude to Doom*. Ed Raul Hilberg, Stanislaw Staron, and Josef Kermisz. Trans. Staron and staff at Yad Vashem. New York: Stein and Day.

Dahrendorf, Ralf. 1967. *Society and Democracy in Germany*. New York: Doubleday.

Dallalfar, Arlene. 1994. "Iranian Women as Immigrant Entrepreneurs." *Gender and Society* 8:541–61.

Das, Veena. 2000. "The Act of Witnessing: Violence, Poisonous Knowledge and Subjectivity." In *Violence and Subjectivity*, ed. Das et al., 205–25. Berkeley: University of California Press.

Das, Veena, M. Kleinman, M. Ramphele, and P. Reynolds, eds. *Violence and Subjectivity*. Berkeley: University of California Press.

Daum, Menachem, and Oren Rudavsky, dirs. 1997. *A Life Apart: Hasidism in America*. New York: First Run Features.

Davidman, Lynn. 1993. *Tradition in a Rootless World: Women Turn to Orthodox Judaism*. Berkeley: University of California Press.

Davidman, Lynn, and Shelley Tenenbaum. 1996. *Feminist Perspectives on Jewish Studies*. New Haven: Yale University Press.

Davie, Maurice R. 1947. *Refugees in America: Report of the Committee for the Study of Recent Immigration from Europe*. New York: Harper.

Davis, Moshe. 1963. *The Emergence of Conservative Judaism: The Historical School in the Nineteenth Century*. Philadelphia: Jewish Publication Society of America.

Dawidowicz, Lucy S. 1981. *The Holocaust and the Historians*. Cambridge, Mass.: Harvard University Press.

Diamond, Etan. 2000. *And I Will Dwell in Their Midst: Orthodox Jews in Suburbia*. Chapel Hill: University of North Carolina Press.

Dimsdale, Joel E. 1980. "The Coping Behavior of Nazi Concentration Camp Survivors." In *Survivors, Victims, and Perpetrators: Essays on the Nazi Holocaust*, ed. Dimsdale. Washington: Hemisphere Publishing Corporation.

Diner, Dan. 2000. *Beyond the Conceivable: Studies on Germany, Nazism, and the Holocaust*. Berkeley: University of California Press.

Dinnerstein, Leonard. 1982. *America and the Survivors of the Holocaust*. New York: Columbia University Press.

Dominguez, Virginia A. 1993. "Questioning Jews." *American Ethnologist* 20:618–24.

Donat, Alexander. 1978. *The Holocaust Kingdom: A Memoir*. New York: Holocaust Library.

Douglas, Lawrence. 1995. "Film as Witness: Screening Nazi Concentration Camps before the Nuremberg Tribunal." *Yale Law Journal* 105:449–81.

Douglas, Mary. 1986. *How Institutions Think*. Syracuse: Syracuse University Press.

Dubb, Allie A. 1994. *The Jewish Population of South Africa: The 1991 Sociodemographic Survey*. Cape Town: Kaplan Centre Jewish Studies and Research, University of Cape Town.

Dunning, Eric, and Stephen Mennell. 1998. "Elias on Germany, Nazism and the Holocaust: On the Balance between 'Civilizing' and 'Decivilizing' Trends in the Social Development of Western Europe." *British Journal of Sociology* 49:339–57.

Duranti, Alessandro, and Donald Brennis. 1986. "Special Issue: The Audience as Co-author; An Introduction." *Text* 6:239–47.

Durkheim, Émile. 1974. *Sociology and Philosophy*. Trans. D. F. Pocock. New York: Free Press.

Eckhardt, Alice, and A. Roy Eckhardt. 1980. "The Holocaust and the Enigma of Uniqueness: A Philosophical Effort at Practical Clarification." *Annals of the American Academy of Political and Social Sciences* 450:165–78.

Einwohner, Rachel L. 1999. "Gender, Class, and Social Movement Outcomes: Identity and Effectiveness in Two Animal Rights Campaigns." *Gender and Society* 13:56–76.

——. 2003. "Opportunity, Honor, and Action in the Warsaw Ghetto Uprising of 1943." *American Journal of Sociology* 109:650–75.

Eitinger, Leo. 1964. *Concentration Camp Survivors in Norway and Israel*. London: Allen and Unwin.

——. 1980. "The Concentration Camp Syndrome and Its Late Sequelae." In *Survivors, Victims, and Perpetrators: Essays on the Nazi Holocaust*, ed. Joel E. Dimsdale, 127–62. Washington: Hemisphere Publishing Corporation.

Ellenson, David. 1996. "Envisioning Israel and the Liturgies of North American Liberal Judaism." In *Envisioning Israel: The Changing Ideals and Images of North American Jews*, ed. Allon Gal, 117–48. Jerusalem: Magnes.

Elman, R. Amy. 1999. "Lesbians and the Holocaust." In *Women and the Holocaust: Narrative and Representation*, ed. E. Fuchs, 9–17. Lanham, Md.: University Press of America.

Erickson, Kai T. 1976. *Everything in Its Path: Destruction of Community in the Buffalo Creek Flood*. New York: Simon and Schuster.

Espiritu, Yen Le. 1989. "Beyond the 'Boat People': Ethnicization of American Life." *Amerasia Journal* 15:302–38.

——. 2003. *Home Bound: Filipino American Lives Across Cultures, Communities, and Countries*. Berkeley: University of California Press.

Espiritu, Yen Le, and Diane L. Wolf. 2000. "The Paradox of Assimilation: Children of Filipino Immigrants in San Diego." In *Ethnicities: The New Second Generation*, ed. A. Portes and R. Rumbaut, 157–86. Berkeley: University of California Press.

Espiritu, Yen Le, and Thom Tran. 2002. "Vietnam, Nuoc Toi (Vietnam, My Country):

Vietnamese Americans and Transnationalism." In *The Changing Face of Home: The Transnational Lives of the Second Generation*, ed. Peggy Levitt and Mary C. Waters, 367–98. New York: Russell Sage Foundation.

Evans, Sara. 1980. *Personal Politics: The Roots of Women's Liberation in the Civil Rights Movement and the New Left*. New York: Vintage.

Evron, Boas. 1995. *Jewish State or Israeli Nation?* Bloomington: Indiana University Press.

Fader, Ayala. 2006. "Learning Faith: Language Socialization in a Community of Hasidic Jews." *Language and Society* 35:205–29.

Faist, Thomas. 2000. *The Volume and Dynamics of International Migration and Transnational Social Spaces*. Oxford: Oxford University Press.

Farber, David. 1994. *The Sixties: From Memory to History*. Chapel Hill: University of North Carolina Press.

Feher, Shoshanah. 1998. "From the Rivers of Babylon to the Valleys of Los Angeles: The Exodus and Adaptation of Iranian Jews." In *Gatherings in the Diaspora: Religious Communities and the New Immigration*, ed. R. S. Warner and J. G. Wittner, 71–94. Philadelphia: Temple University Press.

Fein, Helen. 1977. *Imperial Crime and Punishment: The Massacre at Jallianwala Bagh and British Judgment, 1919–1920*. Honolulu: University of Hawaii Press.

——. 1979. *Accounting for Genocide: National Responses and Jewish Victimization during the Holocaust*. New York: Free Press.

——. 1993. *Genocide: A Sociological Perspective*. London: Sage.

——, ed. 1987. *The Persisting Question: Sociological Perspectives and Social Contexts of Modern Antisemitism*. Berlin: De Gruyter.

Feitlowitz, Marguerite. 1998. *A Lexicon of Terror: Argentina and the Legacies of Torture*. New York: Oxford University Press.

Feldman, Jackie. 1995. "It Is My Brothers Whom I Am Seeking: Israeli Youth's Pilgrimages to Poland of the Shoah." *Jewish Folklore and Ethnology Review* 17:57–66.

Fernandes, Leela. 1999. "'Reading 'India's Bandit Queen': A Trans/National Feminist Perspective on the Discrepancies of Representation." *Signs* 25:123–54.

——. 2000. "Nationalizing the 'Global': Media Images, Cultural Politics and the Middle Class of India." *Media, Culture and Society* 22:611–28.

Findlay, Allan M. 1995. "Skilled Transients: The Invisible Phenomenon." In *The Cambridge Survey of World Migration*, ed. R. Cohen, 515–22. Cambridge: Cambridge University Press.

Findlay, Allan M., and F. I. N. Li. 1998. "A Migration Channels Approach to the Study of Professional Moving to and from Hong Kong." *International Migration Review* 32:682–703.

Findling, Deborah. 1999. "A Hermeneutic Exploration of the Past as Present and Future: The March of the Living as Text." PhD diss., University of San Francisco.

Finke, Roger. 1989. "Demographics of Religious Participation: An Ecological Approach, 1850–1980." *Journal for the Scientific Study of Religion* 28:45–58.

Finkelstein, Norman G. 2000. *The Holocaust Industry: Reflections on the Exploration of Jewish Suffering*. London: Verso.

Finkielkraut, Alain. 1994. *The Imaginary Jew*. Trans. Kevin O'Neill and Daniel Suchoff. Lincoln: University of Nebraska Press.

Fishman, Sylvia. 2000. *Jewish Life and American Culture*. Albany: State University of New York Press.

Fleck, Christian, Albert Müller, and Nico Stehr. 2005. Afterword to *The Society of Terror: Inside the Dachau and Buchenwald Concentration Camps*, by Paul Martin Neurath, ed. Fleck and Stehr, 279–311. Boulder, Colo.: Paradigm.

Fogelman, Eva. 1994. *Conscience and Courage: Rescuers of Jews during the Holocaust*. New York: Anchor Doubleday.

Fonsec, Isabel. 1995. *Bury Me Standing: The Gypsies and Their Journey*. New York: Knopf.

For those Returning Home [in Hebrew]. 1995. Insert in *Yisrael Shelanu*.

Foster, John Burt. 1995. "Cultural Multiplicity in Two Modern Autobiographies: Friedlander's *When Memory Comes* and Denisen's *Out of Africa*." *Southern Humanities Review* 29:205–18.

Foucault, Michel. 1978. *The History of Sexuality*. Trans. Robert Hurley. New York: Pantheon.

——. 1980. *Power / Knowledge: Selected Interviews and Other Writings, 1972–1977*. Trans. Alan Sheridan. New York: Pantheon.

Frankentel, Salley. 1998. "Constructing Identity in Diaspora: Jewish Israeli Migrants in Cape Town, South Africa." PhD diss., University of Cape Town.

Frankfurt Institute for Social Research. [1956] 1972. *Aspects of Sociology*. Trans. J. Viertel. Boston: Beacon.

Fraser, Angus. 1992. *The Gypsies*. Oxford: Blackwell.

Fraser, Nancy, and A. Honneth. 1998. *Redistribution or Recognition? A Political-Philosophical Exchange*. London: Verso.

Freedman, Samuel G. 2000. *Jew versus Jew: The Struggle for the Soul of American Jewry*. New York: Simon and Schuster.

Friedländer, Saul. 1979. *When Memory Comes*. Trans. Helen R. Lane New York: Farrar, Straus, Giroux.

——. 1992. Introduction to *Probing the Limits of Representation: Nazism and the "Final Solution,"* ed. Friedlander, 1–20. Cambridge, Mass.: Harvard University Press.

——. 1997. *Nazi Germany and the Jews: The Years of Persecution, 1933–1939*. New York: HarperCollins.

Friedländer, Saul, and Adam Seligman. 1994. "The Israeli Memory of the Shoah: On Symbols, Rituals, and Ideological Polarization." In *Now Here: Space, Time and Modernity*, ed. R. Friedland and D. Boden, 356–71. Berkeley: University of California Press.

Friedman, Debra, and Doug McAdam. 1992. "Collective Identity and Activism: Networks, Choices and the Life of a Social Movement." In *Frontiers in Social Movement Theory*, ed. A. D. Morris and C. M. Mueller, 156–73. New Haven: Yale University Press.

Friedman, Jonathon. 1990. "Being in the World: Globalization and Localization." *Theory, Culture and Society* 7:311–28.

Friedman, Kathie. 2000. "Complicating Diasporic Identities: The Voice of Two Russian Refugee Women in the U.S." Paper presented at the "Diasporas and Transnational Identities" conference, October 19–22, University of Western Ontario, London, Canada.

Friedman-Kasaba, Kathie. 1996. *Memories of Migration: Gender, Ethnicity, and Work in the Lives of Jewish and Italian Women in New York, 1870–1924.* Albany: State University of New York Press.

Friesel, Evyatar. 1996. "The German-Jewish Encounter as a Historical Problem: A Reconsideration." *Leo Baeck Institute Year Book* 16:263–76.

Fromm, Erich. 1941. *Escape from Freedom.* New York: Farrar and Rinehart.

Frydman, Marcel. 1999. *Le traumatisme de l'enfant caché.* Gerpinnes, Belgium: Éditions Quorum.

Fujitani, T., Geoffrey M. White, and Lisa Yoneyama. 2001. Introduction to *Perilous Memories: The Asia-Pacific War(s)*, ed. Fujitani, White, and Yoneyama, 1–29. Durham, N.C.: Duke University Press.

Fulbrook, Mary. 1999. *German National Identity after the Holocaust.* Cambridge: Polity.

Fuss, Diane. 1990. *Essentially Speaking: Feminism, Nature, and Difference.* New York: Routledge.

Gal, Susan. 1991. "Between Speech and Silence: The Problematics of Research on Language and Gender." In *Gender at the Crossroads of Knowledge: Feminist Anthropology in the Postmodern Era*, ed. M. di Leonardo, 175–203. Berkeley: University of California Press.

Gallant, Mary and Jay Cross. 1992. "Surviving Destruction of the Self: Challenged Identity in the Holocaust." *Studies in Symbolic Interaction* 13:221–46.

Gamson, William A. 1992. *Talking Politics.* New York: Cambridge University Press.

——. 1995. "Hiroshima, the Holocaust, and the Politics of Exclusion: 1994 Presidential Address." *American Sociological Review* 60:1–20.

Gans, Herbert J. 1988. *Middle American Individualism: The Future of American Democracy.* New York: Free Press.

——. 1992. "Second-Generation Decline: Scenarios for the Economic and Ethnic Futures of the Post-1965 American Immigrants." *Ethnic and Racial Studies* 15:173–92.

——. 1999. "Filling in Some Holes: Six Areas of Needed Immigration Research." *American Behavioral Scientist* 42:1302–13.

Gedi, Noa, and Yigal Elam. 1996. "Collective Memory: What Is It?" *History and Memory* 8:30–39.

Gellner, Ernest. 1998. *Language and Solitude: Wittgenstein, Malinowski, and the Hapsburg Dilemma.* New York: Cambridge University Press.

Gerhardt, Uta. 1993. "Introduction: Talcott Parsons's Sociology of National Socialism." In *Talcott Parsons on National Socialism*, ed. Uta Gerhardt, 1–78. New York: Aldine de Gruyter.

——. 1996. "Scholarship, Not Scandal." *Sociological Forum* 11:623–30.

——. 2002. *Talcott Parsons: An Intellectual Biography.* Cambridge: Cambridge University Press.

——, ed. 1993. *Talcott Parsons on Nationalism Socialism.* New York: Aldine de Gruyter.

Gerson, Judith M. 2001. "In Between States: National Identity Practices among German Jewish Immigrants." *Political Psychology* 22:179–98.

Gerth, Hans. 1940. "The Nazi Party: Its Leadership and Composition." *American Journal of Sociology* 45:517–41.

Giddens, Anthony. 1991. *Modernity and Self-Identity: Self and Society in the Late Modern Age.* Stanford: Stanford University Press.

Gilroy, Paul. 1993. *The Black Atlantic: Modernity and Double Consciousness.* Cambridge, Mass.: Harvard University Press.

Glaser, Hermann. 1990. *The Rubble Years: The Cultural Roots of Postwar Germany.* Trans. F. Freige and P. Gleason. New York: Paragon House.

Gleason, Philip. 1980. "American Identity and Americanization." In *Harvard Encyclopedia of American Ethnic Groups*, ed. Stephan Thernstrom, 31–58. Cambridge, Mass.: Belknap.

Gold, Steven J. 1992. *Refugee Communities: A Comparative Field Study.* Newbury Park, CA: Sage.

——. 1994a. "Israeli Immigrants in the U.S.: The Question of Community." *Qualitative Sociology* 17:325–63.

——. 1994b. "Patterns of Economic Cooperation among Israeli Immigrants in Los Angeles." *International Migration Review* 28:114–35.

——. 1994c. "Soviet Jews in the United States." In *American Jewish Year Book*, ed. American Jewish Committee, 3–57. New York: American Jewish Committee.

——. 1995a. *From the Workers' State to the Golden State: Jews from the Former Soviet Union in California.* Boston: Allyn and Bacon.

——. 1995b. "Gender and Social Capital among Israeli Immigrants in Los Angeles." *Diaspora* 4:267–301.

——. 1997a. "Community Formation among Jews from the Former Soviet Union in the United States." In *Russian Jews on Three Continents: Migration and Resettlement*, ed. Noah Lewin-Epstein, Yaacov Ro'i, and Paul Ritterband, 261–83. London: Frank Cass.

——. 1997b. "Transnationalism and Vocabularies of Motive in International Migration: The Case of Israelis in the U.S." *Sociological Perspectives* 40:409–26.

——. 1999. "From 'The Jazz Singer' to 'What a Country!' A Comparison of Jewish Migration to the U.S., 1880 to 1930 and 1965 to 1998." *Journal of American Ethnic History* 18:114–41.

——. 2000. "Transnational Communities: Examining Migration in a Globally Integrated World." In *Rethinking Globalization(s): From Corporate Transnationalism to Local Intervention*, ed. P. S. Aulakh and M. G. Schechter, 73–90. New York: St. Martin's.

——. 2001. "Gender, Class, and Network: Social Structure and Migration Patterns among Transnational Israelis." *Global Networks* 1:57–78.

——. 2002. *The Israeli Diaspora.* Seattle: University of Washington Press.

Gold, Steven J., and Bruce A. Phillips. 1996. "Israelis in the United States." *American Jewish Year Book* 96:51–101.

Goldberg, J. J. 1996. *Jewish Power: Inside the American Jewish Establishment*. Reading, MA: Addison-Wesley.

Goldberg, Michael. 1995. *Why Should Jews Survive? Looking Past the Holocaust toward a Jewish Future*. New York: Oxford University Press.

Goldberg, Simcha R. 1981. "Jewish Acculturation and the Soviet Immigrant." *Journal of Jewish Communal Service* 57:154–63.

Goldhagen, Daniel J. 1996. *Hitler's Willing Executioners: Ordinary Germans and the Holocaust*. New York: Knopf.

Goldscheider, Calvin. 1996. *Israeli's Changing Society: Population, Ethnicity and Development*. Boulder, Colo.: Westview.

———. 2003. "Are American Jews Vanishing Again?" *Contexts* 2:18–24.

Goldstein, Joseph. 1995. *Jewish History in Modern Times*. Brighton, UK: Sussex Academic Press.

Goodwin, Charles. 1986. "Audience Diversity, Participation and Interpretation." *Text* 6:283–316.

Gordon, Milton M. 1964. *Assimilation in American Life*. New York: Oxford University Press.

Gosse, Van, ed. 2003. "Terror and History." *Radical History Review*, no. 85.

Grebler, Leo. 1976. *German Jewish Immigrants to the United States during the Hitler Period: Personal Reminiscences and General Observations*. New York: Leo Baeck Institute.

Grobman, Alex. 2004. *Battling for Souls: The Vaad Hatzala Rescue Committee in Post-Holocaust Europe*. Jersey City: KTAV.

Groves, Julian M. 2001. "Animal Rights and the Politics of Emotion: Folk Constructs of Emotions in the Animal Rights Movement." In *Passionate Politics: Emotions and Social Movements*, ed. Jeff Goodwin, James M. Jasper, and Francesca Polletta, 212–29. Chicago: University of Chicago Press.

Gruber, Ruth. 2000. *Haven: The Dramatic Story of One Thousand World War II Refugees and How They Came to America*. New York: Three Rivers Press.

Grubsztein, Meir, ed. 1971. *Jewish Resistance during the Holocaust: Proceedings of the Conference on Manifestations of Jewish Resistance*. Jerusalem: Yad Vashem.

Gruenspecht, Alfred. 1993. "Alfred Gruenspecht Memoir" (RG-10.123/Box 18). Unpublished Memoir. Washington, DC: United States Holocaust Memorial Museum.

Grynberg, Michal, ed. 2002. *Words to Outlive Us: Voices form the Warsaw Ghetto*. New York: Henry Holt.

Guarnizo, Luis Eduardo. 1996. "The Mexican Ethnic Economy in Los Angeles: Capitalist Accumulation, Class Restructuring and the Transnationalization of Migration." Working paper presented in series 1, California Communities Program, Department of Human and Community Development, University of California, Davis.

Gugelberger, George, and Michael Kearney. 1991. "Voices for the Voiceless: Testimonial Literature in Latin America." *Latin American Perspectives* 70:3–14.

Gurfein, M. I., and Morris Janowitz. 1946. "Trends in Wehrmacht Morale." *Public Opinion Quarterly* 10:78–84.

Gurock, Jeffrey S. 1996. *American Jewish Orthodoxy in Historical Perspective*. Hoboken, N.J.: KTAV.

Gutman, Israel. 1982. *The Jews of Warsaw, 1939–1943*. Bloomington: Indiana University Press.

——. 1989a. "The Genesis of the Resistance in the Warsaw Ghetto." In *The Nazi Holocaust: Historical Documents on the Destruction of European Jews*, ed. Michael R. Marrus, 118–59. Westport, Conn.: Meckler.

——. 1989b. "Youth Movements in the Underground and the Ghetto Revolts." In *The Nazi Holocaust: Historical Documents on the Destruction of European Jews*, ed. Michael R. Marrus, 160–84. Westport, Conn.: Meckler.

——. 1994. *Resistance: The Warsaw Ghetto Uprising*. Boston: Houghton Mifflin.

Haas, Aaron. 1990. *In the Shadow of the Holocaust*. Ithaca: Cornell University Press.

Habermas, Jürgen. 1998. *The Inclusion of the Other: Studies in Political Theory*. Ed. Garan Cronin and Pablo De Greiff. Cambridge: MIT Press.

Hagan, Jacqueline. 1998. "Social Networks, Gender, and Immigrant Incorporation: Resources and Constraints." *American Sociological Review* 63:55–67.

Hakohen, Israel Meir. 1893. *Nidhe Yisrael*. Warsaw: M. I. Halter and M. E. Galevsky.

Halbwachs, Maurice. [1950] 1980. *The Collective Memory*. Trans. Francis J. Ditter Jr. and Vida Yazdi Ditter. New York: Harper and Row.

——. 1992. *On Collective Memory*. Trans. and ed. L. A. Coser. Chicago: University of Chicago Press.

Halter, Marilyn. 2000. *Shopping for Identity: The Marketing of Ethnicity*. New York: Schocken.

Hamilton, Richard F. 1982. *Who Voted for Hitler?* Princeton, N.J.: Princeton University Press.

Handelman, Don, ed. *Models and Mirrors: Towards an Anthropology of Public Events*. Cambridge: Cambridge University Press.

Handelman, Don, and Elihu Katz. 1990. "State Ceremonies of Israel: Remembrance Day and Independence Day." In *Models and Mirrors: Towards an Anthropology of Public Events*, ed. Handelman, 191–233. Cambridge: Cambridge University Press.

Handlin, Oscar. 1961. "Historical Perspectives on the American Ethnic Group." *Daedalus* 90:220–32.

Hartman, Geoffrey. 1992. "The Book of the Destruction." In *Probing the Limits of Representation*, ed. Saul Friedlander, 318–34. Cambridge, Mass.: Harvard University Press.

——. 1996. *The Longest Shadow: In the Aftermath of the Holocaust*. Bloomington: Indiana University Press.

Hartshorne, Edward Y., Jr. 1937. *The German Universities and National Socialism*. London: Allen and Unwin.

Hass, Aaron. 1996. *The Aftermath: Living with the Holocaust*. Cambridge: Cambridge University Press.

Hausmann, Ernst. 1996. "A Family during Troubled Times: The Hausmanns and the Weingartners, 1934–1944." Unpublished Manuscript. New York: Leo Baeck Institute.

Hawkins, S. A., and R. Hastie. 1990. "Hindsight: Biased Judgments of Past Events after the Outcomes Are Known." *Psychological Bulletin* 107:311–27.

Heberle, Rudolf. [1945] 1970. *From Democracy to Nazism: A Regional Case Study on Political Parties in Germany.* New York: H. Fertig.

Hegi, Ursula. 1997. *Tearing the Silence: On Being German in America.* New York: Simon and Schuster.

Heilbut, Anthony. 1983. *Exiled in Paradise: German Refugee Artists and Intellectuals in America, from the 1930s and Present.* New York: Viking.

Helmreich, William B. 1992. *Against All Odds: Holocaust Survivors and the Successful Lives They Made in America.* New York: Simon and Schuster.

Hendricks, Burton J. 1923. *The Jews in America.* New York: Doubleday, Page.

Herman, Pini. 1988. "Jewish-Israeli Migration to the United States since 1948." Paper presented at the annual meeting of the Association of Israel Studies, June 7, New York.

——. 1998. *Los Angeles Population Survey '97.* Los Angeles: Jewish Federation of Los Angeles.

——. 2000. "The Jews of the Jews: Characteristics of Los Angeles Households of Israelis by Birth and Israelis Not by Birth." Paper submitted to the Division E Contemporary Jewish Society the Thirteenth World Congress of Jewish Studies, December.

Herman, Simon N. 1989. *Jewish Identity: A Social Psychological Perspective.* New Brunswick, N.J.: Transaction.

Hermand, Jost, and Wigand Lange. 1999. *"Wollt ihr Thomas Mann wiederhaben?" Deutschland und die Emigranten.* Hamburg: Europäische Verlagsanstalt.

Hertzberg, Arthur. 1989. *The Jews in America: Four Centuries of Uneasy Encounter; A History.* New York: Simon and Schuster.

——. 1998. *Jews: The Essence and Character of a People.* San Francisco: Harper.

Herzog, Hanna. 2000. "Sociology and Identity: Trends in the Development of Sociology in Israel." *Soziologie: Forum der Deutschen Gesellshaft fur Soziologie* 2:5–17.

Hesford, Wendy, and Wendy Kozol, eds. 2001. *Haunting Violations: Feminist Criticism and the Crisis of the "Real."* Urbana: University of Illinois Press.

"HIAS Facts and Figures: Migration Figures, 1945–1995." 1997. Hebrew Immigrant Aid Society, www.hias.org.fact_fig/annual.htm (accessed March 15, 2000).

Hilberg, Raul. 1961. *The Destruction of European Jews.* Chicago: Quadrangle.

Hillgruber, Andreas. 1986. *Zweierlei Untergang: Die Zerschlagung des deutschen Reiches und das Ende des europäischen Judentums.* Berlin: Siedler.

Hiltzik, Michael A. 2000. "Israel's High Tech Shifts into High Gear." *Los Angeles Times,* August 13.

Hirsch, Eric L. 1990. "Sacrifice for the Cause: The Impact of Group Processes on Recruitment and Commitment in Protest Movements." *American Sociological Review* 55:243–55.

Hirsch, Marianne. 1996. "Past Lives: Postmemories in Exile." *Poetics Today* 17:659–86.

——. 1997. *Family Frames: Photography, Narrative, and Postmemory.* Cambridge, Mass.: Harvard University Press.

Hirsch, Marianne, and Leo Spitzer. 1993. "Gendered Translations: Claude Lanzmann's

Shoah." In *Gendering War Talk*, ed. Miriam Cooke and Angela Woollacott, 3–19. Princeton: Princeton University Press.

Hirsch, Marianne, and Valerie Smith. 2002. "Feminism and Cultural Memory: An Introduction." *Signs* 28:1–19.

Hobsbawm, Eric, and Terence Ranger, eds. 1983. *The Invention of Tradition*. New York: Cambridge University Press.

Hoffrage, Ulrich, and Ralph Hertwig. 1999. "Hindsight Bias: A Price Worth Paying for Fast and Frugal Memory." In *Simple Heuristics That Make Us Smart*, by Gerd Gigerenzer, Peter M. Todd, and ABC Research Group, 191–208. New York: Oxford University Press.

Hofstätter, Peter R. 1957. "Zum 'Gruppenexperiment' von Friedrich Pollock: Eine kritische Würdigung." *Kölner Zeitschrift für Soziologie und Sozialpsychologie* 9:97–104.

Hogman, Flora. 1988. "The Experience of Catholicism for Jewish Children during World War II." *Psychoanalytic Review* 75:511–32.

Hollinger, David. 2001. "Not Universalists, Not Pluralists: The New Cosmopolitans Find Their Own Way." *Constellations* 8:236–48.

Hondagneu-Sotelo, Pierrette. 1994. *Gendered Transitions: Mexican Experiences of Immigration*. Berkeley: University of California Press.

Horowitz, Bethamie. 1993. *The 1991 New York Jewish Population Study*. New York: United Jewish Appeal–Federation.

Horowitz, Irving Louis. 1982. *Taking Lives: Genocide and State Power*. 3d ed. New Brunswick, N.J.: Transaction.

———. 1984. "Genocide and the Reconstruction of Social Theory: Observations on the Exclusivity of Collective Death." *Armenian Review* 37:1–21.

Howe, Irving. 1976. *World of Our Fathers*. New York: Harcourt Brace Jovanovich.

Hughes, Everett C. 1962. "Good People and Dirty Work." *Social Problems* 10:3–10.

Hungerford, Amy. 1999. "Surviving Rego Park: Holocaust Theory from Art Spiegelman to Berel Lang." In *The Americanization of the Holocaust*, ed. Hilene Flanzbaum, 102–24. Baltimore: Johns Hopkins University Press.

Hutner, Yitzchok. 1977. "'Holocaust': A Study of the Term, and the Epoch It Is Meant to Describe." Trans. Chaim Feuerman and Yaakov Feitman. *Jewish Observer*, October.

Hyman, Paula E. 1998. *The Jews of Modern France*. Berkeley: University of California Press.

Irwin, Michael D., Charles M. Tolbert, and Thomas Lyson. 1999. "There's No Place Like Home: Nonmigration and Civic Engagement." *Environment and Planning* 31:2223–38.

Isaacman, Clara. 1984. *Clara's Story*. Philadelphia: Jewish Publication Society of America.

Jackson, Livia E. Bitton. 1980. *Elli: Coming of Age in the Holocaust*. New York: Times Books.

Jacobs, Janet Liebman. 2004. "Women, Genocide, and Memory: The Ethics of Feminist Ethnography in Holocaust Research." *Gender and Society* 18:233–38.

Jacobson, Matthew Frye. 1998. *Whiteness of a Different Color: European Immigrants and the Alchemy of Race*. Cambridge, Mass.: Harvard University Press.

Janowitz, Morris. 1946. "German Reactions to Nazi Atrocities." *American Journal of Sociology* 52:141–46.

Jasper, James M., and Dorothy Nelkin. 1992. *The Animal Rights Crusade: The Growth of a Moral Protest*. New York: Free Press.

Jasper, James M., and Jane D. Poulsen. 1995. "Recruiting Strangers and Friends: Moral Shocks and Social Networks in Animal Rights and Anti-nuclear Protests." *Social Problems* 42:493–512.

Jay, Martin. 1984. *Adorno*. Cambridge, Mass.: Harvard University Press.

——. 1990. *Permanent Exiles: Essays on the Intellectual Migration from Germany to America*. New York: Columbia University Press.

Jenkins, Richard. 1996. *Social Identity*. New York: Routledge.

——. 1997. *Rethinking Ethnicity: Arguments and Explorations*. Thousand Oaks, CA: Sage.

Joas, Hans. 1998. "Bauman in Germany: Modern Violence and the Problems of German Self-Understanding." *Theory, Culture and Society* 15:47–55.

Johnson, Eric A. 2000. *Nazi Terror: The Gestapo, Jews and Ordinary Germans*. New York: Basic Books.

Joselit, Jenna Weissman. 1990. *New York's Jewish Jews: The Orthodox Community in the Interwar Years*. Bloomington: Indiana University Press.

Joseph, Samuel. 1914. *Jewish Immigration to the United States from 1881 to 1910*. New York: Arno.

Jung, Carl G. 1989. *The Psychology of Nazism: Essays on Contemporary Events*. Trans. R. F. C. Hull. Princeton: Princeton University Press.

Juteau, Danielle. 1999. "From Nation-Church to Nation-State: Evolving Sex-Gender Relations in Quebec." In *Between Woman and Nation: Nationalisms, Transnational Feminisms, and the State*, ed. Caren Kaplan, Norma Alarcón, and Minoo Moallem, 142–61. Durham, N.C.: Duke University Press.

Kahn, Liselotte. 1970. "Memoirs." Unpublished Memoir. New York: Leo Baeck Institute.

Kaplan, Chaim A. 1999. *Scroll of Agony: The Warsaw Diary of Chaim A. Kaplan*. Trans. A. I. Katsh. Bloomington: Indiana University Press.

Kaplan, Harold. 2001. "The Americanization of the Holocaust." In *Remembering for the Future: The Holocaust in an Age of Genocide*, ed. J. K. Roth and E. Maxwell, 309–21. New York: Palgrave.

Kaplan, Marion. 1998. *Between Dignity and Despair: Jewish Life in Nazi Germany*. New York: Oxford University Press.

Karpf, Anne. 1996. *The War After: Living with the Holocaust*. London: Heinemann.

Kasinitz, Philip. 1992. *Caribbean New York: Black Immigrants and the Politics of Race*. Ithaca: Cornell University Press.

Kasinitz, Philip, et al. 2002. "Transnationalism and the Children of Immigrants in Contemporary New York." In *The Changing Face of Home: The Transnational Lives of the Second Generation*, ed. Peggy Levitt and Mary C. Waters, 96–122. New York: Russell Sage Foundation.

Kasinitz, Philip, Aviva Zeltzer-Zubida, and Zoya Simakhoskaya. N.d. "The Next Generation: Russian Jewish Young Adults in Contemporary New York." Russell Sage Foundation working paper.

Kästner, Erich. 1959. *Gesammelte Schriften.* Vol. 5, *Vermischte Beiträge.* Zurich: Atrium.

———. 1998. *Werke. Splitter und Balkan: Publizistik.* Munich: Carl Hanser.

Katznelson, Ira. 2003. *Desolation and Enlightenment: Political Knowledge after Total War, Totalitarianism, and the Holocaust.* New York: Columbia University Press.

Kaufman, Debra. 1996. "Introduction: Gender, Scholarship and the Holocaust." *Contemporary Jewry* 17:3–18.

———. 1998. "Gender and Jewish Identity among Twenty-Somethings in the United States." In *Religion in a Changing World: Comparative Studies in Sociology,* ed. Madeleine Cousineau, 49–56. Westport, Conn.: Praeger.

———. 1999. "Embedded Categories: Identity among Jewish Young Adults in the U.S." *Race, Gender and Class* 6:76–87.

———. 2003. "Post-Holocaust Memory: Some Gendered Reflections." In *Replacing Ourselves: Gender, Place, Memory in the Modern Jewish Experience,* ed. J. T. Baumel and T. Cohen, 187–96. London: Frank Cass.

———. 2005. "The Place of Judaism in American Jewish Identity." In *Cambridge Companion to American Judaism,* ed. Dana Evan Kaplan, 171–88. Cambridge: Cambridge University Press.

Kelley, Ron, and Jonathan Friedlander, eds. 1993. *Irangeles: Iranians in Los Angeles.* Berkeley: University of California Press.

Kelner, Shaul J. 2002. "Almost Pilgrims: Authenticity, Identity and the Extra-ordinary on a Jewish Tour of Israel." PhD diss., City University of New York.

Kemple, Thomas M., ed. 1975. *Karl Marx: Texts on Method.* Oxford: Blackwell.

Kenny, Michael. 1999. "A Place for Memory: The Interface between Individual and Collective History." *Comparative Studies in Society and History* 41:420–37.

Kermish, Joseph. 1971. "The Place of the Ghetto Revolts in the Struggle against the Occupier." In *Jewish Resistance during the Holocaust: Proceedings of the Conference on Manifestations of Jewish Resistance,* ed. Meir Grubsztein, 306–23. Jerusalem: Yad Vashem.

———, ed. 1986. *To Live with Honor and Die with Honor!—: Selected Documents from the Warsaw Ghetto Underground Archives "O.S." (Oneg Shabbath).* Trans. M. Z. Prives et al. Jerusalem: Yad Vashem.

Kilminster, Richard, and Ian Varcoe. 1998. "Three Appreciations of Zygmunt Bauman." *Theory, Culture and Society* 15:23–28.

Kim, Claire Jean. 2000–2001. "Playing the Racial Trump Card: Asian Americans in Contemporary U.S. Politics." *Amerasia Journal* 26:35–65.

Kimhi, Shaol. 1990. "Perceived Change of Self-Concept, Values, Well-Being and Intention to Return among Kibbutz People Who Migrated from Israel to America." PhD diss., Pacific Graduate School of Psychology, Palo Alto, Calif.

Kirkpatrick, Clifford. 1946. "Sociological Principles and Occupied Germany." *American Sociological Review* 11:67–78.

———. 1948. "Reactions of Educated Germans to Defeat." *American Journal of Sociology* 54:36–47.

Kirschenblatt-Gimblett, Barbara. 1998. *Destination Culture: Tourism, Museums, and Heritage*. Berkeley: University of California Press.

———. 2001. "Imagining Europe." In *Divergent Jewish Cultures: Israel and America*, ed. D. D. Moore and S. I. Troen, 155–91. New Haven: Yale University Press.

Klajman, Jack, with Ed Klajman. 2000. *Out of the Ghetto*. London: Vallentine Mitchell.

Kleinman, David P. 1991–92. "Jewish Identity, Continuity, and Outreach: Some Theoretical and Personal Reflections." *Journal of Jewish Communal Service* 68:140–47.

Klemperer, Victor. 1998. *I Will Bear Witness Volume 1: A Diary of the Nazi Years, 1933–1941*. Trans. M. Chalmers. New York: Random House.

———. 2000. *I Will Bear Witness: A Diary of the Nazi Years, 1941–1945*. Trans. M. Chalmers. New York: Random House.

Kless, Shlomo. 1988. "The Rescue of Jewish Children in Belgium." *Holocaust and Genocide Studies* 3:275–87.

Kleßmann, Christoph. 1982. *Die doppelte Staatsgründung: Deutsche Geschichte 1945–1955*. Göttingen: Vandenhoeck and Ruprecht.

Koebner, Thomas, Gert Sautermeister, and Sigrid Schneider, eds. 1987. *Deutschland nach Hitler: Zukunftspläne im Exil und aus der Besatzungszeit, 1939–1949*. Opladen, Germany: Westdeutscher.

Kogon, Eugen. 1946. "Gericht und Gewissen." *Frankfurter Hefte* 1:25–37.

Kohler, Lotte, and Hans Saner, eds. 1992. *Hannah Arendt / Karl Jaspers Correspondence, 1926–1969*. Trans. Robert Kimber and Rita Kimber. New York: Harcourt Brace Jovanovich.

Koonz, Claudia. 1987. *Mothers in the Fatherland: Women, the Family and Nazi Politics*. New York: St. Martin's.

Korczak, Janusz. 1978. *Ghetto Diary*. New York: Holocaust Library.

Kosmin, Barry. 1990. *The Class of 1979: The "Acculturation" of Jewish Immigrants from the Soviet Union*. New York: Council of Jewish Federations.

Krall, Hanna. 1986. *Shielding the Flame: An Intimate Conversation with Dr. Mark Edelman, the Last Surviving Leader of the Warsaw Ghetto Uprising*. New York: Henry Holt.

Kranzler, David. 1976. *Japanese, Nazis and Jews: The Jewish Refugee Community of Shanghai, 1938–1945*. New York: Yeshiva University Press.

———. 1987. *Thy Brother's Blood: The Orthodox Jewish Response during the Holocaust*. New York: Mesorah.

Krauss, Celine. 1993. "Women and Toxic Waste Protests: Race, Class, and Gender as Resources of Resistance." *Qualitative Sociology* 16:247–62.

Krystal, Henry. 1968. "Patterns of Psychological Damage." In *Massive Psychic Trauma*, ed. Krystal, 149–75. New York: International Universities Press.

Kugelmass, Jack. 1993. "The Rites of the Tribe: The Meaning of Poland for American Jewish Tourists." In *Going Home: Yivo Annual 21*, ed. Kugelmass, 395–453. Evanston, Ill.: Northwestern University Press.

———. 1994. "Why We Go to Poland: Holocaust Tourism as Secular Ritual." In *The Art of Memory: Holocaust Memorials in History*, ed. J. Young, 174–83. New York: Prestel.

Kuper, Leo. 1981. *Genocide: Its Political Use in the Twentieth Century*. New Haven: Yale University Press.

Kurzke, Hermann. 2002. *Thomas Mann: Life as a Work of Art; A Biography*. Princeton: Princeton University Press.

Kurzman, Dan. 1993. *The Bravest Battle: The Twenty-eight Days of the Warsaw Ghetto Uprising*. New York: Da Capo.

LaCapra, Dominick. 1998. *History and Memory after Auschwitz*. Ithaca: Cornell University Press.

Laguerre, Michel S. 1998. *Diasporic Citizenship: Haitian Americans in Transnational America*. New York: St. Martin's.

Lamont, Michèle, and Marcel Fournier, eds. 1992. *Cultivating Differences: Symbolic Boundaries and the Making of Inequality*. Chicago: University of Chicago Press.

Lamont, Michèle, and Virag Molnar. 2002. "The Study of Boundaries in the Social Sciences." *Annual Review of Sociology* 28:167–95.

Langer, Lawrence. 1991. *Holocaust Testimonies: The Ruins of Memory*. New Haven: Yale University Press.

——. 1995. *Admitting the Holocaust: Collected Essays*. New York: Oxford University Press.

Latina Feminist Group. 2001. *Telling to Live: Latina Feminist Testimonios*. Durham, N.C.: Duke University Press.

Le Rider, Jacques. 1993. *Modernity and Crises of Identity: Culture and Society in Fin-de-Siècle Vienna*. Trans. Rosemary Morris. New York: Continuum.

Lentin, Ronit. 2000. *Israel and the Daughters of the Shoah: Reoccupying the Territories of Silence*. New York: Berghahn.

——. 2004a. "Introduction: Postmemory, Unsayability and the Return of the Auschwitz Code." In *Re-presenting the Shoah for the Twenty-first Century*, ed. Lentin, 1–24. New York: Berghahn.

——. 2004b. "Memory, Forgetting and Mourning Work: Deviant Narratives of Silence in the Gendered Relations between Israeli Zionism and the Shoah." In *Re-presenting the Shoah for the Twenty-first Century*, ed. Lentin, 59–76. New York: Berghahn.

——, ed. 2004. *Re-presenting the Shoah for the Twenty-first Century*. New York: Berghahn.

Lesser, Jeffrey. 1999. *Negotiating National Identity: Immigrants, Minorities, and the Struggle for Ethnicity in Brazil*. Durham, N.C.: Duke University Press.

Levi, Primo. [1958] 1996. *Survival in Auschwitz*. Trans. S. Woolf. New York: Touchstone.

Levine, Etan. 1983. "Introduction: The Jews in Time and Space." In *Diaspora: Exile and the Jewish Condition*, ed. Levine, 1–11. New York: Jason Aronson.

Levine, Rhonda F. 2001. *Class, Networks, and Identity: Replanting Jewish Lives from Nazi Germany to Rural New York*. Lanham, Md.: Rowman and Littlefield.

Levitt, Peggy. 2001. *The Transnational Villagers*. Berkeley: University of California Press.

Levitz, Irving N. 1995. "Jewish Identity, Assimilation and Intermarriage." In *Crisis and Continuity: The Jewish Family in the Twenty-first Century*, ed. N. Linzer, Levitz, and D. J. Schnall, 73–94. Hoboken, N.J.: KTAV.

Levy, Andre. 1997. "To Morocco and Back: Tourism and Pilgrimage among Moroccan-Born Israelis." In *Grasping Land: Space and Place in Contemporary Israeli Discourse and Experience*, ed. Eyal Ben-Ari and Yoram Bilu, 25–46. Albany: State University of New York Press.

Levy, Daniel. 1999. "The Future and the Past: Historiographical Disputes and Competing Memories in Germany and Israel." *History and Theory* 38:51–66.

Levy, Daniel, and Natan Sznaider. 2001. *Erinnerung im globalen Zeitalter: Der Holocaust*. Frankfurt: Suhrkamp.

———. 2002. "Memory Unbound: The Holocaust and the Formation of Cosmopolitan Memory." *European Journal of Social Theory* 5:87–106.

———. 2004. "The Institutionalization of Cosmopolitan Morality: The Holocaust and Human Rights." *Journal of Human Rights* 3:143–57.

———. 2005. *The Holocaust and Memory in the Global Age*. Trans. Assenka Oksiloff. Philadelphia: Temple University Press.

Lewin, Abraham, and Antony Polonsky. 1988. *A Cup of Tears: A Diary of the Warsaw Ghetto*. Oxford: Blackwell.

Li, Peter. 1977. "Occupational Attainment and Kinship Assistance among Chinese Immigrants in Chicago." *Sociological Quarterly* 18:478–89.

Lifton, Robert Jay. 1993. *The Protean Self*. New York: Basic Books.

Light, Ivan, et al. 1994. "Beyond the Ethnic Enclave Economy." *Social Problems* 41:65–80.

Light, Ivan, and Steven J. Gold. 2000. *Ethnic Economies*. San Diego: Academic.

Linden, Robin Ruth. 1993. *Making Stories, Making Selves: Feminist Reflections on the Holocaust*. Columbus: Ohio State University Press.

Linenthal, Edward. 1995. *Preserving Memory: The Struggle to Create America's Holocaust Museum*. New York: Viking.

Linn, Ruth, and Nurit Barkan-Ascher. 1996. "Permanent Impermanence: Israeli Expatriates in Non-event Transition." *Jewish Journal of Sociology* 38:5–16.

Lipkis, Galit. 1991. "Business Envoys Whet U.S. Appetites." *Jerusalem Post*, November 26.

Lipset, Seymour Martin. 1960. *Political Man: The Social Bases of Politics*. New York: Doubleday.

———. 1990. "A Unique People in an Exceptional Country." In *American Pluralism and Jewish Community*, ed. Lipset, 3–29. New Brunswick, N.J.: Transaction.

Lixl-Purcell, Andreas. 1994. "Memoirs as History." In *Leo Baeck Institute Year Book*, vol. 39, 227–38. London: Secker and Warburg.

London, Perry, and Robert Chazan. 1990. *Psychology and Jewish Identity Education*. New York: American Jewish Committee.

Lowenstein, Sharon R. 1986. *Token Refuge: The Story of the Jewish Refugee Shelter at Oswego, 1944–1946*. Bloomington: Indiana University Press.

Lowenstein, Steven M. 1989. *Frankfurt on the Hudson: The German-Jewish Community of Washington Heights, 1933–1983*. Detroit: Wayne State University Press.

Lubetkin, Zivia. 1981. *In the Days of Destruction and Revolt*. Trans. Ishai Tubkin. Tel Aviv: Beit Lohamei Haghetaot.

Luchterhand, E. 1980. "Social Behavior of Concentration Camp Prisoners: Continuities and Discontinuities with Pre- and Postcamp Life." In *Survivors, Victims, and Perpetrators: Essays on the Nazi Holocaust*, ed. Joel E. Dimsdale, 259–82. Washington: Hemisphere Publishing Corporation.

Lyotard, Jean F. 1984. *The Postmodern Condition: A Report on Knowledge.* Trans. Geoff Bennington and Brian Massumi. Minneapolis: University of Minnesota Press.

Maerten, Fabrice, Franz Selleslagh, and Mark Van den Wijngaert, eds. 1999. *Entre la peste et le choléra: Vie et attitude des catholiques belges sous l'occupation.* Gerpinnes, Belgium: Éditions Quorum.

Malkki, Liisa H. 1995a. *Purity and Exile: Violence, Memory, and National Cosmology among Hutu Refugees in Tanzania.* Chicago: University of Chicago Press.

——. 1995b. "Refugees and Exile: From 'Refugee Studies' to the National Order of Things." *American Review of Anthropology* 24:495–523.

Mann, Klaus, and Erika Mann. 1939. *Escape to Life.* Boston: Houghton Mifflin.

Mann, Thomas. 1963. *Thomas Mann's Addresses Delivered at the Library of Congress, 1942–1949.* Washington, D.C.: Library of Congress.

——. [1947] 1997. *Doctor Faustus: The Life of the German Composer Adrian Leverkühn as Told by a Friend.* Trans. John E. Woods. New York: Random House.

——. 1999. *Fragile Republik: Thomas Mann und Nachkriegsdeutschland.* Ed. S. Stachorski. Frankfurt: Fischer.

Mannheim, Karl. 1952. "The Problem of Generations." In *Essays on the Sociology of Knowledge*, ed. Paul Kecskemeti, 276–322. New York: Oxford University Press.

——. 1936. *Ideology and Utopia: An Introduction to the Sociology of Knowledge.* Trans. L. Wirth and E. A. Shils. New York: Harcourt Brace World.

Margalit, Gilad. 2002. *Germany and Its Gypsies: A Post-Auschwitz Ordeal.* Madison: University of Wisconsin Press.

Markle, Gerald E. 1995. *Meditations of a Holocaust Traveler.* Albany: State University of New York Press.

Markowitz, Fran. 1988. "Jewish in the USSR, Russian in the USA." In *Persistence and Flexibility: Anthropological Perspectives on the American Jewish Experience*, ed. W. P. Zenner, 79–95. Albany: State University of New York Press.

——. 1993. *A Community in Spite of Itself: Soviet Jewish Emigrés in New York.* Washington: Smithsonian Institution Press.

Marks, Jane. 1993. *The Hidden Children: The Secret Survivors of the Holocaust.* New York: Fawcett Columbine.

Marrus, Michael R. 1987. *The Holocaust in History.* New York: Penguin.

——, ed. 1989. *The Nazi Holocaust: Historical Articles on the Destruction of European Jews.* Vol. 7, *Jewish Resistance to the Holocaust.* Westport, Conn.: Meckler.

Marullo, Sam. 1991. "Gender Differences in Peace Movement Participation." *Research in Social Movements, Conflict, and Change* 13:135–52.

Marx, Emanuel. 1998. Preface to *The Great Immigration: Russian Jews in Israel*, ed. D. Siegel, ix–xii. New York: Berghahn.

Marx, Karl. 1993. *Grundrisse: Foundations of the Critique of Political Economy (Rough Draft)*. Trans. M. Nicolaus. London: Penguin.

Marx, Karl and Friedrich Engels. [1848] 1964. *The Communist Manifesto*. Trans. Paul M. Sweezy. New York: Monthly Review Press.

Mastuda, Mari. 1993. "We Will Not Be Used." *UCLA Asian American Pacific Islands Law Journal* 1:79–84.

Mayer, Egon. 2001. "Secularism among America's Jews: Insights from the American Jewish Identity Survey." Paper presented at the annual meeting of the Association for Jewish Studies, Washington, D.C.

McAdam, Doug. 1982. *Political Process and the Development of Black Insurgency*. Chicago: University of Chicago Press.

———. 1988. *Freedom Summer*. New York: Oxford University Press.

McAdam, Doug, John D. McCarthy, and Mayer N. Zald, eds. 1996. *Comparative Perspectives on Social Movements*. Cambridge: Cambridge University Press.

Meed, Vladka. 1979. *On Both Sides of the Wall: Memoirs from the Warsaw Ghetto*. New York: Holocaust Library.

Melson, Robert. 2000. *False Papers: Deception and Survival in the Holocaust*. Urbana: University of Illinois Press.

Melucci, Alberto. 1989. *Nomads of the Present: Social Movements and Individual Needs in Contemporary Society*. Ed. John Keane and Paul Mier. Philadelphia: Temple University Press.

———. 1995. "The Process of Collective Identity." In *Social Movements and Culture*, ed. H. Johnston and B. Klandermans, 41–63. Minneapolis: University of Minnesota Press.

———. 1996. *Challenging Codes: Collective Action in the Information Age*. Cambridge: Cambridge University Press.

Menchú, Rigoberta. 1984. *I, Rigoberta Menchú: An Indian Woman in Guatemala*. London: Verso.

Menéndez, Ana. 2001. *In Cuba I Was a German Shepherd*. New York: Grove.

Meyer, Jacob C. 1953. "The DP Story: The Final Report of the United States Displaced Persons Commission." *Mississippi Valley Historical Review* 39:793–94.

Meyer, Michael A. 1990. *Jewish Identity in the Modern World*. Seattle: University of Washington Press.

Michman, Dan, ed. 1998. *Belgium and the Holocaust: Jews, Belgians, Germans*. Jerusalem: Yad Vashem.

Mills, C. Wright. 1959. *The Sociological Imagination*. New York: Oxford University Press.

Mintz, Jerome. 1998. *Hasidic People: A Place in the New World*. Cambridge, Mass.: Harvard University Press.

Mitchell, Timothy, ed. 2000. *Questions of Modernity*. Minneapolis: University of Minnesota Press.

Mittelberg, David, and Mary C. Waters. 1992. "The Process of Ethnogenesis among Haitian and Israeli Immigrants in the United States." *Ethnic and Racial Studies* 15:412–35.

Moaz, Shlomo and Avi Temkin. 1989. "Olim and Yordim." *Jerusalem Post*, May 9.

Model, Suzanne. 1988. "The Economic Progress of European and East Asian Americans." *Annual Review of Sociology* 14:363–80.

Modigliani, Andre, and François Rochat. 1995. "The Role of Interaction Sequences and the Timing of Resistance in Shaping Obedience and Defiance to Authority." *Journal of Social Issues* 51:107–23.

Moeller, Robert G. 2001. *War Stories: The Search for a Usable Past in the Federal Republic of Germany*. Berkeley: University of California Press.

Mohanty, Chandra Talpade. 1991. "Under Western Eyes." In *Third World Women and the Politics of Feminism*, ed. Mohanty, Ann Russo, and Lourdes Torres, 51–80. Bloomington: Indiana University Press.

Moore, Barrington, Jr. 1978. *Injustice: The Social Bases of Obedience and Revolt*. White Plains, N.Y.: M. E. Sharpe.

Morris, Aldon D. 1984. *The Origins of the Civil Rights Movements*. New York: Free Press.

Morse, Arthur D. 1968. *While Six Million Died: A Chronicle of American Apathy*. New York: Random House.

Mullins, Nicholas C., and Carolyn J. Mullins. 1973. *Theories and Theory Groups in Contemporary American Sociology*. New York: Harper and Row.

Naficy, Hamid. 1999. "Framing Exile: From Homeland to Homepage." In *Home, Exile, Homeland: Film, Media, and the Politics of Place*, ed. Naficy, 1–13. London: Routledge.

Nash, June. 1979. *We Eat the Mines and the Mines Eat Us: Dependency and Exploitation in Bolivian Tin Mines*. New York: Columbia University Press.

Neaman, Elliot Yale. 1999. *A Dubious Past: Ernst Jünger and the Politics of Literature after Nazism*. Berkeley: University of California Press.

Neuhouser, Kevin. 1998. "'If I had Abandoned My Children': Community Mobilization and Commitment to the Identity of Mother in Northeast Brazil." *Social Forces* 77:331–58.

Neumann, Franz L. [1944] 1963. *Behemoth: The Structure and Practice of National Socialism, 1933–1944*. 2d ed. New York: Octagon.

Neurath, Paul Martin. 2005. *The Society of Terror: Inside the Dachau and Buchenwald Concentration Camps*. Ed. Christian Fleck and Nico Stehr. Boulder, Colo.: Paradigm.

Niederland, William C. 1964. "Psychiatric Disorders among Persecution Victims: A Contribution to the Understanding of Concentration Camp Pathology and Its After-Effects." *Journal of Nervous and Mental Diseases* 139:458–74.

Nonini, Donald, and Aihwa Ong. 1997. "Introduction: Chinese Transnationalism as an Alternative Modernity." In *Ungrounded Empires: The Cultural Politics of Modern Chinese Transnationalism*, ed. Ong and Nonini, 3–33. New York: Routledge.

Nora, Pierre. 1989. "Between Memory and History: Les Lieux de Mémoire." *Representations* 26:7–24.

Novick, Peter. 1999. *The Holocaust in American Life*. Boston: Houghton Mifflin.

"Number of Arrivals by Origin." 2001. Hebrew Immigrant Aid Society, www.hias.org/pages/factsfigs.htm (accessed January 12, 2002).

Oberschall, Anthony. 2000. "Preventing Genocide." *Contemporary Sociology* 29:1–12.

Ochs, Elinor, and Lisa Capps. 1996. "Narrating the Self." *Annual Review of Anthropology* 25:19–43.

Ofer, Dalia, and Lenore J. Weitzman, eds. 1998. *Women in the Holocaust*. New Haven: Yale University Press.

Okihiro, Gary Y. 1994. *Margins and Mainstreams: Asians in American History and Culture.* Seattle: University of Washington Press.

Okin, Susan. 2000. "Feminism, Women's Human Rights, and Cultural Differences." In *Decentering the Center: Philosophy for a Multicultural, Postcolonial and Feminist World*, ed. U. Narayan and S. Harding, 26–46. Bloomington: Indiana University Press.

Olick, Jeffrey K. 1999a. "Collective Memory: The Two Cultures." *Sociological Theory* 17:333–48.

——. 1999b. "Genre Memories and Memory Genres: A Dialogical Analysis of May 8, 1945 Commemorations in the Federal Republic of Germany." *American Sociological Review* 64:381–402.

——. 2005. *In the House of the Hangman: The Agonies of German Defeat, 1943–49.* Chicago: University of Chicago Press.

Olick, Jeffrey K., and Daniel Levy. 1997. "Collective Memory and Cultural Constraint: Holocaust Myth and Rationality in German Politics." *American Sociological Review* 62:921–36.

Olick, Jeffrey K., and Joyce Robbins. 1998. "Social Memory Studies: From 'Collective Memory' to the Historical Sociology of Mnemonic Practices." *Annual Review of Sociology* 24:105–40.

Ong, Aihwa. 1999. *Flexible Citizenship: The Cultural Logics of Transnationality.* Durham, N.C.: Duke University Press.

Oppenheimer, Martin. 1997a. "Footnote to the Cold War: The Harvard Russian Research Center." *Monthly Review* 48:7–17.

——. 1997b. "Social Scientists and War Criminals." *New Politics* 6:77–83.

Orbuch, Terry. 1997. "People's Accounts Count: The Sociology of Accounts." *Annual Review of Sociology* 23:455–78.

Orleck, Annelise. 1987. "The Soviet Jews: Life in Brighton Beach, Brooklyn." In *New Immigrants in New York*, ed. N. Foner, 273–304. New York: Columbia University Press.

——. 1999. *The Soviet Jewish Americans.* Westport, Conn.: Greenwood.

Ostow, Robin. 1989. *Jews in Contemporary East Germany: The Children of Moses in the Land of Marx.* New York: St. Martin's.

——. 1990. "The Shaping of Jewish Identity in the German Democratic Republic, 1949–1989." *Critical Sociology* 17:47–59.

——. 1996. "Imperialist Agents, Anti-fascist Monuments, Eastern Refugees, Property Claims: Jews as Incorporations of East German Social Trauma, 1945–1994." In *Jews, Germans, Memory: Reconstructions of Jewish Life in Germany*, ed. Y. M. Bodemann, 227–41. Ann Arbor: University of Michigan Press.

Ottenheimer, Fritz. 1995. "Hineini: Here I am!" Unpublished Memoir. New York: Leo Baeck Institute.

Paetel, Karl O., ed. 1946. *Deutsche innere Emigration: Anti-nationalsozialistische Zeugnisse aus Deutschland.* New York: Friedrich Krause.

Paldiel, Mordecai. 2000. *Saving the Jews: Amazing Stories of Men and Women Who Defied the "Final Solution."* Rockville, Md.: Schreiber.

Panish, Paul. 1981. *Exit Visa: The Emigration of the Soviet Jews.* New York: McCann, Coward, and Geoghegan.

Parsons, Talcott. [1942] 1993a. "Democracy and Social Structure in Pre-Nazi Germany." In *Talcott Parsons on National Socialism,* ed. Uta Gerhardt, 225–42. New York: Aldine de Gruyter.

———. [1942] 1993b. "Max Weber and the Contemporary Political Crisis." In *Talcott Parsons on National Socialism,* ed. Uta Gerhardt, 159–87. New York: Aldine de Gruyter.

———. [1942] 1993c. "Propaganda and Social Control." In *Talcott Parsons on National Socialism,* ed. Uta Gerhardt, 243–74. New York: Aldine de Gruyter.

———. [1942] 1993d. "Some Sociological Aspects of the Fascist Movements." In *Talcott Parsons on National Socialism,* ed. Uta Gerhardt, 203–18. New York: Aldine de Gruyter.

Patraka, Vivian. 1997. "Situating History and Difference: The Performance of the Term Holocaust in Public Discourse." In *Jews and Other Differences: The New Jewish Cultural Studies,* ed. J. Boyarin and D. Boyarin, 54–78. Minneapolis: University of Minnesota Press.

Pawełczyńska, Anna. [1973] 1979. *Values and Violence in Auschwitz: A Sociological Analysis.* Trans. C. S. Leach. Berkeley: University of California Press.

Penkower, Monty. 2000. "The Holocaust in American Life." *American Jewish History* 88:127–32.

Perlman, Joel, and Roger Waldinger. 1997. "Second Generation Decline? Children of Immigrants, Past and Present: A Reconsideration." *International Migration Review* 31:893–923.

Pessar, Patricia. 1994. "Engendering Migration Studies: The Case of New Immigrants in the United States." *American Behavioral Scientist* 42(4):577–600.

Peters-Rothschild, Lotte. 1986. "Untitled." Unpublished Memoir. New York: Leo Baeck Institute.

Phillips, Bruce A. 1991. "Sociological Analysis of Jewish Identity." In *Jewish Identity in America,* ed. D. Gordis and Y. Ben-Horin, 3–25. Los Angeles: University of Judaism.

Plaut, W. Gunther. 1996. "Jewish Ethnics and International Migration." *International Migration Review* 30:18–26.

Plekhanov, George. 1897. *The Materialist Conception of History.* Trans. A. Blunden. New York: International Publishers.

Plummer, Ken. 1995. *Telling Sexual Stories: Power, Change, and Social Worlds.* New York: Routledge.

Pollins, Harold. 1984. "The Development of Jewish Business in the United Kingdom." In *Ethnic Communities in Business: Strategies for Economic Survival,* ed. R. Ward and R. Jenkins, 73–88. Cambridge: Cambridge University Press.

Pollock, Friedrich, ed. 1955. *Gruppenexperiment: Ein Studienbericht*. 2d ed. Frankfurt: Europäische Verlagsanstalt.

Porter, Jack Nusan. 1994. "Toward a Sociology of National Socialism." *Sociological Forum* 9:505–11.

———. 1996. "Talcott Parsons and National Socialism: The Case of the 'Ten Mysterious Missing Letters.'" *Sociological Forum* 11:603–11.

Porter, Jack Nusan, and Steve Hoffman. 1999. *The Sociology of the Holocaust and Genocide: A Teaching and Learning Guide*. Washington: American Sociological Association.

Portes, Alejandro. 1992. "Disproving the Enclave Hypothesis." *American Sociological Review* 57:418–20.

Portes, Alejandro, and Min Zhou. 1993. "The New Second Generation: Segmented Assimilation and Its Variants." *Annals of the American Academy of Political and Social Sciences* 50:74–97.

Portes, Alejandro, and Rubén Rumbaut. 1990. *Immigrant America: A Portrait*. Berkeley: University of California Press.

———. 1996. *Immigrant America: A Portrait*. 2d ed. Berkeley: University of California Press.

Prell, Riv-Ellen. 1999. *Fighting to Become Americans: Jews, Gender, and the Anxiety of Assimilation*. Boston: Beacon.

Rabinowitz, Dorothy. 1976. *New Lives: Survivors of the Holocaust Living in America*. New York: Knopf.

Radler, Melissa. 2001. "NY Israelis Fly to Polls—or Don't." *Jerusalem Post*, January 28.

Ragin, Charles, and Howard Becker. 1992. *What Is a Case?: Exploring the Foundations of Social Inquiry*. Cambridge: Cambridge University Press.

Rapaport, Lynn. 1997. *Jews in Germany after the Holocaust: Memory, Identity, and Jewish-German Relations*. Cambridge: Cambridge University Press.

Rappaport, Joanne. 1990. *The Politics of Memory: Native Historical Interpretation in the Columbian Andes*. Cambridge: Cambridge University Press.

———. 1994. *Cumbe Reborn: An Andean Ethnography of History*. Chicago: University of Chicago Press.

Rebhun, Uzi. 2001. *Hagirah, kehilah, hizdahut: Yehudei*. Jerusalem: Magnes.

Reuther, Thomas. 1947. *"Die ambivalente Normalisierung": Deutschlanddiskurs und Deutschlandbilder in den USA, 1941–1955*. Stuttgart: Franz Steiner.

Ricoeur, Paul. 1988. *Time and Narrative*. Vol. 3. Trans. Kathleen McLaughlin and David Pellover. Chicago: University of Chicago Press.

Ringelblum, Emmanuel. 1958. *Notes from the Warsaw Ghetto: The Journal of Emmanuel Ringelblum*. Ed. and trans. J. Sloan. New York: McGraw-Hill.

Ritterband, Paul. 1986. "Israelis in New York." *Contemporary Jewry* 7:113–26.

———. 1997. "Jewish Identity among Russian Immigrants in the U.S." In *Russian Jews on Three Continents: Migration and Resettlement*, ed. Noah Lewin-Epstein, Yaacov Ro'i, and Ritterband, 325–43. London: Frank Cass.

Robertson, Roland. 1995. "Globalization: Time-Space and Homogeneity-Heterogeneity."

In *Global Modernities*, ed. M. Featherstone, S. Lash, and R. Robertson, 25–44. London: Sage.

Robnett, Belinda. 1997. *How Long, How Long? African American Women in the Struggle for Civil Rights*. Oxford: Oxford University Press.

Rosen, Sherry. 1993. *The Israeli Corner of the American Jewish Community*. New York: Institute on American Jewish-Israeli Relations and the American Jewish Committee.

Rosenberg, Alan, and Gerald E. Myers. 1988. *Echoes from the Holocaust*. Philadelphia: Temple University Press.

Rosenberg, Maxine B. 1994. *Hiding to Survive: Stories of Jewish Children Rescued from the Holocaust*. New York: Clarion.

Rosenfeld, Alan. 1995. *The Americanization of the Holocaust*. Ann Arbor: Jean and Samuel Frankel Center for Judaic Studies at the University of Michigan.

Rotem, Simha. 1994. *Memoirs of a Warsaw Ghetto Fighter: The Past within Me*. New Haven: Yale University Press.

Roth, Guenther. 1990. "Partisanship and Scholarship." In *Authors of Their Own Lives: Intellectual Autobiographies by Twenty American Sociologists*, ed. B. M. Berger, 383–409. Berkeley: University of California Press.

Rubin-Dorsky, Jeffrey, and Shelley Fisher Fishkin. 1996. "Reconfiguring Jewish Identity in the Academy." In *People of the Book: Thirty Scholars Reflect on Their Jewish Identity*, ed. Rubin-Dorsky and Fishkin, 3–11. Madison: University of Wisconsin Press.

Rumbaut, Rubén, Frank D. Bean, Leo Chavez, Min Zhou, Jennifer Lee, Susan Brown, Louis Desipio, and Min Zhou. 2002. "Immigration and Intergenerational Mobility in Metropolitan Los Angeles." New York: Russell Sage Foundation.

Rumbaut, Rubén D., and Rubén G. Rumbaut. 2004. "Self and Circumstance: Journey and Visions of Exile." In *The Dispossessed: An Anatomy of Exile*, ed. P. I. Rose, 331–56. Amherst: University of Massachusetts Press.

Rumbaut, Rubén G. [1976] 2004a. "The One-and-a-Half Generation: Crisis, Commitment, and Identity." In *The Dispossessed: An Anatomy of Exile*, ed. P. I. Rose. Amherst: University of Massachusetts Press.

——. 2004b. "Ages, Life Stages, and Generational Cohorts: Decomposing the Immigrant First and Second Generations in the United States." *International Migration Review* 38:1160–204.

Rumbaut, Rubén G., and Kenji Ima. 1988. *The Adaptation of Southeast Asian Refugee Youth: A Comparative Study*. Washington: U.S. Office of Refugee Resettlement.

Ryvkina, Rozalina V. 1998. "Jews in Present-Day Russia." *Russian Social Science Review* 39:52–68.

Sabar, Naama. 2000. *Kibbutzniks in the Diaspora*. Trans. Chaya Naor. Albany: State University of New York Press.

Safran, William. 1991. "Diasporas in Modern Societies: Myths of Homeland and Return." *Diaspora* 1:83–99.

——. 1999. "Comparing Diasporas: A Review Essay." *Diaspora* 8:255–91.

Salomon, Kim. 1991. *Refugees in the Cold War: Towards a New International Regime in the Early Postwar Era*. Lund, Sweden: Lund University Press.

Sanders, Jimy M., and Victor Nee. 1992. "Problems in Resolving the Enclave Economy Debate." *American Sociological Review* 57:415–18.

Sanford, Victoria. 2003. *Buried Secrets: Truth and Human Rights in Guatemala*. New York: Palgrave Macmillan.

Saxe, Leonard. 2004. "Birthright: A Gift that Keeps Giving." *Jewish Week* (www.thejewishweek.com), January 23.

Saxe, Leonard, et al. 2002. *A Mega-experiment in Jewish Education: The Impact of Birthright Israel*. Waltham, MA: Maurice and Marilyn Cohen Center for Modern Jewish Studies at Brandeis University.

Saxe, Leonard, Charles Kadushin, Juliana Pakes, Shaul Kelner, Lawrence Sternberg, Bethamie Horowitz, Amy Sales, and Archie Brodsky. 2001. *Birthright Israel Launch Evaluation: Preliminary Findings*. Waltham, Mass.: Maurice and Marilyn Cohen Center for Modern Jewish Studies at Brandeis University.

Schama, Simon. 1995. *Landscape and Memory*. New York: Vintage.

Schiff, Alvin I. 1980. "Language, Culture and the Jewish Acculturation of Soviet Jewish Emigrés." *Journal of Jewish Communal Service* 57:44–49.

Schmool, Marlena, and Frances Cohen. 1998. *A Profile of British Jewry: Patterns and Trends at the Turn of the Century*. London: Board of Deputies of British Jews.

Schwartz, Barry. 1991. "Social Change and Collective Memory: The Democratization of George Washington." *American Sociological Review* 56:221–36.

Schwarzschild, Henry. 1993. Letter to the editor. *New York Times Book Review*, October 7, 2–3.

Schweid, Eliezer. 1994. *Bien hurban liyeshu'ah: Teguvot shel Hagut haredit Lashoah Bizemanah*. Tel Aviv: Hakibbutz Hame-uhad.

Segev, Tom. 1993. *The Seventh Million: The Israelis and the Holocaust*. Trans. H. Watzman. New York: Hill and Wang.

Seidler-Feller, Chaim. 1991. "Response to Perry London and Allissa Hirchfeld." In *Jewish Identitiy in America*, ed. D. Gordis and Y. Ben-Horin, 61–65. Los Angeles: Susan and David Wilstein Institute of Jewish Policy Studies.

Shain, Yossi. 2000. "American Jews and the Construction of Israel's Jewish Identity." *Diaspora* 9:163–201.

Shandler, Jeffrey. 2001. "Producing the Future: The Impresario Culture of American Zionism before 1948." In *Divergent Jewish Cultures: Israel and America*, ed. D. D. Moore and S. I. Troen, 53–71. New Haven: Yale University Press.

Shavit, Uriva. 2001. "Westward Ho!" *Ha'aretz*, August 22.

Sheffer, Gabriel. 1998. "The Israeli Diaspora Yordim (Emigrants) Are the Authentic Diaspora." In *The Jewish Year Book*, ed. S. Massil, xix–xxxi. London: Vallentine Mitchell.

Shils, Edward A., and Morris Janowitz. 1948. "Cohesion and Disintegration in the Wehrmacht in World War II." *Public Opinion Quarterly* 12:280–315.

Shokeid, Moshe. 1988. *Children of Circumstances: Israeli Immigrants in New York*. Ithaca: Cornell University Press.

———. 1998. "My Poly-ethnic Park: Some Thoughts on Israeli-Jewish Ethnicity." *Diaspora* 7:225–46.

Sicher, Efraim. 2000. "The Future of the Past: Countermemory and Postmemory in Contemporary American Post-Holocaust Narratives." *History and Memory* 12:56–91.

Siegel, Dina. 1998. *The Great Immigration: Russian Jews in Israel*. New York: Berghahn.

Siegel, Richard, ed. 2002. *Commission Report on the Future of Jewish Culture in America: Preliminary Findings and Observations*. New York: National Foundation for Jewish Culture.

Silber, Irina Carlota. 2004. "Mothers/Fighters/Citizens: Violence and Disillusionment in Postwar El Salvador." *Gender and History* 16:561–87.

Silberman, Charles E. 1985. *A Certain People: American Jews and Their Lives Today*. New York: Summit Books.

Silberstein, Laurence. 1994. "Others Within and Others Without: Rethinking Jewish Identity and Culture." In *The Other in Jewish Thought and History: Constructions of Jewish Culture and Identity*, ed. Silberstein and R. L. Cohn, 1–34. New York: New York University Press.

Sklare, Marshall. 1955. *Conservative Judaism: An American Religious Movement*. Glencoe, Ill.: Free Press.

Smith, Dennis. 1998. "Zygmunt Bauman: How to Be a Successful Outsider." *Theory, Culture and Society* 15:39–45.

———. 1999. *Zygmunt Bauman: Prophet of Postmodernity*. Cambridge: Polity.

Smith, Michael Peter, and Luis Eduardo Guarnizo, eds. 1998. *Transnationalism from Below*. New Brunswick, N.J.: Transaction.

Snow, David A., Louis A. Zurcher Jr., and Sheldon Ekland-Olson. 1980. "Social Networks and Social Movements: A Microstructural Approach to Differential Recruitment." *American Sociological Review* 45:787–801.

Sobel, Zvi. 1986. *Migrants from the Promised Land*. New Brunswick, N.J.: Transaction.

Sofsky, Wolfgang. 1997. *The Order of Terror: The Concentration Camp*. Trans. W. Templer. Princeton: Princeton University Press.

Sontheimer, Kurt. 2002. *Thomas Mann und die Deutschen*. Munich: Langen Mueller.

Soysal, Yasmin N. 1994. *Limits of Citizenship: Migrants and Postnational Membership in Europe*. Chicago: University of Chicago Press.

Spivak, Gayatri. 1988. "Can the Subaltern Speak?" In *Marxism and the Interpretation of Culture*, ed. Cary Nelson and Lawrence Grossberg, 271–97. Urbana: University of Illinois Press.

Stahlberg, D., and A. Maass. 1998. "Hindsight Bias: Impaired Memory or Biased Reconstruction?" In *European Review of Social Psychology*, vol. 8, ed. W. Stroebe and M. Hewstone, 105–32. Chichester, UK: Wiley.

Stein, Arlene. 1997. *Sex and Sensibility: Stories of a Lesbian Generation*. Berkeley: University of California Press.

Steinberg, Lucien. 1977. "Jewish Rescue Activities in Belgium and France." In *Rescue Attempts during the Holocaust: Proceedings of the Second Yad Vashem International Historical Conference, April 1974,* ed. Y. Guttman and E. Zuroff, 603–15. Jerusalem: Yad Vashem.

Steinberg, Maxime. 1986. *La traque des Juifs 1942–1944,* Vol. 1. Brussels: Éditions Vie Ouvrière.

Steinberg, Stephen. 1989. *The Ethnic Myth: Race, Ethnicity, and Class in America.* Exp. ed. Boston: Beacon.

Steinle, Jürgen. 1995. *Nationales Selbstverständnis nach dem Nationalsozialismus: Die Kriegsschuld-Debatte in West-Deutschland.* Bochum, Germany: Universitätsverlag Dr. N. Brockmeyer.

Stephen, Lynn. 1994. "The Politics and Practice of Testimonial Literature." In *Hear My Testimony: María Teresa Tula, Human Rights Activist of El Salvador,* by María Teresa Tula, 223–34. Boston: South End Press.

Stern, Lewis. 1985. "The Overseas Chinese in Vietnam, 1920–75: Demography, Social Structure, and Economic Power." *Humboldt Journal of Social Relations* 12:1–30.

Stier, Oren Baruch. 1996. "The Propriety of Holocaust Memory: Cultural Representations and Commemorative Responses." PhD diss. University of California, Santa Barbara.

———. 2003. *Committed to Memory: Cultural Mediations of the Holocaust.* Amherst: University of Massachusetts Press.

Stoll, David. 1999. *Rigoberta Menchú and the Story of All Poor Guatemalans.* Boulder, Colo.: Westview.

Strauss, Herbert A. 1982. Foreword to *Jewish Immigrants of the Nazi Period in the USA,* vol. 3, part 2, ed. Strauss, xiii–xxi. New York: K. G. Saur.

Strich, Christian, ed. 1989. *Das Erich Kastner Lesebuch.* Zurich: Diogenes.

Stump, Roger W. 1984. "Regional Migration and Religious Commitment in the United States." *Journal for the Scientific Study of Religion* 23:292–303.

Sturken, Marita. 1997. *Tangled Memories: The Vietnam War, the AIDS Epidemic, and the Politics of Remembering.* Berkeley: University of California Press.

Suleiman, Susan Rubin. 1996. "Monuments in a Foreign Tongue: On Reading Holocaust Memoirs by Emigrants." *Poetics Today* 17:639–57.

———. 2002. "The 1.5 Generation: Thinking about Child Survivors and the Holocaust." *American Imago* 59:277–95.

Sykes, Charles J. 1992. *A Nation of Victims: The Decay of the American Character.* New York: St. Martin's.

Syrkin, Marie. 1948. *Blessed Is the Match: The Story of Jewish Resistance.* New York: Knopf.

Szereszewska, Helena. 1997. *Memoirs from Occupied Warsaw, 1940–1945.* Trans. Anna Marianska. London: Vallentine Mitchell.

Sznaider, Natan. 2001. *The Compassionate Temperament: Care and Cruelty in Modern Society.* Lanham, Md.: Rowman and Littlefield.

Szpilman, Wladyslaw. 1999. *The Pianist: The Extraordinary True Story of One Man's Survival in Warsaw, 1939–1945.* New York: Picador.

Szwajger, Adina B. 1990. *I Remember Nothing More: The Warsaw Children's Hospital and the Jewish Resistance*. New York: Pantheon.

Tai, Hue-Tam Ho. 2001. "Introduction: Situating Memory." In *The Country of Memory: Remaking the Past in Late Socialist Vietnam*, ed. Tai, 1–17. Berkeley: University of California Press.

Taylor, Charles. 1993. *Multiculturalism and the Politics of Recognition*. Princeton, N.J.: Princeton University Press.

Taylor, Telford. 1992. *The Anatomy of the Nuremberg Trials*. Boston: Little, Brown.

Taylor, Verta. 1989. "Social Movement Continuity: The Women's Movement in Abeyance." *American Sociological Review* 54:761–75.

Taylor, Verta, and Nancy Whittier. 1992. "Collective Identity in Social Movement Communities: Lesbian Feminist Mobilization." In *Frontiers in Social Movement Theory*, ed. A. D. Morris and C. M. Mueller, 104–29. New Haven: Yale University Press.

——. 1995. "Analytical Approaches to Social Movement Culture: The Culture of the Women's Movement." In *Social Movements and Culture*, ed. Hank Johnston and Bert Klandermans, 163–87. Minneapolis: University of Minnesota Press.

Tec, Nechama. 1984. *Dry Tears: The Story of a Lost Childhood*. New York: Oxford University Press.

——. 1986. *When Light Pierced the Darkness: Christian Rescue of Jews in Nazi-Occupied Poland*. New York: Oxford University Press.

——. 1990. *In the Lion's Den: The Life of Oswald Rufeisen*. New York: Oxford University Press.

——. 1993. *Defiance: The Bielski Partisans*. New York: Oxford University Press.

——. 2003. *Resilience and Courage: Women, Men and the Holocaust*. New Haven: Yale University Press.

Teitelbaum-Hirsch, Viviane. 1994. *Les larmes sous le masque*. Brussels: Éditions Labor.

Thompson, John L. P., and Gail A. Quets. 1990. "Genocide and Social Conflict: A Partial Theory and a Comparison." *Research in Social Movements, Conflict and Change* 12:245–66.

Thomson, Susan. 2002. "War Chills Israeli Study Programs Here: University of Illinois, Missouri University No Longer Send Students." *St..Louis Post-Dispatch*, April 15.

Tobin, Gary A., Adam Z. Tobin, and Lorin Troderman. 1995. *American Jewish Philanthropy in the 1990s*. Waltham, MA: Cohen Center for Modern Jewish Studies, Brandeis University.

Tomlinson, John. 1999. *Globalization and Culture*. Chicago: University of Chicago Press.

Tonkin, Elizabeth. 1992. *Narrating Our Pasts: The Social Construction of Oral History*. Cambridge: Cambridge University Press.

Tönnies, Ferdinand. [1887] 1957. *Community and Society*. Trans. C. P. Loomis. New York: Harper Torchbooks.

Toren, Nina. 1980. "Return to Zion: Characteristics and Motivations of Returning Emigrants." In *Studies of Israeli Society*, vol. 6, *Migration, Ethnicity and Community*, ed. Ernest Krausz, 39–50. New Brunswick, N.J.: Transaction.

Torpe, John C. 2006. *Making Whole What Has Been Smashed: On Reparation Politics.* Cambridge, Mass.: Harvard University Press.

Tress, Madeleine. 1991. "United States Policy toward Soviet Emigration." *Migration* 3/4: 93–106.

Trinh T. Minh-ha. 1991. *When the Moon Waxes Red: Representation, Gender and Cultural Politics.* New York: Routledge.

Trofimov, Yarolslav. 1995. "Booming Economy Lures Israelis Home from U.S.: Jewish State Now More Inviting." *San Francisco Examiner,* October 8.

Tuan, Mia. 1998. *Forever Foreigners or Honorary Whites? The Asian Ethnic Experience Today.* New Brunswick, N.J.: Rutgers University Press.

Tugend, Tom. 1989. "Peretz: Integrate Yordim into Jewish Community." *Jerusalem Post,* November 29.

Tula, María Teresa. 1994. *Hear My Testimony: Human Rights Activist of El Salvador.* Ed. and trans. Lynn Stephen. Boston: South End Press.

Ungar, Sanford J. 1989. "Freedom's Door Shut in Face of Soviet Jews." *Los Angeles Times,* November 12.

United States Displaced Persons Commission. 1952. *The DP Story: The Final Report of the United States Displaced Persons Commission.* Washington: U.S. Government Printing Office.

United States Holocaust Memorial Museum. n.d. *Homosexuals: Victims of the Nazi Era.* Washington: United States Holocaust Memorial Museum.

Uriely, Natan. 1994. "Rhetorical Ethnicity of Permanent Sojourners: The Case of Israeli Immigrants in Chicago Area." *International Sociology* 9:431–45.

——. 1995. "Patterns of Identification and Integration with Jewish Americans among Israeli Immigrants in Chicago: Variations across Status and Generation." *Contemporary Jewry* 16:27–49.

Vaad Hatzala. 1957. *Disaster and Salvation: The History of the "Vaad Hatzala" in America* [Churbn un retung: Di geshikhte fun "Va'ad Hatsala" in Amerike]. New York: Vaad Hatzala Book Committee.

Van Hear, Nicholas. 1998. *New Diasporas: The Mass Exodus, Dispersal, and Regrouping of Migrant Communities.* Seattle: University of Washington Press.

Varcoe, Ian. 1998. "Identity and the Limits of Comparison: Bauman's Reception in Germany." *Theory, Culture and Society* 15:57–72.

Vertovec, Steven and Robin Cohen, eds. 2002. *Conceiving Cosmopolitanism: Theory Context, and Practice.* Oxford: Oxford University Press.

Vickerman, Milton. 1999. *Crosscurrents: West Indian Immigrants and Race.* New York: Oxford University Press.

Viviani, Nancy. 1984. *The Long Journey: Vietnamese Migration and Settlement in Australia.* Beaverton, Oreg.: International Scholarly Book Services.

Vromen, Suzanne. 1986. "Maurice Halbwachs and the Concept of Nostalgia." *Knowledge and Society: Studies in the Sociology of Culture Past and Present* 6:57–59.

Wagner-Pacifici, Robin. 1996. "Memories in the Making: The Shapes of Things that Went." *Qualitative Sociology* 19:301–21.

Wahlbeck, Osten. 2002. "The Concept of Diaspora as an Analytical Tool in the Study of Refugee Communities." *Journal of Ethnic and Migration Studies* 28:221–39.

Wajnryb, Ruth. 2001. *The Silence: How Tragedy Shapes Talk.* Crows Nest, New South Wales: Allen and Unwin.

Waldinger, Roger. 1994. "The Making of an Immigrant Niche." *International Migration Review* 28:211–32.

Wardi, Dina. 1992. *Memorial Candles: Children of the Holocaust.* New York: Routledge.

Warhaftig, Zorach. 1988. *Refugee and Survivor: Rescue Efforts during the Holocaust.* Jerusalem: Yad Vashem.

Waterman, Stanley. 1997. "The 'Return' of the Jews into London." In *London: The Promised Land? The Migrant Experience in a Capital City,* ed. A. J. Kershen, 143–60. Aldershot, UK: Avebury.

Waterman, Stanley, and Barry Kosmin 1986. "The Jews in London." *Geographical Magazine* 58:21–27.

Waters, Mary. 1990. *Ethnic Options: Choosing Identities in America.* Berkeley: University of California Press.

Waxman, Chaim I. 1983. *America's Jews in Transition.* Philadelphia: Temple University Press.

———. 1989. *American Aliya: Portrait of an Innovative Migration Movement.* Detroit: Wayne University Press.

———. 1998. "The Haredization of American Orthodox Jewry." *Jerusalem Letters/Viewpoints* 376.

———. 2001. *Jewish Baby Boomers: A Communal Perspective.* Albany: State University of New York Press.

Wdowinski, David. [1963] 1985. *And We Are Not Saved.* New York: Philosophical Library.

Webber, Jonathan. 1992. *The Future of Auschwitz: Some Personal Reflections.* Yarnton, UK: Oxford Centre for Postgraduate Hebrew Studies.

———. 2001. "Holocaust Memory, Representation and Education: The Challenges of Applied Research." In *Remembering for the Future: The Holocaust in an Age of Genocide,* ed. J. K. Roth and E. Maxwell, 237–247. New York: Palgrave.

Weber, Max. 1978. *Economy and Society: An Outline of Interpretive Sociology,* ed. Guenther Roth and Claus Wittich. Trans. Ephraim Fischoff et al. Berkeley: University of California Press.

Weinberger, Moses. 1982. *People Walk on Their Heads: Moses Weinberger's Jews and Judaism in New York.* Trans. and ed. Jonathan. D. Sarna. New York: Holmes and Meier.

Weiner, Jon. 1989. "Talcott Parsons' Role Bringing Nazi Sympathizers to the U.S." *Nation,* March 6.

Weiss Halivni, David. 1996. *The Book and the Sword: A Life of Learning in the Shadow of Destruction.* Boulder, Colo.: Westview.

Weitzman, Lenore J. 2001. "Double Identities: The Experiences of Jews Who Survived the Holocaust by Passing as Non-Jews in Germany and Poland." Paper presented at the "Sociological Perspectives on the Holocaust and Post-Holocaust Jewish Life" conference, Rutgers University, New Brunswick, N.J.

Weitzman, Lenore J., and Dalia Ofer. 1998. "Introduction: The Role of Gender in the Holocaust." In *Women in the Holocaust*, ed. Ofer and Weitzman, 1–18. New Haven: Yale University Press.

Welch, Michael R., and John Baltzell. 1984. "Geographic Mobility, Social Integration, and Church Attendance." *Journal for the Scientific Study of Religion* 23:75–91.

Werner, Harold. 1992. *Fighting Back: A Memoir of Jewish Resistance in World War II*. New York: Columbia University Press.

White, Hayden. 1990. *The Content of the Form: Narrative Discourse and Historical Representation*. Baltimore: Johns Hopkins University Press.

——. 2000. *Figural Realism: Studies in the Mimesis Effect*. Baltimore: Johns Hopkins University Press.

White, Naomi Rosh. 1988. *From Darkness to Light: Surviving the Holocaust*. Melbourne: Collins Dove.

Whittier, Nancy. 1995. *Feminist Generations: The Persistence of the Radical Women's Movement*. Philadelphia: Temple University Press.

Wiesel, Elie. 2000. "A Sacred Magic Can Elevate the Secular Storyteller." *New York Times*, June 19.

Wieviorka, Michel. 1992. "Case Studies: History or Sociology?" In *What Is a Case? Exploring the Foundations of Social Inquiry*, ed. C. Ragin and H. Becker, 159–72. Cambridge: Cambridge University Press.

Wiggershaus, Rolf. 1998. *The Frankfurt School: Its History, Theories, and Political Significance*. Trans. M. Robertson. Cambridge: MIT Press.

Wilkomirski, Binjamin. 1996. *Fragments: Memories of a Wartime Childhood*. Trans. C. B. Janeway. New York: Schocken.

Williams, Richard. 2002. "Review Essay: The Dignity of Working Men and Black Identities." *Sociological Forum* 17:351–66.

Wimmer, Andreas, and Nina Glick Schiller. 2003. "Methodological Nationalism, the Social Sciences, and the Study of Migration." *Global Networks* 2:301–34.

Wirth, Louis. [1936] 1985. "Preface" to *Ideology and Utopia: An Introduction to the Sociology of Knowledge*, by Karl Mannheim. New York: Harcourt, Brace.

Wischnitzer, Mark. 1948. *To Dwell in Safety: The Story of Jewish Migration since 1800*. Philadelphia: Jewish Publication Society of America.

Wolf, Alfred. 1969. *Alfred Wolf Memoirs*. New York: Leo Baeck Institute.

Wolf, Diane L. 1997. "Family Secrets: Transnational Struggles among Children of Filipino Immigrants." *Sociological Perspectives* 40:455–82.

——. 2000. "When Post-memory Comes: The Politics of Holocaust Memory Production." Unpublished paper, Department of Sociology, University of California, Davis.

——. 2002a. Introduction to *From Auschwitz to Ithaca: The Transnational Journey of Jake Geldwert*. Bethesda, Md.: CDL Press.

——. 2002b. "'This Is Not What I Want': Holocaust Testimonials, Post-memory and Jewish Identity." In *Diasporas and Exiles: Varieties of Jewish Identity in the Diaspora*, ed. H. Wettstein, 191–220. Berkeley: University of California Press.

Wolin, Richard. 1993. *The Heidegger Controversy: A Critical Reader*. Cambridge: MIT Press.

Wolitz, Seth L. 1991. "The American Jew Is American First." *Jerusalem Post*, February 20.

Wolkomir, Michelle. 2001. "Emotion Work, Commitment, and the Authentication of the Self: The Case of Gay and Ex-gay Christian Support Groups." *Journal of Contemporary Ethnography* 30:305–34.

Wolman, Ruth. 1996. *Crossing Over: An Oral History of Refugees from Hitler's Reich*. New York: Twayne.

Woo, Elaine. 1989. "Anticipated Reunion Turns into a Nightmare for Soviet Emigré." *Los Angeles Times*, November 24.

Woocher, Jonathan S. 1985. "Sacred Survival: American Jewry's Civil Religion." *Judaism: A Quarterly Journal* 34:151–62.

——. 1986. *Sacred Survival: The Civil Religion of American Jews*. Bloomington: Indiana University Press.

Wrong, Dennis H. 1996. "Truth, Misinterpretation, or Left-Wing McCarthyism?" *Sociological Forum* 11:613–21.

Wu, William F. 1982. *The Yellow Peril: Chinese Americans in American Fiction, 1850–1940*. Hamden, Conn.: Archon.

Wuthnow, Robert, and Kevin Christiano. 1979. "The Effects of Residential Migration on Church Attendance in United States." In *The Religious Dimension: New Directions in Quantitative Research*, ed. Wuthnow, 257–75. New York: Academic Press.

Yerushalmi, Yosef Hayim. 1996. *Zakhor: Jewish History and Jewish Memory*. Seattle: University of Washington Press.

Yiftachel, Oren. 1998. "Nation Building and the Division of Space: Ashkenazi Domination in the Israeli 'Ethnocracy.'" *Nationalism and Ethnic Politics* 4:33–58.

Young, James E. 1988. *Writing and Rewriting the Holocaust: Narrative and the Consequences of Interpretation*. Bloomington: Indiana University Press.

——. 1993. *The Texture of Memory: Holocaust Memorials and Meaning*. New Haven: Yale University Press.

——. 1994. *The Art of Memory: Holocaust Memorials in History*. New York: Jewish Museum with Prestel.

——. 1997. "Between History and Memory." *History and Memory* 9:47–58.

Zahler, Gayle. 1989. "Jewish Identity and the Soviet Emigré Newcomer." Paper presented at the National Conference of Jewish Communal Workers, Boca Raton, Fla.

Zanna, Mark P., and James M. Olson, eds. 1994. *The Psychology of Prejudice*. Hillsdale, N.J.: L. Erlbaum.

Zeldich, Morris. 1950. "Immigrant Aid." *American Jewish Year Book* 51:193–200.

Zerubavel, Eviatar. 1991. *The Fine Line: Making Distinctions in Everyday Life.* New York: Free Press.

——. 1996. "Social Memories: Steps to a Sociology of the Past." *Qualitative Sociology* 19:283–99.

——. 2006. *The Elephant in the Room: Silence and Denial in Everyday Life.* New York: Oxford University Press.

Zerubavel, Yael. 1995. *Recovered Roots: Collective Memory and the Making of Israeli National Tradition.* Chicago: University of Chicago Press.

——. 2002. "The 'Mythological Sabra' and Jewish Past: Trauma, Memory and Contested Identities." *Israel Studies* 7:115–44.

Zhou, Min. 1997. "Growing Up American: The Challenge Confronting Immigrant Children and Children of Immigrants." *Annual Review of Sociology* 23: 63–95.

Zhou, Min, and Carl L. Bankston III. 1998. *Growing Up American: How Vietnamese Children Adapt to Life in the United States.* New York: Russell Sage Foundation.

Zilversmit, Kitty. 1995. *Yours Always: A Holocaust Love Story.* Bethesda, Md.: CDL Press.

Zuckerman, Yitzhak. 1993. *A Surplus of Memory: Chronicle of the Warsaw Ghetto Uprising.* Berkeley: University of California Press.

Zuckmayer, Carl. 1966. *Als wär's ein Stück von mir: Horen der Freundschaft.* Frankfurt: Fischer.

Zuroff, Efraim. 2000. *The Response of Orthodox Jewry in the United States to the Holocaust: The Activities of the Vaad ha-Hatzala Rescue Committee, 1939–1945.* New York: Michael Scharf Publication Trust of the Yeshiva University Press.

Zussman, Robert. 2000. "Autobiographical Occasions: Introduction to the Special Issue." *Qualitative Sociology* 23:5–8.

Zvielli, Alexander. 1989. "The Mark of Cain." *Jerusalem Post,* September 26.

CONTRIBUTORS

Richard Alba is Distinguished Professor of Sociology and Public Policy at the University at Albany, SUNY, where he directs the Center for Social and Demographic Analysis and the Lewis Mumford Center for Comparative Urban and Regional Research. He received Fulbright grants and fellowships from the Guggenheim Foundation and the German Marshall Fund. His books include *Ethnic Identity: The Transformation of White America* (1990); *Italian Americans: Into the Twilight of Ethnicity* (1985); and *Remaking the American Mainstream: Assimilation and Contemporary Immigration* (2003), co-written with Victor Nee. He has been President of the Eastern Sociological Society and Vice President of the American Sociological Association.

Caryn Aviv is a Marsico Lecturer and affiliated faculty with the Center for Judaic Studies at the University of Denver. Her research focuses on global Jewish identities, gender and sexuality, and Israel Studies. She is the co-editor, with David Shneer, of *Queer Jews* (2002) and *American Queer: Now and Then* (2006). She is the co-author, with Shneer, of *New Jews: The End of the Jewish Diaspora* (2005). Her current research explores the relationships between gender, national identity, and social movement participation by looking at transnational conflict resolution programs for Israeli and Palestinian adolescents.

Ethel Brooks is an Assistant Professor of Women's and Gender Studies and Sociology at Rutgers University. She studies the relations of gender, race, class, labor practices, citizenship and nation-state formations, with a focus on Central America, South Asia and the United States. Her research explores critical political economy, globalization, social movements, feminist theory, comparative sociology, nationalism, urban geographies and postcolonialism, with close attention to epistemology. Brooks's publications include *Unraveling the Garment Industry: Transnational Organizing and Women's Work* (2007).

Rachel L. Einwohner is an Associate Professor of Sociology at Purdue University and is affiliated with Purdue's Jewish Studies Program. Her research focuses on the dynamics of protest and resistance, a topic that she has explored with theoretically-driven analyses of a diverse set of movements and cases of protest including the U.S. animal rights movement, the college-based anti-sweatshop movement, and the Warsaw Ghetto Uprising. Currently she is engaged in a study of the efforts to create resistance movements in the Jewish ghettos of Nazi-occupied Warsaw, Vilna, and Łódź.

Yen Le Espiritu received her PhD in Sociology from the University of California, Los Angeles in 1990. She is currently a Professor of Ethnic Studies at the University of California, San Diego. Her latest book is *Home Bound: Filipino American Lives Across Cultures, Communities, and Countries* (2003), which received two national book awards. Her current research projects explore public commemorations of the Vietnam War and Vietnamese and Vietnamese American transnational lives.

Leela Fernandes is an Associate Professor of Political Science at Rutgers University. She is the author of *Producing Workers: The Politics of Gender, Class and Culture in the Calcutta Jute Mills* (1997), *Transforming Feminist Practice* (2003) and *The Rise of India's New Middle Class: Democratic Politics in an Era of Economic Reform* (2006). She has also written numerous essays and articles on gender, labor, cultural politics, social identity and globalization in India and is currently working on a research project on religion and politics.

Kathie Friedman is an Associate Professor of International Studies at the Henry M. Jackson School of International Studies, University of Washington, Seattle. She is author of *Memories of Migration: Gender, Ethnicity, and Work in the Lives of Jewish and Italian Women in New York, 1870–1924* (1996). Her research focuses on migration, ethnic identities, and gender. She is currently working on a project about Bosnian refugee families, collective memory and the production of post-migration identities.

Judith M. Gerson is an Associate Professor of Sociology and Women's and Gender Studies at Rutgers University where she is also an affiliate faculty member of the Department of Jewish Studies. She was a visiting fellow at the Center for Advanced Holocaust Studies, U.S. Holocaust Memorial Museum. Currently she is completing a book manuscript about Jewish refugees who fled Germany during the Holocaust and resettled in the U.S., entitled *By Thanksgiving We Were Americans.*

Steven J. Gold is a Professor and Associate Chair in the Department of Sociology at Michigan State University. Having served as President of the International Visual Sociology Association and Chair of the International Migration Section of the American Sociological Association, he is co-editor of *Immigration Research for a New Century: Multidisciplinary Perspectives* (2000) (with Rubén G. Rumbaut and Nancy Foner); and the author of four books: *Refugee Communities: A Comparative Field Study* (1992); *From the Worker's State to the Golden State* (1995); *Ethnic Economies* with Ivan Light (2000); and *The Israeli Diaspora* (2002).

Debra Renee Kaufman is a Professor of Sociology and Matthews Distinguished University Professor at Northeastern University. Her work in the area of religion, women and identity politics includes: *Rachel's Daughters* (1991; 1993); guest editor of "Women and the Holocaust" in *Contemporary Jewry* (1996). She organized an international conference and edited the proceedings entitled: *From the Protocols of Zion to Holocaust Denial Trials* (2007). She is currently writing a book about contemporary post-Holocaust identity among Jews.

Rhonda F. Levine is a Professor of Sociology at Colgate University, where she has been teaching since 1982. Her most recent books include *Enriching the Sociological Imagination: How Radical Sociology Changed the Discipline*, ed. (2005) and *Class, Networks, and Identity: Replanting Jewish Lives from Nazi Germany to Rural New York* (2001). She is currently studying the hopes, fears, and educational experiences of African American teenagers in a diverse small-city high school in the northeastern United States.

Daniel Levy is an Associate Professor in the Department of Sociology at the State University of New York–Stony Brook. He has written *The Holocaust and Memory in the Global Age* with Natan Sznaider (2005). In addition, he co-edited *Challenging Ethnic Citizenship: German and Israeli Perspectives on Immigration* with Yfaat Weiss (2002) and *Old Europe, New Europe, Core Europe: Transatlantic Relations after the Iraq War* with Max Pensky and John Torpey (2005).

Jeffrey K. Olick is a Professor of Sociology at the University of Virginia. He is author of *In the House of the Hangman: The Agonies of German Defeat, 1943–1949* (2005) and *The Politics of Regret: Collective Memory and Historical Responsibility in the Age of Atrocity* (2007), and editor of *States of Memory: Continuities, Conflicts and Transformations in National Retrospection* (2003). He is currently working on a translation of Theodor Adorno's essay *Schuld und Abwehr* (Guilt and Defense) as part of a project on the Frankfurt School and public opinion.

Martin Oppenheimer, Emeritus Professor of Sociology at Rutgers University, currently is a Lecturer in the Graduate Program, College of General Studies at the University of Pennsylvania. He is the author of *The Sit-In Movement of 1960* (1989), *The Urban Guerrilla* (1969), *White Collar Politics* (1985), *The State In Modern Society* (2000), and most recently, *The Hate Handbook: Oppressors, Victims, and Fighters* (2005).

David Shneer is an Associate Professor of History and Director of the Center for Judaic Studies at the University of Denver. His books include *New Jews: The End of the Jewish Diaspora* (2005), co-authored with Caryn Aviv; *Yiddish and the Creation of Soviet Jewish Culture* (2004); and *Queer Jews* (2002), and *American Queer: Now and Then* (2006), both co-edited with Caryn Avia. Shneer's next project, *On the Frontlines: Soviet Jewish Photographers Confront World War II and the Holocaust*, examines the lives and works of a dozen Soviet photojournalists who documented the war and Nazi genocide for the Soviet reading public.

Irina Carlota Silber is an Assistant Professor at City College of New York Center for Worker Education (CWE). Her research and book-length manuscript, *Desencanto Revolu-*

cionario: Gender, Violence and Memory, examines postwar reconstruction processes in Chalatenango, El Salvador, a former conflict zone. She has held Postdoctoral Fellowships at the Rutgers Center for Historical Analysis and a Rockefeller Fellowship at the Virginia Foundation for the Humanities. A new project, "The Texture of Illness" is a study of childhood genetic illness and disability, which explores the politics of suffering and embodied trauma in everyday life.

Arlene Stein is an Associate Professor of Sociology at Rutgers University. Her last book, *The Stranger Next Door: The Story of a Small Community's Battle Over Sex, Faith, and Civil Rights* (2001), a community study of a town embroiled in a battle over gay/lesbian civil rights, was awarded the Ruth Benedict Prize. A collection of her essays, *Shameless: Sexual Dissidence in American Culture* (2006) has recently been published. She is currently studying the lives of descendents of Holocaust survivors in relation to the burgeoning public discussion of the Holocaust in the U.S.

Natan Sznaider is a Professor of Sociology at the Academic College of Tel-Aviv-Yaffo. His recent publications include *The Compassionate Temperament: Care and Cruelty in Modern Society* (2001). He co-edited *Global America: The Cultural Consequences of Globalization* with Ulrich Beck and Rainer Winter (2003). He is the co-author of *The Holocaust and Memory in the Global Age* with Daniel Levy (2005).

Suzanne Vromen is Professor Emeritus of Sociology at Bard College. She has held visiting positions at Vassar College, at the University of Haifa, and recently taught as a Fulbright Senior Specialist at the Buber Institute, Free University of Brussels. Her publications address collective memory, nostalgia and commemoration, Georg Simmel, Maurice Halbwachs and recently Hannah Arendt's Jewish identity. Her book on Jewish children hidden in Belgian convents during the Holocaust is forthcoming from Oxford University Press.

Chaim I. Waxman until recent retirement was a Professor of Sociology and Jewish Studies at Rutgers University. He is the author of *The Stigma of Poverty: A Critique of Poverty Theories and Policies* ([1977] 1983); *America's Jews in Transition* (1983); *American Aliya: Portrait of an Innovative Migration Movement* (1989), and *Jewish Baby Boomers: A Communal Perspective* (2001). He co-authored the *Historical Dictionary of Zionism* (2000), and co-edited *Jews in Israel: Contemporary Social and Cultural Patterns* (2004), among others. He is past President of the Association for the Sociological Study of Jewry.

Richard Williams is an Associate Professor of Sociology at Rutgers University, New Brunswick/Piscataway. His research is in the areas of sociological theory, the social construction of identity and visual sociology. He is the author of *Hierarchical Structures and Social Value: The Creation of Black and Irish Identities in the United States*. He is currently working on a book that reverses the traditional concern with the problems identities raise for "deviants." His focus is on problems that identities necessarily raise for "identity normals," those who are fully socialized into an identity.

Diane L. Wolf is a Professor of Sociology at the University of California, Davis and a member of the Jewish Studies Program. She is the author of *From Auschwitz to Ithaca: The Transnational Journey of Jake Geldwert* (2002) as well as *Beyond Anne Frank: Hidden Children and Postwar Families in Holland* (2007).

Feldman, Jackie, 77

Feminist scholarship, 340, 341–42

Findlay, Allan M., 228

"First International Gathering of Children Hidden during World War II" (1991), 141

Fischer, Joschka, 328

Foucault, Michel, 90

Frankfurt Institute for Social Research, 12–13, 291–92

Fraser, Angus, 27

Freedom Summer, 279, 280

Freud, Sigmund, 304

Friedlander, Jonathan, 232

Friedländer, Saul, 157

Fromm, Erich, 334

Front de l'Indépendance (FI), 135

Gal, Susan, 181

Gamson, William, 32–33 n.7

Gans, Herbert J., 209

Garment workers, 186, 190

Gay men and women, 26, 27, 36, 84–85

Geldwert, Jake, 25; in America, 162–66; Holocaust testimonial of, 157–69, 170–73, 180–82, 189; as labor camp prisoner, 159–60, 167–68; reflections of, on family relationships, 165–66, 167, 168; VHF testimony of, 170–73, 182, 189

Gender: and Belgian resistance, 149; and feminist scholarship on representations of violence, 340, 341–42; and Holocaust memorials, 26; and Jewish identity, 48–49; and reactions to migration and settlement, 232–33; and rural German Jewish refugee wives, 198, 201, 203, 212, 213; scholarship, 24–26; and Warsaw Ghetto uprising, 279, 284–85, 287

Genealogical research, 121

Generations: and collective memory of the Holocaust, 6, 9 n.2; and Jewish children,

134–53; "1.5" generation, 6, 9 n.2, 132 n.8; and second-generation identity issues, 6, 22–23; and young Jewish American adults, 39–54, 67–83

Genocide: comparative sociological/historical approaches to, 7, 19, 32–33 n.7, 131, 132 n.4, 177; and context of Warsaw Ghetto uprising, 289; and politics of genocide representation, 340–41

Gerhardt, Uta, 15, 32 nn.4–5

German Jewish refugees: and anti-Semitism, 204; class resources and business skills of, 200–204; and collective self-definitions, 123–24; and ethnic identity, 29, 207–8, 214; ethnic mobility patterns of, 210; ethnic networks and resources of, 204–7, 211–14, 261; and German citizenship, 121–22; Holocaust memoirs of, 115, 117–33; and natural landscapes, 125–26, 177–78; post-Holocaust adaptation of, 197–214, 260–61, 267; pre–1941, 117–18, 187; preparations of, for immigration, 122–23; and racial definitions, 210–13; and self-blame (hindsight bias), 124–25; social world of, 207–8; and women's economic roles, 198, 201, 203, 212, 213

German national perspectives on the Holocaust, 318–19, 324–26; and the Balkan Wars, 328; and Cold War pressures, 325–26; defensive and tropes, 293–99, 311 n.1; and the formation of Holocaust memory, 318–19; and the Mann affair, 293–99, 304; and moral agonies of defeat, 292–93, 310; and shame, 325–26; and student movement and Nazi legacy (1960s), 325–26; and uniqueness of the Holocaust, 318–19, 325–26; and universalization, 325–26

Germany and collective guilt, 291–312, 338, 342; and "boundary work," 299, 311; and

40, 143; and female escorts, 149; and financial incentives, 142; international recognition and memorialization of, 135, 141, 142, 146, 151–53, 188; and memories of the nuns, 138–39; motivations for hiding, 142, 145; names of, 137–38, 148; in the Netherlands, 172; and nuns' fears, 147, 151; parents' separation from, 137, 140–41, 148–49, 172, 182–83; postwar, 140–43; reasons to focus on Belgian stories of, 134–35; and secrecy issues, 146; and sociological issue of testimony, 150–51

Hilberg, Raul, 334

Hillel House, 47

Hillgruber, Andreas, 291

Hirsch, Marianne: and cultural memory, 5; and post-Holocaust identity narratives, 40–41, 52; post-memory concept, 6, 35, 39–40, 52, 53 n.2, 169–70, 270

Histadrut (Labor Zionist trade union), 69

Hoffman, Steve, 32 n.2

Hofstätter, Peter, 291

Holidays, Jewish, 47, 162, 249

Holocaust, as term, 9 n.1, 119, 132 n.3, 318, 329

Holocaust deniers, 157

Holocaust memoirs, 111–12, 115–33, 176–78, 185, 187–88, 190; and anecdotal references and collective belonging, 122–23; and collective self-definitions, 123–24; and comparable jokes, 115–16, 131 n.1; and comparative techniques, 116, 120–26, 130; and comparisons of Holocaust and September 11 attacks, 126–30; content analysis of, 120; and debate over Holocaust's uniqueness, 116–17, 131, 289; and explicit comparisons made by memoir writers, 120–23, 130, 187–88; and generalizability, 116, 120; on German citizenship, 121–22; and interpretative problems of avoiding comparisons, 123–

26; and nature, 125–26, 177–78; reading, within sociohistorical contexts, 120; and references to preparations for immigration, 122–23; and returning to "normal," 127–28, 133 n.16; and self-blame (hindsight bias), 124–25; and study design and sample, 117–20, 132–33 n.10

Holocaust Memorial Day (Yom Ha'Shoah), 63–64, 76, 77, 89, 98–99

Holocaust remembrance and national perspectives, 313–30, 338–39; and the Balkan Wars, 327–29; and the Cold War, 322, 325, 326–27; commemorative trend in (1980s), 317; and cosmopolitanism, 314–17; and cosmopolitanization, 314–15; and "cosmopolitan memories," 317, 326–27, 329–30; and demands for reparations/public apologies, 329–30, 330 n.6; and differences in national perspectives, 315, 319–26; and formation of global Holocaust memory, 317–19, 329–30; and formation of Holocaust awareness (1960s), 317; German, 324–26, 328; and globalization, 314–15, 330 n.1, 338–39; and human rights issues, 323, 325, 326; of immediate postwar period, 317–18, 319–20; Israeli, 319–21, 327–28, 329; and particularism/universalism, 313–14, 317, 322–24, 325–26; and the uniqueness of the Holocaust, 318–19, 322, 325–26; and universal identity politics, 316–17; U.S., 321–24, 327–28; and violence and nation-states, 338–39

Holocaust studies, 3–10, 11–33, 331–36; and academic ghetto, 6; and academic marketplace and "Holocaust industry," 332–34; and advantages of scholarly interchange, 6, 7–9; and collective/cultural memory, 5–6, 28–30; comparative historical approaches to, 3–9, 18–19, 21, 32 n.7; and concept of survivor, 4; and cos-

Holocaust studies (*cont.*)

mopolitan memories, 317, 326–27, 329–30; and dearth of comparative sociology research, 3, 6–7, 11, 331–34; and gender analysis, 24–26; and historicity of the Holocaust, 5; and the "Holocaust narrative," 334–35; and immigration studies, 3–4, 6, 21–22; and Jewish studies, 3, 8, 109, 225, 333; and legitimacy issues, 332–34; and second-generation issues, 6, 22–23; sociological concepts shaping, 4–5, 7–8; sociology-of-knowledge approach to, 275, 331–36; and uniqueness of the Holocaust, 6–7, 30, 116–17, 131, 289. *See also* Sociology and Holocaust study

Holocaust testimonies, 113–14, 185–92; and agency, 167, 182, 190; and biblical roots of giving witness, 157; of camp survivors, 17–18, 133 n.12, 151, 157, 159–60; and collective memory, 29, 155–56; and comparative techniques, 116, 120–26, 130; and concentration camps, 17–18, 133 n.12, 151, 157, 159–60; and concepts of diaspora and home, 173; and control of the circulation of memory, 187; and emotional transnationalism, 169; and family relationships, 165–66, 167, 168; as form of remembering, 156–57; implications of, for pedagogy, 183–84; and Jake Geldwert's narrative, 157–69, 170–73, 180–82, 189; and Latin American *testimonios*, 156, 179–80, 189; and oral history methods, 157–58; as political witnessing, 156–57, 181; and postmemory creation, 169–73; and production of memory/identity, 112–13, 151, 154–75, 179–82, 185, 189, 190; sociological analyses of, 154–55, 173–74, 175 n.2; and survivors in aftermath of violence, 113, 176–84; and the terms *immigrant, refugee, survivor,* 118–20, 133 n.11, 187;

and transnational frameworks/discourse, 169, 173; and trauma stories, 36–37, 84–91; and VHF interviews, 154, 155, 170–73, 174, 182, 189. *See also* Hidden children; Holocaust memoirs; Identity narratives, post-Holocaust; Trauma

Horkheimer, Max, 12, 335

Horowitz, Irving Louis, 19, 32 n.7, 132 n.4

Hughes, Everett C., 16

Human rights movement: and autonomy of post-Holocaust immigrants, 225–26; and Holocaust remembrance in the United States, 323, 325, 326; and representation of violence, 339

Hungerford, Amy, 43

I. G. Farben, 158, 167–68

Identity, Jewish, 35–37; and anti-Semitism, 45, 250–52, 269; defining, 65 n.3; and gender differences, 48–49; and Holocaust memorials, 45–47, 50–51, 85, 88–89; Holocaust testimonies and production of, 112–13, 154–75, 179–82, 185, 189, 190; inherited, 100–102; and non-Orthodox Jews from Central Europe, 94–99; and Orthodox Jews, 36, 55–66, 93–99, 106; and "outlook," 43–44; role of the Holocaust in, 5–6, 41–43, 50, 54 n.5, 92, 109 n.3, 322; and social constructionism, 37, 92–110; and social/political engagement, 48, 52, 53; and trauma stories, 36–37, 84–91; and victimology, 42, 43, 45, 49, 51. *See also* Diaspora business and Jewish identity travel; Identity and social constructionism; Identity narratives, post-Holocaust; Orthodox Jews and American Jewish identity; Soviet Jewish refugees in the United States; Trauma

Identity and social constructionism, 37, 92–110; collective identity, 93, 280, 286–88;

collective identity trauma, 37, 107–9, 110 n.7; collective resistance, 280, 285–88; and creation of identity, 105–6; and debate over Holocaust's uniqueness, 92, 105–6, 107; and heterogeneous/homogenous identities, 93–106

Identity narratives, post-Holocaust, 35–36, 39–54, 89, 93–94, 99–102, 106; and anti-Semitism, 45; as bearing witness, 40–41; and collective memory and history, 39, 40, 51, 53 nn.1, 3–4; and concepts of homogeneity/heterogeneity, 93–106; and ethnic identifications, 101–2; and gender differences, 48–49; and historical precedents to the Holocaust, 52; and Holocaust as historical marker, 47; and Holocaust themes in popular culture, 43; and identity politics and social/political engagement, 48, 52, 53; and inherited Jewish/American identities, 100–102; and Judaism and Jewish survival, 52; and liberation themes, 45–47, 48; and "outlook," 43–44; and postmemory, 35–36, 39–40, 52, 53 n.2, 89; and the postmodern space of cultural memory, 40, 43–50; and sample respondents' characteristics, 44; and trauma stories and postwar identities, 36–37, 84–91; and U.S. society, 100–102; and victimology and political identity, 42, 43, 45, 49, 51; and victor ideology, 52–53. See also Holocaust testimonies

Identity travel. See Diaspora business and Jewish identity travel

Immigrant, as term, 118–20, 133 n.11, 187

Immigration and transnational practices, 4, 193–96, 215–35, 262–64; and "context of reception," 260; and diaspora circuits and ethnic networks, 212–14, 266–72; and diaspora-to-diaspora migrants, 217–18; ethnic/racial factors, 22, 210–13,

270–72; and family diasporic memories, 242; and identity travel, 69, 78–80; and immigrant adaptation, 209–14; and immigration studies, 3–4, 6–8, 21–23, 209–14; and mobility patterns and economic opportunities, 210; and notions of diaspora, 3–4; and paradigmatic status of immigration, 260–65; and post-Holocaust Jewish migration, 215–35, 262–64; and process of "incorporation," 260; and "racial middleness," 270–72; and relationships to "home," 253–56, 269; and terms *immigrant, refugee, survivor*, 118–20, 133 n.11, 187; and transnational immigration literature/diaspora studies, 4, 6, 236–37, 238–41, 258–59; and transnationalism and identity, 4, 234, 237, 241–45, 257, 263; and twice-minorities, 267–69, 272 nn.1–2; and twice refugees, 169. *See also* Post-Holocaust Jewish migration; Rural German Jewish refugees and post-Holocaust adaptation; Soviet Jewish refugees and post-Holocaust migration; Soviet Jewish refugees in the United States

Immigration Reform and Control Act (IRCA), 217

Immigration studies, 3–4, 6–8, 21–23, 209–14

India, globalization in, 338–39

Intermarriage, 256, 265

International Gathering of Hidden Children (1991), 152

Interpretative methods in sociology, 12, 23–31

Intifada, second, 73, 80–82, 223

Iranian Jews in Los Angeles, 229, 232

Israel: and diaspora business, 69, 70–71, 74–75, 77–78, 103; and Soviet Jewish refugees, 247, 253; state politics of, and

Mullins, Nicholas C., 32 n.2
Münchner Zeitung (newspaper), 296
Museum of Tolerance–Beit Hashoah (Los Angeles), 47, 50

Naficy, Hamid, 269
National Committee for Free Germany, 294
National Coordinating Committee of Refugee Problems, 65 n.2
National Council of Jewish Women, 65 n.2
National Jewish Population Survey (1990), 58, 60, 61, 70, 72
National perspectives. *See* Holocaust remembrance and national perspectives
National Refugee Service, 65 n.2
National Society of Hebrew Day Schools (Torah Umesorah), 59
Nation-states: and birth of sociology discipline, 330 n.1; and Fein's analysis of the Final Solution, 18–19; and globalization, 330 n.1, 338–39
Nature, 125–26, 177–78
Nazism: and anti-Semitism, 15, 19; and authoritarianism and personality, 12–13; and conformity and deviance, 15–16; and democracy, 16–17; and denazification/Allied reeducation policies, 299, 300, 301–2, 311 n.4; and German universities, 14; legacy of, and German student movement (1960s), 325–26; and party membership, 13–14, 20–21; sociological scholarship on, 12–17, 19, 20–21, 334. *See also* Germany and collective guilt
Neue Zeitung, 301, 305, 306–7
Neumann, Franz, 334
Neurath, Paul, 17–18
"Never again," 133 n.15, 179
New York: and diaspora tourism, 82; and Orthodox Jews, 56, 58, 60, 62; and rural German Jewish Refugees, 197–214; and West Indian immigrants, 213–14

New York State Cattle Dealers Association, 207
Noczyk Synagogue (Warsaw), 76
Nonini, Donald, 229
Nora, Pierre, 40
North American Jewish Federation, 72
Novick, Peter, 41, 42, 50, 54 n.5, 133 n.12, 322
"Nuremberg and the Historians" (Kästner), 312 n.9
Nuremberg trials, 301, 306, 311–12 n.6, 312 n.9, 317, 325

Oberschall, Anthony, 32–33 n.7
Ofer, Dalia, 24
Okihiro, Gary, 271
Oneg Shabbat archives, 278, 289 n.1
"1.5" generation, 6, 9 n.2, 132 n.8
Ong, Aihwa, 229
Orthodox Jews and American Jewish identity, 36, 55–66, 93–99, 106; and assimilation issues, 95–96; and concepts of homogeneity and heterogeneity, 95–99; and Eastern European immigration, 55–56, 94–99; and extrinsic/intrinsic culture, 55, 65 n.1; and family incomes, 61; and Holocaust commemoration, 63–64; and immigration patterns, 55, 57–60, 94–99; and influence on American Jewish national identity, 87–88; and Jewish day school movement, 59–60; and Jewish organizational memberships, 58; in New York area, 56, 58, 60, 62; and Orthodox and non-Orthodox rifts, 60–61, 96–99; and post-World War II population, 55; and reestablishing yeshivas, 59; and resettlement locations, 58; and responses to the Holocaust, 62–64; role of, in American Jewish culture, 64–65; and suburban communities, 61–62; and

uniqueness of the Holocaust, 64; during World War II, 97–98

Oslo Peace Accords (1993), 224

Ostow, Robin, 29

Rabin, Yitzhak, 216, 221

Race and immigration: and immigrant adaptation, 210–13; and postwar "whitening," 270–72, 272 n.4; and "racial middleness," 270–72

Radical History Review, 335

Rapaport, Lynn, 21, 22–23

Rappaport Memorial (former Warsaw Ghetto), 76

Reagan, Ronald, 292

Reform Judaism, 56, 80

Refugee Act (1980), 226

Refugee, as term, 118–20, 133 n.11, 187

Refugees. *See* Diaspora; Immigration and transnational practices

Reparations and public apologies, 329, 330 n.6

Ricoeur, Paul, 105

Ringelblum, Emmanuel, 289 n.1

Roma (Gypsies), 26–27

Roosevelt, Franklin D., 294

Rosenberg, Allan, 51

Rosenfeld, Alvin, 42

Rosenzweig, Franz, 316

Rotem, Simha, 283, 284, 287–88

Roth, Guenther, 29

Rufeisen, Oswald, 23

Rumbaut, Rubén G., 9 n.2

Rural German Jewish refugees and post-Holocaust adaptation, 197–214, 260–61, 267; and anti-Semitism, 204; and cattle breeders, 205–6; and cattle dealing, 199–208, 260–62; and class resources and business skills, 200–204; and ethnic identity, 207–8, 214; and ethnic mobility patterns, 210; and ethnic networks and resources, 204–7, 211–14, 261; and extension of credit, 200, 203–4; and knowledge of cows, 200, 202–3; and milk market/dairy industry in postwar New York state, 199–200; and racial

definitions and process of adaptation, 210–13; and raising capital, 200–201, 203; and slaughterhouses and auctions, 206–7; social world of, 207–8; and women's economic roles, 198, 201, 203, 212, 213

Sanford, Victoria, 179

Schindler's List (film), 85, 154, 340

Schwarzschild, Henry, 124

Segev, Tom, 293

September 11, 2001 terrorist attacks, 61, 81, 126–30

Shain, Yossi, 233

Shandler, Jeffrey, 70

Sheffer, Gabriel, 234

Shils, Edward, 14

Sho'ah, as term, 9 n.1, 119, 132 n.3

Shoah (film), 41

Shoah Foundation Institute for Visual History and Education (VHF), 82 n.8, 154, 155, 170–73, 174, 182, 189; focus of, on wartime experiences, 170–73; and formulaic structure of interviews, 172–73, 174; and Jake Geldwert's testimony, 170–73, 182, 189

Shokeid, Moshe, 219, 230–31

Siegel, Dina, 223

Silberman, Charles, 42

Simple maillon, Un [Just a Link] (film), 149

Six-Day War (1967), 320, 321

Sklare, Marshall, 57

Smith, Valerie, 5

Social constructionism and Jewish identity, 37, 92–110

Sociology and Holocaust study, 3–10, 11–33, 31 nn.1–2, 331–36; and academic marketplace and "Holocaust industry," 332–34; and the advantages of specificity, 27–28; and collective memory and collective identity, 5–6, 28–30; and comparative historical approaches, 3–9, 18–19, 21, 32 n.7; and cultural studies, 335; and dearth of comparative Holocaust research, 3, 6–7, 11, 331–34; defining, 31 n.1; and diaspora studies, 4, 6, 239–41, 258–59; and foreign language knowledge, 333; and the Frankfurt School, 12–13, 291–92; and gender scholarship, 24–26; and genocide studies, 19, 32–33 n.7, 131, 132 n.4; and Holocaust atrocities, 17–19; and immediate postwar studies, 12–16; and immigrant adaptation, 209–14; and immigration studies, 3–4, 6–8, 21–23, 209–14; important books on, 334; and interdisciplinary scholarship, 6–8, 23; and interpretative approaches (case studies), 12, 23–31; and legitimacy issues, 332–34; macrohistorical positivist approach to, 11–12, 13–23, 335–36; and missing research, 335–36; and Nazism/fascism, 12–17, 19, 20–21, 334; in the 1970s, 17–19; in the 1960s, 16–17; and social organization of mass murder, 19–20; and sociology of knowledge, 331–36; and studies of the second-generation, 22–23; uniqueness/comparability debates, 6–7, 10 n.3, 30, 116–17, 131, 289; World War II era, 12–16. *See also* Holocaust studies

Sofsky, Wolfgang, 20

South Africa's Truth and Reconciliation Commission, 90

Soviet Jewish refugees and post-Holocaust migration, 215–35, 262–64, 267–68; and anti-Semitism as motive for emigration, 250–51, 269; and destinations other than Israel, 217–18; education levels of, 229; enhanced status/autonomy of, 222, 223, 224; ethnographic study of, 234–35 n.1; and history of Israeli positions, 227–28; and Jewish nationality/identity, 231; and memories of leaving Russia, 245–47; and migration to Israel (Soviet aliyah), 223, 224; and religiosity/Jewishness, 222–23; and U.S. resettlement staff, 219, 222; world attention to plight of, 225–26

Soviet Jewish refugees in the United States, 236–59, 264–65, 267, 269–70; and anti-Russian prejudice, 251–53, 255, 271; and children of former refugees, 245–56, 258, 264–65; and empirical data/interviews, 237, 259 n.2; and encounters with Jewish American institutions, 247–50; and family diasporic memories, 242; first generation, 241–45, 257–58; friendships of, 254; Israel in the ethnic self-understanding of, 247, 253; and Jewish holidays, 249; and Jewish identity and Russianness, 242–44; and marriage, 250, 256, 257–58; and multilayered identities and in-betweenness, 255–56, 258; and parochial school educations, 247–48; and project of self-identification, 245–47, 254–56; and relationships to "home," 253–56, 269; and self-deprecating humor, 248–49; transnational identities of, 237, 257; and transnational immigration literature, 236–37, 238–41, 258–59

Spielberg, Steven. *See Schindler's List* (film); Shoah Foundation Institute for Visual History and Education (VHF)

Spitzer, Leo, 40–41

Spivak, Gayatri, 187, 191–92

Steinberg, Maxime, 137

Steinberg, Stephen, 213

Stern, Lewis, 268

Stier, Oren, 53 n.3, 74, 78

Stoll, David, 180

Sturken, Marita, 88, 155

Survivor, as term, 4, 118–20, 129, 187

338, 340–41; and the ethics of representation, 343; in films and other cultural representations, 339–40; framing debates on human rights, 339; and globalization and Holocaust memory, 338–39; and nation-states, 338–39; notions of the "real" in representations of, 337–38; perpetrators of, 342; and questions of agency and resistance, 341

Visual History Foundation. *See* Shoah Foundation Institute for Visual History and Education (VHF)

Viviani, Nancy, 268

Von Molo, Walter, 296–98, 311 n.4

Wagner-Pacifici, Robin, 151

Wajnryb, Ruth, 87

Waldinger, Roger, 210

Warsaw Ghetto uprising and collective resistance, 277–90, 338, 341; and availability for activism, 279–80, 282–85, 288; and case selection and data sources, 278–79, 288; and emergence of armed resistance, 281–82; establishment of, 281–82; and female couriers, 284–85, 287; and friendship ties, 283; and gender, 279, 284–85, 287; and identity processes and motives, 280, 285–88; and individual/collective resistance, 278; and masking of Jewish identity, 286–88; and previous activist experience, 282–85; sociological study of, 279–80, 288–89; usefulness of, for sociological inquiry, 278, 289

Warsaw Jewish cemetery, 76

Waters, Mary, 259 n.1

Wdowinski, David, 281

Webber, Jonathan, 42

Weber, Max, 105

Weinberger, Rabbi Moses, 56

Weitzman, Lenore J., 24

West Indian immigrants in New York City, 213–14

Wiesel, Elie, 47

Wilowsky, Rabbi Jacob David, 57

Wirth, Louis, 332

Women. *See* Gender

World Jewish Congress, 227

World War I, 121–22

World Zionist Organization, 69

Yad Vashem, 119, 135, 142, 151–52

Yerushalmi, Yosef Hayim, 157

Yiddish language study, 89

YIVO Institute for Jewish Research (New York City), 158

Yom Ha'Shoah, 63–64, 76, 77, 89, 98–99

Young, James E., 51, 77, 150

Young Guard (Ha'shomer Hatza'ir), 68, 283

Young Judea, 68

Young Pioneer (HeHalutz HaTza'ir), 283, 290 n.2

Zeldich, Morris, 58

Zerubavel, Eviatar, 151

Zerubavel, Yael, 53 n.4

Zionism: constructions of Holocaust memory, 320; and diaspora business/identity travel, 68–70, 78, 80; questioning of, 227; and racism, 321; and transnationalism, 263

Zolberg, Aristide, 264

Zuckerman, Yitzhak, 283, 285, 286

Zussman, Robert, 120

Żydowska Organizacja Bojowa (ŻOB), 282–88

Żydowski Związek Wojskowy (ŻZW), 282–84, 286

Library of Congress Cataloging-in-Publication Data

Sociology confronts the Holocaust : memories and identities in Jewish diasporas /
edited by Judith M. Gerson and Diane L. Wolf.

p. cm.

Includes bibliographical references and index.

ISBN 978–0-8223–3982–3 (cloth : alk. paper)

ISBN 978–0-8223–3999–1 (pbk. : alk. paper)

1. Holocaust, Jewish (1939–1945)—Historiography—Congresses. 2. Holocaust, Jewish
(1939–1945)—Personal narratives—History and criticism—Congresses. 3. Holocaust, Jewish
(1939–1945)—Influence—Congresses. 4. Holocaust survivors—Biography—Congresses. 5.
Sociology—Biographical methods—Congresses. I. Gerson, Judith Madeleine. II. Wolf,
Diane L.

D804.348.S63 2007

940.53'18142—dc22   2006101924